A Month-to-Month Guide

Fourth-Grade Math

A Month-to-Month Guide

Fourth-Grade Math

4

Lainie Schuster

Math Solutions Publications
Sausalito, CA

Math Solutions Publications
150 Gate 5 Road
Sausalito, CA 94965
www.mathsolutions.com

The publisher would like to acknowledge sources of adapted or borrowed material:

Massachusetts Comprehensive Assessment System (MCAS) 2005 Released Test Questions, Mathematics, Grade 4, Items no. 20 and 26: Reprinted with permission from the Massachusetts Department of Elementary and Secondary Education.
Tangram Explorations, Pentomino Explorations, and Fraction Kit Investigations activities, and Cover Up, Digit Place, Place-Value Game, and Uncover Versions 1 and 2 games: Adapted from *About Teaching Mathematics: A K–8 Resource, Third Edition*, by Marilyn Burns (Math Solutions Publications, 2007)

Continued on page 489, which is an extension of the copyright page.

Library of Congress Cataloging-in-Publication Data
Schuster, Lainie.
  A month-to-month guide: fourth-grade math / Lainie Schuster.
      p. cm.
Includes bibliographical references and index.
Summary: "Provides teachers with an overall sense of planning a math curriculum and managing classroom instruction for the whole year, including what is going to be taught each month and what specifically to teach each day. Topics include problem solving, numeration and place value, geometry, measurement, multiplication, division, fractions, decimals, algebraic thinking, and more"—Provided by publisher.
  ISBN 978-0-941355-83-4 (alk. paper)
  1. Mathematics—Study and teaching (Primary) 2. Fourth grade (Education)—Curricula. I. Title.
  QA135.6.S4349 2008
  372.7—dc22
                                                                    2008024554

Editor: Toby Gordon
Production: Melissa L. Inglis-Elliott
Cover and interior design: Catherine Hawkes/Cat and Mouse
Composition: Macmillan Publishing Solutions

Printed in the United States of America on acid-free paper
12 11 10 09 08   SB   1 2 3 4 5

A Message from Marilyn Burns

We at Math Solutions Professional Development believe that teaching math well calls for increasing our understanding of the math we teach, seeking deeper insights into how children learn mathematics, and refining our lessons to best promote students' learning.

Math Solutions Publications shares classroom-tested lessons and teaching expertise from our faculty of Math Solutions Inservice instructors as well as from other respected math educators. Our publications are part of the nationwide effort we've made since 1984 that now includes

- more than five hundred face-to-face inservice programs each year for teachers and administrators in districts across the country;
- annually publishing professional development books, now totaling more than seventy titles and spanning the teaching of all math topics in kindergarten through grade 8;
- four series of videos for teachers, plus a video for parents, that show math lessons taught in actual classrooms;
- on-site visits to schools to help refine teaching strategies and assess student learning; and
- free online support, including grade-level lessons, book reviews, inservice information, and district feedback, all in our *Math Solutions Online Newsletter*.

For information about all of the products and services we have available, please visit our website at *www.mathsolutions.com*. You can also contact us to discuss math professional development needs by calling (800) 868-9092 or by sending an email to *info@mathsolutions.com*.

We're always eager for your feedback and interested in learning about your particular needs. We look forward to hearing from you.

Math Solutions.

"Ah," my father murmured. He was silent for a moment. Then he said quietly, "Reuven, listen to me. The Talmud says that a person should do two things for himself. One is to acquire a teacher. Do you remember the other?"
"Choose a friend," I said.
The Chosen,
Chiam Potok 1967, 74

To my teacher, Larry E. Grimes, PhD
Bethany College
Department of English
Bethany, West Virginia

To my friend, Suzanne H. Chapin, EdD
Boston University
School of Education
Boston, Massachusetts

And to my grandmother, Edith Ladd Armstrong, who was both.

Contents

Foreword

One of the challenges of teaching mathematics is planning a coherent year of instruction. Not only must we address the important mathematics children need to learn, but we also need to help children learn to think, reason, and become proficient problem solvers. And we also want to inspire children to enjoy mathematics and see it as useful to their lives. Accomplishing this is a tall order that calls for understanding the full scope of the mathematics curriculum, having a rich repertoire of instructional options, being skilled at managing instruction in the classroom, and understanding the needs of the individual students in your class.

This book is a month-by-month guide for planning a year of math instruction. It is one of a four-book series, each written by a master teacher to address teaching mathematics in grades 1, 2, 3, and 4. The author of each book acknowledges that her suggestions do not comprise the only approach to accomplish planning, or necessarily the best approach for others to follow. Rather, each suggests a thoughtful, practical, and very personal approach to planning that has grown out of her years of experience in the classroom.

The authors of this series are truly master teachers—experienced, caring, hardworking, and incredibly accomplished. They bring their wisdom and experience to their books in unique ways, but as teachers they share common experiences and outlooks. Each has offered many professional development classes and workshops for teachers while also choosing to make classroom teaching the main focus of her career. For all of them, mathematics was not their initial love or strength. However, they each came to study and learn to appreciate mathematics because of their need to serve their students. They are committed to excellence in math instruction, they understand children, they know how to manage classrooms, and they are passionate about teaching. It is a great pleasure to present these books to you.

—MARILYN BURNS

Acknowledgments

We teach in an era of wonderful resources and standards-based curricula. I would like to acknowledge two curricula in particular: Everyday Mathematics (Everyday Learning Corporation) and Investigations in Number, Data, and Space (Scott Foresman). Although no curriculum can meet every need and demand, these two present the very best of instructional frameworks.

I would like to give special thanks to Joan Carlson, my reader, and Toby Gordon, my editor. You both have helped me time after time to refine my thinking and improve my writing. Who knew the editing process could be so painless and rewarding?!

I cannot think of any one person who has influenced how I think about mathematics as much as Marilyn Burns. She is as passionate and masterful a teacher as I have ever known. Thank you, Marilyn, for taking me along on your mathematical journey.

It is my fourth-grade students, however, for whom I wrote this book. You have amazed, delighted, and entertained me with your thinking about mathematics. I have been blessed to teach in a school with remarkable eight-, nine-, and ten-year-olds . . . but then again, aren't they all? They are truly my teachers.

Introduction

"I'll give you one more chance. I have eight coconuts, eight monkey nuts, and eight nutty idiots like you. How many nuts do I have altogether? Answer me quickly."

Poor Wilfred was properly flustered. "Wait!" he cried. "Please wait! I've got to add up eight coconuts and eight monkey nuts . . ." He started counting on his fingers.

"You bursting blister!" yelled the Trunchbull. "You moth-eaten maggot! This is not adding up! This is multiplication! The answer is three eights! Or is it eight threes? What is the difference between three eights and eight threes? Tell me that, you mangled little wurzel and look sharp about it!"

Matilda
Roald Dahl 1988, 218

Fourth graders delight in Matilda's undoing of the Trunchbull in Roald Dahl's *Matilda*. They are enthralled by her magic, her ingenuity, and her pranks. It is also not surprising that they can identify with Wilfred's confusion and panic when put on the spot to solve a math problem! Fourth graders are like that. They, like Matilda, are gaining mastery in their world. They will work hard on a logical reasoning problem and prepare for a chapter test in math, but they can continue to struggle with 13 − 8. They cherish their successes, but can be reluctant to take risks. They are learning to be loyal friends but can easily dissolve into a puddle of tears because of an unkind word or action. They are concerned with the fairness of their world but can have difficulties assessing the fairness of their own behavior. Fourth graders, like all the rest of us, have their own developmental growing pains. And we have the pleasure of teaching them!

The mathematics explored in the fourth grade is rich and varied. The procedural expectations continue to increase, as does the need for conceptual understanding and sense making of the mathematics. An Advanced Placement calculus teacher once told me that she felt there were two crucial years in one's mathematical education—Algebra 1 . . . and fourth grade! I tell my new students and their parents that each September. We have much work to do in the fourth grade.

I have been teaching fourth grade for the past twenty-something years. (This is when an estimate is just fine!) Each and every year my fourth graders amaze and astound me. I am impressed and delighted with their persistence, effort, and insatiable curiosity. There are days when I collapse into a chair in my classroom at day's end and smile. Not every lesson goes swimmingly. Not every child leaves class with complete understanding of the concept investigated that day. Not every homework assignment makes it into the backpack. But every child has given me his best that day. Every child has laughed some, shared some, and uncovered something new about the mathematics. The students have left school wondering a little more about fractions . . . or division . . . or multiplication. That's a good day.

Designing and implementing a yearlong mathematics curriculum for your fourth graders can be a daunting task. Even though most of us have our prescribed curricula, we realize early in our careers that one size does not always fit all. Although I follow a similar road map each year, I continue to tweak my program a bit to meet the needs of my current class and the academic standards and expectations of my school.

As September approaches, I often think back to my years as a young student of mathematics and shudder. My early mathematical years were fraught with tears, stomachaches, and shallow understandings. For years, my math classes had been those in which material was delivered—never explored, questioned, or discussed. I was constantly reminded of what I could not do, rather than what I could.

I was searching for connections and there were few to be found.

Then good mathematics happened. I was stunned when a college mathematics professor stopped class one day early in the semester to ask me what I did *not* understand about whatever it was we were discussing. I was making the same mistake over and over again, and he noticed it. He cared enough about me and cared enough about the mathematics to stop class and ask me about it. Although it was difficult to actually articulate what I did *not* understand because I had never been asked that question before, I realized in the process how strong my logical reasoning and language skills were and that they could actually help me demystify the mathematics. During that interchange and subsequent epiphany, a concept was explored, a discussion was had, a connection was made! Good mathematics.

This may be a good time to take a few minutes to think about *yourself* as a mathematician. What is it that you like about learning mathematics? What frustrates you about learning mathematics? What helps or hinders your understanding of a concept? What topics do you like best in math? What topics do you like least? Are you a visual learner? Do you need charts and diagrams to support your thinking? How successful are you at defending your procedures and solutions? How willing are you to rethink those procedures and solutions? How much practice do you need? Who was your favorite math teacher in school? Why? We spend so much time focusing on our teaching (which we do need to do, by the way) that we often forget who we are in the process.

Our fourth graders are well aware of our efforts in getting to know *them* as mathematicians. In their own nine-year-old ways, they are appreciative when we acknowledge their persistence in completing tangram puzzles, their interest in batting averages, or their frustration with long division. Getting to know, understand, and validate our young mathematicians can set the stage for a year of mathematical growth and progress.

A Month-to-Month Guide: Fourth-Grade Math represents my yearlong journey. It is a window into my classroom and a description of mathematical routines, strategies, and practices that I have found to be successful and engaging. It is my hope that you will be able to apply or adapt much of what you read as you move through your year of teaching mathematics. Developing powerful mathematical thinkers requires patience, persistence, and practice from all those involved—teachers, students, parents, and administrators. Teaching mathematics well—or perhaps better phrased, teaching good mathematics—is just plain hard work. Designing and implementing a meaningful mathematics program takes mindful and comprehensive planning and selective resourcing. I am hopeful that this book will help you with both.

"You!" the Trunchbull shouted, pointing a finger the size of a rolling-pin at a boy called Wilfred. . . . "Stand up, you!" she shouted at him.

Wilfred stood up.

"Recite the three-times table backwards!" the Trunchbull barked.

"Backwards?" stammered Wilfred. "But I haven't learnt it backwards."

"There you are!" cried the Trunchbull, triumphant. "She's taught you nothing! Miss Honey, why have you taught them absolutely nothing at all in the last week?"

"That is not true, Headmistress," Miss Honey said. "They have all learnt their three-times table. But I see no point in teaching it to them backwards. The whole object of life is to go forwards." (Dahl 1988, 217)

And forwards we shall go, making sense of life . . . and fourth-grade mathematics.

Chapter 1

BEFORE THE CHILDREN ARRIVE

Providing effective mathematics instruction calls for thinking about what's required to support and facilitate student learning—organizing the physical classroom, establishing a safe environment for learning, helping students establish productive learning habits, structuring effective lessons, and more.

About Teaching Mathematics
Burns 2007, 51

Planning Your Math Program

As you begin planning your math program, please remember that this book presents an overview of the mathematical concepts, procedures, and topics fourth-grade mathematicians may encounter in a given school year. It is not meant to be a prescribed curriculum, but rather a thoughtful collection of lessons and investigations based on topics and units covered in most fourth-grade classrooms as well as those recommended by the National Council of Teachers of Mathematics (NCTM) standards. It is my ultimate hope, however, that this yearlong overview will give you the opportunity to think about how to approach and develop the teaching and learning of mathematics in your classroom.

Chapter Focus and Time Span

The mathematical content covered in *Fourth-Grade Math* focuses on the following units of study commonly presented in fourth grade:

problem solving and logical reasoning

number relationships and operations

geometry

measurement

multiplication

division

fractions and decimals

algebraic thinking

data collection and interpretation

The number of weeks devoted to each topic may vary from year to year and from class to class. You will also find that number relationships and operations (addition, subtraction, multiplication, and division) and algebraic thinking can spiral through each unit because of their connectedness to other concepts and procedures covered in the proposed units of study. Many of the concepts and procedures are introduced, practiced, or applied in a problem-solving context that can support and develop greater meaning of the mathematics. Following is a possible scope and sequence of an academic year:

September (4 weeks)   welcome back activity

problem solving

algebraic/logical reasoning

addition and subtraction fact review and yearlong extensions

estimation strategies

October (4 weeks)	numeration review and yearlong extensions
	multiplication and division fact review
November/December	geometry
(6 weeks)	area/perimeter
	measurement
January (4 weeks)	multiplication (multidigit)
February (4 weeks)	division (long)
March (4 weeks)	fractions
April (4 weeks)	decimals
May (4 weeks)	algebraic thinking
	data collection and interpretation
June (2 weeks)	multiplication and division revisited

The following nine chapters are sequenced according to content. You may need to adjust the length of study or placement of various units within the year according to the needs, strengths, weaknesses, and interests of your particular class or school. It is important, however, to keep your yearlong syllabus in mind and plan accordingly as you move through each unit, whatever it might be. Your school or district may establish curriculum guidelines according to the scheduling of state-mandated or standardized testing. You may need to base your curricular decisions on those guidelines and time constraints. If you feel you can spend only four weeks on multiplication, then spend only four weeks on multiplication! And believe me, this is easier said than done.

As teachers of young children, we focus on teaching for understanding with meaning, passion, and creativity—and all of that takes time. In my perfect world, I would teach math for ninety minutes each and every day, but I have yet to teach in a school in which that has been possible or even plausible. Daily lesson planning and integration of math into other subject areas become increasingly important as we look at our yearlong itinerary and our commitment to its follow-through. Planning your math time each day may or may not be in your control, depending on the day-to-day logistics of your school. I would highly suggest devoting sixty minutes to math teaching each day. I also establish the flexibility of working through a ninety-minute block one day a week, which allows for longer and more in-depth investigations.

TEACHER-TO-TEACHER TALK   I have recently discovered an inverse correlation between the number of years I have been teaching and the number of units I cover within any given year. As my years of teaching have increased, the number of units I cover within a year has decreased. NCTM's *Curriculum Focal Points for Prekindergarten Through Grade 8 Mathematics* (2006) proposes a similar pedagogical shift in thinking. This document presents a small number of significant mathematical targets for each grade level instead of listing a multitude of goals, standards, objectives, or learning expectations. (*Curriculum Focal Points* is available at www.nctm.org.) Over the past five years or so, I have made a conscious effort to allow children more time to investigate and explore fewer concepts and procedures in more depth. It takes careful lesson, unit, and yearlong planning to create meaningful contexts in which new concepts and procedures can be explored and previously covered material can be reviewed, practiced, and applied. I have also found that certain mathematical problems take on a life of their own. What begins as a twenty-five-minute lesson may actually turn into a two-day investigation—and I want and need to allow that to happen every now and again.

Chapter Structure

Each chapter is sequenced in a similar fashion and contains the following sections.

The Learning Environment

Each chapter begins with a discussion of the classroom climate and culture and its importance to the learning of mathematics. Different topics and different procedures often lend themselves to different teaching, learning, and communication styles and practices. Is this a day for small-group work? Or is this a day for individual paper-and-pencil work? Is this a day for student-led discussions? Or is this a day for teacher-facilitated conversations? How will misconceptions be addressed? How will varying abilities be accommodated? How will classroom discussions be fostered and nurtured? Research continues to remind us of the importance of context and natural learning environments to the teaching and learning of mathematics (Stoessiger and Edmunds 1993). What real-world and problem-solving contexts will you provide to help your students construct greater meaning of the mathematics? How will you establish expectations in regard to quality of work, achievement, participation, and behavior?

Not only do you need to establish a positive, challenging, and comfortable classroom climate in September, but you must maintain it throughout the year—and that can be the tricky part! Also, it's important to set up those routines that make things run smoothly throughout the year. How will homework routines be handled? What about collecting and distributing papers? How will students put away manipulatives and other tools?

The Mathematics and Its Language

As children move through the fourth grade, the process and progress of mathematical learning becomes increasingly entrenched in the mathematical content. Because of this, a teacher's understanding and identification of the mathematics being taught, explored, and discovered takes on significant importance. The mathematics of each chapter is discussed as well as the possible misconceptions that may manifest themselves as children work with the material. It is your understanding of the mathematics and the pace at which your students are moving through it that will help to direct lesson planning. Exploring, defining, manipulating, and refining mathematical language help children learn with greater understanding and meaning. Children need to speak the mathematics, represent the mathematics, and write the mathematics. Acquiring the necessary vocabulary and language usage will help children develop the conceptual and procedural skills required for mathematical growth and success. This section also discusses how to introduce the mathematical language of the unit.

Investigations and Literature-Based Activities

Sample investigations, games, and literature-based activities are offered to support the unit of study. The investigations modeled in each unit may also help you develop activities of your own.

Some lessons are more traditional and teacher directed, while others are open-ended and student directed, depending on the mathematics being addressed. The questions that you pose to your students can often open up more traditional textbook lessons. Good questioning can expand a traditional lesson into a rich mathematical investigation. A listing of the mathematical objectives and materials is offered prior to the description of each activity.

Games

Frequent practice and application of skills is necessary as children strive to develop conceptual and procedural mastery. Games can offer a rich context for such practice and application. Not only are games motivating and challenging, but carefully chosen and constructed games can also support important mathematical ideas and help children further develop reasoning and procedural skills. Using games to practice number skills can greatly reduce the need for worksheets and rote practice of skills, which can be tedious and ineffective.

Calculation Routines and Practices

Paper-and-pencil routines and practices are shared in this section. The emphasis here is on the *representation* of the calculations and numerical reasoning, not necessarily on the repetition or drill of one specific algorithm. Calculation methods need to be appropriate to the numerical or problem-solving situation. There are certainly those times when calculation practice is needed as children work to master procedures. Arithmetic skills, however, need to extend beyond memorization and computational proficiency. Our students need to learn to use their calculation skills as they develop number sense and solve problems efficiently and accurately.

Mathematics Writing

Representing the mathematics is integral to the work students do in my classroom. This section discusses this important practice. How do your children document their thinking as they are working through a lesson? This includes not only writing about their thinking but also charting, drawing, and diagramming their thinking. As the year progresses, so too does its conceptual challenges. We need to offer opportunities for students to improve the sophistication of their mathematical representations in written explanations and recorded work. This is a tricky business! We need to listen to our students as they talk through the mathematics so that we can help them represent their thinking with clarity and organization. A great deal of airtime has been given to the importance of writing in math class—but this is easier said than done. Learning to write about mathematics takes time, practice, and patience. I have found it necessary to occasionally devote an entire period to one short writing assignment. I model. The children write. We share. The children rethink and revise. We share. We generate a list of writing accountabilities together. This section addresses writing guidelines, possible journal prompts, and mechanical expectations for each month's course of study.

Parent Communication

Creating a partnership between school and home supports the mathematical education of everyone involved. Communication with families needs to be regular and ongoing in order to report all the good mathematics going on in the classroom. You can establish a working relationship with parents through informational forms that present the mathematical goals of an upcoming unit and explain how parents can help at home; newsletters; formal reports; phone calls; and conferences. Parents often spend time doing mathematics with their children at home, but in a more traditional context within which they feel comfortable. Many do not understand how today's mathematics class will help their children in and out of school. We have an opportunity (and an obligation) to educate families about the importance of teaching mathematics with meaning and understanding. Suggestions and samples of home-school communication are offered in this section.

Come August, I begin to draft my "Welcome Back to Math Class" newsletter to the parents of my students (see Figure 1–1). I have now been doing this for so many years that I simply revise the previous year's letter. So even if this is your first attempt at such a letter, save it and rework it for the following year. It will be well worth the time and effort spent in writing a comprehensive and informative first draft! There are many parents who are genuinely interested in what you are doing in math class. With every letter sent home (about four a year), I attach a relevant article or summary of related research. NCTM's journals often have articles that are extremely informative and describe current best practices in mathematics education.

FIGURE 1–1 ◄

September's "Welcome Back to Math Class" newsletter.

September 5

Dear Fourth-Grade Parents,

We have had a busy and successful start to the school year. Your fourth-grade mathematicians have already started their year with a probability activity generated by a very endearing yellow lab named Martha . . . who talks, by the way. We will spend most of September working through problem-solving protocol and expectations as we review basic math facts and develop estimation strategies. We will then begin our year's work with the Everyday Mathematics program. A parent information form is currently posted on the electronic bulletin board under "Lower School Homework" that explains the goings-on in fourth-grade math in greater detail. Parent information forms will be posted prior to the beginning of each new unit.

I have included below some of my classroom quirks and policies. Some of these may be new to you; some may not. Please feel free to discuss any questions or concerns about your child in math this year with me at your convenience.

Class Policies

- *Homework:* Homework will be assigned three nights a week. I do give the children an opportunity to start most assignments in class in order for them to ask any necessary questions. I do ask that *little* parental supervision be given to the children as they complete their math homework. Please refer to the handout in your child's registration packet for further "helpful hints" about helping with math homework. If children are having a tough time with the assignment, please have them stop, and send in a note with your child the next morning. (Email works fine, too!) I would rather *not* have them "dissolve" over an assignment after a long day of school! The fourth graders will have "Terrific Tuesday" each week—a no-math-homework night.

- *Pencils: All classwork and homework is to be done in pencil.* The end.

- *Homework passes:* These are very valuable pieces of paper! Five consecutive perfect (+10) quizzes earn a homework pass that can be turned in anytime in lieu of an assignment. I encourage the children to save these passes for those emergency nights: a birthday dinner, a late hockey practice, a special outing.

- *Quizzes:* Ten-point quizzes will be given in grade 4 so frequently that they will soon be thought of as daily procedure. Five consecutive perfect quizzes earn a homework pass.

- *Math notebooks:* All students in grade 4 will be asked to keep a math notebook. The graph paper notebooks will be distributed to the children in class. This notebook will become a valuable tool as the children move throughout the year. Quizzes, homework, seatwork, and other written activities will be completed in their notebooks. A quick look-see at the notebook will give you an excellent reference as to where we have been in class and the degree of progress that your child is making. The children will carry their math notebooks to and from class each day.

FIGURE 1–1 ▶

**September's "Welcome
Back to Math Class"
newsletter, continued.**

- *Mathematician's Logs:* At the beginning of each term, each fourth grader will receive a new Mathematician's Logs. Prompts writing focus areas will be given for each entry. Students will be asked to respond to a mathematical prompt in writing and with diagrams or pictures. Each entry will be evaluated for content and mechanics—an effort grade will be given for each by way of a fraction:

$$\frac{content}{mechanics}$$

- *Language demands of the mathematics:* The exploring, defining, manipulating, and refining of mathematical language can help children learn with greater understanding and meaning. Children need to speak the mathematics, represent the mathematics, and write about the mathematics. Acquiring the necessary vocabulary and language usage will help your fourth grader develop the conceptual and procedural skills required for mathematical growth and success. Working through the mathematical language of each particular unit of study will be a primary teaching and learning objective.

- *Assessment:* Assessment is a constant process in my classroom. The children are asked to write about the math, to show the math, and to defend their solutions about the math. Each fourth grader will develop a math portfolio throughout the year. Corrected homework, classwork, and tests are housed in each child's portfolio. You are welcome at any time to view your child's work. All quizzes, tests, and project due dates will be posted on the online Lower School WebEvent calendar.

- *Exams:* Unit exams will be given in grade 4 upon the completion of each major unit. Study sheets will *always* be handed out two or more days prior to *every* exam. With the use of a study sheet, each child can be well prepared for every test. No surprises will appear on the test— what is on the study sheet is what is on the test. Test self-reflections follow every exam and are stapled to the front of each child's exam. The finished product is then sent home. I ask that the children return these to me in order to file them in their portfolios. The children are asked to assess their preparation and performance on their test reflection sheet. I have actually learned more about the children from reading these than by correcting their tests! They are often brutally honest and right on the mark as they self-reflect.

- *Portfolios:* Yet another assessment tool . . . all loose papers, corrected homework and class work, and tests are kept in manila folders in my room. The children love folder day because they greatly enjoy collecting and commenting on completed work. It is always fun to hear the children talk about their own work. "This was so easy!" "Remember when we did this?" "This took me the longest time to understand!" Written personal assessments follow each unit in the fourth grade. These writing tasks develop important reflective skills that help children not only assess their work but own their work and progress, as well.

- *Calculators:* I love playing with calculators, and the children do, too. It is very important in these times of increased technology that our children know their way around a calculator. We use calculators in class quite often when I am not as concerned about the calculations as I am about the *process* of reaching a solution. We are now using the TI-15 in class. It is not necessary to have the same calculator at home. I would actually prefer to have the children learn to use other styles and brands as well. Please keep your calculator choice simple, however.

■ *Heffalumps and Woozles:* As most of you may know, Heffalumps and Woozles are the *optional* problem-solving activities posted in my room every two weeks. Children are encouraged to pick up problems and work on them on their own, with a friend, or even as a family. I have received some wonderful family solutions! Please remind your children that they *must* show and explain their thinking when completing their problems.

Additional Supplies

■ colored pencils
■ mechanical pencils
■ compass and ruler for at-home constructions

I would like to close this epic with a paragraph from *Raising Cain: Protecting the Emotional Life of Boys* (Kindlon and Thompson 1999). Even though this book explores the emotional life of boys, it provides insights into the development of all young people.

> The most important thing to remember, the guiding principle, is to try to keep your son's self-esteem intact while he is in school. That is the real risk to his success and to his mental health. Once he's out of school, the work will be different. He'll find a niche where the fact that he can't spell well, or didn't read until he was eight, won't matter. But if he starts to hate himself because he wasn't good at schoolwork, he'll fall into a hole that he'll be digging himself out of for the rest of his life. (36)

My goal as a teacher (and as a mother of two sons, too) is to send *all* of our fourth graders off into the mathematical world feeling confident and self-assured. They may struggle some with fractions or remainders, but they also realize that they have the skills, perseverance, and self-confidence to wrestle with these concepts, knowing that understanding will come in time. I cannot praise this book enough. I laughed. I sighed. I even wept while reading certain chapters. I rarely say this about a book, but it is a must-read if you have sons, know sons, or are a son.

Thank you all—children and parents—for your continued support. This is a very difficult job to do well and it would be all the more impossible without your support.

Please sign off on the form provided.

Mathematically yours,

Lainie Schuster

Lainie Schuster

Assessment

Embedding informal assessment measures into day-to-day routines as well as establishing formal assessment practices help us identify and document the mathematical growth of our students. Assessment routines can also give us important information about the effectiveness of our teaching and the math curriculum. We need to listen to and learn from our students as they tell us what makes sense to them and show us what they can do with the mathematics. This section discusses possible methods of formal and informal assessment as well as how to use the information you gather for in-house or reporting purposes.

> **TEACHER-TO-TEACHER TALK**   Although our ultimate goal for our fourth-grade students is conceptual and procedural proficiency and efficiency, the road to that end can be a long one! Are wrong answers always wrong? Again, it is the mathematics and our understanding of it as teachers that need to drive our assessment practices. Perhaps Kirsten got the wrong answer, but how was her thinking? How was her approach to solving the problem? How was her number sense? How was she applying what she knew to what she did not? There are those times when a quick look at the answers will do when correcting math work. But there are also those times when we need to *study* the work of our children. Where was the breakdown in their thinking? Where was the miscalculation? Where did the fragile understanding of the concept or the procedure manifest itself? Once we have this information, our follow-up interactions with children become crucial to their rethinking, learning, and success.

Resources

There are wonderful mathematical resources available on the market. A resource listing at the end of each chapter offers additional materials to support the concepts and procedures covered in the respective unit of study. Understanding the needs of your students and the targeted mathematics will help you seek out relevant and valuable resources to further enrich your instruction.

Homework

Homework is *not* be addressed in this yearly overview. Homework policies can be district based, school based, discipline based, or teacher based. My homework routines have remained simple over the years and have largely been adjusted by homework practices set forth in Annette Raphel's *Math Homework That Counts* (2000). I give math homework three nights a week—Monday, Wednesday, and Thursday. Every Tuesday is Terrific Tuesday—a night off with no math homework. Thursdays are designated for journal writes. Many of my homework assignments require some type of parent interaction. I want parents to know what is going on in math class. Initially, this was difficult to implement, but the parents now enjoy it, appreciate it, and expect it.

Setting Up Your Classroom

Setting up your classroom before the children arrive sets the stage for the yearlong mathematical journey ahead—literally! Even after thirty-something years of teaching, it still feels like Christmas when I open up the supply boxes and begin to organize my room for the upcoming year. New books, pencils, reams of graph paper, rulers, and glue sticks are reminders of new beginnings and hope-filled first days of school.

Valuing mathematical communication and sense making requires us to pay close attention to the physical organization of our classrooms. Table groupings are helpful in facilitating mathematical conversations. Easy access to mathematical tools and resources can help keep children engaged in the task without having to search out needed materials. Availability of several types of paper is helpful for the representation and charting of the mathematics. Suggestions for student materials and the organization of student work and teaching materials follow.

Furniture Arrangement

Table or desk groupings of four children work very well in my classroom. This configuration allows for small-group work, partner sharing, as well as individual work. Desks of the same height can be grouped together, as can rectangular or trapezoidal tables. Random seating assignments can set the expectation that all students are to work cooperatively with each other. You can pull name cards or color-coded craft sticks from a cup to determine table groups. I change my table groupings every two weeks to offer consistency within the randomness.

Teaching Materials

Math Manipulatives and Tools

Although my choice of manipulatives has remained fairly consistent over the years, my organizational practices and containers change fairly frequently. In an active mathematics classroom, certain materials should be available and accessible at all times. The organization of materials is a personal choice but one that needs to be shared with your students. Establishing routines early in the year for use, organization, and cleanup of materials will be well worth your time and effort.

Your choice of manipulatives should rely on instructional purpose. How will their use support the teaching and learning of mathematics? Although I use base ten blocks when I introduce decimals later in the year with my class, I do not use them enough to warrant having a set housed in my classroom, so I borrow a set from one of my colleagues when we begin the decimals unit. Pooling materials with other teachers can stretch your budget dollars and allow for a greater selection of materials.

Here is my personal list of must-have manipulatives followed by a list of materials that are nice to have, which I usually borrow from others.

Must-Have Manipulatives

- Cuisenaire rods
- pattern blocks
- small translucent chips
- decimal cards
- dice
- number card decks, made up of four of each of the numbers 0–12—see Blackline Masters (Playing card decks also work well. You may also find that your prescribed curriculum offers card decks. Have enough for one deck per pair of children and a few extra decks for card replacements.)

Optional Manipulatives

- color tiles
- linking cubes
- geoboards

Years ago, a colleague introduced me to using plastic dishpans as an organizing system. I keep pattern blocks and Cuisenaire rods in separate dishpans (one color for pattern blocks and another color for Cuisenaire rods) for each table grouping. I stack them in open shelves for easy access. Chips, decimal cards, dice, and number card decks are organized in a similar fashion but in smaller color-coordinated tubs for easy access.

Calculators and 6- and 12-inch rulers are kept in an inexpensive plastic three-drawer unit. Each drawer is labeled. Each year I add a few new calculators to my collection so that each child can have access to a calculator. I purposefully keep several styles of calculators in my room, from the basic four-function model to those with a few more bells and whistles. I want to give the children the opportunity to manipulate and investigate different models. I find it interesting that even though the children are intrigued by the fancier calculators, they go straight for the four-function models when solving problems. They like the user-friendliness and comfort level the simple models offer.

An overhead projector continues to be my most coveted teaching tool even in this technological era of document cameras, LCD projectors, and interactive whiteboards. I have a supply of overhead manipulatives (pattern blocks, Cuisenaire rods, color tiles, and Decimal Squares) housed under the projector in zip-top baggies (in a plastic bin, of course!).

Supplies

As with manipulatives, you should rely on instructional purpose and budget to choose supplies and determine accessibility. How will children record their day-to-day math? How will you organize math writing? What paper will you use if students will be making posters or presentations? Will these materials be exclusive to mathematics or can they be shared with the other disciplines you teach? You will also need to address organization and storage as you determine class and logistical needs and constraints.

My paper supply is perhaps my most costly line item in my yearly order. In my classroom, paper is organized in a five-tier tray, which saves considerable space on the countertop. Quarter-inch graph paper, centimeter graph paper, plain white paper, and lined notebook paper fill the tiers. I keep a roll of 1-inch graph paper on hand for projects requiring a large work area. A supply of 16-by-24-inch newsprint for poster making and presentations is also handy. I also keep a tablet of lined chart paper available for use with whole-group instruction. I do not have room for a free-standing easel for the chart paper, so I just mount individual sheets on the whiteboard when necessary. I also order four to five reams of colored card stock for special projects and math journals (see "Student Materials" below for more information).

Art supplies such as scissors, glue sticks, and markers are also available in plastic bins on the countertop. I ask that each child supply her own colored pencils. The children and I have agreed over the years that markers are best suited for poster making, but colored pencils are preferred for day-to-day work. Colored pencils do not bleed and can be sharpened. I ask that only colored pencils be used on paper-and-pencil activities that require coloring.

TEACHER-TO-TEACHER TALK   I ask my fourth graders to use pencil for *all* of their math work—with the exception of check writing later on in the year. I also encourage the children to use mechanical pencils when possible, upon the suggestion of a past parent who was also an occupational therapist. Mechanical pencils may be tricky for the children to use at first, so be prepared. The children frequently break their lead and fiddle with replacement procedures. In time, however, they master the usage of these tools. Mechanical pencils are a great help to those children who have grip and excessive pencil-pressure issues. If you push down too hard, the lead breaks! Mechanical pencils now come with rubber grips that are also helpful for some.

Student Materials

I supply each student with a spiral $\frac{1}{4}$-inch graph paper notebook. We do just about everything on graph paper. This allows students to develop organizational practices on paper and helps them align their calculations. I ask that they always place one digit per box. When working with decimal numbers, I ask that they give the decimal point its own box (because it is that important!). This may take a little vigilance on your part. Children may grumble at first with your corrections and constant reminders. But once the ground rules are set, written work tends to be neat and well organized. Most of our written work in and out of class is completed in this notebook. It becomes a comprehensive and well-documented written record of the year.

Each child also receives a *Mathematician's Log* that I publish and collate myself. For years, I have searched for a math journal that would suit my needs, but I have never found one. So I headed to my computer and the copy machine and created my own. I have been very happy with this format but find that I tweak it a little each year. I print the front and back covers on primary-colored card stock (see Figures 1–2 and 1–3). The inside pages are two-sided copies (see Figure 1–4). When the log is opened, the prompt and writing focus areas are taped on the left side. The children

FIGURE 1–2   ▶

Front cover of Mathematician's Log.

A Mathematician's Log

Mathematician:_____

Fall 2006
Grade 4

Editing Checklist

Checking for Organization and Readability

Read your entry aloud to yourself.

_____ Does your introductory sentence restate the problem or question?

_____ Have you written a concluding solution statement defining your position?

_____ Do you have an example(s) or a diagram(s) to support your solution?

Checking for Punctuation and Mechanics

Read one sentence at a time.

_____ Does every sentence begin with a capital letter?

_____ Does every sentence end with proper punctuation?

_____ Do all your sentences express one clear idea?

Checking for Spelling

_____ Circle lightly any words that do not look correct.

_____ Use a dictionary to verify spelling.

Helpful Words for Mathematical Writing

_____   _____

_____   _____

_____   _____

_____   _____

_____   _____

_____   _____

_____   _____

_____   _____

_____   _____

_____   _____

_____   _____

FIGURE 1–3 ◄

Back cover (editing checklist) and first page of Mathematician's Log.

FIGURE 1–4   ▶

**Inside facing pages of
Mathematician's Log.**

Prompt:

Writing Focus:

Assessment: content
                     ―――――
                     mechanics

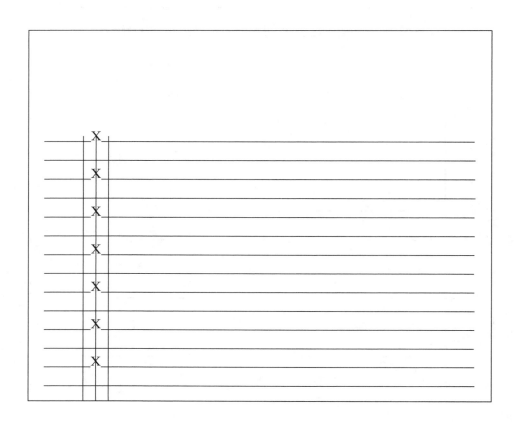

are to construct their response and diagrams on the right. I prefer that the children write on every other line and not write on the lines beginning with Xs. I find the entries easier to read and edit when written in this format. I collate the books with a binding machine (an office supply store or printing company could also do this for you). New journals are distributed at the beginning of each grading period. This gives students a sense of accomplishment because they can view the previous journal as a finished product. Completed journals are filed in portfolios.

Organization of Student Work

Each child has a math portfolio. There are numerous options for this practice. Currently, I am using hanging folders—one for each child—that are housed in one of my two lateral filing cabinets. Crates and individual filing boxes also work just fine. My system does place a constraint on easy access, but it reduces clutter. The good news is that the filing cabinet is very near my phone. When phone conferencing with a parent, I can easily and quickly retrieve his child's portfolio and make reference to student work as we speak.

I distribute a manila folder to each child at the beginning of each trimester in which to place that trimester's corrected homework and tests, test reflections, and major projects. One of my students' favorite activities is to decorate their manila folders at the beginning of each trimester. I ask each child for her favorite one- or two-digit number. With a permanent broad-tipped black marker, I write the number big in the middle of the cover of the folder. The children then use markers (any color except black) to create a picture around that number. I have seen 5s become baseball players and ladies with big hats. I have seen 3s transformed into colorful butterflies. My students call this folder day and are delighted when it is announced at the beginning of class. While they are drawing, I can be handing out work and having quiet conversations with children about their progress or about a piece of work of which they should be particularly proud.

Organization of Teaching Materials

As we gain years of experience, we begin to develop our own organizational systems for teaching materials. I used to keep files and files of student handouts, unit projects, and activities. I still do, but I now keep the bulk of my unit planning materials in three-ring notebooks—one for each unit. Each notebook has the unit printed on the spine and on the front. There are similar dividers in each notebook designating the following categories:

- *Lesson plans and teaching notes:* I usually type these up on Friday afternoon, to reflect on the week that has just ended. They are cryptic but address the mathematics of the lesson, contain important text page numbers, homework given, and personal notes about the success of the lesson.

- *Vocabulary:* I keep a listing of new vocabulary encountered in the unit.
- *Student handouts:* I keep copies of handouts given in class for in- or out-of-class work. They are referenced in the lesson plans and teaching notes.
- *Parent handouts:* I file newsletters that have been sent home during that unit in this section. Also included is the parent information form for the unit.
- *Unit project:* If a project is assigned in this unit, I file away the student information sheets and rubrics in this section.
- *Formal assessments:* Copies of study sheets, quizzes, and the unit test are filed in this section.
- *Reference articles:* I file any articles that support the teaching of this unit in this section.

This notebook becomes my teacher's manual for the unit. Personally, I have found that such a notebook system makes referencing activities, articles, and dates that certain material was covered much easier and more accessible from year to year. I add to the notebooks each year and remove and archive dated material. Each unit will quickly become your own as you collect materials to support and document your teaching and progress.

Literature Display

I have recently acquired a book display rack that sits on the corner of the math counter. For years, my math picture books were on a bookshelf too high for the children to reach. But when the library was discarding several book racks, I commandeered one for my classroom. Now the math picture books are available for student use at all times. I often find children under my desk or huddled together at a table sharing a book in their free time. I love the fact that some of the books are tattered and well worn. Much like the Skin Horse in *The Velveteen Rabbit*, these are sure signs of being loved.

For me, a classroom is a sacred place. I am very fortunate because I do not have to share my space with other teachers. Therefore, I have been able to make it truly my own. My classroom is a manifestation of who I am as a teacher and who my students are as mathematicians. A friend of mine from another school came to visit one day and could not find me. She wandered into several rooms and then waited for me in what "had" to be my room. "It just looked like you," she admitted. That was the warmest compliment I could have received.

Chapter 2

September

PROBLEM SOLVING

Teachers should present . . . problems for children to discuss and find solutions to, without the distraction of numerical symbols. This needs to be done frequently, several times a week throughout the entire year, at all grade levels. The goal is for the children to generalize for themselves—from many, many experiences—how the arithmetic operations are described in the language of the real world. Also, students should be encouraged to find their own ways to arrive at solutions and make sense of situations numerically.

About Teaching Mathematics
Burns 2007, 14

The Learning Environment

Establish expectations for working in a problem-solving environment.

Much of September is devoted to modeling, creating, and establishing problem-solving routines and protocol. Many concepts and procedures covered throughout the year can be introduced and explored in problem-solving contexts. It is important to help children understand just how that process will work right from the beginning, and this will facilitate and support instruction as well.

Before you have class discussions with the children about classroom protocol and communication expectations, it is important that you identify those behaviors and proficiencies that you value and want to see develop in the children. Problem solving offers opportunities for children to:

- solve problems in ways that make sense to them
- talk about and represent mathematics
- work with a partner or small group
- realize that the process of solving a problem is often as important as the solution
- apply previously covered concepts and procedures to new situations
- learn to be patient with themselves
- persevere when the solution is not immediately evident

These behaviors and attitudes may represent a shift from what you have expected from students in the past. Establishing an environment that supports cooperative problem solving will allow children to develop, practice, and apply these procedural practices as well as thinking and reasoning skills to the problems that they solve.

Each September, I ask my fourth graders what they think good problem-solving behavior looks like and sounds like. I place two pieces of chart paper on my whiteboard titled "Looks Like" and "Sounds Like." I then solicit ideas from the children about what they should see and hear in the classroom when solving mathematical problems either together or individually. Establishing your own goals and expectations prior to this conversation will allow you to facilitate conversations with greater ease. You may find, in fact, that little restructuring of conversations is needed. Fourth graders love to talk about themselves and their opinions. They will feel empowered by helping establish their own classroom guidelines. After the conversations, I rewrite the agreed-upon behaviors and characteristics on chart paper, have each child sign it, and keep it posted throughout the year on a wall or bulletin board. I also type up a similar copy and send it home for parents. (See Figure 2–1.)

In math class, cooperative problem solving	
Looks Like	*Sounds Like*
• Having fun • Working hard, not hardly working • Staying at your table groups • Focusing on the math task • Listening to each other • Appropriate use of math tools • Paying attention to each other *and* Mrs. Schuey	• Calm—not *too* quiet • Disagreeing with another's ideas respectfully • Indoor voices • Talking through the mathematics • Should *not* hear "I can't …"

Emma Griffin Norah Sarah Jarod Peter
Kavan Matthew Quentin Vidya
Ava Willy Rebecca Mrs. Schuster Kira
Jackson Ben Hayden Mac Nicholas
Michael Nolan

FIGURE 2–1 ◀

Class list of desired mathematical behaviors.

Build a community of learners who can justify and explain their solutions and who see mistakes and misconceptions as opportunities to learn from.

You may need to consistently address these two issues within the first few weeks of school:

■ how to handle misconceptions
■ how to explain and justify solutions or processes

Misconceptions offer some of the very best teaching and learning experiences for mathematical communities. It is important, however, to coach your children on how to disagree with a classmate—or you! A safe classroom environment needs to be established and maintained throughout the year so that children feel free to risk making mistakes. Once again, I solicit ideas from my students about how to disagree with one another, keeping in mind my expectations. We brainstorm possible behaviors and expectations. I collate the responses and post them in the classroom. Here is an example of a list of expectations and behaviors:

- You are free to disagree with another class member's *ideas*.
- You will be asked to support your position with examples.
- You will be asked to converse with the person with whom you are disagreeing.
- You are expected to be respectful.

Once expectations are set, you'll have to be vigilant in their follow-through. These expectations are applicable not only for whole-group discussions but for small-group work as well. It will be necessary to circulate among groupings as children solve problems to model and support these behaviors.

Ask clarifying questions to help students better articulate their thinking and reasoning.

In the first weeks of school, students need to have plenty of practice explaining and justifying their solutions. Asking clarifying questions as students talk through their thinking will help them develop the skills and language to articulate their thoughts and justify their reasoning. The following questions will focus children on the reasoning of their solutions and ideas:

- Why do you think that?
- Will this work with every number?
- When will this strategy *not* work?
- Can you give a counterexample?
- How do you know you have an answer?
- Can you solve this another way?

The Mathematics and Its Language

Children begin to establish problem-solving routines, practices, and strategies in a variety of meaningful contexts.

The mathematics explored in September helps establish yearlong routines and expectations. The mathematical focus for September is helping students establish problem-solving routines and strategies such as the following:

- Guess and check.
- Organize data using tables, charts, and lists.

- Look for a pattern, generalize, and predict.
- Make a model or draw a picture.
- Act out the problem.
- Solve a simpler problem.
- Write a number sentence.
- Work backward.

Choosing rich problems will offer opportunities to develop problem-solving behaviors as well as estimation, calculation, and reasoning skills.

Presenting, facilitating, and monitoring these routines and strategies with your fourth graders can be a yearlong task. Modeling a routine or two when they apply to a problem the class is discussing will help your children identify other situations when those strategies are appropriate. It is also important to remind the children throughout the year to use strategies and routines that they know to find out answers they do not.

While solving a rather involved logic problem with the use of a matrix a while back, a particular group of children kept getting lost in all the presented information. It was a puzzle concerning colors of towels, shoe types, colors of shoes, and who had what. Emily came up to me begging for help; the group just could not keep all the information straight even though they knew exactly what they needed to do. As I sat with them, I asked them what the difficulty was in solving this puzzle. "It's too big!" they all cried. I asked the children to think of how they could make the problem smaller. Asking them to redirect their approach seemed to open up a new possibility for solving the problem. Emily began to make three smaller matrixes—one for towel color, one for shoe type, and one for shoe color. And off they went. When problems with lots of information began to bog down the children later on in the year, I ask them to think back to when they had encountered this same issue when solving logic puzzles. "Make it smaller!" they would all call out. We need to help our young mathematicians make these connections as they move through the year. Seemingly simple questions that help them make these connections, such as "How is this like . . . ?" or "What have you done before when something like this was difficult?" can support children as they work to apply previously used strategies to new situations and problems.

Children refine, practice, and apply mathematical skills as they solve problems.

The class work presented in September offers children opportunities to practice and further refine the following mathematical skills:

- addition with and without regrouping
- subtraction with and without regrouping
- estimation procedures
- basic addition and subtraction fact review

- collecting, representing, and analyzing collected data
- investigating odd and even numbers and their sums
- writing and talking about the discovered mathematics

It may be very helpful to keep anecdotal records for each class member as the students work on the activities at this time in the school year. You may wish to note your students' basic fact automaticity, computational strengths and weaknesses, interpersonal nuances, flexibility of thinking, and willingness to self-correct.

Children focus on the use of mathematical language as they talk and work through the mathematics.

As children work together, it will become increasingly important for them to use the language and the vocabulary of the mathematics appropriately and precisely. When children speak of answers to an addition problem, encourage them to use the word *sum*. When children speak of quantities being the same, encourage them to use the word *equivalent*. When children speak of the number of times a letter occurs in a paragraph, encourage them to use the word *frequency*. Developing a word wall of math terms for each unit will help students focus on precise mathematical language.

TEACHER-TO-TEACHER TALK   My students often refer to math as a "foreign language." And I guess for some, it is! Learning a new language requires immersion and usage. I have always enjoyed the study of vocabulary. Because of that, word study has become an important component in my curriculum. When choosing problems for students to solve in September, I look for those that require similar language. The new vocabulary that we encounter in one investigation can then be applied to another. I was delighted to hear a former student use the word *consecutive* with another student in the hall one day—it was a word that we had worked with the previous year as we investigated patterns in Pascal's triangle. As children begin to realize how concise mathematical language can help them better articulate their ideas, they will want to make use of their newly expanding vocabulary.

Investigations and Literature-Based Activities

Martha Blah Blah

Duration: 2–3 class periods

I begin the year with a read-aloud of *Martha Blah Blah* (Meddaugh 1996). Martha, a dog who is able to talk as a result of eating a bowl of alphabet soup each day, finds herself in a pickle when the owner of the soup company reduces the number of letters in each can of alphabet soup. Fourth graders are tickled by Martha's amusing but unintelligible speech as a result of the missing letters. Martha takes it upon herself to solve the problem of the missing letters and is soon able to order her favorite burgers once again. Students then investigate letter frequencies in paragraphs. This investigation offers students opportunities to:

- collect, represent, and analyze data
- write about the collected data
- create words out of randomly chosen letters
- work in pairs

Materials
- *Martha Blah Blah*, by Susan Meddaugh
- 1 sheet of writing prompts for *Martha Blah Blah*, per student (see Blackline Masters)
- 1 sheet of newsprint per pair of students
- 25 pieces of alphabet pasta per pair of students
- 1 small paper cup per pair of students
- 1 9-by-12-inch piece of construction paper per pair of students

Following the reading of *Martha Blah Blah*, we have a class discussion about letter distribution in words. What letters occur most frequently? Why might that be? Do we notice any frequency patterns between consonants and vowels? How could we investigate this? How could we collect data? How could we chart the collected data? If Granny Flo was determined to eliminate the least-used letters from her soup, how could our data help her make an informed decision (at least for talking dogs)? After posing these questions, I ask the children to talk with their neighbor about ideas for carrying out such an investigation. As the children talk, I circulate around the room, listening and handing out the writing prompts.

I call the class back together so students can share their ideas and discuss the writing task. I ask each pair to choose a paragraph in a book. Many choose a paragraph from a book they are presently reading or from one of the books in the classroom book display. I ask that the paragraphs be relatively short. At this point in the school year, I am more concerned about the manageability of the task than the length of the paragraph. Each pair is given a piece of newsprint on which to post their collected data in whatever format they choose. I remind the children that they will not only post their collected data on the newsprint but also write summarizing statements as well as post one last task on it later. I explain that they will have the opportunity to decorate their poster at the end of the investigation.

Depending on how much experience your children have had in working collectively, you might want to brainstorm with your class as to how to collect the data. Does one child read the words and the other tally the letters? Do they take turns after each sentence? How might they chart the letter frequencies? Invariably, students suggest that all the letters of the alphabet be written in a T-chart with the letters on the left and the distribution tallied on the right. I ask the children if it is necessary to write down all the letters in the alphabet or just the ones that are used in the paragraph. Rich discussions can occur as to the importance of being able to quickly assess the holes in the collected data. Once we have agreed on what they are being asked to do, the children set off to collect and represent their data.

Before all the children have finished collecting their data, I ask for their attention, and we discuss the written part of the task. I ask the children to write two summarizing statements about their data collection on their sheet of newsprint. What do they notice? Is there a pattern of any kind? Where are the "lumps, bumps, and holes"? They then complete the writing prompts. Each child completes her own sheet, but they may certainly discuss and compare opinions and answers.

FIGURE 2–2   ▼

Norah's completed
Martha Blah Blah
assignment.

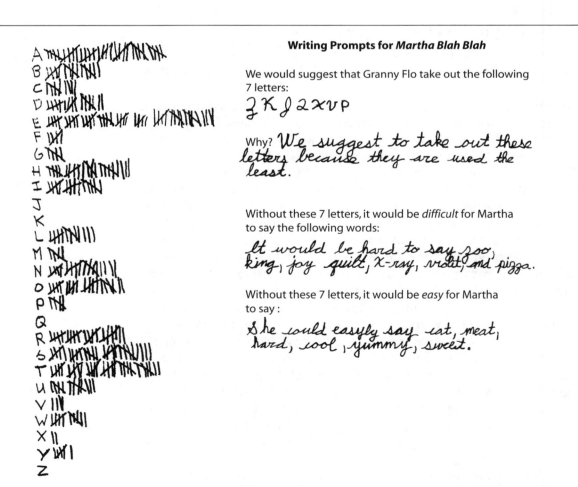

Writing Prompts for *Martha Blah Blah*

We would suggest that Granny Flo take out the following 7 letters:

Z K J Q X V P

Why? We suggest to take out these letters because they are used the least.

Without these 7 letters, it would be *difficult* for Martha to say the following words:

It would be hard to say zoo, king, joy quilt, x-ray, violet, and pizza.

Without these 7 letters, it would be *easy* for Martha to say:

She could easyly say eat, meat, hard, cool, yummy, sweet.

As the children move on to the writing part of the task, it may be necessary to circulate around the room to offer assistance. Talking about the mathematics is one thing—writing about it can be quite another. I begin to push students to use "because" statements as they write: "I would remove these letters *because* . . ." It may also be necessary to remind students to refer to their collected data as they write. How is their collected data influencing their decisions and writing? (See Figure 2–2.)

I call the students back together for a class discussion of their findings and decisions. Most agree that more consonants should be removed than vowels. As the children share their findings, help them refer to their data. Questions such as "Why do you think so?" and "On what are you basing this opinion?" can help children better articulate the mathematical proof on which their opinions are based. Asking whole-class questions such as "Do you agree with Beth? Why or why not?" can focus the children on the mathematics offered by another child. Encourage the children to turn and speak to each other, not just to you.

TEACHER-TO-TEACHER TALK   Holding the children's attention while another student is speaking can be a challenge, not only for the teacher but for the children as well. Chapin, O'Connor, and Anderson (2003) present five user-friendly talk moves that promote listening skills and help students make sense of mathematics:

- revoicing
- restating another's reasoning
- agreeing or disagreeing with another's reasoning
- adding on to another's reasoning
- using wait time (11–16)

Mathematical talk can be engaging, animated, and instructional for everyone involved. The implementation of talk moves helps children keep their focus on one another as well as on the mathematics. As I implement a talk move, I explain to the class what I am doing. After asking a few children to restate what another classmate has offered, I explain to the class that I want them to focus on what each child is saying. I sometimes tell the children that asking them to respond to another classmate's comments also keeps them on their toes! Listening is hard work. Listening *well* is *really* hard work.

The activity concludes with a word search made from a cupful of alphabet pasta. Each pair gets a paper cup with twenty-five pieces of alphabet pasta in it. They pour the pasta on their desktops and construct as many words as they can from the letters. Then they glue their pasta onto a piece of construction paper (old-fashioned white glue works best) and write their words underneath. This can also be mounted on the newsprint containing the group's frequency chart and summary statements.

Math and Literature, Grades 4–6 (Bresser 2004) contains another series of activities focusing on Martha Blah-Blah's dilemma in which students analyze letter frequencies and apply their findings to the game of Boggle.

Estimation Practice with Linking Cubes

Duration: 1–2 class periods

This problem-solving activity, adapted from *Mathematical Thinking at Grade 4* (Tierney 1998), offers students opportunities to articulate and test out estimation practices in small-group settings.

Materials

- several teacher-created objects made from linking cubes
- approximately 100 linking cubes per group of four students
- 1 note card per student
- 1 *How Many Cubes in Each Object?* record sheet per student (see Blackline Masters)

Because my table groupings are arranged in fours, each table group works together on this activity. Before the lesson, I create several objects from the cubes to use as examples. For the first example, I often make a desk or a chair—a simple object that the students can easily identify. I place a container of linking cubes on each table and allow the children a little free building time with the cubes to satisfy their curiosity. While the children are building, I pass out a note card to each child.

After about five minutes of free building time, I ask the children to dismantle their constructions into single cubes and place them in the container once again. I present my first object to the class and ask, "How many cubes do you think I have in this desk?" Children offer random guesses, and invariably a child will ask to hold the object. I tell the students that they can touch my object, but they cannot count the cubes one by one. They will be able to do that later. I want them to estimate the total number of cubes using some sort of estimation strategy. I ask, "What could we do to estimate how many cubes are in my desk?" I write students' ideas on the board. Most suggest counting in groups, then adding up the groups. Pushing the children to explain what groupings to count can very often uncover some creative thinking. Some may suggest counting layers. Some may suggest counting up parts (the legs, then the top). A few may even look at the object as sitting within a cube and then delete the "empty" spaces around the object.

Next I present the following task:

1. Each child will make a structure.

2. On the note card, the student will write the name of his structure.

3. Each student will place his structure and the note card on the table in front of him when he is finished.

I have found that giving the children a time limit (ten minutes works well) helps them stay focused on the task at hand. As the children are building, I pass out one *How Many Cubes in Each Object?* record sheet to each student.

Once time is called, I ask the children to do a gallery walk around the room to investigate the objects made by their classmates. Once settled back at their seats, the next phase of the investigation begins. The students at each table move around their table, filling in their record sheets. They look at each object, name the object, and make an estimate as to how many cubes are in that object. Before they begin, I ask the children to think about an estimation strategy that they could apply to all the objects in order to make their estimations more efficient and accurate. Encourage the children to talk about their estimations, compare estimations, and explain estimation strategies with each other. Once the children have moved around their table (the children move—not the objects!), they return to their seats. In turn, each tablemate takes apart her structure and counts the cubes in it. The tablemates then record this count on their sheets.

Then I call the children together for a whole-class discussion. I ask for a show of hands—"Who are good estimators? Who are not so good estimators? Why do you think that is so? Who had a good estimation strategy?" I ask a volunteer to describe his strategy. I then pull out one of my already-made objects. I ask a child *other* than the one who offered the strategy to estimate the number of cubes in my object using the proposed strategy. We then break down the structure and count the cubes. I repeat this process several times with the remaining objects, asking for a new strategy and a new volunteer to apply that strategy to each one.

Asking for and then writing practices and characteristics of good estimators on the board or a piece of chart paper can be helpful to the class. Your list might look like this:

Good Estimators

- Group before they count.
- Count in groups of fives.
- Break the object down into smaller groups before they count.
- Ask themselves if their estimate makes sense.

Follow-Up Journal Write

Suppose someone was trying to estimate how many cubes were in an object. What advice would you give that person? (See "Mathematics Writing" on page 48 for more information about journal writes.)

Thinking in 3s

Duration: 1–2 class periods

This paper-and-pencil calculation task, adapted from *Awesome Math Problems for Creative Thinking* (Gavin et al. 2000), offers students opportunities to:

- practice calculation skills
- apply logical reasoning skills based on number sense
- identify multiples
- construct generalizations about multiples
- work cooperatively in small groups

Materials

- 1 *Thinking in 3s* activity sheet per student (see Blackline Masters)
- 1 *Thinking in 4s* activity sheet per student (see Blackline masters)
- 1 overhead transparency of *Thinking in 3s* activity sheet
- 1 *Thinking About Thinking in 3s* record sheet per student (see Blackline Masters)

As the class begins, I explain to the children that they will be working on a calculation task with a partner. I give each child a copy of the *Thinking in 3s* handout. The assignment asks students to cross out two numbers in the array so that the sum of the numbers in each row and column is a multiple of three. This is a meaningful opportunity to introduce new mathematical vocabulary such as *sum* and *multiple*: discuss what the words mean and how they apply to the task. I also remind the children that this is a cooperative activity and that I expect them to talk to their partner about the mathematics. When they make a decision to cross out a number, they need to justify their decision mathematically.

I give the children a time frame—approximately 15 minutes—and they set off to work. If children finish early, I hand them a nearly blank array titled *Thinking in 4s* and ask them to try to fill it in. The same rules apply; there must be two numbers that do *not* fit into the array, in which the sums of the rows and columns should be multiples of four. This task can be more challenging and engaging than the first because multiple solutions can apply. If students don't finish the challenge task, they can put it away and pull it out at another time of the day.

Using an overhead transparency of the *Thinking in 3s* activity sheet, we process the task. I have a volunteer come up and cross out two numbers. Does everyone agree with the student's choices? Are there any other solutions? Initially, students are unprepared for this question, so I often offer a counterexample to move the discussion along. I cross out two other numbers and ask, "Will this work? Why or why not?" Some children dive right in to the calculating and others try to reason their way to a solution. When enough hands are raised, I begin to ask for solutions. I ask, "How do you know?" after each answer to encourage children to explain their strategies as well as their mathematical reasoning. I implement talk moves to keep the discussion focused.

Next, I distribute the *Thinking About Thinking in 3s* record sheet. I ask students to work with the same partner, but each child is responsible for completing his own written work. This is a time when the children can be moved from thinking about the *specifics* of the task to making *generalizations* about multiples of three, and they may struggle a bit with this line of questioning initially. First they were asked about sums, and now they are being asked about odd and even numbers within the context of this problem. (See Figure 2–3.)

FIGURE 2–3 ▼

Ava's completed *Thinking in 3s* assignment.

Thinking in 3s

Cross out two of the numbers in the array below so that the sum of the numbers in each row and column is a multiple of 3.

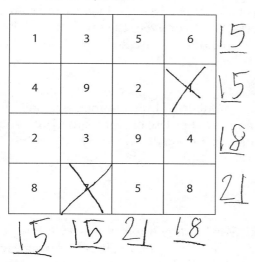

$3, 6, 9, 12, 15, 18, 21, 24, 27, 30, 33, 36, 39$

Thinking about Thinking in 3s

1. Is a multiple of 3 always an odd number? Why or why not? Use examples to justify your thinking.

   No, it goes odd, even, odd, even, ec For example 3×4=12 and 6×3=18.

2. What numbers could you substitute for the crossed-out numbers to make sums of all the rows and columns divisible by 3? Are there other solutions?

   We could turn the ones we had to cross out into multipuls of three.

3. Could you have a row (or column) of four *odd* numbers whose sum is a multiple of 3? Why or why not? Give examples to justify your thinking.

   Yes, you could make them all odd multipuls of three 3,9,15,21, or 27,27,33 because they equal multipuls of three

4. Could you have a row (or column) for four *even* numbers whose sum is a multiple of 3? Why or why not? Give examples to justify your thinking.

   Yes, it is posilive.

The study of odd and even numbers can set the stage for further study of number theory and relationships. When we ask our students to investigate patterns of odd and even numbers, we are asking them to think beyond the fact that a number is simply odd or even. When we calculate sums and ask children to investigate the addends, we are asking our students to make generalizations about properties of whole numbers. When children report that an odd number plus an odd number equals an even number, we can help them better articulate their thinking by asking them to give numerical examples that support their thinking, such as $3 + 5 = 8$ or $5 + 5 = 10$. Some children may be intrigued by a matrix describing the sums:

+	Odd	Even
Odd	e	o
Even	o	e

Some children will be able to apply these generalizations to columns of numbers, as in the *Thinking in 3s* task. When asked to identify the sum of a row (or column) of four numbers as odd or even, they will reason their way to an answer rather than calculate. (See Figure 2–4.)

Follow-Up Journal Write

Chris is calculating the sum of five numbers. Three numbers are odd and two are even. What could those numbers be? Use examples to justify your thinking. Will your sum be odd or even? How do you know?

$1.00 Word Riddles

Duration: 1–3 class periods

This lesson is based on *The $1.00 Word Riddle Book* (Burns 1990), which presents a system for decoding words into monetary values by giving each letter a value: A is worth one cent, B is worth two cents, C is worth three cents, and so on. The answers to the riddles in the book are all worth one dollar. This investigation offers students opportunities to practice addition within a language arts context.

FIGURE 2–4 ▶

Tree diagram showing sums of odd and even numbers.

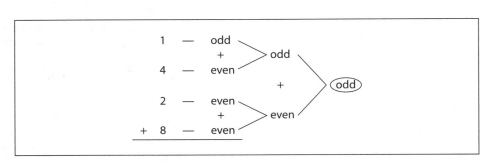

Materials

- piece of chart paper with a vertical listing of the letters of the alphabet
- at least 1 copy of *The $1.00 Word Riddle Book* (multiple copies if possible), by Marilyn Burns
- enough crayons, markers, or colored pencils for the class to share
- enough magazines to cut up for the class to share
- enough glue sticks for the class to share

I begin the class by asking the children how they might make up a secret code if they wanted to send a top secret message to a classmate. Some suggest making up a new alphabet or the use of some form of hieroglyphics, but someone usually suggests some sort of numerical code, especially since this is math class! If the children do not offer the code used in *The $1.00 Word Riddle Book*, I post the chart paper on which the letters of the alphabet are listed. I write in $0.01 next to the A. Then I reveal that the B is $0.02. The children quickly catch on and offer all the other values of the letters. I ask them to open up their math notebooks to a clean sheet, label the page *$1.00 Words*, and list the letters and their values for future reference.

I begin the lesson by reading the book's introduction aloud to the class. Before we begin to work on the riddles, I ask each child to calculate the "price" of his or her first name. Calculators are not permitted, and I ask the students to keep track of their calculations in their math notebooks. Before they begin, it may be helpful to spend a few minutes to talk about ways of keeping track of their work.

There is always a great deal of excitement as the children calculate the value of their names. We talk about who is worth more and why. Who is worth one dollar? Does a long name mean a higher price? What vowels are more valuable? Why might my nickname be worth more than my formal name? We also take the time to talk about our calculation strategies. We share strategies and discuss the efficiency of each. Processing strategies can be very helpful for some children. Children may discard the strategy they were using for another if they think another strategy is more efficient.

We then look at the cover of *The $1.00 Word Riddle Book*. I write the caption of the picture on the board: *Whenever Henrietta whistled, trembling costumed elephants merrily performed*. I ask the children why they think this caption is on the front of the book. They find it hard to believe that each word is worth one dollar, so I assign each word to a pair of students and they calculate the word's value.

We then move to the riddles in the book. Once again, I ask the children to work with a partner. Over the years I have collected enough copies of *The $1.00 Word Riddle Book* so that each pair of children can share one. Making transparencies from the pages is an alternative. There are visual riddles attached to pictures and word riddles that can easily be written on the board or reproduced as a handout.

When the children have solved some of the riddles in the book, I offer them a choice of two different activities:

- Work through the story of "Robin Hood and the Hot-Blooded Hawkers," which can be found at the end of *The $1.00 Word Riddle Book*. There are forty-two $1.00 words in the story. Can you find them? (Directions are included on page 9 of the riddle book.)
- Create or mount cutout pictures on white drawing paper with captions. Captions may be one word or a few, but each word or words within a caption must be worth $1.00.

Students need to agree with their partner on their choice and settle in to complete the task.

I try to give the children a full class period in which to work, reminding them that we will process our work in the next class period. They have little difficulty sustaining their focus and interest for forty-five minutes to an hour. I also remind the children that they will be asked to present their work to the class and share their calculating strategies.

By this time in September, the children begin to look forward to whole-class discussions. A mathematical community is beginning to develop. They now approach classroom conversations with anticipation and an understanding of discussion expectations. All focus needs to be centered on the student who is sharing, and all comments or questions should be addressed to that child. I structure the conversations by determining the order of presentation and asking leading or probing questions. The focus of this particular conversation is addition strategies. If children become frustrated with this task, it is often because they are using inefficient adding strategies. I also question the partners about their cooperative strategies—how they worked together or did not!

Follow-Up Journal Write

Nicole claims that *attitude* is a $1.00 word. Nick claims that *altitude* is a $1.00 word. Without adding, can you determine who is correct? Why or why not? Explain your thinking.

Games

Games can be an important instructional tool in every fourth-grade classroom. Not only are games motivating and challenging for children, but they also contain and support mathematical knowledge and help children further develop procedural and reasoning skills. Playing games over and over again helps children clarify their mathematical understandings and fine-tune their skills. A game can be introduced and played in one class session and then offered again in a menu format. In September, I focus my game choices on the following mathematical skills:

- basic fact recall
- mental multidigit addition and subtraction strategies
- place value
- classification and properties of numbers
- number sense
- equality

Name That Number

This game, adapted from *Everyday Mathematics* (Everyday Learning Corporation 2007a), asks children to combine numbers using whole number operations to represent a target number. There is no scoring in this game, which can eliminate some of the competitiveness games can elicit. *Name That Number* offers students opportunities to:

- represent a target number by combining numbers using addition, subtraction, multiplication, or division
- represent equality

Materials
- *Name That Number* directions (see Blackline Masters)
- 1 deck of 0–12 number cards, containing 4 of each number (if using a regular deck of playing cards, aces can represent 1, jacks 11, queens 12, and kings 0.)
- number of players: 2–3

Number sense, estimations skills, and fluency of basic math facts are all involved in playing this game. Rather than compete against each other, students often help each other to use as many cards as possible to reach their target number.

Each student must to record her number sentences as she plays the game. I have students do this in their math notebooks to establish the routine of keeping written records of games in their notebooks.

Sample Round

Player's cards: 4, 5, 8, 2, 10

Target number: 12

Possible solutions:

10	*2*	*8*		*4*	*5*	*10*	*2*
(10 × 2) − 8		*or*	*(4 × 5) − (10 − 2)*				
(3 cards used)			*(4 cards used)*				

When representing their number sentences, students can be encouraged to begin with the target number:

$$12 = (10 \times 2) - 8$$
$$12 = (4 \times 5) - (10 - 2)$$

Students can be uncomfortable representing number sentences in this manner. Some have yet to understand the meaning of the equals sign. For many fourth graders, the symbol is synonymous with "the answer is . . ." when, in fact, the equals sign represents a *relationship*, not an *operation*. The sign indicates the balance of an equation. Both sides of the equation represent the same value. In this case, both sides of the equation represent the value of twelve.

Although students may have played similar games in earlier grades, *Name That Number* is well worth playing. As fourth graders, the children should now have greater fluency with their basic facts. Their number sense and estimation skills are also better established. Replaying games in subsequent years should not to be automatically dismissed because of the children's familiarity with the games. If you choose to play a game that the children have played in previous years, articulate your mathematical expectations to the class. Let them know that strategies should be different now that they are more proficient mathematicians. You may also want to let them know prior to playing the game that you will be asking them about how their strategies in the fourth grade differ from those used in previous years.

Close to 100

This game, adapted from *Mathematical Thinking at Grade 4* (Tierney 1998), involves arranging digits to make two two-digit numbers whose sum is as near to hundred as possible. *Close to 100* offers students opportunities to:

- add and subtract
- estimate
- create two-digit numbers whose sum is one hundred or close to one hundred

Materials
- *Close to 100* directions (see Blackline Masters)
- 1 deck of 0–9 number cards, containing 4 of each number
- 1 *Close to 100* score sheet per player (see Blackline Masters)
- number of players: 2–3
- optional: 1 deck of overhead 0–9 number cards

Observing the children's strategies will help you gain some useful insights about their mathematical thinking. Do children choose cards randomly, or are they narrowing down numbers to make numbers more reasonable? Do they add mentally, or do they need to write down the numbers? Do students consider the sum of the tens digits when choosing numbers? If so, how do they compensate with the ones digits? It may be helpful to play a game with several groups of students in order to get a better window on their thinking. If time allows, ask children to share strategies with the class. Using a set of overhead cards is helpful as children explain to the class how they think about and choose their numbers.

Digit Draw

This whole-group activity, adapted from *Nimble with Numbers, Grades 4–5* (Childs and Choate 1998), has become one of my classroom favorites. It is similar to *Close to 100* in that children are asked to create two two-digit numbers from drawn cards whose sum equals a target number or close to it. *Digit Draw* offers students opportunities to:

- practice two-digit addition mentally and/or on paper
- choose positions for digits based on estimation skills, understanding of place value, and logical reasoning skills

Materials
- *Digit Draw* directions (see Blackline Masters)
- 1 *Digit Draw* record sheet per team (see Blackline Masters)
- deck of 0–9 number cards, containing 2 of each number
- number of players: entire class, divided into teams of 2–3
- optional: overhead transparency of *Digit Draw* record sheet
- optional: overhead deck of number cards

Playing *Digit Draw* in a whole-class format offers an opportunity for rich mathematical discussion. Opening up a discussion about strategies not only will direct the conversation but may encourage children to adopt what they think will be better strategies as well. If a team scores a difference of 0, I often stop and ask the team members about their strategy. What worked well? Where did they place "high" numbers? Why? Where did they place "low" numbers? What did they do with 5s? Every year, *Digit Draw* quickly becomes one of my class's favorite games. I am always amazed at how efficient some groups become at playing this game. I ask that the children keep their record sheet taped on a blank page in their math notebook for easy access.

Capture the Outlaw

This game, adapted from *Math Homework That Counts* (Raphel 2000), requires students to decide which number in a group does not belong.

When children offer an "outlaw," they must also explain their reasoning. I often play this game with the entire class. I present the first few sets of numbers, then ask for volunteers to present sets of their own. There are often multiple solutions and multiple possible outlaws, which makes this activity engaging. It is the *reasoning* in determining the outlaw that becomes so interesting. *Capture Outlaw* offers students opportunities to classify properties of numbers.

Materials

- none

Sample Round

Capture the outlaw in this set of numbers: 3, 4, 7, 12

Possible Solutions

- The outlaw is 12, because 3, 4, and 7 constitute an addition/subtraction fact family.
- The outlaw is 7, because 3, 4, and 12 constitute a multiplication/division fact family.
- The outlaw is 7, because it is the only two-syllable word.
- The outlaw is 12, because it is the only two-digit number.

Capture the outlaw in this set of numbers: 8, 18, 27, 90

Possible Solutions

- The outlaw is 27, because it is odd.
- The outlaw is 8, because the sum of its digits does not equal 9.
- The outlaw is 90, because it is the only multiple of 10.
- The outlaw is 8, because it is the only single-digit number.

I ask the children to open to a clean page in their math notebooks and label the page *Capture the Outlaw*. I encourage the children to make sets of four numbers that they could use in this activity in their free time. It takes even greater classification and reasoning skills to put together a set of numbers with multiple solutions than to determine an outlaw. Journal writes and homework assignments can easily be developed from this activity.

> **TEACHER-TO-TEACHER TALK**   There are many wonderful resources on the market for math games. Do not be afraid to try out different games with your class! If I am trying out a new game, which I do quite often, I ask the class for a thumbs-up or thumbs-down after the game. I also ask the children to explain their positions about the game. Why did they like it? Why was it too easy? What could we do to make the game

more fun? It is important for teachers to understand what mathematical skills and procedures a game addresses. Some games lack the mathematical rigor we want for our students; some games lack the engagement. When conducting back-to-school nights in September, I often present a math game to the parents. After we play the game, I ask the parents to brainstorm about the math skills necessary to play it. I also ask the parents about the strategies they used while playing. Would they stick with the same strategy if we played the game again? Why or why not? The follow-up conversation helps parents understand the merit and mathematical importance of playing games in math class. Assigning math games for homework is another way to engage families in their children's math education.

Calculation Routines and Practices

Basic addition and subtraction fact review and the application of mental addition and subtraction strategies as well as estimation skills are the focus of September's calculation routines and practices. Deciding when to *reteach* or when to *review* can be a challenge. Although it is important for children to practice and review skills, they should do so in the spirit of working toward more complex mastery of those skills. Redundant review and unnecessary reteaching can be inherently boring and insulting to fourth graders and can be most effective in turning our young mathematicians off to learning (Jacobs 1997).

Each September, I expect that my fourth graders will enter my class with a developed fluency of the basic addition and subtraction facts. This, as you may well know, can be a dangerous expectation! What is fluent for a fourth grader can look quite different from fluency for a third or fifth grader. And fourth-grade fluency can look quite different from one class to the next as well. It is the automaticity of fact recall that becomes increasingly important as children move through the procedural challenges of the fourth-grade year. We need to be aware of the fundamental difference between *automaticity* and *memorization*. According to Fosnot and Dolk (2001b), the automaticity of fact recall relies on thinking about number relationships and number sense. Answers to facts must be automatic—produced in only a few seconds. When fact recall is automatic, it is *not* reliant on memorization, repetitive drill, and practice without contextual meaning.

The automaticity of fact recall can be assessed by observing and listening to the mathematical conversations of your students during the first few weeks of school. Although this first month of fourth-grade mathematics focuses on problem-solving routines and practices, each activity also contains multiple opportunities for children to apply basic fact knowledge and understandings. Observing counting routines as children tally letter frequencies can give you a window into their fact fluency. Do they count letters one by one, or do they count by groups? Do your students compose and decompose numbers for ease of counting or adding or subtracting when estimating the number of cubes in an object? For example, do they look at eighteen as "twenty with two less"? Do some students continue to count on their fingers in order to compute a sum? Are students relying on their number sense to assess the reasonableness of answers?

If you feel that your students' fact recall is not what it should be, now is the opportune time to call together the class for a discussion about your expectations. Make your expectations known to your children. Let your students know why fact recall is so important in the study of mathematics. I often share with my students my personal difficulties with the multiplication facts when I was in school. I realized only years later that my youthful frustrations and disgust with math were intrinsically related to my inability to conjure up products with any regularity, let alone meaning! Have a plan in place to share with your students that will give them opportunities to practice and automatize their facts.

> **TEACHER-TO-TEACHER TALK**   I am forever looking for books, workbooks, and publications that offer activities and practice pages that will help students with fact recall. Although I do give an occasional page of repetitive addition or subtraction facts, I usually choose problems based on the students' needs or difficulties. More often than not, fourth graders struggle more with the automaticity of their subtraction facts than that of addition. Therefore, I might give the class a page of subtraction facts with a final question such as *How does knowing 8 + 5 help you in knowing 13 − 8?* I prefer number puzzles and riddles that require numerical reasoning and application of number sense to pages of fact practice. For example, I like to introduce students to "Sum Squares" (Childs and Choate 1998). (See Figure 2–5.) Completing a series of sum squares offers opportunities for both addition and subtraction fact practice within a puzzle context. Try keeping a reference notebook of successful practice pages organized by content and skill—it will quickly become invaluable.

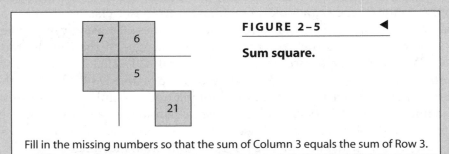

FIGURE 2–5   ◀

Sum square.

Fill in the missing numbers so that the sum of Column 3 equals the sum of Row 3.

Weekly Warm-Ups

Although much of September is devoted to problem-solving practices and routines and creating a mathematical community and culture, attention to paper-and-pencil proficiency cannot be ignored. As I began to incorporate more problem-solving investigations and small-group work into my curriculum, I began to worry about the *apparent* lack of paper-and-pencil work in my classroom. I was delighted, impressed, and motivated by the mathematical thinking and reasoning of my children, but I was always aware that the world of education puts additional constraints on our teaching and students. As a result, I began to develop a series of weekly warm-ups for my students that focus on paper-and-pencil thinking, reasoning, and accuracy with addition and subtraction. Using published as well as teacher-generated activities and worksheets, I collate a selection of five to seven activities that are to be completed by the children over a given period of time. The children and I refer to these as warm-up packets. I often distribute them on Monday morning and collect them on Friday afternoon. Children may work on these packets together or independently. Once the routine becomes established within the classroom, the children often find time to work on their packets themselves within the schedule of the schoolday.

Because some children may be unsure of how to work productively with other children on an independent math activity, you may need to spend time discussing how and when that can be done. I ask that children do not give other children answers. Comparing answers is fine, however, and even encouraged. Having children read the directions or the problem to each other can help focus their attention on the mathematics. Children can ask for my assistance only if they *both* agree that they need help. Allotting time in the schoolday for completion of the warm-ups can help establish routines and expectations. Soon, the children will settle into routines and even set up some of their own! Warm-ups can also be assigned for homework, which can help children establish time-management practices as they learn how efficiently they can move through the activities.

Although I am forever striving to be creative, innovative, and open-ended in my teaching, there are certainly times when the use of a worksheet is appropriate and good practice. But there are good worksheets and not so good ones. Good worksheets embed computational and procedural practice in a problem-solving format. They can offer practice of new skills or the application of previously learned concepts and procedures. Good worksheets can even cause intrigue and wonder about the presented mathematics. Annette Raphel (2000, 9–12) describes good worksheets as those that:

- are mathematically rich
- are interesting
- stimulate mathematical connections
- are rooted in problem formation, problem solving, or mathematical reasoning
- promote communication

- advance student understanding
- are *not* intimidating
- do not require children to do arithmetic for arithmetic's sake

It may be helpful to consult this list when assessing worksheets prior to assigning them. Asking for the opinions of your fourth graders after they have completed a worksheet can once again be helpful in your assessment of its quality. Their brutal honesty is often insightful and enlightening! Once again, instructional decisions need to be rooted in the mathematics of the task. We need to present meaningful mathematics tasks within an engaging context.

Choice Time

Children greatly benefit from and enjoy the independent problem-solving opportunities that choice time can offer. Choice time can also allow us to differentiate instruction in those areas and at those times when we see the need to support struggling learners or challenge advanced learners. Assigning choice time partners with similar needs can help us focus the instruction on specific skills or tasks. Students with beginning skills may need tasks with more opportunities for direct instruction or practice. They may require activities that are hands-on and require only simple reading skills. Students with the ability to extend their skills, on the other hand, may require tasks that are open-ended, abstract, and move beyond the mere practice of previously mastered skills and understandings.

The tasks you offer will differentiate the experiences for the children. Good tasks are those that can be easily adjusted within the context of the task, investigation, or problem. Adjusting the numbers within a problem for different students can quickly offer additional practice or challenge. Adjusting the journal prompt following an activity for groups of children can also offer further review or additional challenge.

Choice time can be organized in a menu format that offers a collection of content-specific activities that students complete independently without classroom instruction. Offering children a choice of several tasks following class instruction can be equally effective. Whatever the format of your choice time, independent activities from which children can choose will offer additional opportunities for your students to interact with targeted mathematical ideas, concepts, and procedures.

Addition and Subtraction Menu

A menu is a collection of activities that students can do independent of classroom instruction. Menu choices are often content specific. In this case, an addition and subtraction menu can offer additional independent calculation and problem-solving practice. Menu items are not hierarchical and do not conceptually build upon one another. Rather, they pose problems, set up situations, and ask questions that help students interact with targeted mathematical ideas (Burns 2007).

When choosing items for a menu, I try to create an eclectic mix of games, investigations, and paper-and-pencil practice. Introducing the menu format to your class can take time, but it is important to set up expectations and routines prior to the students' first experience. I use the menu format throughout the year, so this initial session is well worth the time and effort. Prior to class time, I list the menu items on chart paper. I have found that keeping the wording of the tasks simple helps minimize confusion. It is also important to determine which menu items are *required* and which are *optional*. I try to include both on each menu. Learning to make choices and then having to honor those choices is important business! Each required item is labeled with a yellow arrow. The arrows can be taped to the menu or mounted with Velcro for easy removal. Optional items have no label. Each item is also labeled as an *individual* or *partner* (cooperative) task. These labels are also mounted next to each item. I use the same labels for all of my menus. (See Figure 2–6.) Suzy Ronfeldt (2003) offers her third graders a "dinner" menu, consisting of required items, as well as a "dessert" menu of optional items for those children with a firmer grasp of concepts who are seeking further challenge.

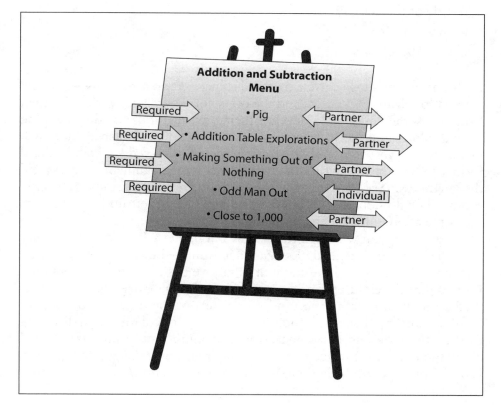

FIGURE 2–6 ◄

Master listing of menu items.

FIGURE 2–7   ▶

Menu task card for
Addition Table
Explorations.

FIGURE 2–7

Menu task card for *Addition Table Explorations.*

Addition Table Explorations

You need:

several addition charts per pair of students
1 *Addition Table Explorations* worksheet per student
a partner
colored pencils (optional)

Directions
Using the addition chart, you and a partner will explore patterns found on the chart and make generalizations about those patterns. You may wish to color in patterns as you discuss them with your partner.

Required ⟶   ⟵ Partner

I write individual tasks on 12-by-18-inch tagboard so that I can reuse them year to year. Each task card contains the following:

- title of the activity
- materials list
- directions (see Figure 2–7)

Each station has a task card, a materials bin, and two other bins—one designated for clean worksheets and the other for completed work. Although I often ask the children to develop their own methods for documenting their thinking and work, I have found that creating worksheets for each menu item saves time and frustration for all involved. A standardized format for completing written work also helps me document progress and thoroughness. (See Figure 2–8.) The stations are set up around the classroom. They do not take up much space and can be left up for the necessary time allotted for menu completion.

Once again, you will need to set time parameters. I prefer to introduce a menu during an extended block; a ninety-minute block works well. I can introduce the menu and the children can move right into the mathematics. I prefer that the children work on menu items as an entire class for a specified amount of time, not in random pockets of the day. It allows me to focus on the mathematics and to spend time circulating and listening to their thinking and reasoning. Timing is important—and difficult. If I allow too much time for completing menu items, the students can get restless; if I provide too little time, they can get frustrated. I try to complete

FIGURE 2–8 ◄

Worksheet for *Addition Table Explorations*.

Addition Table Explorations

Name_____

Describe general rules or shortcuts you have discovered to find the following:

The sum of any three horizontally adjacent numbers:

The sum of any three vertically adjacent numbers:

The sum of any three diagonally adjacent numbers:

The sum of any four diagonally adjacent numbers:

The sum of any five diagonally adjacent numbers:

The sum of any 2-by-2 array of numbers:

The sum of any 3-by-3 array of numbers:

The sum of any cross of five numbers:

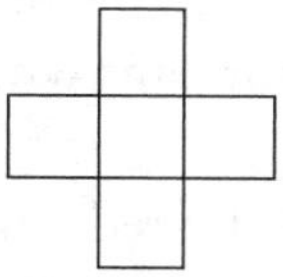

menu activities within a two-day window. In addition to the initial ninety-minute block, another period or two may be needed. I ask the children to complete the required items first; then they can pick and choose between the optional offerings.

Record keeping can and should be kept to a minimum when facilitating a menu. A standardized class listing with columns designating each menu item can be kept on a clipboard or in your lesson plan book. At the end of each day, you can quickly collect the completed worksheets from each station and check the tasks off on your class listing. I keep all the collected work until the menu time is completed. Then each child receives a collated set of worksheets that he can file in his portfolio or take home. I often send home the first set of menu worksheets with a letter stapled to the front explaining the activity and process. A quick reflective journal write can also accompany this packet home. The prompt can be as simple as *List three things you learned about yourself or the mathematics as you worked through this menu.*

Items for an addition and subtraction menu focus on just that—skills and concepts related to addition and subtraction. Items can be extensions of topics covered in class, a game already introduced in class, or an investigation based on a piece of children's literature with which the children are familiar. Here are some sample items for an addition and subtraction menu:

- *Pig* (Directions can be found in Burns 2007, 99.): A game of chance for two or more players. The goal of the game is to be the first to reach 100 by rolling two dice. Rolling a 1 or double 1s can cause scores to be partially or completely erased. (required; cooperative)

- *Addition Table Explorations* (Directions can be found in Burns 2007, 164.): Using a 10-by-10 addition chart, students identify patterns and generalize rules. (required; cooperative)

- *Making Sense of Nothing* (Directions can be found in Raphel 2000, 8.): A paper-and-pencil task that requires students to work without numbers. Children assess possible configurations of numbers (represented by □s) and determine if the numbers could be added, subtracted, or if it's impossible to know. (required; cooperative)

- *Odd Man Out:* A paper-and-pencil task that presents the children with a page of addition problems with the following directions: Only calculate those problems whose sums will be even numbers. (required; individual)

- *Close to 1,000* (Adapted from Economopoulos, Mokros, Akers, and Russell 2004, 48.): A game played much like *Close to 100* (a game the children have already played in class), but with three-digit numbers. (optional; cooperative)

Processing menu items as a class will help the children deepen new mathematical insights and understandings. Processing practices also validate the time and thought that the children have put into their work. When processing items, it is important to have familiarized yourself with the targeted mathematical concepts and procedures of each item. Being aware of the applied mathematics will help you direct conversations and pose good questions to better facilitate the articulation of reasoning, strategies, and solutions. Processing *Making Sense of Nothing* is always an interesting exercise. Disagreements will undoubtedly arise as to what operation a configuration can represent. Children often need to be reminded that they can disagree with another child's *idea,* but disagreements need to be supported by reasoning and handled respectfully. Rather than processing every problem on this particular menu item, choose one or two that can be discussed in depth.

The menu format has advantages for students and teachers alike. The independent format gives students opportunities to make choices, learn to manage their time, and work at their own rate. Menu time allows teachers to work with individuals as well as small groups of students. The discussions you have with children can offer valuable insights into their thinking, understanding, and even misunderstanding of the mathematics involved.

Heffalumps and Woozles

Some children just love problem solving! Years ago I started offering two optional problem-solving extensions for those fourth graders who enjoyed the extra challenge. Initially, I played on the names of candies for the names of the problems. We had Problems for Dum-Dums, Problems for Smarties, Problems for Nerds, and the ever popular Problems for Kisses. As we ran out of candies, one student recommended renaming the problems Heffalumps and Woozles. There were two extensions; the easier one became known as the Heffalump, and the more challenging, the Woozle. The names have stuck over the years—and so has the interest and enthusiasm in solving the problems. What started as a fourth-grade activity is now a math event for grades 1–5.

I write two problems on chart paper and post them on a bulletin board in my classroom. I also reproduce the problems on half sheets of paper for the children to take with them from class. Students slip their completed work into a slotted box on the counter under the bulletin board. Each solution is to be accompanied by an explanation of the thinking or reasoning used in solving the problem; answers without an explanation are not considered. Students must also write the final solution in sentence form with the necessary labels or units. Heffalumps and Woozles are often posted on Mondays and due within a two-week time span. I post the names of students with correct solutions outside my classroom. The children listed receive a special math pencil for each problem solved with clarity and accuracy.

I continue to be amazed at the excitement in the halls when new Heffalumps and Woozles are posted. The completion of these problems has turned into a family event for many children. Students frequently turn in solutions with help from parents, older siblings whom I have had in class years before, and even entire families.

The problems I select often revolve around a theme. Many problems in September, for example, have a baseball theme. I try to choose problems that address mathematical concepts and procedures other than the ones we are currently studying. I have gathered quite a collection of books and copies of open-ended problems over the years. The pieces of student work in Figures 2–9 and 2–10 on the next page are examples of problems and solutions offered by fourth graders.

FIGURE 2–9 ▶

Heffalump problem and fourth grader's solution.

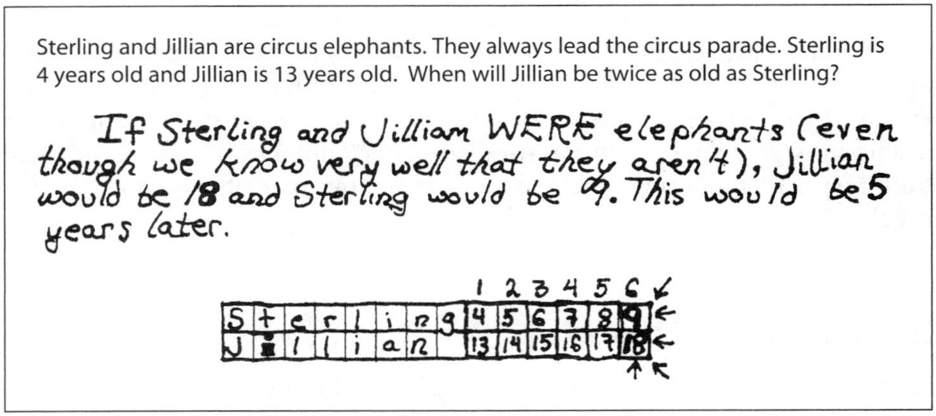

Sterling and Jillian are circus elephants. They always lead the circus parade. Sterling is 4 years old and Jillian is 13 years old. When will Jillian be twice as old as Sterling?

If Sterling and Jillian WERE elephants (even though we know very well that they aren't), Jillian would be 18 and Sterling would be 9. This would be 5 years later.

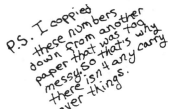

FIGURE 2–10 ▶

Woozle problem and fourth grader's solution.

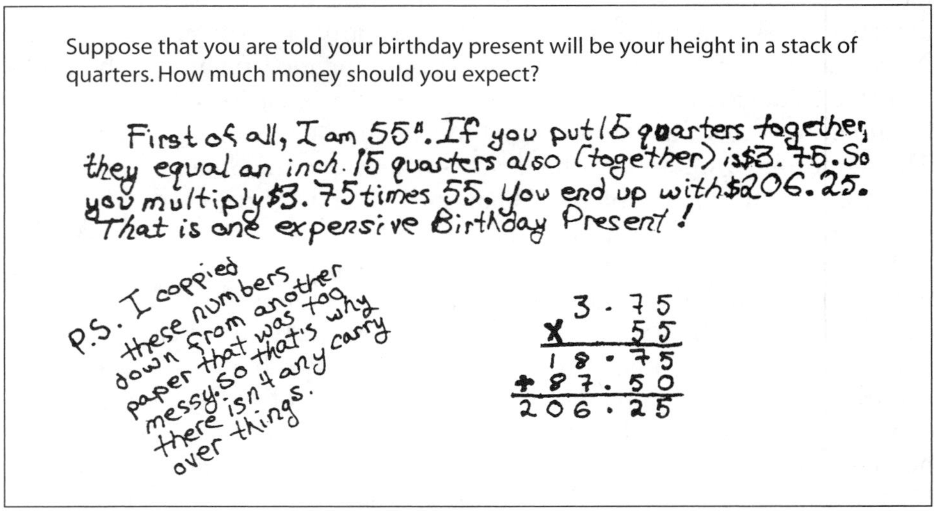

Suppose that you are told your birthday present will be your height in a stack of quarters. How much money should you expect?

First of all, I am 55". If you put 15 quarters together, they equal an inch. 15 quarters also (together) is $3.75. So you multiply $3.75 times 55. You end up with $206.25. That is one expensive Birthday Present!

P.S. I coppied these numbers down from another paper that was too messy. So that's why there isn't any carry over things.

$$
\begin{array}{r}
3.75 \\
\times\ \ 55 \\
\hline
18.75 \\
+\ 87.50 \\
\hline
206.25
\end{array}
$$

Mathematics Writing

In *Writing in Math Class*, Marilyn Burns (1995) explains:

> The process of writing requires gathering, organizing, and clarifying thoughts. It demands finding out what you know and don't know. It calls for thinking clearly. Similarly, doing mathematics depends on gathering, organizing, and clarifying thoughts, finding out what you know and don't know, and thinking clearly. . . . The mental journey is, at its base, the same—making sense of an idea and presently it effectively. (3)

Writing in math class offers children the opportunity to reflect on their work, think about mathematical ideas, and deepen their understanding. It is a chance for students to make learning their own and to establish their mathematical voices.

Because I so value writing as a teaching and learning tool, teaching students *how* to write mathematically is an important objective of my instructional practices in September. Offering clear structures and expectations early in the year will help children organize their thinking and writing as well as offer opportunities for the children to make greater sense of the mathematics they are writing about. Initially, your students may grouch a little about the amount of writing they are expected to complete in math class. I find it helpful and important to take class time to discuss the reasoning behind the writing requirements. For some children, it is reassuring to hear that many times I am less concerned with the right answer and more concerned with their thinking about the problem, strategy, or mathematical idea. As children write more and learn to write with greater clarity, support, and organization, they will better recognize their understandings and even their misunderstandings! Many a child has handed me a paper with an apologetic face, realizing that her fragile understanding of the concept or procedure is right there in front of her. This gives us the opportunity to sit together and go over the concept or procedure again.

I give three types of writing assignments in the fourth grade:

- journal writes
- problem solutions
- explanations of procedures or mathematical ideas

Each is described in greater detail later in this section.

It may be helpful to customize writing assignments to meet the needs of your prescribed curriculum or particular class. There have been many times when I have opted to have my children write about an idea, procedure, or problem in lieu of completing a recommended worksheet. Once again, it is important that we understand the mathematical objectives targeted by a lesson in order to successfully align our writing request.

Posting a word wall in your classroom will help students not only with vocabulary development and language usage but also with spelling. You could use a piece of chart paper headed with the unit name and listing vocabulary words below or use laminated sentence strips secured to the board with magnetic tape, which are more likely to last from year to year. September's words can be titled "Problem Solving" and include words encountered when working through class investigations. If wall space is at a premium, you can remove a previous unit's list when you begin a new unit. I have found, however, that keeping the lists available throughout the year encourages children to continue to refer to them. It also helps children make important connections between the vocabulary of various concepts and procedures and see how those words relate to one another.

I ask students to proofread their pieces *aloud* in a "twelve-inch voice" (a voice that can be heard only from 12 inches away or less) before handing them in. In doing so, children often pick up on the grammatical errors (plural forms, verb tense, etc.) that are easily noticeable when heard. It does take time and effort to repeatedly ask the children, "Have you read this aloud?" Increased attention to this practice helps it to become routine. Proofreading is a valuable writing skill not only in math class but in all other disciplines as well. Please remember that a final written product in math class may look a little different than a final product in language arts or social studies. There may be spelling errors, incomplete sentences, or arrows pointing to parts of calculations. It is the thinking, the understanding, and its representation that should guide our evaluation.

To grade or not to grade, that is a great question! Sometimes I do, and sometimes I do not. If grading journal writes, for example, I evaluate the representation of the mathematics (content) as well as the structure of the writing (mechanics). A checkmark system ($\sqrt{+}$, $\sqrt{}$, and $\sqrt{-}$) represented as a fraction has worked well in my class:

$$\frac{content}{mechanics}$$

For example, a grade of $\frac{\sqrt{+}}{\sqrt{}}$ would indicate a piece of writing rich in mathematical content with grade-appropriate use of writing mechanics. When assessing student work, whether I am grading it or not, I am mindful to comment on each child's writing. I try to stay away from general comments like "Excellent" and "Nice job" and rather comment on the clarity of the mathematics being presented. Our students value our feedback—and require it to become better mathematical thinkers and writers. I often comment on the thoroughness of a response (or lack thereof), on a presented insight, or on a creative strategy. My students have come to identify my assessments with the presence of my purple pen and look for it on returned work. The more assessment of student writing that you do, the more efficient you will become with the process. I try to turn around writing assessments in a day or two so that the assignment and ideas are still fresh in everyone's mind. When evaluating writing, we need to understand the task and the mathematics involved in understanding or explaining it. It is also important to ask ourselves, "Has the child answered the question being asked?" I have read a plethora of wonderful answers to never-asked questions! Having children refer to the prompt or question multiple times while responding will help them focus their responses on the task at hand.

Class discussions are important in helping children develop writing skills and techniques specific to the task and to manifest their mathematical understandings. Perhaps even more important, however, is the role class discussions can have in helping children decide about what to write! Discussing a task in a whole-class format can help children frame the assignment and understand what is being asked of them. Listening to others' ideas and opinions prior to writing can help reluctant writers start. These conversations are crucial in September, when the writing task may appear overwhelming to some. Circulating around the classroom as your children write will help you identify those who need a little extra support or clarification. Class discussions following an assignment can be equally helpful. Giving students a chance to share their thinking and to consider the ideas of others can help them improve the clarity of their written and oral communication.

Modeling writing assignments with the children in the first weeks of school is extremely helpful. Responding to a prompt as a class can help give structure to future tasks. We read the prompt together and determine what it is asking. I write on the board or overhead as the children write in their journals or math notebooks. We write, we proof, we edit, and then we discuss the final product and process. You may find it helpful to model an assignment from each of the following writing categories. Although the children may not be able to distinguish one category from another initially, it will help *you* to identify your guidelines and requested structures.

Journal Writes

Journal writes are completed in each child's *Mathematician's Log*. I give a prompt with a set of three or four areas on which to focus. Possibilities can range from complete sentences, correct spelling, or transitional words to the use of calculations, diagrams, pictures, and so on.

Journal writes can easily be used for assessment purposes. They can ask children to summarize ideas, to apply concepts and procedures to novel situations, or to justify a position or thinking. I assign journal writes routinely and frequently. They can also be easily assigned for homework on a regular basis. I assign journal writes every Thursday night for homework.

Prompts can be developed from class investigations, discussions, or student-posed questions. *Good Questions for Math Teaching* (Sullivan and Lilburn 2002) contains easily adaptable open-ended questions organized by strand. Figure 2–11 is an example journal entry.

Problem Solutions

Problem solutions are written opportunities for children to apply mathematical skills to problem-solving situations. When solving problems, children should be required to not only present the answer but also justify and document their reasoning. The focus of these tasks is on the clarity of thinking and reasoning. You may find that as children write with greater mathematical sophistication, the mechanics of their writing demonstrate improvement as well. Figure 2–12 is one student's problem solution.

Explanation of Procedures or Mathematical Ideas

Students' writing about procedures or mathematical ideas gives us valuable insights into their thinking and mathematical sophistication. Encourage

Prompt

Here are the results of a survey of the 4th grade. What could the survey have been? Why would that choice make sense given the results on the line plot?

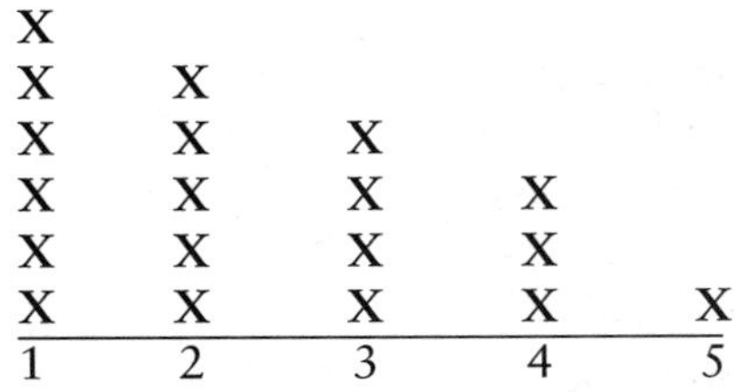

```
X
X    X
X    X    X
X    X    X    X
X    X    X    X
X    X    X    X    X
1    2    3    4    5
```

Writing Focus

1. Concise introductory sentence
2. Two examples that support your position
3. Correct spelling

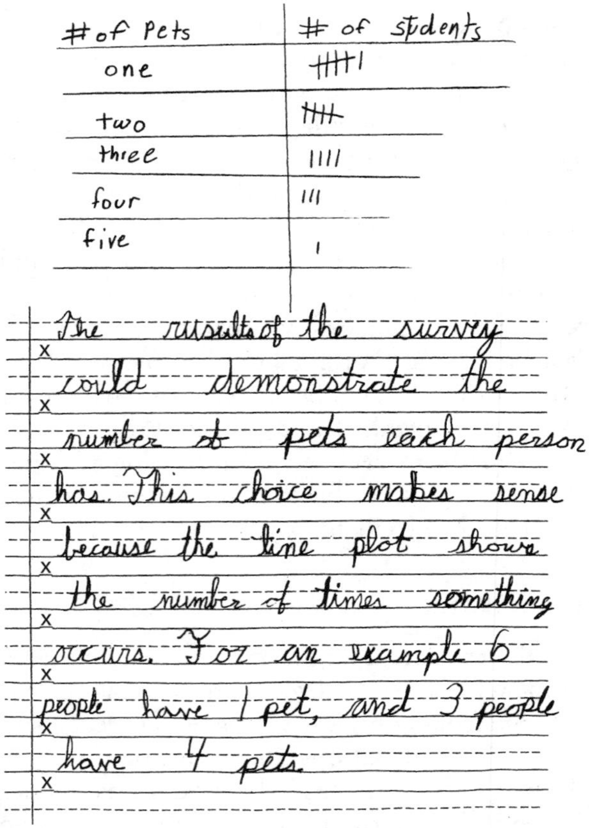

# of Pets	# of students
one	++++ l
two	++++
three	llll
four	lll
five	l

The results of the survey could demonstrate the number of pets each person has. This choice makes sense because the line plot shows the number of times something occurs. For an example 6 people have 1 pet, and 3 people have 4 pets.

FIGURE 2–11   ▲

Emily's journal entry from September.

children to offer examples as they support their thinking and reasoning with mathematical proof. Drawings and diagrams with detailed captions are also helpful. Figure 2–13 shows one student's explanation.

Our students' writing provides us with insights into how they think and reason mathematically. Reading and evaluating students' writing can help teachers to:

1. evaluate how well the instructional program is supporting learning goals and objectives

2. learn about individuals' understandings and skill development

3. communicate with parents about what their children are learning and how they are progressing (Burns 1995, 29–30)

Writing is an integral component of my instructional practice. I place a high premium on communication in my classroom. It is the integration of discourse, writing, and the representation of the mathematics that helps develop our students into thoughtful mathematicians and capable problem solvers.

Prompt

What is the "outlaw" in this group (something that does not belong)? Why do you think so?

$$\frac{1}{2} \quad 0.6 \quad 0.5$$

Writing Focus

1. Complete sentences
2. Strong introductory and concluding sentences
3. Illustration or diagram to support your thinking

$0.5 \left(\dfrac{5}{10}\right) \; \frac{1}{2} \left(\dfrac{5}{10}\right) 0.6 = \left(\dfrac{6}{10}\right)$

They are equal.

This is not equal to $\frac{5}{10}$.

The outlaw is 0.6 because it does not have the same value as 0.5 and ½. When I look at numbers I think of value not how the numbers are written. ½ and 0.5 are two different ways of writing the same thing. 0.6 is equal to ⁶⁄₁₀, not ½.

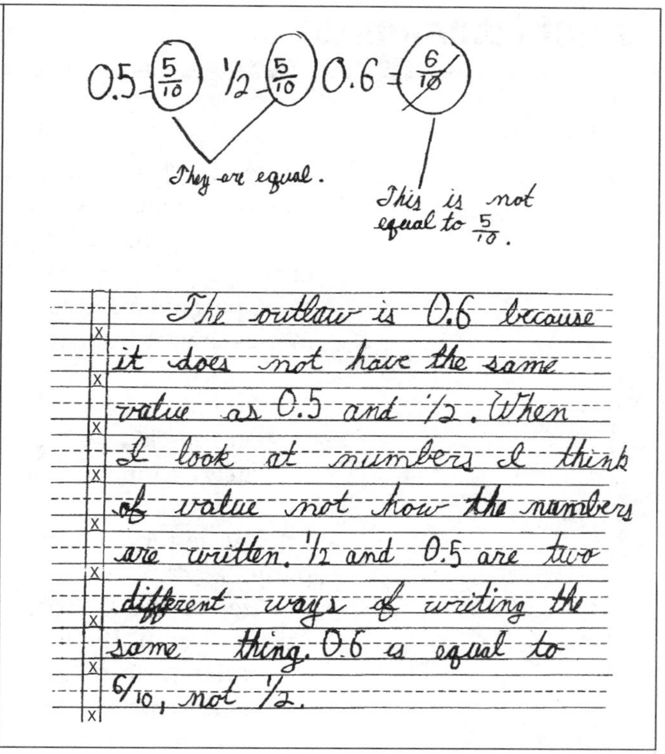

FIGURE 2–12 ▲

Diana's problem solution.

Prompt

$$\square \times \triangle = \triangle \times \square$$

True or false? Why? (You might want to substitute numbers to support your thinking.)

Writing Focus

1. Strong introductory sentence
2. An example to support your conjecture
3. Strong concluding sentence that summarizes the original question

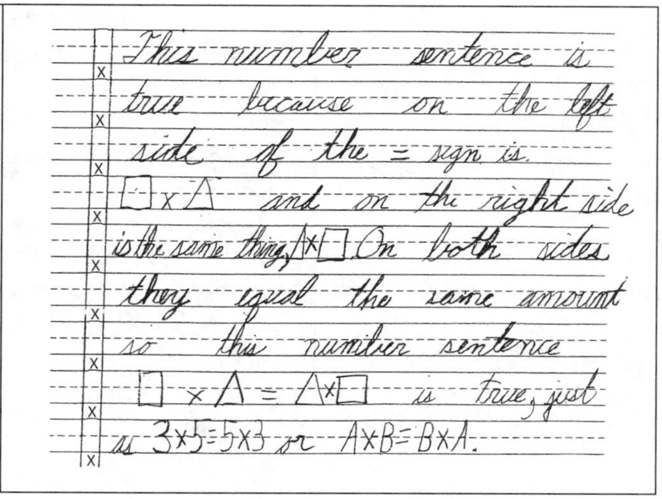

This number sentence is true because on the left side of the = sign is □ × △ and on the right side is the same thing, △ × □. On both sides they equal the same amount so this number sentence □ × △ = △ × □ is true, just as 3×5=5×3 or A×B=B×A.

FIGURE 2–13 ▲

Alexander's explanation.

Parent Communication

I work in a school in which parent communication is not only recommended but required. Teachers who actively inform and educate parents about what goes on in math class create families who are excited about mathematics. A colleague of mine frequently reminds me that we are not teaching "our fathers' math." Because of that, we need to be mindful of the confusion some parents may feel when they encounter a different approach to mathematics than the one to which they were exposed. Nancy Litton writes:

> When teachers forge successful partnerships with parents, students are the ultimate beneficiaries as everyone joins together in the sometimes confusing but ultimately exciting and satisfying task of making sense of mathematics. (1998, 4)

Newsletters continue to be my favorite form of communication with parents. Prior to the start of school, I craft my back-to-math-class newsletter (see Chapter 1, Figure 1–1). I send this newsletter home with the children in the first week of school. It is a quick overview of the year, an explanation of some of my classroom management routines, and an enthusiastic preview of the year's mathematical opportunities and growth. I send home several other newsletters throughout the year. I often send home one when we tackle multiplication and division, one as we begin our work with fractions, one prior to our standardized testing dates, and a final newsletter in celebration of the year's journey and achievements. The content of these letters is discussed in the relevant chapters of this book.

TEACHER-TO-TEACHER TALK   I have also been known to send home letters enlisting parental support and help when I am not particularly satisfied with a class's progress. I do not use the letter as a forum to complain or whine—that would not do anybody any good! I do, however, present my concerns and their mathematical relevance. I recently had a class, for example, that demonstrated no urgency about the mastery of basic addition and subtraction facts, let alone multiplication and division. In late September, I sent home a letter describing the importance of fact fluency and how its lack could affect our later work with multiplication and division. I included a list of activities in which families could engage to improve fact fluency. By enlisting family support and help, I began to develop a yearlong dialogue and partnership with the families of that class.

I passed a father in the hall one day and he asked, "How is thirteen minus eight going this week?"

It was nice to be able to say, "Better. . . ."

Parent information forms can also help develop home-school partnerships. They can be sent home with your children or posted electronically if your school has an accessible website for parents. Every parent information form is presented in the same format and sent home or posted prior to the beginning of each new unit. Parents greatly appreciate the section of the form that suggests how they can help at home. Once again, this practice gives us the opportunity to enlist help and support from home that will ultimately benefit our students. Figure 2–14 contains a sample September parent information form. A blank template for the form is included in the Blackline Masters.

Back-to-School Night offers a forum for you to set the stage for your year of mathematics. School policy may dictate what you need to present that night. Whatever the format or expectations, do commit yourself to the charge of engaging parents in meaningful mathematics that night.

FIGURE 2-14   ◄

Parent information form for September.

Parent Information and Involvement Form

From: Lainie Schuster
To: Parents of Fourth Graders
Re: Mathematics Curriculum
Month: September

During the next month, the major topics we will be studying are:

- problem solving
- fact review and yearlong routines
- estimation

My goal in studying these topics is for the students to be able to:

- develop and model positive problem-solving attitudes and behavior
- talk, write, and draw the mathematics
- recall and apply basic math facts
- develop mental strategies to help along the recall process for fact "demons" (facts with which an individual child struggles)
- develop estimation strategies appropriate to a given task
- determine when an estimate or an exact number is an appropriate solution

Parents can help at home by:

- posting and referring to the "Good Problem-Solving Behaviors" list at home
- reviewing basic addition, subtraction, multiplication, and division facts
- engaging children in problem solving related to home life, for example: *A box of brownie mix requires 2 eggs. We are going to triple the recipe. How many dozen eggs will we need to buy? Why?* (Be careful!)
- devising a consistent homework time and place with your children

---

Nancy Litton (1998, 38–40) suggests that we keep in mind five major ideas when planning presentations for Back-to-School Night:

1. The goal of the year is to have each child love and understand mathematics.

2. Appropriate materials will be available that will enable your child to explore mathematical concepts studied in fourth grade.

3. Each child will be an active participant in the learning process.

4. School mathematics may look different from the mathematics program parents experienced as children.

5. Forming a partnership between home and school is important to support each child's growth in mathematics.

Having the parents do mathematics initially will scaffold the discussion of these major points. Choose an activity that will quickly engage parents. Having parents play a game that the children have already played in class can make speaking about the mathematics of the activity with the parents a little easier. You and they will have a common experience on which to draw as you address the group.

Assessment

We have many questions about the mathematical strengths, weaknesses, and needs of each new class. How fluent are they with their basic addition and subtraction facts? How easily do they apply their understandings of addition and subtraction to problem-solving situations? How do they apply number sense to their calculation strategies and practices? How efficient are their calculation strategies? What dictates their choice of strategies? Do they repeatedly apply the same strategies? Or do the numbers or the context of problems determine the procedures they use? How well do they articulate their understandings? What methods do they use to represent their mathematical work and thinking? We are ultimately asking ourselves, How do our students *know* and *do* mathematics?

As teachers, we are diagnosticians of student growth and achievement. In *Developing Judgment: Assessing Children's Work in Mathematics*, Jean Moon writes:

To understand how children learn, we need to be good diagnosticians of their work. The instructional tasks we use in our classrooms for assessment purposes should give students an opportunity to demonstrate their progress toward agreed-upon instructional goals in mathematics, and teachers must know how to interpret that progress and adjust their instructional goals accordingly. (1997, 61)

Because some assessment formats are better than others in isolating specific characteristics of children's mathematical thinking, it is important to understand and identify the difference between the *purpose* of an assessment (Why am I giving this assessment?) and its *design* (How can I structure the assessment to achieve my purposes?).

I have found the most important purpose of assessment in September is gaining initial information about our students that will help us understand the level of sophistication of their mathematical thinking in order to help direct instruction. Informal assessments are most helpful as we move through the early weeks of school. Talking and listening to our students will help us make informal assessments in regard to their understanding and sense making of the mathematical tasks we ask them to perform. Asking open-ended questions can help us assess the flexibility and efficiency of their thinking and reasoning skills. Reviewing written work can help us make judgments about the articulation of their thoughts and the accuracy of their calculations.

I have borrowed many practices from my favorite first-grade teacher, Dava Dunne. Many years ago, Dava shared with me her system of keeping anecdotal records in reading and writing. Dava uses a spiral notebook with a section of pages tabbed for each child. She takes notes as she circulates throughout the room while children work or as she conferences individually with each child, and dates each entry. I have adopted a similar practice in my fourth-grade math class. In September, I often comment on the following issues in my notes:

- number sense
- fact fluency
- application of appropriate and efficient strategies
- reasoning ability
- ability and willingness to self-correct
- enthusiasm level
- interpersonal skills
- frustration level

I try to comment on the same skills for each child so that I have a standard for comparison. I can then assess each child individually as well as the whole class. Data collected from student conversations and observations can also be used for assessment in much the same way written assessments can be used. You may find that your prescribed curriculum offers materials with which to record and archive anecdotal notes as well.

We need to have a clear understanding of what our students *know* and *can do* mathematically from early on in the school year. We need to collect and analyze evidence that goes beyond test scores. We must draw inferences from this collected evidence in order to make sound assessments and instructional decisions. This is a difficult business, but one that is necessary and enlightening to our professional practice.

TEACHER-TO-TEACHER TALK   September is exhausting! But I am not sure that there is any other way to do it well. September is a time for creating a mathematical community. Routines and practices that are established in September will create structure and familiarity for the months to come. It is also a time, however, for us to focus our attention on getting to know our students—and I mean *really* know them. What makes them smile? What makes them hesitate? What makes them cower? What makes them confident? What makes them persevere? And then there is the issue of getting to know them mathematically . . . but we have the luxury of a whole school year for that. Until we make some personal connections, the mathematics almost seems irrelevant. I truly believe that a child's success in mathematics is highly dependent on the relationship and connection that she has established with her teacher. Establishing those relationships helps us create mathematically safe classrooms in which students and teachers can develop mathematical inquiry, thoughtfulness, and competence.

Resources

About Teaching Mathematics (Burns 2007)

A comprehensive resource for teachers that offers classroom-tested activities as well as strategies for teaching math within a problem-solving context.

Math Matters (Chapin and Johnson 2006)

A resource that examines mathematical concepts covered in grades K–6 and can help teachers clarify their own understanding of the mathematics they teach. It can also help teachers pose better questions, explain ideas more accurately, and stress important relationships and concepts.

Young Mathematicians at Work: Constructing Number Sense, Addition, and Subtraction (Fosnot and Dolk 2001b)

Although this series is targeted for teachers of children ages four to eight, the authors provide comprehensive descriptions of development, progressive strategies, and emerging models that can easily be applied to the teaching of fourth graders.

Good Questions for Math Teaching (Sulllivan and Lilburn 2002)

This resource includes a plethora of open-ended questions that promote thinking, reasoning, and creativity covering sixteen mathematical topics.

Nimble with Numbers (Childs and Chaote 1998)

This resource offers engaging math activities that provide meaningful practice that is necessary for students as they develop greater number sense, operation sense, and computational competence.

Awesome Math Problems for Creative Thinking (Gavin et al. 2000)

Each book in this series for grades 3–5 presents math problems in engaging contexts. I choose problems from the grades 3, 4, and 5 books depending on the strengths and needs of a given class.

Teaching Children Mathematics (National Council of Teachers of Mathematics)

This monthly journal is published by the National Council of Teachers of Mathematics and focuses on the teaching and learning of mathematics in the elementary school. This resource presents activities, lesson ideas, teaching strategies, and problems through in-depth articles, departments, and features. An NCTM membership can include a subscription to this publication.

Chapter 3

October

NUMERATION AND PLACE VALUE

Children must be able to make sense of the various ways numbers are used. They need to develop a sense of number that enables them to recognize relationships between quantities; to use the operations of addition, subtraction, multiplication, and division to obtain numerical information; to understand how the operations are related to one another; to be able to approximate and estimate when appropriate; and to be able to apply their understandings to problem situations.

About Teaching Mathematics
Burns 2007, 157

The Learning Environment

Facilitate conversations about the importance of risk taking and making mistakes in the learning of mathematics.

It is best to introduce conversations about the importance of risk taking and the making of mistakes after you have established an emotionally and mathematically safe and trusting environment. As children grow mathematically, it becomes increasingly important for them to practice and apply their newly acquired mathematical concepts and procedures without fear of ridicule or negative feedback. Empowerment and courage also come from children witnessing their teachers making mistakes and learning from them. I cannot tell you how many times I have miscalculated or misunderstood something that was going on in class. I, too, need to stop, regroup, rethink, and then move on, just as I ask the students to do. The practice of learning from mistakes can then become embedded in the culture of your classroom. The willingness and patience to work through misconceptions and misunderstandings with persistence and confidence make for stronger mathematical thinkers and problem solvers.

Foster mathematical curiosity.

Mathematical curiosity is a wonderful thing that should be alive and well in every fourth-grade classroom! Questions can encourage and support the insatiable curiosity of fourth graders. How does that work? Will this work with every number? Can you show me why this works? Can you think of another way to solve this? Encouraging children to ask questions as they work and think will help everyone move instruction in more meaningful directions. Sometimes student-generated questions take on a life of their own and are deserving of their own investigation. Robert wondered one day if one million teddy bears could fit in our classroom. The question took me by surprise . . . and then I realized what a fun (and mathematically meaningful!) investigation that could be. We spent the next day exploring his question. We used what we knew about the measurements of one teddy bear (Robert brought his to school for the investigation) to predict how many bears we would need to fill the room. Conversations about multiplication, volume, and calculator use became part of that day's lesson. What seemed to be a simple question led us to some wonderful mathematics!

Develop good questioning practices.

Good questioning practices are valuable teaching tools. Well-crafted questions can help a teacher support and direct instruction. Simply asking, "What do you notice?" or "Why do you think that?" can help students dig deeper into the mathematics. Good questions are intentional and thoughtful. They demonstrate a teacher's understanding of the mathematics and help the children make better sense of a concept or procedure. Good questions not only require the application of facts and procedures but encourage students to make connections and generalizations. To question well is to teach well. And both take time and patience.

The Mathematics and Its Language

Children represent large numbers in a variety of ways using pictures, place-value mats, stories, base ten blocks, and numbers.

During October, I ask students to think about the relationships between numbers and quantity. I emphasize the representations and notations of large numbers as well as further applications of estimation and approximation routines. Big numbers are interesting to fourth graders. As their understanding of place value increases, so too does their interest in the magnitude of numbers.

Children articulate, apply, and demonstrate their understanding of addition and subtraction procedures in problem-solving contexts.

The application of addition and subtraction routines and strategies continues in problem-solving contexts. The children solve both addition and subtraction problems that involve regrouping and articulate and demonstrate their understanding of their chosen procedures. Fourth graders will delight and amaze you as they demonstrate fluency, flexibility, and confidence in their chosen strategies. They may employ one addition method to a given problem and then employ another when the context or numbers change—and be completely comfortable with their strategies and the sense that they make. You need to present mathematical contexts that will allow students to be flexible in their approach to the numbers and the strategies with which they combine and compare them.

Children apply their knowledge of mathematical language and relationships to the solving of problems requiring logical reasoning.

The process of logical thinking is basic to all mathematics. It is important for children to understand that mathematics is a way of thinking rather than a body of facts and procedures that need to be memorized and performed. Activities that require children to think logically help them develop clarity and precision in their thinking (Burns 2007). This is helpful not only in the study of mathematics but in other curricular areas as well.

Reading and language fluency can influence the success with which children solve problems requiring reasoning and logical thinking. It is important to remind ourselves that no mathematical activity is ever void of language! Encouraging children to work cooperatively and to think out loud can help us identify and support those children who are having difficulty with the nuances of the mathematical language and the articulation of their thinking and understanding.

TEACHER-TO-TEACHER TALK   As children move through the fourth grade, issues with reading comprehension and other language-related difficulties may begin to present themselves for the first time. For years, these children have been *learning to read*. The tables have now turned a bit in that we often ask our students to *read to learn*. Even though I had heard this from several reading specialists over the years, it was not until I experienced it in the teaching of mathematics that I began to truly understand it. Although language nuances may seem minor to us, they can really become an issue for some children as they are expected to read, retain, and integrate ever more complex mathematical information. I recently noticed a few students who were struggling with the difference between "three more" and "three times as many."

Fourth graders are learning that while reading a piece of literature, a few omitted or added words may not significantly alter the meaning of the context. In reading mathematical text, however, each word, number, and symbol, and the order in which they appear take on significant importance. Therefore, we need to be mindful that difficulties with the mathematics may be caused by difficulties with the language.

Investigations and Literature-Based Activities

Building Place Value

Duration: 2 class periods

This investigation offers students opportunities to:

- build large numbers based on a triples system
- practice and refine understanding of place value of large numbers

Materials

- collection of base ten blocks, enough to represent a few three-digit numbers
- 1 place-value mat per student (see Blackline Masters)
- 1 set of digit cards per child (you may wish to copy these on colored card stock or copy paper) (see Blackline Masters)

- 1 roll of transparent tape per group of students
- *How Much Is a Million?* (Schwartz 1985)

I begin the class by reading aloud *How Much Is a Million?* to set the stage for thinking about large numbers. There may be much discussion about the concepts and images presented in the read-aloud. The word *million* is often randomly used to mean "a lot." But how much is a lot? This is a wonderful time to discuss the need for precision in our choice of mathematical language. I try to be on the alert for examples of mathematical misuse of the word *million* by the children when not in math class. It may raise an eyebrow or two if you ask the perpetrator, "Do you really mean a million? Or is it more like ten . . . twenty . . . or perhaps just a mere one thousand?"

Have the base ten blocks available on a front desk or table. Write a three-digit number on the board, such as *487*, and ask the children to tell you everything that they know about that number to set up this lesson. Recording the children's responses will slow down the discussion and allow some additional thinking and reflection about the number. If a student does not offer to decompose the number into its ones, tens, and hundreds, ask for a volunteer to build 487 with the base ten blocks. As the child is building, ask others to support and justify his choice of blocks. Ask, "Will this method of building work for every number?" to help children generalize place-value concepts and understandings from one number to the next.

Distribute a place-value mat and a set of digit cards to each child. Instruct the children to cut out the digit cards and cut the place-value mats in half along the dotted line. Next, have the children tape their place-value mats together to form a row of seven boxes.

Ask, "How could this mat help you build four hundred eighty-seven?" Children will more than likely begin to place a 4-card, an 8-card, and a 7-card on the mat to represent 487. Most children will place the digit cards in the appropriate places on the mat. Playing devil's advocate can facilitate some interesting and meaningful discussion. Ask, "What if I put my cards here?" and place the cards in the thousands, ten thousands, and hundred thousands places on a mat. Ask, "What happens to the value of the number?" Move the children to the realization that for this activity, labeling each place can make this idea make more sense. Have the children label the ones, tens, and hundreds places to help them identify the first *triple*. Some children may suggest that the next triple—thousands, ten thousands, and hundred thousands—be labeled as well. Ask the children, "Why do these labels make sense?" to once again open up discussions about the necessity of precision and standardization in our place-value system.

The following activity can continue for several rounds.

1. Ask, "Can someone give me a four-digit number?"

2. Have the children build the number on their place-value mats.

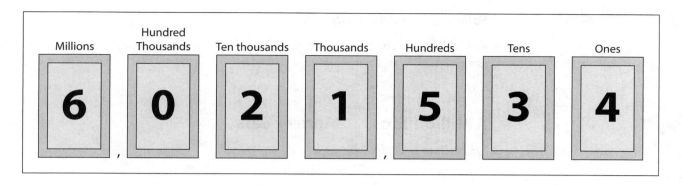

Millions	Hundred Thousands	Ten thousands	Thousands	Hundreds	Tens	Ones
6	0	2	1	5	3	4

3. Direct students to switch the ones digit with the hundreds digit (or the tens with the hundreds, etc.).

4. Have the children make a few more switches.

5. Ask, "What is the new number?"

6. Ask, "What does this number represent?"

FIGURE 3–1 ▲

A labeled place-value mat.

Writing on the board the students' responses to the last question allows you to symbolically and visually represent the decomposition of the number, for example: $4{,}089 = 4{,}000 + 000 + 80 + 9$.

Move the activity along with several other four-digit numbers. Then move to five-digit numbers and six-digit numbers. Follow each new number with questions and recording. Ask several children to each read the large final numbers to keep the class engaged. I often ask the children to *not* raise their hands. I inform the children that I am going to call on them randomly—not to put them on the spot, but rather to move the discussion along and to support those who may need help. Children often look at a number and assume that they can read it out loud, but that is not always the case! Having established a trusting and mathematically safe environment in the first month of school will help students take risks during activities like this.

Extension

Once you have constructed and read several numbers, ask the children to then add or subtract multiples of ten to or from their new number. For example, say, "Add one thousand to your number," or "Subtract one hundred from your number." Then ask, "What is your new number now?" Have the children use their digit cards to build their new numbers. If students don't have all the digit cards necessary to build the new number, engage them in thinking of an operation to perform that will allow them to use the cards they have available.

Follow-Up Journal Write

Represent 824 in five different ways. You can use words, numbers, diagrams, and drawings.

A Million Taps . . . More or Less

Duration: 1–2 class periods

This investigation, adapted from *Everyday Mathematics* (Everyday Learning Corporation 2007a), offers students opportunities to:

- estimate the length of time it would take to tap a pencil one million times given a sample of experimental data
- apply understanding of conversion factors of time
- collect and analyze data
- practice multiplication with a calculator

Materials

- 1 calculator per pair of students
- 1 stopwatch per pair of students or a clock with a second hand
- 1 *A Million Taps . . . More or Less* record sheet per student (see Blackline Masters)
- 1 *What Would I Do with One Million?* worksheet per student (see Blackline Masters)

A million is a lot! Children use the quantity often in their everyday speech, but their understanding of the magnitude of one million is usually a little fragile. Begin this investigation by posing a question: "How long do you think it would take you to tap your desk with the eraser on your pencil one million times?" As the children think about their guesses, distribute the *A Million Taps . . . More or Less* record sheets. Have the children record their guesses on their sheets. Inform the children that they are now going to assess their guesses with a data collection activity.

The record sheet walks the children through the tapping activity. The children will use their sample count to estimate how long it will take them to tap one million times. It is helpful for children to work with partners. As one partner taps and counts, the other partner can time the activity, telling when to start and stop. Partners then reverse roles. Encourage children to round numbers when helpful and to use calculators for their calculations. If a student taps forty-three times in ten seconds, it might be more manageable to round that count down to forty. This is a meaningful context in which to discuss rounding practices and routines. As children develop mathematically, they need to learn to identify situations in which rounding is appropriate. And in this case, it is!

Time conversions can be difficult for some fourth graders. Although they do have the use of a calculator, the children still need to understand how the numbers are working and what is to be multiplied by what and why. The "Useful Information" box at the top of the record sheet can guide their calculations. As you circulate throughout the room, be cognizant of those pairings who have a tenuous understanding about what to multiply and why.

When students complete their record sheets, have them complete the follow-up *What Would I Do with One Million?* worksheet. This will allow you to work with pairings who need extended time. This worksheet can also be assigned as homework. Make sure to offer a time for the students to share their responses to this worksheet.

As always, I call the students together to debrief their findings after all have finished the tapping and calculating. I begin with a question such as "Were you surprised at what you found out?" to direct the discussion. Keep the discussion focused on the magnitude of one million with questions such as the following:

- What if I asked you how long it would take to tap your desk one billion times? How could we set up that investigation and calculation?

- Could we use the data that we have already collected to help us with that calculation? How?

Follow-Up Journal Write

Having 1,000,000 _____ would be great! Why would that be so?

Number Riddles

Duration: 2 class periods

All children seem to enjoy riddles, so why not engage them with riddles involving numbers! Although number riddles can address just about any mathematical concept, these riddles focus on place value and number relationships. Solving and writing number riddles offer students opportunities to:

- identify mathematical attributes of targeted numbers
- compare and combine large numbers
- apply mathematical language and relationships in the writing of riddles
- publish a class collection of number riddles

Materials

- *One Riddle, One Answer*, by Lauren Thompson (2001)
- several pieces of chart paper

One Riddle, One Answer is the tale of a Persian princess named Aziza who loves riddles and numbers. When it is time for her to marry, Aziza makes a proposition to her father, the sultan. Aziza will pose a riddle and he who can solve it will become her husband. The context of the story sets up the activity of solving and writing number riddles.

Prior to the lesson, write the riddle that Aziza poses on chart paper to help focus the follow-up discussion of possible solutions, of which there are two.

Placed above, it makes things small.

Placed beside, it makes things greater.

In matters that count, it always comes first.

Where others increase, it keeps all things the same.

What is it?

Begin the lesson with a read-aloud of *One Riddle, One Answer*. In the story, the scholar suggests that the answer to Aziza's riddle is the sun. A discussion of why the scholar's answer is incorrect will encourage students to reevaluate each clue. In order for an answer to be true, the response has to fit every clue. Although it could be argued that the sun is an acceptable response to the first clue ("Placed above, it makes things small"), it does not make sense as a response to the second ("Placed beside, it makes things greater"). Next, discuss why Ahmed's response of one is true. The number one makes each statement true.

Although zero is not considered a counting number, it can make true statements of each clue as well. If during the discussion no student offers zero as a solution, ask if any other number could constitute a true answer.

Placed above, it can make things small, as in the case of multiplication.

$$
\begin{array}{cc}
0 & 0 \\
\times\ 1 & \times\ 99 \\
\hline
0 & 0 \\
\end{array}
$$

Placed beside, it makes things greater, as in multiples of 10.

10   20   30

In matters that count, it always comes first.

0, 1, 2, 3, 4, 5 . . .

Where others increase, it keeps all things the same, as in the case of addition.

0 + 1 = 1   *0 + 5 = 5*

Once you have discussed the format and the process of solving a riddle, introduce another riddle, perhaps one that you have created or one found in your curricular text. Here's one example:

I am a two-digit number.

I am a multiple of 5.

The sum of my digits is 3.

I am an even number.

You can count by 10s to get to me.

Who am I?

Starting a word bank on chart paper will help children identify, use, and interpret the mathematical vocabulary we can use to solve and create number riddles. A look at the vocabulary can be an entry point in solving this riddle. What is a *two-digit number*? A *multiple*? A *sum*? An *even number*? Asking children to then solve the riddle with a neighbor will give all students a chance to try out their solutions with each clue.

The students can then turn to writing their own riddles. The process of writing riddles will help reinforce, support, and clarify students' mathematical understanding and savviness. Determining where to start when creating a riddle may be an issue. If so, ask the class, "Where should we start?" Some may suggest starting with the targeted number and working backward with the clues. Some may suggest random clues highlighting certain properties of a possible number (e.g., the number is even or the sum of the digits of the number is nine). Honor and model class suggestions. Do not shy away from modeling unreasonable suggestions, as well. Discussing such responses may empower the children to identify the flaws in their own thinking. When students find errors in their ideas, encourage them to adjust or rethink their suggestions together with the class.

This is an excellent opportunity for highlighting the importance of clear and precise language. For example, if a student says, "Add two numbers to get my number," ask if she could use the word *sum*. Ask, "How would that streamline our clue? Could we ask classmates to add two *odd* numbers or two *even* numbers? Would that eliminate certain numbers from being the solution? How could we reword 'Subtract two hundred thirty-five from five hundred sixty-six' with better clarity? Does 'Find the difference between two hundred thirty-five and five hundred sixty-six' mean the same thing?" Keep an ongoing list of words and phrases that increase the clarity of the clues on a piece of chart paper or on the board. The children can easily refer to the words and phrases as they write.

Once a riddle has been completed, determining the number of possible solutions may be another issue that needs to be addressed. Ask the student, "Does your riddle have only one solution? Or are there several possible solutions?"

It is important to offer the children a listing of specific riddle guidelines. Keep in mind that the focus of this activity is on comparing and combining large numbers. Some possible guidelines include:

Your riddle will need to contain clues with…

- Hints about place value:

  There is a number greater than 7 in the tens place.

  The number in the ones place is 6 less than the number in the thousands place.

- Addition and/or subtraction task(s):

  When you add 68 to my number, it becomes a 5-digit number.

  If you subtract 1 from my number, it becomes an even number.

- Information that can help eliminate a number of possible solutions:

  My number is greater than 9,950 and less than 9,999.

Asking children to work in pairs works well with this activity. Children are more actively involved in the process when working with only one partner. When children have completed a riddle, have proofed it, and are happy with it, I ask them to copy it onto a clean sheet of composition paper—neatly, of course! I also ask them to write the solution in a box on the back of the paper. I collect the riddles and look them over for spelling or mathematical errors. Then I collate the pages and publish them as a class riddle book. I often ask an artist in the class to create a cover for the book.

Follow-Up Journal Write

The solution to my riddle is 342. My first four clues are:

- I am a 3-digit number.
- All my digits are less than 5.
- I am an even number less than 400.
- My digits are consecutive numbers but not in consecutive order.

What could the final clue be? Why does that make sense?

TEACHER-TO-TEACHER TALK   I keep copies of all collated books and samples of student work from year to year. They are helpful to have as models for students in following years. Their greatest use, however, is to assess *my* progress as a teacher. Each year, similar projects tend to be better in one way or another. Reviewing these projects gives me the opportunity to reflect on my practices from year to year. Because of my concern with mathematical language and its use in both oral and written expression, I look for good examples of it in the children's work. Did one class write particularly well because the students were just better writers, or did I teach math writing differently or perhaps better that year? Why do some pieces of work appear to be better organized than others? Could the increased organization be attributed to my preparation or presentation? What did I do differently that year than others? Time for reflective practice is often not available to us during the schoolday. If you work with a team of fourth-grade teachers, gathering to share student work once a term or semester would give you a forum for reflection. Then again, quiet time spent with student work and a cup of coffee in mid-July can also help us better evaluate our own progress and practice.

Color Tile Riddles

Duration: 1–2 class periods

This activity, adapted from *A Collection of Math Lessons: From Grades 1 Through 3* (Burns and Tank 1988), offers students opportunities to:

- apply logical reasoning skills within a problem-solving context
- solve and create color tile riddles

Materials
- 1 tub of color tiles per group of students
- several color tile riddles written on overhead transparencies

This activity emphasizes language and reasoning skills. The language of mathematics can be intriguing as well as frustrating to some children. Does *three more* mean the same thing as *three times as many*? Does *half as many* mean the same thing as *two less*? We often assume that our students' understanding of the nuances of mathematical language is as developed as their understanding of the nuances of everyday language. This is not always the case.

Place a tub of color tiles at each table grouping. If this is the first time in the year that the tiles have been used, allow the children a little free exploration time before the lesson begins. I allow a little playing time with all manipulatives before every activity throughout the year. When I call time, students push the manipulatives back to the center of the table and play ceases.

I present the first riddle on an overhead, clue by clue.

Clue 1: I have fewer than 10 tiles.

Clue 2: I have an even number of tiles.

Clue 3: There are three colors.

Clue 4: I have more yellow tiles than blue tiles.

Clue 5: I have one more yellow tile than red tile.

Clue 6: I have the same number of blue tiles as yellow tiles.

As I present the clues, I ask the children to manipulate their tiles. I encourage students to rethink their choice of color tiles with each clue. A new clue can cause children to take new tiles, replace colors, or return tiles to the tub. After I've revealed all the clues, I reread them while the children evaluate the tiles before them. Then we discuss the activity. Does their choice of tiles match the given clues? How many clues were necessary before they were able to make an informed choice of tiles? Were there tile choices that could be eliminated right from the first few clues? How many clues make up a good riddle? Why? I present several other riddles following the same process.

Because the children have had experience creating riddles of their own in previous activities, they are quick to ask when they can make up their own. I instruct the students to work with a partner and create a series of color tile riddles for their classmates to solve following the same format as the riddles presented on the overhead. It is important for the children to manipulate the tiles as they create their riddles. The tiles keep them focused on the process and help them formulate their clues.

I collect the riddles and check them over. I make several overheads of children's riddles to present to the class for the following lesson. We go through the riddles clue by clue just as we did the day before. The remaining riddles can be reproduced on tagboard and placed at a center with a tub of tiles for completion at choice time. Each riddle card includes the author's name.

Charting common riddle phrases on chart paper can help those children who struggle some with the mathematical language of good riddles. Charting phrases and their symbolic representation can help all children move from words to the symbols they'll be required to use as they move into the upper grades. Charting the phrases used in the initial riddle could look like this:

Phrase	Symbolic Representation
fewer than 10 tiles	total tiles < 10
more yellow tiles than blue tiles	yellow (y) $>$ blue (b)
one more yellow than red tiles	yellow (y) $=$ red (r) $+ 1$
same number of blue tiles as yellow tiles	blue (b) $=$ yellow (y)

Add to the chart as you share and discuss riddles. Pairing symbols and words is a skill too often ignored in elementary mathematics. Current research and our national math standards (NCTM 2000) highlight the importance of algebraic thinking in the elementary grades. Here is an opportunity to work with your class on the relational language that is required when we think algebraically.

Logic Puzzles

Duration: 1–3 class periods

In grades 1, 2, and 3, logical thinking is often approached informally. As children move into the middle elementary grades, the need for a representational model of their reasoning becomes greater. Logic puzzles solved with matrices can support that need. This activity offers students opportunities to:

- apply logical reasoning while solving problems with differing contexts
- represent reasoning with a matrix model

Materials

- 1 booklet of 5–10 logic puzzles per student
- optional: a few simple riddles written on chart paper

I have yet to come across a fourth grader who could not be engaged by logic puzzles. In this activity, logical reasoning is demonstrated by a child's ability and willingness to generalize solutions in response to a series of clues. Reading comprehension becomes as important as the ability to think relationally as the children solve the puzzles. Working through logic puzzles offers children opportunities to make assumptions and conclusions based on the connectedness of the information presented by the clues.

Introducing logic puzzles in a whole-group format with small puzzles of a few clues will help students identify and practice the type of thinking needed to solve logic puzzles. I work through two or three puzzles with the class as an introduction to the task. I duplicate booklets of five to ten puzzles of increasing difficulty for the children to work on in pairs or trios. I have seen many books of puzzles on the market, but I continue to choose puzzles from *Logic, Anyone?* (Post and Eads 1996). I pick and choose puzzles that I think will engage my students. For each puzzle, I type the clues and a blank matrix on a single page. You'll need to decide whether or not to fill in the headings on the matrices. When making this decision, keep in mind that the mathematical focus is on the development of reasoning and logical thinking, not necessarily on the creation of the matrix headings.

The following puzzle can help set the stage for the work of the next few days:

There are three children in the Jones family: Jason, Jonathan, and Jacob.

Use the following clues to find each one's age:

- *Each of the two younger children is half as old as the next.*
- *The oldest is 12.*
- *Jason is not the oldest.*
- *Jason is twice as old as Jacob.*

What is the age of each child? How do you know?

Displaying this puzzle on chart paper can be helpful as the children unravel the clues and relationships. When a child offers an idea, ask what clue or what word or phrase in the clue helped her come to that conclusion so others can follow that child's thinking. Ask for other ways of thinking about the clues to gain insights into your students' thinking. Some children may start with the last clue. Some may start with what they know is not true, given the clues. Some may manipulate the names and some the ages. Asking children to share their strategies with their neighbor will not only help the children articulate their own thinking but offer the children an additional opportunity to consider and perhaps adopt a new strategy. Sharing strategies with a partner prior to a whole-class discussion also lets students try out their thinking before sharing it with the whole group.

Examining the language of logic puzzles becomes extremely important as children work through them. Encourage children to underline words or phrases that they think may be important as they consider the clues to help them focus on relationships presented by the language of the puzzle.

A new puzzle can offer new challenges, such as the following:

Jacob, Jonathan, Jason, and Jessica all have a favorite sport. Each one likes a different sport. Their favorite sports are hockey, swimming, tennis, and golf.

- *Jessica does not like water.*
- *Both Jason and Jonathan like to hit a ball.*
- *Jonathan does not like to play on a playing field that has lines on it.*

What is each one's favorite sport? How do you know?

Asking children to solve this puzzle with a neighbor will encourage them to talk through their thinking. Encourage partners to chart their thinking in some way so that they can re-create their decisions as to who liked what when they are sharing with the class. When the class comes together to quickly discuss the solution and share strategies, remind the children that Jacob was never mentioned in the clues. How did they determine what sport he liked? How did they keep track of their information?

Asking children to share their charting strategies may uncover the use of a matrix or something similar. If not, introduce the use of a matrix to offer students a method of representing their thinking as they work through the puzzles in their booklets. Decide whether to fill in the headings of a blank matrix with your class or to offer a matrix with headings already filled in, based on the needs and strengths of your students.

	Hockey	*Swimming*	*Tennis*	*Golf*
Jacob				
Jonathan				
Jason				
Jessica				

As a decision is made, place a check mark in the appropriate cell. You can then put an X in the other cells in that row and column. We know that Jonathan likes golf, so the matrix at this point would look like:

	Hockey	Swimming	Tennis	Golf
Jacob				X
Jonathan	X	X	X	√
Jason				X
Jessica				X

Continue filling in the matrix with the children until all the sports have been decided upon. Working with a matrix will often encourage children to go back and reread clues if they are not able to fill in the matrix after the first reading.

Distribute a logic packet to each child. Ask the children to work in groups of two or three. Because the puzzles are presented in order of increasing difficulty, I ask the children to work through the booklet in order. As the children move on to more difficult puzzles, they are asked to confer with another group before they ask for my help.

I like to allow two class periods for the completion of the logic packets. The children quickly get caught up in the process of logical thinking that these puzzles require. Allowing them the time to work through the challenges that some of the later puzzles present will not only strengthen reasoning skills but also give them the necessary time to talk and think with each other.

Completion of these packets with partners also allows for differentiation in your instruction. The quality of mathematical talk that accompanies the completion of each puzzle will help you identify those children who need support or those who need an extra challenge.

TEACHER-TO-TEACHER TALK I continue to struggle with determining how much time to allow for a task or activity. The completion of an independent task, such as working through the logic packet, can vary from child to child or pairing to pairing. So how much time is enough? We all deal with scope-and-sequence requirements and guidelines. With those pressures—some imposed by school mandates and some by our own choice—comes the need to move through the curriculum at a particular pace. Too much time allotted to a task can produce restlessness, and not enough can cause frustration.

With this particular activity, I allow the children two class periods. Most are able to finish or almost finish in that amount of time. I call the children together at the end of that second class period. I recommend that those who did not finish the packet find time to work through the remaining puzzles on their own even though we are going to move on to another lesson. Some do and some do not. Even after two class periods, those that struggle some will have been able to get through three or four puzzles. I can live with that—and so can they. This is also an activity that can easily be sent out with the children if they see resource personnel.

The needs and strengths of your class will determine how much processing you do once the booklets are completed. Choosing a puzzle or two that seemed to be difficult for the majority of the class can help direct the processing. Having a matrix set up on an overhead or piece of chart paper for that particular puzzle or two can move along the class discussion.

The study and practice of logical reasoning is closely tied to children's language development, so from time to time, I slip logical reasoning activities into homework assignments and independent work. Learning how to read and interpret the mathematical text in logic puzzles can help children not only fine-tune reasoning skills but sharpen their reading and language skills as well.

Follow-Up Journal Write

Miranda likes ice cream.

Isabella likes pretzels.

Cam likes potato chips.

Alexander likes cookies.

Create a series of logic clues to identify each child with his or her favorite snack.

Games

Close to 1,000

This game, adapted from *Money, Miles, and Large Numbers, Grade 4* (Economopoulos, Mokros, Akers, and Russell 2004), involves arranging digits to create two three-digit numbers whose sum is as close to one thousand as possible. *Close to 1,000* offers students opportunities to:

- add and subtract
- estimate
- create three-digit numbers whose sum is one thousand or close to one thousand

Materials
- directions for *Close to 1,000* (see Blackline Masters)
- 1 deck of 0–9 number cards, containing 4 of each number
- 1 *Close to 1,000* score sheet per player (see Blackline Masters)
- number of players: 2–3

Close to 100 was introduced in September. *Close to 1,000* was offered in the addition and subtraction menu in September as an optional item, but many children have either not played it or not played it much. Because the children are familiar with the format of *Close to 100*, *Close to 1,000* is quick to engage them. The format of the two games is the same. In *Close to 1,000*, students create two three-digit numbers from eight dealt cards whose sum is as close as they can get to one thousand. Their score for a particular round is the difference between their sum and one thousand.

Although *Close to 100* and *Close to 1,000* are similar in their format, the strategies children use when playing one are often different from strategies used when playing the other. As students are playing, observe their strategies. Are they using front-end estimation by beginning in the hundreds place? How do they adjust for regrouping needs in the tens and ones places? Do they create numbers one at a time? Or do they create numbers concurrently? Are their strategies consistent or do they change depending on the cards students draw? Allow time at the end of class for processing this game in a whole-class format. Children may hear strategies that make sense to them and may, in turn, opt to apply those strategies to their estimation routines.

Digit Place

In this game, adapted from *About Teaching Mathematics* (Burns 2007), children take turns guessing a three-digit number based on logical reasoning and previous guesses. *Digit Place* offers students opportunities to apply logical reasoning skills.

Material

- directions for *Digit Place* (see Blackline Masters)

When initially introducing this game to the children, I find it helpful to first model it with the entire class. I choose the number and draw a chart on the board, and the children take turns guessing. It may be helpful to list the digits 0–9 over the chart, but allow the children to decide what to do with that display. Different classes will do different things with the digits. One year my class sent a child up to the board to cross off the digits that they all agreed were not in the number in order to narrow their choices. It is also interesting to observe when a class will decide that a guess with no correct digits is actually a good guess because they can eliminate numbers quickly. Once the correct guess is given, there is often much discussion about how that child came to that decision. That talk can often be directed into a quick sharing of strategies not only from that child but from others willing to share as well.

Digit Place is my class's favorite game year in and year out and a wonderful game to play throughout the year. It can be played with partners, but my students prefer to play in a whole-class format. When we have five to ten minutes at the end of a class, the children will often lobby to play

Digit Place. When a student guesses the number correctly, that child then chooses the new number. The child will come to the front of the class and orchestrate the game while I chart the responses. It can also easily be a homework assignment for children to play with their families.

Calculation Routines and Practices

Although I spend time in the first weeks of school reviewing and strengthening addition and subtraction skills, further development of these operations should continue through October. Because we spend time in October exploring large numbers, calculation and problem-solving practices can have the same focus. I do give an occasional set of context-free addition and subtraction calculations, but I choose the numbers carefully. The regrouping process required when subtracting across zeros can still be problematic for some and the extra practice for the others is beneficial. I may ask the children to give ballpark estimates of the sums or differences before they calculate to push their developing number sense and estimation skills. By this time in the year, my students are aware of my obsession with story problems and context. Even when I assign a set of calculations, I ask students to choose one and write a story problem that fits the number model of the calculation. There are times when any context will do. Sometimes we decide as a class what the context of the problems will be. We have written about dogs, a circus tent, the ocean, the Red Sox, the surprising items that can be found in the closet in my classroom, and many other unrelated topics chosen by the children, with which they have great fun. Having the children compare solutions and share stories at table groups can keep processing time manageable and give equal airtime to each student.

Developing a problem-of-the-day format can further support the development of problem-solving skills (see "Resources" section on page 86) and continue to strengthen calculation skills outside of the time allotted to math class. The chosen problem can be posted as morning work, work to be completed in choice time, or possibly work to be taken home. Again, the focus is on number sense, large number manipulation, and addition and subtraction procedures. Standardizing the written requirements and procedure will help you manage the correction process. Perhaps all problems throughout the year are to be completed in a notebook or on run-off paper with a standardized heading. You can place an icon next to the problem to identify whether the problem should be completed independently or cooperatively.

It may be helpful at this point in the year to become familiar with any required test, either district or state, and the types of calculation tasks it will ask of the children. Constructing an occasional problem of the day that is similar in language and format as questions that the children will eventually encounter on mandated tests will them help develop some ease with the testing process and format.

TEACHER-TO-TEACHER TALK We all eventually wrestle with this question: to teach to the (mandated) test . . . or not? When children are asked high-level questions, we are finding that they often perform better on standardized tests. Perhaps we need to spend time assessing and adjusting our style of *presenting* questions when thinking about preparing children for these tests. If calculation tasks requiring addition and regrouping appear on your test, why not present the class with a problem and its multiple-choice answers in a similar format? Review the reasonableness of each answer option and follow up with questions such as "How do you know that? Can knowing that help you eliminate another possible answer choice or identify the correct response?" Calculation skills are all well and good, but the process of reasoning, the application of number sense, and the way children think about the possible solutions become almost more important as we help them become better test takers. Take this question, for example:

The chart below shows the number of college students who participated in four different sports in the academic year 1998–1999.

Sport	Women	Men
Indoor track	15,460	16,943
Outdoor track	18,220	20,401
Soccer	17,520	18,238
Basketball	14,365	15,710

According to the chart, how many men and women participated in soccer in 1998–1999?

A. 25,758

B. 33,230

C. 35,758

D. 37,921

(Massachusetts Department of Education 2005)

Asking children to think this question through aloud and *without* actual calculation will help students apply number sense and logical thinking to a standardized test question.

For example, using front-end estimation (17 + 18 = 35), we can throw out A *and* B because they are too small. So now we need to choose between C and D, even though D may be too large. So let's focus on C. Adding the ones digits in the table gives us eight, so we can truly eliminate D. C is the answer . . . and we didn't need to perform the entire addition calculation to find it. Why not use what we know to figure out what we don't know? Yes, there may be time constraints from test to test, but when we work with our students outside of the testing format in more cooperative and comfortable settings, we are encouraging them to think and reason rather than to merely calculate.

Mathematics Writing

The documentation and justification of mathematical thinking take on importance with activities that promote and support logical thinking. We need to provide language experiences in order for children to learn how to use words and mathematical notation as tools for mathematical thinking (Bickmore-Brand 1990). We find out what we think when we write, and the same is true for fourth graders. When we ask children to write about their thinking, they can make conclusions, formulate generalizations, and uncover misconceptions.

Questions such as "How do you know?" or "Why does this makes sense?" can follow any writing prompt. Answers to these questions can help us assess the logical reasoning process that a child is using.

Taking the time to process an assigned writing prompt or to model responses with your class as the year progresses can prove to be helpful for all children. Because we want the writing of our students to improve in its clarity and precision, we need to revisit assignments to make our continued expectations known.

Working with a small group of children on the same prompt can support the writing process. Small-group work will also help inform your instructional decisions not only for math class but for language arts lessons as well.

Parent Communication

A parent information form can be sent home or posted electronically for this month of study. Figure 3–2 is a sample information form.

Sending home corrected student work on a regular basis can help keep parents informed of their children's progress in math class. Math notebooks can be sent home as a collected record of student work and progress for parents to view. Ask children to share one entry or one piece of work with a parent to facilitate the communication between school and family as well as between child and parent. If this is something that you think would benefit your classroom community, you may wish to standardize this practice. If doing it every week seems too cumbersome, try every other week or perhaps once a month. If notebooks are sent home, the students can document what they are sharing as well as a parent's response right in the notebook.

Parent conferences may be on the horizon in October. Because we are still getting to know our students in October, I have found that focusing my conversation with parents on *their* mathematical assessment of their children is extremely helpful. This conversation can reveal further insights into my student, but also helps me understand how each family views and values mathematics. That information can prove to be very handy down the road if issues present themselves with progress or behavior in class.

FIGURE 3–2 ◄

Parent information form
for October.

Parent Information and Involvement Form

From: Lainie Schuster
To: Parents of Fourth Graders
Re: Mathematics Curriculum
Month: October

During the next month, the major topics we will be studying are:

- problem solving
- logical reasoning
- place value
- large numbers

My goal in studying these topics is for the students to be able to:

- develop and model positive problem-solving attitudes and behavior
- talk, write, and draw the mathematics
- apply place-value understandings to the reading and interpretation of large numbers
- develop deductive and inductive reasoning skills and strategies

Parents can help at home by:

- continuing to review basic addition, subtraction, multiplication, and division facts
- identifying contexts in which large numbers "count," such as mileage (from Boston to San Francisco) or money (the cost of a new car, the cost of a home).
- asking about the goings-on in math class: "What did you do in math today? Can you explain that game to me? *What* did you think about that? *How* did you think about that? *Why* did you think that?"
- working with your children on Sudoku puzzles—you can find books of them everywhere!

You'll be able to make more standardized observations if prior to the conference you construct questions that you'll ask each parent. You might want to think about using some of these questions:

- What are your goals for your child in math this year?
- What do you see as your child's strengths in math? Weaknesses?
- What were your experiences with math in school? Have you shared these with your child?
- Do you solve math problems as a family? Does that opportunity come up?
- How is math homework approached at home? If your child asks for help, how do you respond?

When we engage parents in these types of conversations, we are inviting them into our classrooms. Some parents want to be there very much;

they just do not know how to make it happen. Having a handout for parents to take along with them after the conference can also be helpful. Figures 3–3 and 3–4 are sample handouts.

FIGURE 3–3 ▶

Parent handout.

How Can I Help My Child Become Mathematically Powerful?

Money

Encourage your child to:

- participate in making family budget decisions
- participate in grocery shopping
- begin to manage his or her allowance
- make decisions about how much her or his allowance can buy

Counting/Number

Encourage your child to:

- Count past 500 by different multiples (count past 500 by 50s, or count past 650 by 20s)
- Make connections between factors and multiples (If I can run 1 mile in five minutes, how many miles can I run in thirty minutes?)

Math Facts

By the end of fourth grade, your child should know the multiplication facts up to 10×10.

Time

These are some of the time concepts that you can help your child learn at home:

- how to read an analog clock (with an hour hand and a minute hand)
- how to schedule time (If you need to do four specific things, how much time will you need? If you have four things to do and they each take twenty-five minutes, how much time will you need to complete them all? What could those four things be?)

Measurement

Involve your child in activities that encourage measurement, such as:

- cooking (fractions, volume, cups, teaspoons, following step-by-step instructions)
- reading a thermometer
- estimating temperatures (It will be 60 degrees today; will you need a coat for recess?)

Problem Solving

Pose meaningful problems attached to real-world contexts whose solutions allow for varied approaches. Follow up solutions with questions such as:

- How did you figure that out?
- How do you know if your answer is correct?
- Can your answer be an estimate or does it have to be an exact number? Why?

FIGURE 3–4 ◀

Parent handout.

What to Say When Your Child Asks for Help with Math Homework

In order to help your child become a strong and flexible problem solver, I assign a variety of math activities as homework.

Often your child will receive homework that is directly connected to our math curriculum. Other assignments may be teacher generated or "borrowed" from other relevant sources. You may also see many writing assignments—something that has not always been associated with math homework!

Games may also be assigned for homework. I use games as motivating ways to help my students learn and master concepts. We play these games in school and I ask that you play them at home with your child, too. Games are to be taken seriously. When your child asks you to play a math game, notice that your child has to remember and explain rules; create, articulate, and justify a strategy; and use math, as well. Often a lot more mathematical thought goes into playing a game than completing a worksheet!

I also assign open-ended problems (multistep story problems) or performance tasks (collecting data). Open-ended problems often challenge your child to try to use much of his or her math knowledge to solve an unfamiliar problem. Sometimes children complain, "The teacher did not teach me how to do this." And in a way, they are correct. I cannot teach your child how to do every kind of problem. Instead, I focus on problem-solving strategies and making connections between similar types of problems and possible strategies used to solve them.

When your child asks you for help, please try not to jump in with an answer, no matter how tempting that may be! Instead, try using some of these prompts to support your child's thinking and perseverance:

- Does this remind you of other problems that you have done in class?
- What have you come up with so far?
- Where do you think you should start?
- What is the problem asking you to do?
- Would drawing a diagram or picture help?
- Why do you think your answer is not correct?

Implementing a well-balanced homework policy takes into account the various needs and expectations of the children. This is a tricky business! It requires mathematics teachers to be thoughtful, purposeful, and respectful in their assignments. The ultimate goal of any homework assignment is to offer opportunities for meaningful mathematical conversations between parents and their children.

Assessment

We are beginning to know our children mathematically by October. Behavioral and work habit expectations have been set and classroom protocol set into motion. Our students quickly become aware of what is valued and important in math class based upon our pedagogical style and expectations.

Informative assessment strategies provide students with the opportunity to demonstrate their conceptual understanding, procedural knowledge, and processing abilities. Many tasks can be used for assessment purposes. Creating color tile riddles, for example, can offer you valuable information about how your children:

- manipulate and apply mathematical language
- create clues based on reasoning and logical thinking
- use physical models (color tiles) to construct clues and a final solution
- assess the appropriateness of clues based upon the final solution
- communicate clues in writing
- communicate with their partner

If you wish to use *Color Tile Riddles* as an assessment, it might be helpful to create an assessment framework such as a rubric that identifies the process and understandings you will assess. A sample rubric for *Color Tile Riddles* appears in Figure 3–5.

Some educators recommend sharing assessment frameworks with their students before the students complete a task, and I agree with them. When frameworks are presented to children prior to the assessment, they become active participants in the assessment process. The children are aware of the mathematical knowledge and performance that are valued for that particular task. They then can make informed decisions as they work to complete the task.

It continues to be important to keep your focus on the mathematics of the task as you create assessment practices and routines. Some tasks are better suited for assessment than others given the richness of the mathematics and the required mathematical understandings. It is also not necessary that every activity be formally assessed with a rubric or other framework. As you work through activities, you will better be able to determine what tasks are best suited for formal assessments. NCTM (2000) describes assessment as a "routine part of the ongoing classroom activity rather than an interruption" (23). Mindfully chosen tasks and carefully designed assessment formats will benefit both the teaching and learning of mathematics.

Name: _Michael_

Task	Yes	Sometimes	No
My clues are well organized and easily understood.	✓		
My clues lead to a solution.	✓		
My mathematical language and word choice are clear and specific.		✳ ✓	
My solution is posted neatly on the back of my riddle.	✓		

Comments:
Great clues, Michael.
Easy to follow.
✳ Sum = answer to an addition problem!!

FIGURE 3–5 ◀

Sample *Color Tile Riddles* rubric.

TEACHER-TO-TEACHER TALK   You might be wondering about tests and quizzes at this point. Yes, I give them both. End-of-unit tests are addressed in the "Assessment" section of Chapter 4. But what about quizzes? If the truth be known, I like quizzes. I give quizzes frequently as class warm-ups. They are short, worth 10 points, and completed in students' math notebooks. They are easy to create and just as easy to correct. Most quizzes for September and October focus on place value, addition, and subtraction. I may give the children five subtraction problems one day, two word problems the next, and two number riddles the next. We begin the class with a quiz. I move around the classroom correcting the quizzes as the children finish them. Years ago, I encountered a Latin teacher who offered homework passes to her students based on the successful completion of one thing or another. In my class, five consecutive 10s earns you a homework pass, which can be passed in at any time of the year in lieu of a homework assignment. If a child earns a 9 on the fifth quiz, he has to start all over again. Some children are devastated when they miss that fifth 10 and are denied a homework pass, but that, too, can be turned into a teachable moment about the importance of perseverance—and of making mistakes in mathematics!

Because I give quizzes so frequently in my class, there is little hoopla about quiz taking. I try to put some fun into the quizzes with story problems about the children or solutions to number riddles that follow a pattern.

Resources

About Teaching Mathematics (Burns 2007)

The "Logical Reasoning" chapter contains a myriad of activities that can be used independently or offered in a menu format.

Awesome Math Problems for Creative Thinking (Gavin et al. 2000)

An excellent resource for logical reasoning problems in an engaging format. Books can be purchased for each child at a very reasonable rate.

Logic Mysteries (Molnar 1999)

Each logic mystery is presented with a matrix. The mysteries are indexed in three levels. Convenient to have on hand for independent work, choice time, or homework.

Logic, Anyone? (Post and Eads 1996)

A fairly comprehensive collection of logic problems. Analogies, matrix logic, table logic, circle logic, syllogisms, and Venn diagrams are all explored.

Chapter 4

November/ December

GEOMETRY AND MEASUREMENT

Young children have considerable experience with geometry before entering school. . . . These initial investigations should be nurtured and extended in children's school learning of mathematics. In their classroom experiences, children should have opportunities to explore shapes and relationships among them. They benefit from problem-solving situations that lead them to investigate patterns and structures in shapes and to develop reasoning processes in spatial contexts. They need experiences that relate geometry to ideas in measurement, number, and patterns. Through these kinds of activities, students grasp how mathematics adds to their understanding of the world.

About Teaching Mathematics
Burns 2007, 107

The Learning Environment

Continue to support and develop a positive and productive classroom culture.

We have come a long way since September in the development of a classroom culture that supports and celebrates meaningful mathematical conversation, routines, and practices. Such a learning community will continue to survive and thrive when its members continue to treat it with care and attention.

Develop routines and practices that promote wait time.

Wait time refers to the quiet thinking time following a question or introduction of a task. Because fourth graders are fourth graders, wait time is understandably difficult for them. Many teachers understand the need to wait at least ten seconds after posing a question before calling on a student for a response. The same amount of time should be given to a student when called upon so she can organize her thoughts (Chapin, O'Connor, and Anderson 2003). Teachers and students are often uncomfortable with the silence of wait time. It is that very silence, however, that allows students to reason and react with purpose and thought. Years ago I had a student whose favorite expression was "Wait! Wait! Don't tell me!" I think of him often as I work to be patient and deliberate with my own wait-time practices.

The Mathematics and Its Language

Children investigate the construction of lines, segments, rays, and angles.

Geometry study in the fourth grade builds on students' informal work with geometry from the earlier grades. A greater emphasis is placed on geometric notation and precision with the use of letters and symbols that identify lines, segments, rays, and angles. Properties of lines, segments, rays, and angles can also be explored with carefully scaffolded instruction. Engaging the children in meaningful activities and conversations will help them make connections between the various notations and concepts.

Children construct and apply understandings of properties and classifications of polygons.

Properties and classifications of polygons are explored and identified. Visual organizers such as two-column T-charts and Venn diagrams can be used to help students articulate and classify similarities and differences among polygons. Hands-on activities and materials give students the opportunity to use models to discuss and even argue their observations and convictions.

Children investigate the relationship between area and perimeter.

Investigations involving fixed areas or perimeters can help children make sense of how one may or may not affect the other. Because fourth graders have had some experience with area and perimeter in earlier grades, they can now explore how the two measurements are related. These investigations can often be a source of disequilibrium for children as they work to make generalizations about the effects of one property on the other. Concrete manipulations, organizing collected data, and meaningful class discussions can help children think beyond assumed generalizations.

Children explore measurement concepts and procedures.

When working with measurement, children need to measure! Length, weight, volume, capacity, and time can be measured and investigated in a menu format.

Children make sense of the complexities found in geometric language.

The language of geometry can be confusing for fourth graders. There are many geometric words with double meanings. Charting those words can help identify those potentially confusing words and their usage. (See Figure 4–1 on the next page.)

More precise mathematical language can grow naturally from exploration, experience, and discussion. Everyday terminology such as *corner* and *lines that cross* can be replaced with more appropriate mathematical vocabulary such as *vertex* and *intersect*. Adding geometric vocabulary to a word wall will continue to support the children as they identify, use, and apply appropriate language. Having access to reference books such as *Math at Hand* (Great Source Education Group, 2004) can also be helpful. When multiple copies of reference books are easily accessible to the class, students will use them. These particular references have excellent glossaries with student-friendly examples, illustrations, and format.

Children apply their knowledge of root words, suffixes, and prefixes to decode, apply, and manipulate the language of geometry.

Geometry lends itself well to the study of root words, prefixes, and suffixes. It can be helpful to remind the children to use what they know about a prefix to help them uncover the meaning of a new word with that same

FIGURE 4–1 ▶

Chart of double-meaning words.

	Double Meanings	
Many math words have a math meaning and another meaning in regular conversation.		

Word	In math it means . . .	It usually means . . .
right	an angle whose measure is 90°	correct; accurate
obtuse	an angle whose measure is greater than 90° and less than 180°	vague

Adapted from *Writing About Mathematics* (O'Connell 2002).

prefix. We use the term *polygon*, for example, quite freely. Do the children realize that *poly* means many? How can knowing that help us to describe a polygon? We know an *octo*pus has eight legs. So, then, how many sides does an *octa*gon have? And how many notes in an *octa*ve, for that matter? If we know that a *bi*cycle has two wheels, what are we doing when we *bi*sect a segment, line, or angle?

If we can help our children get interested in and curious about the study, usage, and application of geometric words, it can pay off in increased motivation and clear articulation. When we model fascination with and application of mathematical language, students will follow our lead. As a result, our classroom discussions and directives will be mathematically richer and more meaningful.

Investigations, Games, and Literature-Based Activities

Polygon Study

Duration: 5–10 class periods

In the fourth grade, we can expect our students to begin to develop more precise definitions of polygons and their properties than they used in the earlier grades. The focus of this polygon study is on developing an understanding of how geometric figures are classified and the relationships that can be found between and among figures. This lesson offers students the opportunity to:

- identify and articulate properties that characterize polygons
- recognize and name polygons by number of sides
- sort and classify polygons in regard to common properties
- develop vocabulary to describe special triangles and quadrilaterals

Materials
- 1 *What Is a Polygon?* worksheet per student (see Blackline Masters)
- 1 set of colored pencils per table group
- 1 glue stick per pair of students
- 1 *Polygons: Must Be True and Cannot Be True* record sheet per student (see Blackline Masters)
- a collection of cutout polygon shapes (made from card stock) per pair of students (see Blackline Masters)
- 1 zip-top sandwich bag per pair of students for polygon collections
- directions for polygon sorting activities (see Blackline Masters)
- 1 geometry template per student (There are many templates on the market, but I particularly like the template created and distributed by Everyday Learning Corporation (2007a). It contains regular and nonregular polygons as well as circles and two protractors.)
- 1 *Classifying Triangles* record sheet per student (see Blackline Masters)

- 1 container of several 2-inch, 3-inch, and 4-inch pieces of drinking straws and 1-inch pipe cleaner connectors per table group
- 1 *Classifying Quadrilaterals* record sheet per student (see Blackline Masters)
- 3 12-inch pieces of string per table group for Venn Diagram models
- *The Important Book* by Margaret Wise Brown (1949)
- 1 set of *The Important Book About Polygons* pages per student for final copy; rough drafts can be written on notebook/writing paper (see Blackline Masters)
- optional: geoboards

I introduce this series of lessons with a coloring activity. I distribute the *What Is a Polygon?* worksheets and ask the children to color in the shapes. As they are coloring, the children are asked to begin to think about which shapes can be classified as polygons, which cannot, and why. Through thinking about and discussing why a shape is or is not a polygon, we will develop a set of polygon properties.

I ask the children to make a large T-chart that will fill a page in their math notebook. Although I generally do not like students to work on the backs of notebook pages, I ask the children to complete this activity on two consecutive pages of their notebooks—the back of one page and the front of the next. The two-column T-chart, which is drawn on the left-hand page, is labeled "Polygons and Not Polygons." The children cut out their shapes and place them under their respective headings. I have the students work in pairs. As they cut out and place a shape under its appropriate heading, they must articulate the reasoning behind their placement. Once both partners agree on all of the placements, they glue their shapes onto their T-charts.

Next I hand out the *Polygons: Must Be True and Cannot Be True* record sheets. The children tape the worksheet into their notebook facing the T-chart page, as illustrated in Figure 4–2. We then begin to analyze each shape and why it belongs on one side of the T-chart or the other in a whole-class discussion. As we discuss shape placements, we begin to generate characteristics of polygons (must be true) and characteristics of nonpolygons (cannot be true). Not only are the children defining and classifying polygons, but they're also integrating reasoning in support of their decisions.

The geometric vocabulary that will be introduced and applied in this activity can be rich and varied. You may have the opportunity to introduce and explore new words, such as *convex* and *concave*. And you'll have the opportunity to apply familiar words, such as *open* and *closed*, as the class discusses, defines, and classifies polygons.

Children are easily confused by the term *regular*. Regular polygons have congruent sides and angles. Nonregular polygons do not. Although I adore pattern blocks and take every opportunity to use them, their use can muddy up the concept of nonregular shapes. A hexagon has six sides. The yellow pattern block is a regular hexagon. Not all hexagons are regular,

Use separate piece of paper

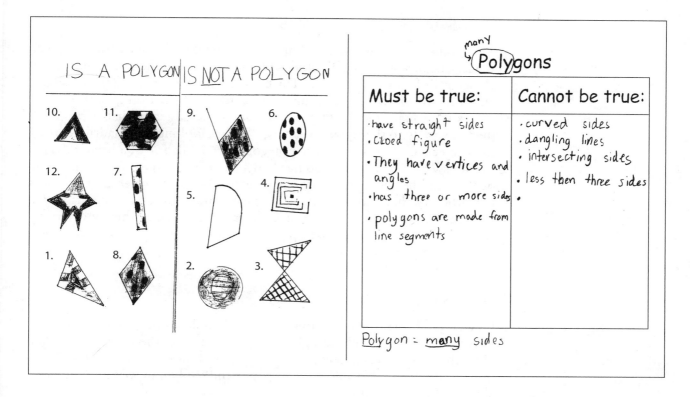

IS A POLYGON | IS NOT A POLYGON

^{many}
Polygons

Must be true:	Cannot be true:
· have straight sides	· curved sides
· closed figure	· dangling lines
· They have vertices and angles	· intersecting sides
· has three or more sides	· less then three sides
· polygons are made from line segments	·

Polygon = <u>many</u> sides

FIGURE 4–2 ▲

Jackson's completed polygon pages in his notebook.

however. Once the term *regular* is introduced as a form of classification, ask the children to construct a nonregular hexagon. What could that polygon look like? A regular quadrilateral can be defined as a *square*. What might a nonregular quadrilateral look like? Play around with the words and the classifications. In order to make sense of these classifications, children will need to compare and contrast shapes and labels.

Hands-on sorting activities help children further develop their visual and reasoning skills as they classify polygons according to agreed-upon properties. Whenever possible, invite the children to determine the sorting principles themselves. Children can work in small groups as they complete some or all of the following tasks (adapted from Van de Walle 2004). These tasks can be presented in a menu from which the children can pick and choose those that they wish to complete. Students will need sets of cutout polygon cards to complete these activities. You can create the cards by duplicating the shapes on card stock and then cutting them out (see Blackline Masters). Keep the polygon cards in zip-top bags when not in use.

This and That

Children each randomly choose two shapes (before they know the task!). The task is to find something that is alike and something that is different between those two shapes.

Valuable Property

The group randomly selects a shape and places it in the center of the workspace. The task is to find all other shapes that are like the target shape, but all according to the same rule. The children can then use that same shape and identify another sorting rule as an extension. For example, the group places the square on the target mat. One child states a sorting property that can apply to the square, such as, "We are looking for quadrilaterals." In turn, each child chooses a polygon that is also a quadrilateral and explains why. Once each child has had a chance to choose a quadrilateral, or there are no more to be chosen, a second child can offer another sorting property that can apply to the square, such as, ". . . a quadrilateral with four right angles." Each child determines whether this new sorting rule can apply to their chosen polygon. Some polygons may fit the sort, and some may not.

Out of Sorts

One student identifies a sorting rule. Each child in the group chooses a polygon that fits the rule and places it in the center of the workspace. Each child then constructs a new polygon on paper that matches the rule. They must write the sorting rule on their paper and explain in writing how their shape adheres to that rule.

I Have a Secret

Children conduct a secret sort. One child creates a small collection of shapes that fit a secret rule. The other group members try to add polygons to the collection as they guess the secret sorting rule.

Guess My Rule

Using about one-third of a set of cutout shapes, create secret-shape folders by pasting each shape inside a folded piece of paper so that the shape is hidden from view. One child is selected as the leader, draws a secret-shape folder, and peeks inside. The other students are to select shapes that they think may match the shape in the folder. They can ask the leader questions about the shape, but the leader can answer only yes or no in response to their questions. The students cannot ask, "Is this the shape?" Questions need to relate to the properties of the secret shape. (See Blackline Masters for a reproducible set of directions for these activities.)

I also give children additional time to explore the shapes found on an available geometry template so they can informally compare and contrast shapes. Creating animals, houses, or other objects with the template shapes will engage the children in observation and discussion. (See Figures 4–3 and 4–4.)

FIGURE 4–3 ◀

Evan made a bear from template shapes.

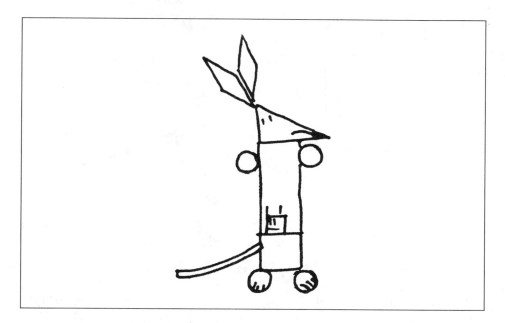

FIGURE 4–4 ◀

Chris created a kangaroo with template shapes.

Triangles

Once properties of various polygons have been explored, instruction can then move on to identifying and classifying special types of polygons, such as triangles. Begin by distributing a *Classifying Triangles* record sheet to each student. This sheet asks the children to classify triangles into two categories: all triangles and some triangles. Place a container of straws and pipe cleaner connectors at each table so children can physically model the properties as they identify them. The class labels, discusses, and traces *equilateral*, *isosceles*, and *scalene* triangles using a geometry template. These special triangles, classified by side length, belong in the Some Triangles column. Triangles can also be classified by angle measurements. Those containing a right angle are identified as *right* triangles. Those containing all angles less than 90 degrees are identified as *acute* triangles. And those with an angle greater than 90 degrees are identified as *obtuse* triangles. (See Figure 4–5.)

FIGURE 4–5 ▶

Kelsey's *Classifying Triangles* worksheet.

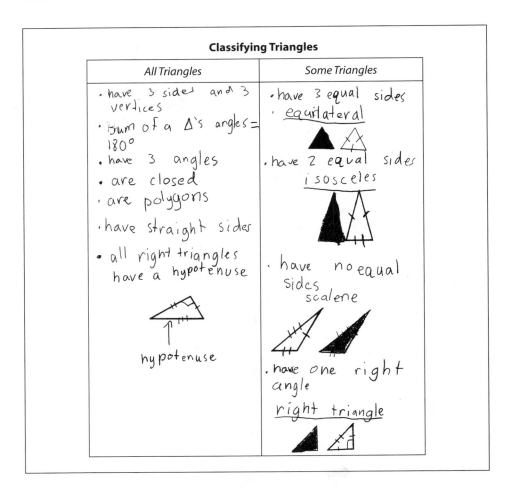

When classifying triangles by their angle measures, children invariably ask: "Can a triangle have two right angles or two obtuse angles?" These questions can set up some wonderful student-initiated mathematical investigations. This is an opportunity for the children to pose their own questions and the activities they wish to pursue as they work to discover the answers. Having geoboards or straws and pipe cleaner connectors available will help children to build triangles as they test out their conjectures.

Follow-Up Journal Write

Isabella says this figure is a triangle. Tyler says it is a polygon. With whom do you agree and why? (See Figure 4–6 for one student's response.)

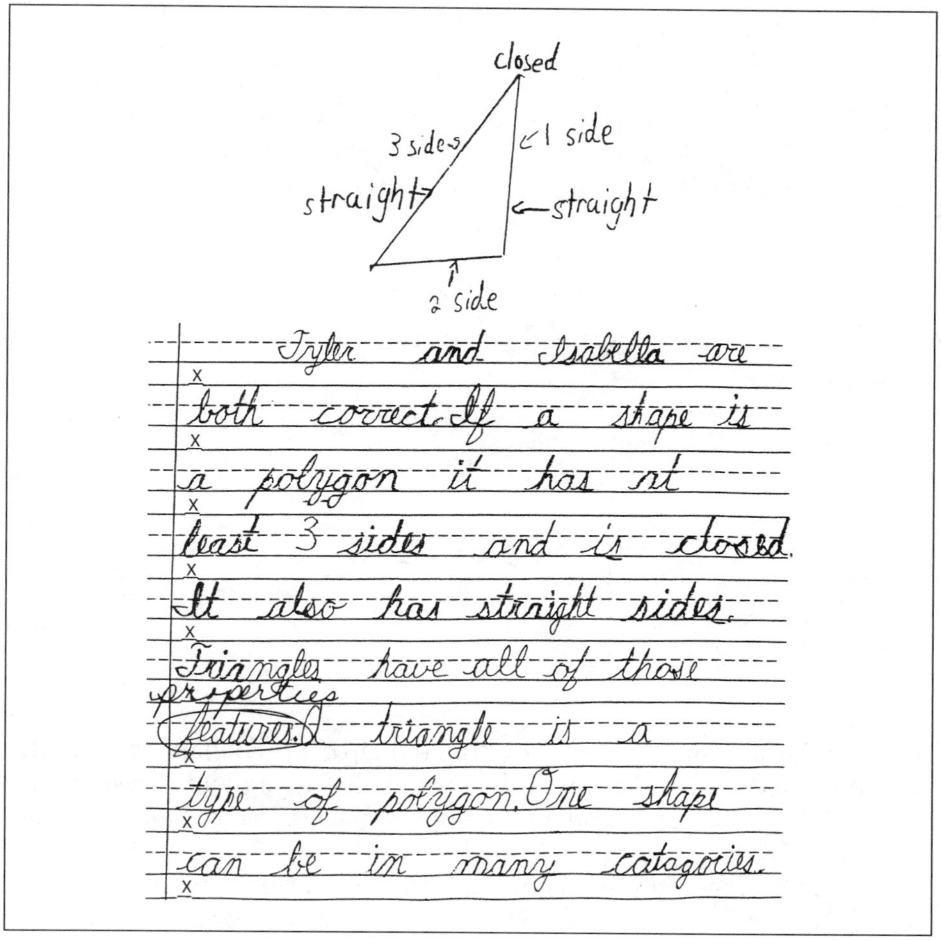
closed
3 sides
1 side
straight
straight
2 side
Tyler and Isabella are both correct. If a shape is a polygon it has at least 3 sides and is closed. It also has straight sides. Triangles have all of those properties features. A triangle is a type of polygon. One shape can be in many catagories.

FIGURE 4–6

Diana's journal write.

Quadrilaterals

It is equally important to take the time to identify, classify, and discuss quadrilaterals. Begin by having students fill out the two-column T-chart on the *Classifying Quadrilaterals* record sheet. Keep in mind that there are two methods of classifying quadrilaterals: by the presence (or absence) of parallel sides *and* by the length of their sides. Fourth graders often focus on the length of sides in their classification. Posing questions such as "What do you notice about a trapezoid's opposite sides?" and "What is similar between a rhombus and a square?" will shift the focus from side length to the presence of opposite parallel sides. Extending the sides of a parallelogram on a visual display for the children can help them identify why its opposite sides are parallel. (See Figure 4–7.) A discussion about the similarity between parallel lines and parallel sides can take place based on prior knowledge and experience with the concept of parallel lines.

We need to be mindful that connections between concepts and terminology will not happen on their own. Our good questions can plant the

FIGURE 4–7   ▶

Visual representation of polygons with parallel and nonparallel sides.

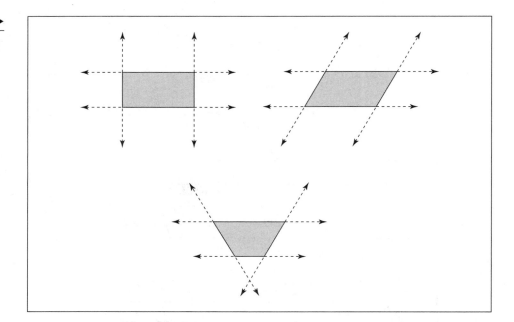

seeds for those connections to grow and to help children make sense of the interconnectedness of the topics the class is discussing and investigating. Figure 4–8 shows one student's completed *Classifying Quadrilaterals* worksheet.

The comparing and contrasting of quadrilaterals in a whole-class discussion is often not enough for fourth graders. Visual organizers such as Venn diagrams are extremely helpful as children work to make sense of all of the overlapping categories of quadrilaterals. Students can draw Venn diagrams or make them with string on tabletops. The set of polygon shapes made for the sorting activities can once again be used to create the Venn diagrams. (See Figure 4–9.)

Once the students have carried out the categorizing tasks that you have determined, ask if they have any category suggestions. Following a child's lead can occasionally take you to unchartered territory, which I believe is the true essence of teaching. Robert wanted to classify squares, rectangles, and rhombi. I was a little nervous about this one because I knew that one was classified as another, but in all my years of teaching math, the square-rhombus delineation remained my nemesis. In order to make sense of it myself, I had to re-create the Venn in much the same way that Robert had asked his classmates to. As we placed our quadrilaterals into the Venn, there was much discussion about the difference and similarity between squares, rectangles, and rhombi. Children were getting up and rifling through reference books to find definitions. Children were moving squares, rectangles, and rhombi in and out of the Venn with much attention to detail—in this case, angle measurement and side length. Needless

Classifying Quadrilaterals

All Quadrilaterals	Some Quadrilaterals
• have 4 sides and 4 angles • have vertices • are polygons • all angles of a quadrilateral add up to 360°	• have 4 right angles square rectangle • have obtuse and acute angle trapezoid rhombus kite parallelogram • have parallel sides • have 2 pairs of parallel sides rectangle square rhombus parellelogram • have no parallel sides kite • have equal sides square rhombus rhombus

FIGURE 4–8 ◄

Matt's *Classifying Quadrilaterals* worksheet.

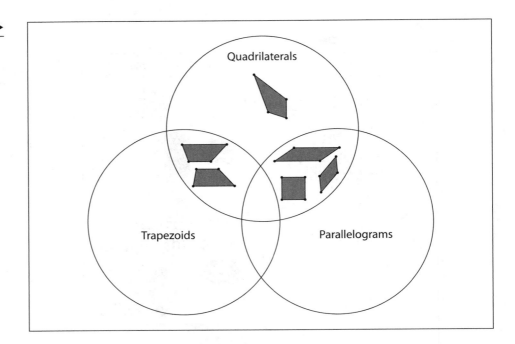

to say, this investigation took on a life of its own! By the end of a very noisy math class, we all agreed on the following facts:

- Squares, rectangles, and rhombi were *all* quadrilaterals and parallelograms.
- Squares were special rectangles. We found that the definition of a *rectangle* (a quadrilateral with two pairs of congruent, parallel sides and four right angles) identified *both* the square and the rectangle.
- The definition of a *square* (a parallelogram with four congruent sides and four right angles) could fit the rectangle *or* the rhombus.
- The definition of a *rhombus* (a parallelogram with all four sides equal in length) described a square. Therefore, a square *is* a rhombus but a rhombus *is not* necessarily a square.

I was quite amazed at how the children manipulated and applied the formal definitions to their drawings, models, and ideas. They understood the words and made their understanding visible by identifying the properties in the models themselves. (See Figure 4–10.)

The Important Book About Polygons

This activity is based on the children's book *The Important Book*, by Margaret Wise Brown (1949). *The Important Book* is a collection of important characteristics about everyday things. For example, Brown writes:

The important thing about snow is that it is white. It is cold, and light, it falls softly out of the sky, it is bright, and the shape of tiny stars, and crystals. It is always cold. It melts. But the important thing about the snow is that it is white. (9–10)

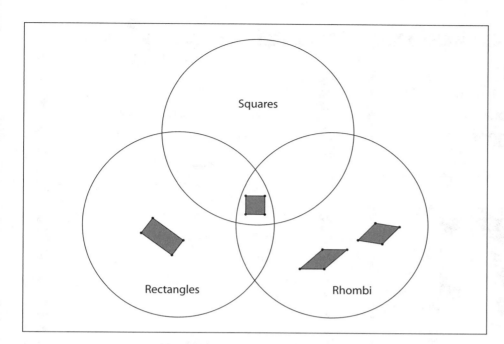

FIGURE 4–10   ◄

A Venn diagram categorizing squares, rectangles, and rhombi.

Each of Brown's observations begins and ends with the same important thing. This book lends itself beautifully to thinking about important things about polygons. Each child will create an *Important Book About Polygons*. The first page of each child's book describes the important thing about *polygons*, and we craft it together in a whole-class format. Reading the book out loud to the class allows me the opportunity to focus on the language and format of an entry. The children can then choose four or five other polygons about which to write important things—always beginning and ending with the same important thought, mirroring the original author's style. Books can be illustrated and dedicated. Because many published books contain a page about the author, *The Important Book About Polygons* ends with an "About the Mathematician" page on which the child writes about himself. (See Figures 4–11 and 4–12.)

The writing of *The Important Book About Polygons* offers a creative and interdisciplinary final project to the study of polygons. Because I use this piece of work as a formal assessment, I ask the children to complete rough drafts of each page, to be proofed and corrected. I will often conference with each child once the entire first draft is completed to help direct needed grammatical or mathematical corrections and decisions for the final draft, such as illustration choices and placements. I copy the cover pages on card stock and bind each final copy. Each year, the published copies are displayed in the library alongside Brown's book. Because entire afternoons can be spent working on our books, it makes complete sense to collapse language arts and mathematics into one extended block while students are writing the books.

The
Important Book
About
Polygons

Words by ___Jack___
Pictures by ___Jack___

Vertex   Rectangle (Rec-TANG-GEL)   Vertex

Vertex   Vertex

© Fall 2006

FIGURE 4–11   ▲

Jack's *Important Book About Polygons* cover page.

The important thing about a ___polygon___
is *that it has many sides. It is closed.
It has 3 or more sides. It has no
curves. It has angles and vertices. It
can be regular or irregular. It can
be concave or convex.*

But the important thing about a

___polygon___   is
that it has many sides.

The Important Book About Polygons
Fall 2006

FIGURE 4–12   ▲

Jack's polygon page.

Tangram Explorations

Duration: 3–4 class periods

Tangrams are very old and popular puzzle shapes. The standard set of seven tangrams is cut from a square and can be used for a multitude of rich geometric investigations, from polygon sorts to explorations of area and perimeter. These lessons are adapted from *About Teaching Mathematics* (Burns 2007) and offer students opportunities to:

- investigate part-whole relationships
- identify and articulate properties that characterize polygons
- sort and classify polygons in regard to common properties
- investigate area
- investigate perimeter

Materials

- 1 6-inch square cut out of card stock per student, plus a few extras
- 1 zip-top bag or size 10 envelope per student

- 1 set of tangram cutting instructions per student (see Blackline Masters)
- *Grandfather Tang's Story*, by Ann Tompert (1990) (multiple copies, if possible)
- several sheets of card stock per student
- 1 *Constructing Polygons* worksheet per student (see Blackline Masters)
- piece of chart paper with blank "Constructing Polygons" table
- several sheets of newsprint per student

Having children cut their own set of tangrams not only is a good lesson in following directions but will also convince the children that these seven pieces truly can go back together to make a square . . . and some will still be utterly convinced that this cannot be done! The directions in Figure 4–13 illustrate how to cut the 6-inch card stock square into seven pieces: two pairs of congruent right triangles, one midsize right triangle, one square, and one parallelogram. Each child can keep her set of tangram pieces in a zip-top sandwich bag or an envelope.

Once the pieces are cut, the children will automatically begin to explore shapes that can be made by using some or all of the pieces. As the children are creating new shapes, ask them to be mindful of the relationships they see in shape and size among the pieces. Even in this early stage of the lesson, you will notice which children manipulate the pieces with ease and those for whom this is difficult. Having children make their own shapes as an initial investigation provides accessibility of the lesson to all of the children. This free exploration time can also provide us with some valuable insights about how various students interact with the manipulatives and the task. Spatial organization or difficulty with such may influence a student's performance on a variety of nonmathematical school tasks as well as the tasks that follow this exploration.

Grandfather Tang's Story is a lovely tale told by Grandfather Tang to his granddaughter, Little Soo. Each has a set of tangrams, and together they make up a story about two fox fairy friends. If you do not have access to a classroom set of books, it might be helpful to reproduce copies

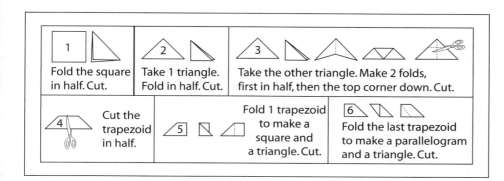

FIGURE 4–13 ◀

Tangram cutting instructions (Ronfeldt 2003).

of each tangram animal listed in the story from which the children can work. As I read the story out loud, the children manipulate their puzzle pieces to create the animal about which I am reading. I am always amazed at how engaged the children are with this storytelling technique. Some children listen as I read a page and then set off to create the animal. Some prefer to create the animal while I am reading. There is something very soothing about hearing the shuffling of the puzzle pieces and the whispers of children as they compare finished constructions with one another.

Tangram Puzzle Cards

Have the children explore making shapes using all seven tangram pieces. When they find one that pleases them, have them trace around the outline of the shape on a sheet of card stock. Have the children name it and sign the front. The outlines can be placed in a class tangram box so that others can try to fit their pieces into the shape. Students can sign their names on the backs of the cards as they complete them. (See Figure 4–14.)

Constructing Polygons

Hand out a *Constructing Polygons* worksheet to each student. Having this posted on chart paper will allow you quick reference as you introduce and process the task. Using just the three smallest triangles, the children are asked to make a square, a right triangle, a trapezoid, and a parallelogram. They are then asked to use the five smaller pieces (all but the two large triangles) to make the same shapes. Then they repeat the procedure with all seven pieces.

Being mindful of the geometric and spatial strengths and needs of your students will help you direct and differentiate instruction. Assigning groups of children with similar strengths and needs to complete certain tasks or certain parts of tasks will help them develop the skills addressed by each activity. An achieving group of children, for example, can sketch their polygons when completing the *Constructing Polygons* task. Those

FIGURE 4–14　▶

Jane's tangram puzzle card (front) and explanation of puzzle (back).

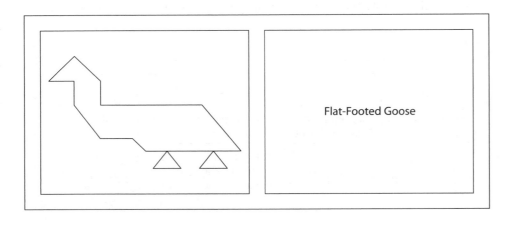

Flat-Footed Goose

whose spatial skills are at a beginning level can simply check off the various constructions as they complete them. The sketching of the completed polygons can introduce a whole new level of frustration for some. It may also be helpful to identify your specific objectives for this activity before determining the students' recording process.

Using All Seven

There are thirteen different convex polygons that you can make with the seven tangram pieces. Ask students to find them. Tracing each shape onto newsprint will offer mathematical proof of each construction. Having children compare and contrast their completed polygons with each other will offer opportunities for rich mathematical dialogue. Students now have a meaningful context within which to apply geometric vocabulary such as *rotation*, *adjacent*, and *congruent*.

Making Squares

You can construct a square with just 1 tangram piece or by using all 7. Can students make a square using 2, 3, 4, 5, or 6 pieces? Tell them that one of these is impossible, and ask them to find which one it is and why it is not possible.

Show Me the Money

Assign a value of $0.05 to a small triangle. Have the children determine the value of each of the other pieces—and the value of the square made from all seven pieces (a total of $0.80). Using these assigned values, ask the students to create shapes with varying values. Students can be asked to make a polygon worth $0.25 or $1.05. Having students post their shapes and dollar amounts on a class chart will add to the richness of the investigation and discussion.

Exploring Area and Perimeter with Tangrams

Have the children build a triangle, a trapezoid, a parallelogram, a square, and a rectangle from the two small triangles and the medium triangle. What do the children know about the areas of the polygons, given their previous work with area in the previous activity? (All areas are the same—the same three shapes are used to create each polygon.) Order the polygons according to perimeters only using the tangrams as units of measure. The square will have the smallest perimeter and the triangle, trapezoid, and parallelogram will have the largest (Chapin and Johnson 2006, 276). (See Figure 4–15.)

This activity can scaffold understandings about the relationship between perimeters of shapes that have the same area. This relationship can be further investigated in the *Area Stays the Same* activity (page 112).

FIGURE 4–15 ▶

Perimeters of tangrams (Chapin and Johnson 2006).

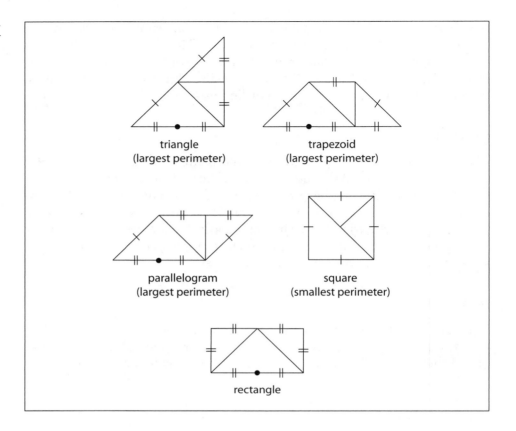

Pentomino Explorations

Duration: 3–4 class periods

Work with pentominoes offers continued hands-on experiences with spatial visualization and reasoning. These lessons are adapted from *About Teaching Mathematics* (Burns 2007) and offer students opportunities to:

- apply logical reasoning to spatial tasks
- investigate the concept of congruence
- explore translations (slides), rotations (turns), and reflections (flips)
- investigate area
- investigate perimeter

Materials

- 1 set of color tiles per table group
- 1 set of overhead color tiles
- several sheets of 1-inch graph paper per student
- 1-inch graph paper copied on card stock, 2 sheets per pair of students

- 1 copy of *Pent-Tris* directions per pair of students (see Blackline Masters)
- 1 die per pair of students
- 1 colored pencil per student
- a few pieces of chart paper

Creating a Set of Pentominoes

This lesson focuses on the creation of a complete set of pentominoes—arrangements of five squares. Using overhead color tiles can help you introduce and model the activity in a whole-class format. Place a container of color tiles and several sheets of 1-inch graph paper at each table and then create a pentomino on the overhead. Ask the children what they notice about this shape. You will want to use this opportunity to specify the constraints of the shapes.

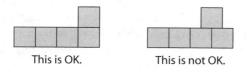

This is OK.   This is not OK.

At least one whole side of each square must touch a whole side of another. The children will have to decide if two shapes are the same or different. They can compare their shapes by flipping or turning them. If one shape can fit on top of another once flipped or turned, then the two shapes are said to be *congruent*. The ability to identify congruent shapes will be important when the children are later asked to find all the possible different pentomino configurations.

If the children have not yet recognized that a pentomino is constructed from five squares, asking them to identify the word's prefix and root word will help them articulate the word's derivation. Playing around with various other -*omino* words will give you the opportunity to once again discuss the merits of first solving a simpler problem. Place two color tiles end-to-end either in a central area or on the overhead. Ask, "What have I made?" This shape can be identified as a *domino*. Ask, "What do you think a three-tiled shape could be called?" to move into a discussion of trominoes. Asking about a four-tiled shape may elicit a label such as quadromino. In the world of -*ominoes*, however, a four-tiled shape is identified as a *tetromino*, which may make sense to those children familiar with the computer game Tetris.

Using the tromino as a model, ask the children how many possible arrangements could be made with three tiles. Have the children make the possible arrangements with color tiles. They will find that there are two shapes. Some children may be confused when trying to determine whether one shape is congruent to another. Having children cut out their shapes from 1-inch graph paper can help them see congruence by flipping and turning shapes to determine if they fit on top of one another. Show-and-tell becomes a useful and insightful directive in this lesson!

Repeat this same procedure with tetrominoes. Ask the children to create their tetrominoes. (There are five possible tetrominoes.) Once the children believe that they have a complete set of tetrominoes, have them convince their tablemates that they have found them all. Having 1-inch graph paper available may once again be helpful if children need to flip and turn their arrangements to prove congruence or incongruence.

Next, ask pairs of children to cut out a set of pentominoes from 1-inch graph card stock. Some may wish to start with the color tiles. Others may move right to the graph card stock. Once a pair has decided that it has created a complete set (of which there are twelve), have the students share and compare their set with another pair of children, reminding them that each pentomino must be different from all the others. Try to refrain from revealing that there are twelve arrangements (your students will undoubtedly ask you how many there are) or if a pair has found them all. If children need help, try informing a pair that it has a few congruent shapes or that it needs a few more and then leave the pair to continue its search. The more accustomed your children become to working through problem-solving tasks, the more accustomed they will be to you not giving a definitive answer! I often hear children whisper, "Ahhh . . . she'll never tell us," as I walk by. A smile or a wink lets them know that I have heard them . . . and that they are quite right! Once a group of children are convinced that complete sets have been made, pose the question "How do you know?" to give them further opportunities to convince one another that their sets are complete.

As pairs of children complete their pentomino sets, ask if they can place all of the twelve pieces into a rectangular array. Children may want to use a piece of 1-inch graph paper to align their pieces. A complete set of pentominoes can make several arrays of 60 tiles. Once a pair has made an array, ask the children why this array makes sense. Some may realize that with twelve pentominoes, there are sixty tiles ($12 \times 5 = 60$). A 3-by-20, 4-by-15, 5-by-12, and 6-by-10 array each contains 60 units. If students construct different arrays, ask them to convince each other why all the rectangles are correct. Some children may notice that a few of the pentominoes make creating a 2-by-30 array impossible just by way of their tile arrangements—no flipping or turning will help them to fit. This is an activity the children may wish to return to over the next few days.

Once you have given ample time for the children to create complete sets of pentominoes, have each pair post one of its shapes on the board until all the arrangements have been shared in a whole-class format. Have the children make replacement shapes for the posted arrangements so that each pair of children has a complete set of pentominoes. Once again, discussions about congruence will surface as children determine the twelve different arrangements.

TEACHER-TO-TEACHER TALK "Do I have them all?" and "Is this right?" seem to be the most popular questions a fourth grader asks on any given day or with any given unit! They love the exploration, but the open-ended nature of some investigations can be difficult for some. There is always that risk of missing one pentomino, of misunderstanding a direction, or of giving an incorrect answer. It is important that we understand the emotional as well as mathematical thresholds of our students. Frustration never helps with any learning of any kind. And as we all know, there is a fine line between frustration and intrigue. We have all lived through those lessons that begin swimmingly—and the next thing we know, we're drowning! Differentiating your open-ended lessons can help keep frustration at bay. Presenting the rectangular array task to children who have found a complete set of pentominoes can allow you time to move among those groups of children that need extra guidance in finding all the shapes. Using a menu format for exploration tasks can also help meet the needs of all your learners. Sometimes a quick check in with the class will also help direct your next step in a lesson. I will often call out, "Where are we?" as an exploration is being carried out. By this time in the year, my children often answer without even picking up their heads, "Fine!" "OK!" and even "Awful!" I often use those replies as my cues as I decide when to call the class back together for processing. I often start a processing session by acknowledging that this exploration may have been difficult for some, which is certainly OK. Posing the question "What made this exploration challenging?" will help all children articulate the difficulties they encountered. Follow-up questions such as "How did working with a partner help?" or "If you did this again, what would you do differently?" will offer some closure to the exploration.

Pent-Tris

Outline several of the following rectangles on 1-inch graph paper: 5 by 12, 6 by 10, 3 by 20, and 4 by 15. Make copies of these rectangles to serve as game boards. Two children or teams play against each other, taking turns placing pentomino pieces in a rectangle. The one who has played the most pieces is the winner. Some children may recognize this game as similar to the electronic game Tetris. They might be interested to know that Tetris was, in fact, inspired by a set of pentominoes that Elexy Pazhitnov played with. The first Tetris game was created by Pazhitnov in 1985 at the Moscow Academy of Science's computer center.

Pent-Tris is also adapted from a game played with tetronomoes called "Tumbling Tetronimoes" (Russell and Clements 1997).

The players choose any five pentominoes to use as their game pieces. A roll of a die will determine which piece they must use. Have the children make a key on graph paper for the numbers 1 through 6. They can reproduce each chosen pentomino on the key and label them *1–5*. (See Figure 4–16.)

A roll of 6 earns the player a free choice of whatever pentomino she wishes to use—whether one of the chosen five or any of the other seven. The children choose one game board and identify the bottom of their

FIGURE 4–16   ▶

Sample *Pent-Tris* key.

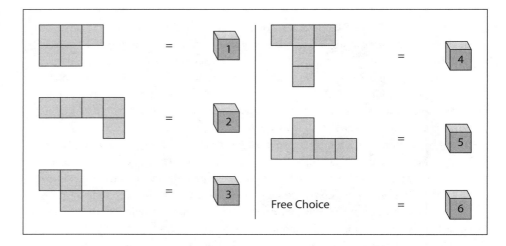

board. Each child also must choose a color with which to color in his pentominoes.

Player 1 rolls the die and colors his pentomino onto the game board. The pentomino must touch either the bottom of the board or another pentomino. Play continues with players alternating turns until no other pentominoes can be placed on the board. A player's score is the number of squares she has colored. The highest score wins.

Pent-Tris quickly becomes a game of cooperation rather than competition between players. Knowing where to place various pentominoes requires spatial visualization skills as children flip and turn the pentominoes to fit them into allotted spaces. Some children may wish to use their set of pentominoes to determine what piece would best fit where and then color them in. Others may go right to the coloring after studying the board for a minute or two. It is fascinating to watch and talk to children as they play this game! I have extra copies of game boards and pentomino sets in my room and in our school library for free choice time. I am always amazed at how many fifth graders remember playing *Pent-Tris* the year before and want to play it again!

Exploring Area and Perimeter with Pentominoes

The gridded construction of the pentominoes lends them well to exploration with area and perimeter. Open-ended tasks such as the following can open up discussions and even expose some misunderstandings about these two concepts. The children use their cutout set of pentominoes as they model and discuss their findings. These activities can easily be presented in a menu format.

- Compare the perimeters of an entire set of pentominoes. What do you notice?
- Describe the shapes with the largest perimeters. Describe those with the smallest perimeters.

- Create a shape with an area of 20 units². Pentominoes must share at least one unit of length. What is the perimeter of that shape? Can you reconfigure the same pentomino pieces to create a new shape with a smaller perimeter? A larger perimeter? What do you notice about the shapes with the smallest perimeter? What do you notice about the shapes with larger perimeters? (Create a classroom poster headed "Areas of 20 Units²" on which the children can mount their various shapes and perimeters. A class discussion will easily follow as children observe and comment on the shapes and their perimeters.)

- Create a shape with a perimeter of 20 units. What is the area of that shape? Can you make another shape with a perimeter of 20 units but with an area different from the one you just made? (Create a classroom poster headed "Perimeters of 20 Units" on which the children can mount their various shapes and areas. A class discussion will easily follow as children observe and comment of the shapes and their areas.)

Follow-Up Journal Write

Jack made a rectangle out of six of his pentominoes. He told Patrick that the area of his rectangle was 32 square units. Patrick told him that he was nuts. Why did Patrick disagree with Jack's statement? Could Jack be correct? Why or why not?

Area and Perimeter

Duration: 3–4 class periods

These activities continue to build upon children's developing understanding of area and perimeter: what they measure, how they are measured, and how they relate to each other. These activities, adapted from Cheryl Rectanus's *Math By All Means: Area and Perimeter* (1997), offer students the opportunity to investigate:

- area
- perimeter
- fixed area and how it is related to perimeter (e.g., shapes with the same area can have different-length perimeters)
- fixed perimeter and how it is related to area (e.g., shapes with the same-length perimeter can have different areas)
- areas and perimeters of irregular shapes

Materials

Brainstorming Webs

- 2 brainstorming web templates per student (see Blackline Masters)
- 2 pieces of chart paper with blank brainstorming webs drawn on them

The Area Stays the Same

- several 5-by-5-centimeter squares cut from index cards per student, plus a few extras for teacher
- several 36-inch pieces of string per pair of students
- 1 12-by-18-inch piece of white construction paper per pair of students
- optional: 1–2 pieces of chart paper
- optional: 12–24 color tiles per student
- optional: a few sheets of 1-inch graph paper per student

The Perimeter Stays the Same

- 1 sheet of centimeter graph paper per student
- 2 pieces of chart paper

Brainstorming Webs

Brainstorming webs, one labeled "Area" and the other labeled "Perimeter," can open up a classroom conversation about the two measures. Distribute two webs to each child and post two blank webs on separate pieces of chart paper. Ask the children to talk at their table groups about what they already know about these two measures. They can begin to fill in their webs as they collect information from one another.

Call the class back together for a whole-class discussion in which students can share information—and misconceptions! Area and perimeter can be a constant source of confusion for young children. What is being measured, the units used to label those measurements, and when to use one or the other are some of the concerns that can complicate matters as children work to make sense of these measures. Perimeter is a measure of length while area is a measure of surface space. It will be helpful to keep these distinctions in mind as you process the information shared by your children. As you post information offered by children on the class webs, be sure to include the respective units of measure each time. Perimeter is measured in units of length, such as inches or centimeters. Area is measured in square units—the number of squares needed to cover a surface. (See Figures 4–17 and 4–18.)

The Area Stays the Same

Prior to the lesson, cut several 5-by-5-centimeter squares from index cards for each child. Also cut several 36-inch lengths of string for each pair of children. Children will work in pairs as they investigate shapes with the same area (25 cm^2) but different perimeters.

To begin the lesson, hold up one 5-by-5-centimeter square and ask, "What is the *area* of this shape? How do you know?" The multiplication is accessible (5×5), as is counting the centimeters on the square. If only

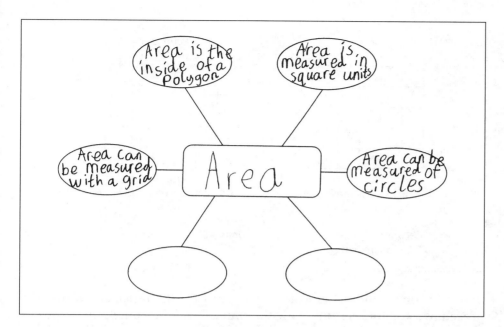

FIGURE 4–17   ◀

Area brainstorming web.

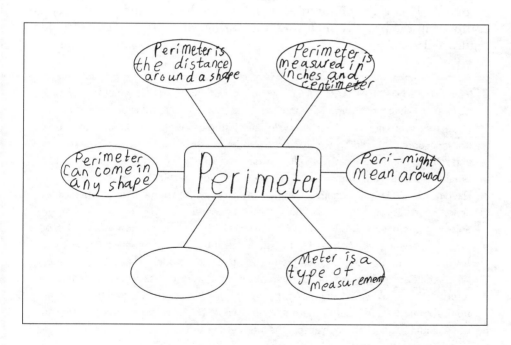

FIGURE 4–18   ◀

**Perimeter brainstorming
web.**

one strategy is shared, push the students to think of another way to find
the area of the square. Then ask, "What is the *perimeter* of this shape?
How do you know?"

Some fourth graders may not have had prior experience manipulating
these two concepts within the same task. Their previous work with area
and perimeter may have taken place in isolated lessons, if at all. You may

FIGURE 4–19   ▶

Class reference chart for area and perimeter.

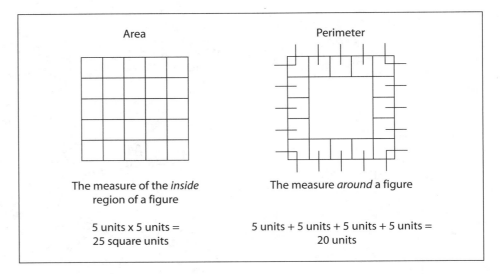

find that some children substitute one word for the other or confuse the procedures for finding one with the other. It might be helpful to post a chart identifying the area and perimeter measurements of the 5-by-5 square. This gives children easy access to the information if they get confused in the process of cutting, measuring, or writing. (See example in Figure 4–19.)

TEACHER-TO-TEACHER TALK   Learning how to access information is an important skill in any discipline. For some reason, children tend to think of math as something that you know or don't know. In social studies, we teach children to access primary sources. In reading, we are forever reminding the children to use context clues and refer to the text. In math ... well, how do we teach children to access information? When class charts are completed, I keep them hanging up throughout the entire unit. Having a positive and negative number line around the room, area and perimeter charts, charts listing properties of polygons, or a geometric vocabulary word wall available as children work through investigations will help them access new information or revisit that which has not yet been assimilated into their mathematical repertoire. A small collection of fourth-grade-friendly math reference books is also quite helpful. When children come to me with a reference question, I often ask several questions in return: "What could you do if I were not here? Where could you go to find this information?" Although I love modern technology and would be lost without my computer, I do not encourage the children to access the Internet. It is just too vast and does not necessarily support the math teaching and learning going on in the classroom. I often tell the children, "Use what you know to figure out what you don't know." And just think, moving into a new unit of study allows you to change your room décor with new charts, posters, and vocabulary!

Inform the students that they will be working with a partner as they cut their square into two or three pieces. Then they'll tape the pieces together to make a new shape different from the square. Ask for suggestions as to how the square could be cut. Cuts may be straight or curved, but *no pieces of the square are to be discarded*. Model how to cut the shape into parts. Then tape the pieces together again to make a new shape. (See Figure 4–20.)

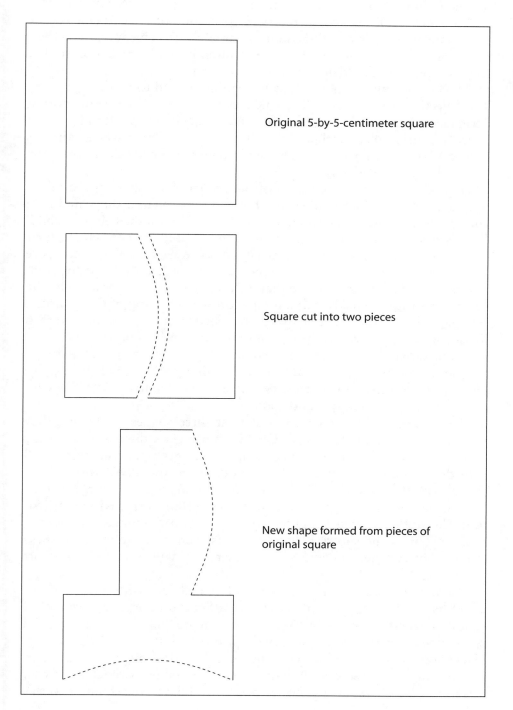

Original 5-by-5-centimeter square

Square cut into two pieces

New shape formed from pieces of original square

FIGURE 4–20 ◀

Cut a square and tape the pieces into a new shape.

Compare the new shape with another 5-by-5 square. When asked about the area of the new shape, most children will agree that it continues to be 25 cm^2. When asked about the perimeter, however, children may have differing opinions. Some may assume that the perimeter has stayed the same since the area has stayed the same. Some may argue that the perimeter looks longer or shorter than the original square's perimeter.

Asking the children how to resolve the question of the perimeter of the new shape will move the discussion to one of measurement and how best to measure this new shape. Once the children have had a chance to offer some suggestions, I hold up a piece of string and ask, "How could this help me?" They quickly see how the string can be shaped to fit the perimeter. The objective here is to establish which shapes have the longest or shortest perimeters. The actual measurement is not needed, which is an interesting concept in itself to some children! I often ask the children when estimates of length, or knowing when something is longer or shorter than something else, is enough in everyday life.

On each table, I place white construction paper, scissors, tape, a tub of 5-by-5 squares, and a tub of string. I model how to cut a shape and then cut a piece of string to the length of the perimeter with the help of a child. By this time in the year, the children are quite used to representing their work in some way. I ask the class what would be the best way to compare the perimeters of our shapes, and they usually realize the need for standardization of representation so that we can all look at the same thing. We often agree rather quickly that a margin drawn at the top of the construction paper is necessary. The shape can be taped in the top margin and then the string can be taped on the line of the margin. When posted, the string will hang down the paper (and sometimes off!) to identify the length of the perimeter. When the papers are lined up side by side, it will be easy to identify the longest and shortest perimeters. (See Figure 4–21.) The children are ready to cut, tape, and compare.

When each pair has completed at least three shapes, I ask that they post their papers on the board. Opening up a class discussion with the ever popular "What do you notice about our shapes and perimeters?" will help direct the conversation. Many children are initially surprised that shapes with the same area (25 cm^2) can have so many different perimeters. And to be quite honest, the variance in perimeters surprised me at first, too! The students often focus on the shapes with the longest perimeters and those with the shortest. If so, ask, "Is there something about these shapes that can help us estimate whether they will have long or short perimeters?"

Making generalizations as to why different shapes with the same area could have differing perimeters may be difficult for some. The results of reconfiguring the initial 5-by-5-centimeter square and then predicting and measuring the perimeter of the new shape often contradicts students' original expectations. I have learned to be very pleased with the generalization that a "longer" or "skinnier" shape will have a longer perimeter and that a "fatter" shape will have a shorter perimeter. I have often found that this

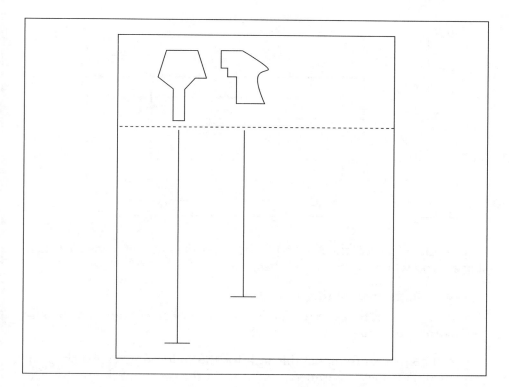

FIGURE 4–21 ◀

The Area Stays the Same.

exploration truly opens up the world of mathematical wonder for some children. Most fourth graders begin this investigation with the belief that a defined area will dictate one defined perimeter. What they thought to be true about the relationship between area and perimeter just isn't!

This exploration can also be extended with the use of color tiles. Ask the children to create a rectangular array with a specified number of tiles—say twelve, sixteen, or twenty-four tiles. (Choosing an area with many factor pairs offers greater shape variations.) Ask the children to create polygons with differing perimeters but with this same area. Before the perimeters are calculated, ask the children to predict whether the perimeter will be a long one or a short one. Students can re-create their shapes on 1-inch graph paper and post them and their perimeters (cut from string) on a class poster titled "The Area Stays the Same." A graph paper model of the original rectangular array and its area measurement should be mounted at the top of the poster. Using color tiles also helps children further visualize and manipulate the square units used to measure area.

The Perimeter Stays the Same

This activity explores the areas of shapes with the same perimeter but differing areas, which is a natural follow-up to the preceding activity. Instruct the children to draw at least three shapes with perimeters of

FIGURE 4–22   ▶

Model of shape with a perimeter of 30 centimeters.

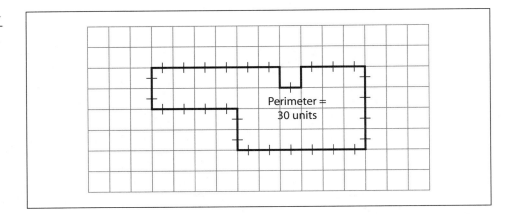

30 centimeters on centimeter graph paper. As the children construct their shapes, you will need to remind them to:

- stay on the lines of the graph paper
- create shapes that can remain in one piece when cut out (having only corners touching is not allowed)

It will be helpful to model this task for the children. Create a shape of your own, labeling its perimeter and area in the center of the shape. The use of slash marks will help children keep count of their perimeter units. (See Figure 4–22.)

The children can work in small groups as they create their own shapes on centimeter graph paper. There may be much erasing and redrawing as children use a trial-and-error approach to construct their shapes. Encourage the children to count frequently! The accuracy of the perimeters is necessary to the success of the lesson. Post two charts on the board: one labeled "Greatest Area" and the other labeled "Least Area," while the children are working.

When children are ready to process, call them together for next phase of the exploration. Inform the children that they will exchange papers with someone else at their table. Each child is to check a tablemate's shapes to be sure that each shape has a perimeter of 30 centimeters. The children should check each other's area measurements. With their group, the children should examine their shapes and take about what they notice about the shapes with the same and different areas. Each table group should cut out the shape with the greatest area and the shape with the least area and post them on the appropriate class chart.

Once all the shapes with the greatest and least areas are posted, begin a whole-class discussion by posing the question, "What patterns do you notice with the posted shapes?" Asking the children to share their observations with a neighbor before they share as a whole class will offer them opportunities to practice the wording of their responses. The children will notice that the shorter, fatter shapes have greater areas while the longer, thinner shapes have lesser areas. I often end the discussion by asking when this generalization would be important to know in everyday life. Gardens and ice-skating ponds tend to come up in my class; I like to garden and my students like to skate!

Resurrecting the area and perimeter brainstorming webs that were used to introduce the lessons will give some closure to the explorations. Ask the children to contribute to the information previously collected on the webs to give them a chance to informally evaluate the investigations, review what they have learned, and even ask questions that they still have about area and perimeter.

The relationship between area and perimeter is an interesting one, more important to be explored than mastered at this point in a child's mathematical career. In this particular investigation and with these particular materials, the polygon with the smallest perimeter is a square when the area is fixed. It is also interesting to note that when a polygon increases in its number of sides, the smaller its perimeter will be as it approaches a circle. Be mindful, however, that here we are focusing on a polygon that is created out of grid paper with whole units of measure; the "fatter" a shape, the smaller its perimeter will be. The "skinner" the shape, the larger the shape's perimeter will be. I still have to stop, explore, and think about these relationships each time I present these lessons.

Exploring Measurement

Duration: 3–4 class periods

In order for children to construct and apply concepts and procedures regarding measurement, they need to measure! *Measuring Up, Down the Drain, It Beats Me*, and *Popcorn Madness* were adapted from *MEGA Projects* (Greenes et al. 1996b). These lessons offer students the opportunity to:

- explore the measurements of weight, capacity, length, time, and volume
- collect, analyze, and represent measurement data

Materials

- 1 copy of directions for each activity per student (Materials needed for each exploration are listed on the corresponding Blackline Master.)
- optional: 1 *Measures of Central Tendency* worksheet per student (see Blackline Masters)

Although these lessons were originally developed for presentation in a modified menu format, they could easily be adapted for whole-class lessons. It may also be helpful to present the explorations as they become applicable to your science curriculum. However and whenever you decide to present the explorations, keep in mind that each investigation may take several class sessions to complete. These explorations can be done by table groupings, but I often assign children to groups of four. This practice offers children the opportunity to work with classmates with whom they haven't worked before. I present the students with the descriptions of all the explorations and ask them to choose three in which they are interested. I quickly go through their choices and assign each group a different task.

Measuring Up

In this investigation, students learn about measuring lengths and determining the size of a "typical" fourth grader.

Down the Drain

In this investigation, students learn about measuring capacity and saving water, by determining how much water they use, on average, each time they brush their teeth.

It Beats Me

In this investigation, students learn about heart rates by exploring how fast their hearts beat and what affects the number of heartbeats in a minute.

Popcorn Madness

In this investigation, students learn about volume by exploring how much more space popped popcorn takes up than unpopped popcorn.

Box It or Bag It

In this investigation, students learn about measuring weight by exploring the average weight of a fourth grader's pencil container.

Each exploration offers small groups of students the opportunity to collect, analyze, and represent measurement data. Guiding questions are presented, as are exploration expectations. The collected data, answered questions, and observations are presented in poster form. Following the completion of the posters and explorations, each group offers an oral presentation to the class recapping its investigation and findings. The handout in Figure 4–23 presents the format of the investigations for the children.

Because some of these measurements and their respective units of measure are new to fourth graders, it may be necessary to develop introductory lessons that address the big ideas of the measurement. Although our students need to be proficient with both the U.S. customary system as well as the metric system, it will be important for you to determine and identify with the children which system of measurement they will be using for their explorations. You may find that your prescribed curriculum offers lessons that will help introduce these measurements and how and why they are used. Your students will gain further competence with measurement concepts and procedures by then engaging in meaningful measurement tasks.

Exploring Measurement

Over the next few days, we will be exploring measurement. You and your partners will:

- choose an investigation that interests your group
- read about the measurement concept or procedure being addressed in the investigation
- carry out the investigation keeping written records of your collected data
- create a poster that represents your data collection and findings
- present your investigation to your classmates

Choosing Your Investigation

You have several investigations from which to choose. The measurement topics include:

- length
- capacity
- volume
- time and rate
- weight

Each investigation is just that—an activity that will help you to investigate the given topic.

Carrying Out Your Investigation

Now for the fun part! Organize and complete the investigation. Remember to keep the questions you are answering in mind at all times. How can your data help you answer the posed questions? *This should take no longer than a period!*

Creating Your Poster

Following the poster guidelines presented in the Measurement Guide, your group will complete a poster that represents the results of your investigation and answers the posed questions. Your poster should be complete, neat, well organized, and creative.

Because all the explorations require students to collect measurement data, they will need to be familiar with measures of central tendency: mean, median, and mode. You might want to require students to complete the *Measures of Central Tendency* worksheet prior to collecting their data.

Because of the interdisciplinary nature of measurement, math and science classes can be collapsed into block period explorations. The explorations listed here may be tweaked and adjusted to align with your science curriculum frameworks. Other explorations can be substituted, as well, if you find that you are comfortable with this format. I continue to adjust the volume exploration. It tends to be messy and needs to be supervised quite closely because of the use of the popcorn popper. But each year, that exploration is the absolute favorite and the one the children remember for years to come.

Follow-Up Journal Write

I looked in my refrigerator and found some items that were about 1 pound in weight. What could these items have been? How do you know?

Calculation Routines and Practices

Although addition and subtraction review and application continue to be important, the big idea that addition and subtraction are related can now be explored and discussed with greater depth and understanding than in the earlier months of the year. As students are given a variety of problems to solve, they will begin to articulate the connection between the two operations and generalize across the problems. Fourth graders are at a developmental crossroads in which they can begin to identify similar problems and generalize strategies and thinking from one problem to another.

The following investigations and discussions can occur throughout the weeks spent on geometry and measurement. Because this approach to thinking about subtraction may be new to some of the children, their interest and intrigue will sustain the instruction and ensuing conversations from week to week. Related homework can also be given on the nonsubtraction days for review and extra practice. I designate one lesson a week for our subtraction work throughout the geometry unit.

Present a subtraction problem to your children on the board such as the following:

$$174 - 67 =$$

Ask, "What can you tell me about this problem?" to open up a discussion about subtraction. Some students may do the calculation, some may complain about the calculation because it requires regrouping, and some may discuss the relationship between the numbers presented. Asking the children to solve the problem with whatever strategy they prefer will give them access to all the numbers in this particular fact family as they move on to discuss and investigate relationships between addition and subtraction.

The lesson can now shift to creating story problems to fit the given number model. As you ask the children to share stories, you may find that they are all similar in plot: "Tommy has 174 hockey pucks. He gives 67 to his brother, Matthew. How many hockey pucks does Tommy have left?" Write one of the shared stories on the board. Ask the children how they know what to do with the numbers presented in the story. Where is the focus? Is it on the cue words, the numbers, the operation, or the context? Many will agree that they focus on the wording—*have left* informs them to subtract.

Offer another story problem:

Becca is reading a mystery novel with 174 pages. She was on page 67 last night when she fell asleep. How many more pages does she have to read in order to finish the novel tonight?

Ask the children if they notice any similarities between the two story problems. Some children may focus on the cue words. Some may focus on the numbers. Some may focus on the subtraction. Posing the question "Can I use addition to solve this problem?" will help focus the conversation on the relationship between addition and subtraction.

Now construct a number line on the board.

Ask, "How can this number line help us think about how many pages Becca has to read in her book tonight?" The number line may be a visual model that the children have not used with large numbers. Your children may need to talk about how pieces of a number line can be used to represent the calculations presented in a problem.

When I presented my class with this model one year, they initially had difficulty identifying it as a number line and focused on the fact that it was a *line*—a geometric construction! Becca wanted to know if she could label the points B and C—her initials, of course. Michael kept reminding us that all lines have arrows because they extend indefinitely in both directions. Matthew added that lines are always straight. This conversation was not exactly headed in the direction in which I intended! I asked the class if I could label the points with numbers instead of letters. What would I have then? They all shouted, "A number line!" Phew! We then made reference to the original subtraction problem, $174 - 67$. "Could I place these numbers on this number line?" I asked. "Where would they go? Why do those placements make sense?"

Once the 67 is placed as one point and 174 as another, ask the children how they can get from one point to the other. Different children will employ different jumping strategies. Placing several number lines on the board and asking children to come up and represent their jumps will open up conversations about jump choices and friendly additions. (See Figure 4–24.)

As children are presenting their strategies, continue to refer to the problem at hand: What are we trying to find out? What is the question being asked? How does this number line model help us answer our question? How can we keep track of our operations on the number line? Where is the solution on this number line? Why does using a number line make sense when solving this problem? Why are we adding in order to subtract?

FIGURE 4–24   ▶

Student solutions using an open number line model.

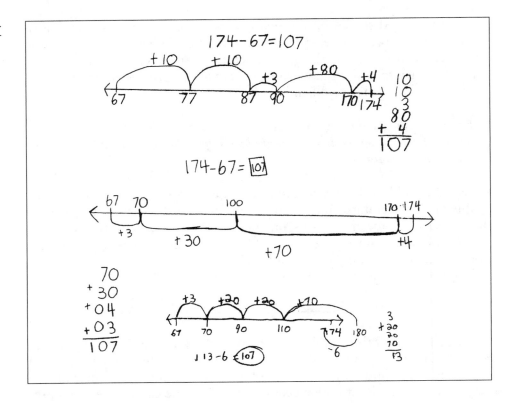

As we were working through this investigation, Rebecca announced to the class that she really liked this procedure. When asked why, Rebecca informed us that she liked *seeing* the answer to a subtraction problem. What she saw as the solution to the problem was the *distance* between the two points. She also informed us that the word *distance* was much more appropriate here than the word *difference*, a word we usually associate with subtraction. I was quite taken aback by her response. Rebecca was one of my stronger students and did not often find it necessary to refer to concrete representations. But the visual model of this subtraction problem deepened Rebecca's understanding of the procedure as well as the language she chose to describe this calculation.

Having a set of related story problems ready for the children following these conversations will give them additional opportunities to apply this adding-on strategy. For example:

Mrs. Schuster loves to read out loud to the fourth graders. She is reading Sid Fleischman's The Ghost in the Noonday Sun. *She is presently on page 42. There are 226 pages in the book. How many more pages does she need to read to finish reading the book to the class?*

Emma could not wait until Mrs. Schuster finished the book. Emma sneaked down to the library and checked out the book herself! Emma is on page 84. How many pages does Emma need to read to finish the book?

FIGURE 4–25 ◀

Students' money story problems and solutions employing number lines.

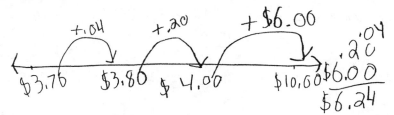

1. Sarah bought a sandwich for $3.76 and gave the cashier $10.00. How much change did she get back?

2. Jackson saw a comic book that was $2.69. If he gave the store worker $5.00, how much change would he get back?

The fourth grade loves pirate stories and loves Sid Fleischman's books, so they agree to read The Giant Rat of Sumatra *next.* The Giant Rat of Sumatra *has 185 pages. How many more pages does* Ghost in the Noonday Sun *have than* The Giant Rat of Sumatra?

Matthew is already reading The Giant Rat of Sumatra. *He is on page 57. How many more pages does Matthew need to read before he finishes the book?*

Once the children have completed the assigned problems, have them make up some of their own to share and solve with their classmates. Some adventurous children may wish to develop story problems within a different context that can also be solved with the use of a number line. Money problems, for example, lend themselves well to this format. When we make a purchase and pay with a larger denomination than the purchase, the adding-on strategy helps us calculate change efficiently. Encourage children to represent their solutions with number lines that show their jumps and addition. (See Figure 4–25.)

Mathematics Writing

Writing about geometric ideas, connections, and observations offers opportunities for children to support their thinking with models and diagrams. Having concrete models available for reference as they write helps children focus and scaffolds their thinking and written responses. Take a minute to examine the following journal write:

Choose a polygon that does not belong in this set. Justify your choice.

It may be helpful to model the writing of a response in a whole-class format. Ask the children to talk with their neighbor about the similarities and differences between the polygons. Have the partners choose their "outlaw" and create a bulleted list as they talk. This initial talk time can help the children organize their thoughts as they prepare to write. Soliciting the class for a sentence starter can help the children begin the writing process. The sentence starter can be as simple as "In this set, the _____ does not belong because . . ."

Once the writing has been completed, ask if anyone would like to share his piece of writing with the class. Inform the class that this time they will show the response they have written on the overhead. Volunteering your work in this format takes some guts! It is one thing to read your work to the class; it is another to display a written copy in front of everyone. Also inform the children that as a class they will rework the response together. But here's the catch: for homework, each child will rewrite her own response. The volunteer will get a copy of his reworked response (simply make a copy of the corrected overhead) and can just recopy it as his final draft. You may get a few more volunteers after this caveat is revealed! Copy the volunteer's response to an overhead to rework it with the class. I ask the volunteer to come up and sit beside me during this revision process.

I adore this exercise, which is adapted from work developed by John Collins (1992). The children quickly become very engaged and focused on the writing process because they become the teachers! We look at mathematical thoroughness and language as well as sentence structure and punctuation. We talk about the importance of concluding sentences and how to construct them. We refer to the polygons themselves as we construct our proof. If the outlaw is identified by only one difference, I ask if someone can find another difference or outlaw. By about now the volunteer is feeling pretty good about volunteering his work. He now has a mathematical masterpiece!

For homework, the children are asked to rework their responses. I ask them to turn in both copies—their in-class piece as well as their revised final copy. This can be completed in their Mathematician's Logs or as a separate piece to be archived in their language arts portfolios. Both copies can also be mounted side by side on a 12-by-18-inch piece of construction paper. These before-and-after writings make for wonderful bulletin board displays.

Language and writing can turn experience into thinking and learning (Reeves 1990). A carefully scaffolded writing lesson can make the mathematics meaningful and visible. In this particular lesson, the mathematical context gives meaning and purpose to the writing process. I am forever amazed and delighted with the myriad writing opportunities that the study of mathematics presents.

Parent Communication

A parent information form can be sent home or posted electronically for this month of study. (See the example in Figure 4–26.)

Parent Information and Involvement Form

From: Lainie Schuster
To: Parents of Fourth Graders
Re: Mathematics Curriculum
Month: November/December

During the next month, the major topics we will be studying are:

- geometry: two-dimensional
- area and perimeter
- geometric measurement
- measurement

My goal in studying these topics is for the students to be able to:

- manipulate tools for geometric constructions
- identify and construct lines, segments, rays, angles
- classify polygons based on their properties
- explore designs with lines and circles
- construct figures with a compass and straightedge
- explore measurements of area and perimeter
- explore metric measurement systems of weight, volume, length, and capacity

Parents can help at home by:

- encouraging the use of rulers for all linear constructions
- encouraging neatness and precision
- discussing and identifying geometry in everyday life, for example, use of patterns in counter tiles, floor tiles, clothing
- identifying units of measure appropriate to that which is being measured, for example, using feet or yards when measuring the perimeter of a gardening bed and using inches when measuring a tile
- continuing to practice basic addition and subtraction facts

FIGURE 4–26 ◀

Parent information form for November/December.

As the year progresses, so too do our needs to keep parents informed of what is going on in math class. The manipulatives students create in various lessons can conveniently be used to complete homework but also to engage parents in the mathematical thinking to which their children are being exposed. Sending home a tangram exploration or a pentomino task can foster geometric conversations and observations. Journal writes can also strengthen the home-school connection. As a journal write, have the children interview someone at home about how he or she uses geometry in everyday activities.

Concern may develop when parents observe their children struggling some with tasks requiring spacial organization or awareness. Encourage parents to continue the development of these skills by engaging their children in activities related to those that they have worked through in class. There are some wonderful puzzles on the market—some that tessellate, some that create quilt blocks, some that have children re-create a presented design. And for your video game aficionados, there is always Tetris! Creating tangram and pentomino activity packets with the directions for the activities completed in class, extensions of those activities, as well as the child's manipulatives can also be very helpful for parents. When sending home such a packet, I often include a cover letter for parents explaining the materials, activities completed in class, and possible extension activities that can be completed at home.

Assessment

Informal assessments continue on a daily basis in the fourth-grade math class. We continue to notice how children interact with the mathematics as well as each other as they move through explorations and lessons. We continue to notice communication strengths and needs as children articulate orally and in written language their understandings of the mathematics. We continue to notice how our children respond to mathematical challenge and frustration. We continue to observe our children doing mathematics, which helps us inform, design, and adjust our teaching.

A monthlong study of geometry lends itself well to more formal assessment practices. Well-orchestrated test practices require purposeful planning. I find it helpful to plan backward in my lesson plan book by designating the projected finish date of the unit and then planning the lessons and explorations within that given time frame. If an end-of-unit test is planned, inform your students that their final assessment will be the completion of a unit exam that will be given in a specified number of weeks.

This is my first math test of the school year. I speak to the children relatively early in the unit about test taking—what is involved, why I test, and how they can be prepared for the test. Your children will want to know this. You will also be surprised at how few eyebrows will be raised if your children have been actively involved in the assessment process since September. Test taking is just one more form of assessment—and one that will be with them for many years to come.

My students receive comprehensive study sheets three to four days prior to each exam. This routine helps everyone—students, parents, and me! The study sheet outlines the big ideas as well as specific concepts and procedures covered in our unit of study. Following the outlined topics of study are several pages of extra practice worksheets and puzzles. Because my prescribed curriculum is frequently adjusted to meet the needs of my particular class, now is a good time to get in all those extra practice worksheets that are included in my teacher's edition!

Designing a good test is interesting and time-consuming work. Just as we need to plan our lessons according to the mathematical needs of our children, state guidelines, and prescribed curriculum expectations, we need to create tests with much the same focus, always keeping in mind the mathematical journey the children have taken through a given unit. I often look over the suggested test questions of my prescribed curriculum before I begin to develop my own. I may find a few questions that I think are interesting, but I often rewrite them to open them up and make them more applicable to our approach in class.

After tests are corrected, each child completes a test reflection. The reflection questions remain fairly standard from year to year and from test to test:

- Did you prepare properly for this test? Explain.
- What did you do *well* on the test? Why?
- What part of the test was difficult for you? Why?
- List three things that you learned about the mathematics or about yourself from this unit.

This writing exercise gives the children an opportunity to reflect upon their work and progress during the unit as well as their preparation for the test. I have found that I sometimes learn more about my children from their test reflection responses than I do from their tests. I read each reflection, often responding in the margins to what the child has revealed. The reflection is stapled to the front of the child's exam and sent home. The children return the packet to me after parents have looked at it, and I file it in their portfolio. Figure 4–27 on the next page is one child's reflection on the geometry exam.

I have come to value the preparation and reflection process far more than that of the test taking. After the children have completed this first test-taking process from beginning to end, I share that thought with them. I open up a quick discussion by asking them why I think that. Those children who utilized their study sheets well are quick to respond that they spent far more time preparing for the test than actually taking it. Those particular children are also aware of how much they really did know and

FIGURE 4–27   ▶

**Chris's geometry test
reflection.**

Stuff to think about:
Did you prepare properly for this test? Explain.

I prepared properly for the test because I did my whole study sheet.

What did you really do *well* on the test? Why?

I did the bonus question well because I listened in class.

What part of the test was difficult for you? Why?

The Journal write was a little bit difficult because I'm not a super writer

List 3 things that you learned about the mathematics or about *yourself*
from this unit:

1. *I learned that geometry is not all about shapes.*
2. *I learned that I can do well if I study hard.*
3. *I learned that a pentomino is a shape that is made of 5 square units.*

understand about geometry as they worked through the puzzles and problems presented in the study sheet. There is a lot of self-pride and confidence to be gained in the completion of the study sheets. The test reflection gives the children the opportunity to revisit and rethink their
preparation and work in our geometry unit. Because I share with the children how much I value this reflection process, they approach it with great
sincerity and often brutal honesty!

Resources

Math Matters (Chapin and Johnson 2006)

Three chapters in *Math Matters* may be of significant support when working through November and December: Chapter 10, "Plane Geometry,"
Chapter 12, "Measurement," and Chapter 3, "Addition and Subtraction."

About Teaching Mathematics (Burns 2007)

Contains a wonderful selection of geometry problem-solving activities including work with pentominoes and tangrams. The activities can be completed independently or in a menu format.

Math By All Means: Area and Perimeter (Rectanus 1997)

Although targeted for fifth and sixth graders, lessons in this book can be easily adapted for use in the fourth grade. Write-ups of *Area Stays the Same* and *Perimeter Stays the Same* are informative and comprehensive. Other activities in this replacement unit may also be easily adaptable to a fourth-grade class.

Math By All Means: Geometry (Rectanus 1994)

Although targeted for third graders, lessons in this book can be easily adapted for use in the fourth grade. If you or your children are not familiar with the *Four Triangle Problem*, it is well worth a look! The *Four Triangle Problem* is also written up in *About Teaching Mathematics* (Burns 2007).

Young Mathematicians at Work: Constructing Number Sense, Addition, and Subtraction (Fosnot and Dolk 2001b)

Chapter 5 ("Developing Mathematical Models") offers excellent support of the importance of making addition and subtraction connections visible and accessible to children.

Good Questions for Math Teaching (Sullivan and Lilburn 2002)

An excellent resource of open-ended questions to be used in math class. Questions can be used for daily warm-up exercises, journal writes, or test questions.

Hot Math Topics: Measurement and Geometry (Greenes, Dacey, and Spungin 2001a)

Creative and engaging problem-solving tasks in worksheet format.

MEGA Projects (Greenes et al. 1996a)

A box of math explorations and group activity projects. Although intended for use in grade 3, the "Shape Explorations" activities are completely appropriate for fourth grade.

Chapter 5

January

MULTIPLICATION

Students need to develop a strong and complete conceptual knowledge of multiplication and division. If they don't, they will have difficulty with more advanced multiplicative situations such as proportions, measurement conversion, linear functions, and exponential growth.

Math Matters
Chapin and Johnson 2006, 97

The Learning Environment

Continue to listen.

Listening, really listening, to your children talk about mathematics is hard work. Strong reasoning and deep thinking as well as misconceptions and fragile understandings can all be apparent in children's mathematical talk. Learning to listen well helps us respond to the mathematical needs of our children.

Talk less and ask more.

We need to frequently remind ourselves how important the asking of good questions can be. Good questions can keep the focus on the thinking and sense making going on in the lesson or with a particular student. The following list of generic questions may help you guide and facilitate mathematical talk:

- Why do you think that?
- How did you know to try that strategy?
- How do you know you have an answer?
- Will this work with every number? Every similar situation?
- When will this strategy not work? Can you give a counterexample?
- Who has a different strategy?
- How is your answer like or different from another student's?
- Can you repeat your classmate's ideas in your own words?
- Do you agree or disagree with your classmate's idea? Why? (Schuster and Anderson 2005, 11)

TEACHER-TO-TEACHER TALK It never fails. When I begin my multiplication unit, a parent will stop by to thank me for finally working through some "real" mathematics. Parents wait for this unit. Students wait for this unit. And I wait for this unit, too—but for very different reasons. Ask any adult what he remembers from fourth grade, and the response will more than likely be "Double-digit multiplication and long division," said with a groan, of course. What most expect to see come out of this unit are computational accuracy and procedural proficiency. Although I certainly expect that as well, my primary focus continues to be on sense making and the conceptual understanding of multiplication and the multiplicative procedures the children choose to perform. This was a difficult stand to take in my first decade of teaching. There was always that child, or that parent, or that administrator who just didn't see eye-to-eye with me about this.

Beginning your multiplication unit midyear gives you the opportunity to establish expectations, routines, and practices with your children, their families, and your administrators. Your children have grown in mathematical maturity since September because of your instructional choices and pedagogical style. By this time in the year, your children know that writing is a big part of learning math. They know that understanding *why* can be as important as understanding *how*. They understand that in your class, computational exercises are more often than not carried out within a problem-solving context. They know when they are learning and when they are not. In her book *About Teaching Mathematics* (2007), Marilyn Burns cites three reasons for teaching arithmetic in the context of meaning and application:

1. When you understand why, your understanding and skills can be applied more easily to new tasks. This requires children to understand why as well as knowing how. It is not an either or situation; both are necessary.

2. Learning the meaning in arithmetic procedures makes them easier to remember. When you understand the reasons behind rules and procedures, you are not keeping a large number of unrelated rules in your memory.

3. Learning to reason is a goal effective in itself and leads to the continued support of learning. (185–86)

Although we need to be patient with our parents, administrators, and students, we also need to stay true to our convictions. It is difficult, if not impossible, to appreciate something that you do not understand. According to Burns, teachers must teach mathematics so that children are encouraged to make sense of all they learn to do. Research continues to remind us that the benefit of teaching for understanding manifests itself for years down the road in a child's mathematical career. By abandoning rote algorithms and meaningless tasks, we are not asking our children to learn less. We are, in fact, asking them to learn more (Fosnot and Dolk 2001a, 102).

The Mathematics and Its Language

Children continue to develop conceptual knowledge of multiplication.

Conceptual knowledge is based on relationships (Chapin and Johnson 2006, 76). When children identify and articulate connections between multiplication and *addition*, their thinking is based on the relationships between the two operations. When children identify and articulate connections between multiplication and *division*, their thinking is based on the relationships between the two operations. Although procedural proficiency is a goal in every fourth-grade math class, it alone is not enough if students are to ultimately understand the hows and whys of multiplication.

Children investigate arrays as geometric representations of multiplication.

Arrays continue to be meaningful models for the study of multiplication. These geometric models can help children explore relationships between factors and products and make important connections between multiplication and division. Arrays can make these relationships visible and tangible.

Children explore and articulate relationships among factors, products, and multiples.

The language of multiplication becomes increasingly important as children gain mathematical maturity. Children need to understand the meanings, roles, and connectedness of factors, products, and multiples as they move through their work with multiplication.

Children explore and apply the commutative and distributive properties of multiplication.

Working through problems that require children to think about the order of factors or how factors can be decomposed offers students opportunities to investigate and internalize the importance of the commutative and distributive properties of multiplication. Both properties can help children solve complex multiplication problems when they realize that factors can be rearranged or broken down into smaller, more manageable parts. Children who have had experiences manipulating and applying these important properties of multiplication transfer this knowledge with greater ease when reintroduced to these properties in pre-algebra and algebra courses than those with no such experiences.

Children choose and carry out efficient and accurate computational strategies based on the task and the particular numbers involved.

It is helpful for children to have several options for completing multiplication computations accurately and efficiently. It is important for children to use logical reasoning, their understanding of number, and mathematical properties to construct procedures to solve multiplication problems. To do so, children also need to become proficient at multiplying by ten, powers of ten, and multiples of ten as well as manipulating their basic multiplication facts. Alternative and standard algorithms can be presented once children have had the opportunity to develop and investigate personal computational strategies.

Children create and solve story problems based on multiplicative models.

Creating and solving multiplication story problems gives students the opportunity to apply their understanding of multiplicative contexts. Not only will children be asked to apply their procedural understandings and proficiencies, but they will have the opportunity to apply their conceptual knowledge as well.

Investigations and Literature-Based Activities

Checking for Multiplication Understanding

Duration: 1 class period

This exercise is adapted from *Teaching Arithmetic: Lessons for Extending Multiplication* (Wickett and Burns 2001). This lesson sets the stage for work with multiplication and gives students the opportunity to think about multiplication. Perhaps more importantly, it can serve as an assessment model throughout the entire unit. The information gathered from these assessments can help guide, direct, and differentiate instruction. This lesson offers students the opportunity to:

- think about the meaning of multiplication
- articulate understandings of what it means to multiply
- represent understandings of multiplication in pictures, drawings, numbers, and/or words

Materials

- 1–2 pieces of chart paper

I begin the lesson by writing 3×5 on the board. I ask the children to raise their hands if they know the answer to this multiplication fact. Asking the children to share their answer with a neighbor invites every member of the class to become part of the conversation.

Next I present the directions for the task to the children. Each child must write down as many ways as she can think of to solve this multiplication problem or to prove her answer. Following are the questions students usually ask and my typical replies.

Question: Can I draw pictures?

Answer: Yes.

Question: Can I write a story?

Answer: Of course!

Question: Can I use circles and stars?

Answer: Absolutely. (I particularly enjoy this request because it extends the work that the children did in third grade with the *Circles and Stars* investigation in *Teaching Arithmetic: Lessons for Introducing Multiplication* [Burns 2001b].)

Question: Can I use addition?

Answer: If it makes sense to you!

Moving around the classroom and taking the time to talk to your children about their strategies will help you better understand their thinking. Encourage the children to include labels and short explanations when representing their strategies. This activity can make your children's understanding visible. The children are to represent their solutions quietly and independently. This does not happen too often in my class and I find that I have to remind the children to not interrupt their neighbor in their desire to share their work.

Strategies that demonstrate sound conceptual knowledge may include, but are not limited to, the following:

Showing multiplication as repeated addition:

5 + 5 + 5

Showing multiplication as a collection of equal groups:

3 groups of 5 stars

Showing a geometric representation of multiplication by use of arrays:

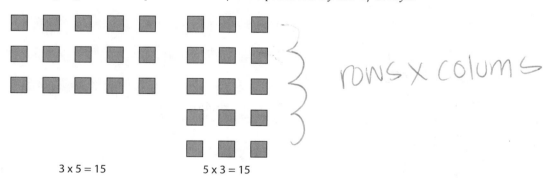

rows x colums

3 x 5 = 15   5 x 3 = 15

Indicating an understanding of the commutative nature of multiplication:

3 × 5 = 5 × 3

Using number sense and reasoning particular to the given numbers:

3 × 5 = 2 × 5 plus 5 more

Making a real-world connection:

3 × 5 = 3 school weeks of 5 days each or 15 school days

Pulling the class together for a whole-class discussion will give your students the opportunity to think and talk together about the meaning and representation of multiplication and of this particular number model. When asked, "Who would like to share your strategy?" more hands will go up than not because of the accessibility of the problem. I try to give every volunteer an opportunity to address the class. Each child's strategy is recorded in front of the class on chart paper. Strategies are labeled with the mathematician's name: "Michael's Method" or "Sarah's Strategy," for example. We can compare, contrast, add on, or revise strategies as we move through the lesson with the help of these visual aids. (See Figure 5–1.)

Having these strategy charts hung up in the room will give your children access to other methods of multiplicative thinking. Not only will this visible information help children fine-tune their own strategies and thinking, but it will also help them devise new methods of finding a product when problem solving.

This activity can be revisited several times within the unit to assess the progress and growth of each child's multiplicative thinking and reasoning. I move from the representation of basic facts to multidigit multiplication by the end of the unit. These informal assessments can also be assigned as homework. If assigned as such, I ask the children to explain their work to a parent once it is completed. I remind the children that it is important for

FIGURE 5–1   ▶

Class strategy chart.

What Do We Know About Multiplication?

Nick's Method:

Repeated addition, aka BIG adding!

$$3 \times 5 = 5 + 5 + 5$$

Sarah's Strategy:

Think of "groups of":

$$3 \times 5 = 3 \text{ groups of } 5$$

Groups must be equal in size!

Jack's Way:

I know my doubles and work from there.

$$3 \times 2 = 6$$
$$3 \times 2 = 6$$

So I double 6 to get 4 groups of 3, which is 12.

Then I add 1 more group of 3 to get 5 groups of 3: $12 + 3 = 15$.

them to be as clear in their thinking and talking with their parent as it is in math class. This gives the children one more opportunity to talk mathematically, and it also gives the parent a window into our classroom. (See Figures 5–2 and 5–3.)

As the children move through the unit, the representations of their multiplicative thinking should increase in sophistication. Instead of two representations, some children may be able to provide three or four. Some children may begin to apply the distributive property as they break down factors into friendlier numbers and then put the partial products back together again to arrive at the solution. Some children may apply the commutative property when they realize that the manipulation of one number is easier for them than the other. Norah, for example, decided to work with 12 × 23 rather than the format she was given of 23 × 12. When asked why she chose to reverse the factors, she quickly responded, "Come on, Mrs. Schuey, why would I play around with an odd number?" Their written language may also demonstrate greater mathematical sophistication. The children may begin to apply the terms *factor* and *product* in their explanations and labels. Keeping children's papers close at hand from the beginning of the unit to the end can provide visible documentation of growth and progress.

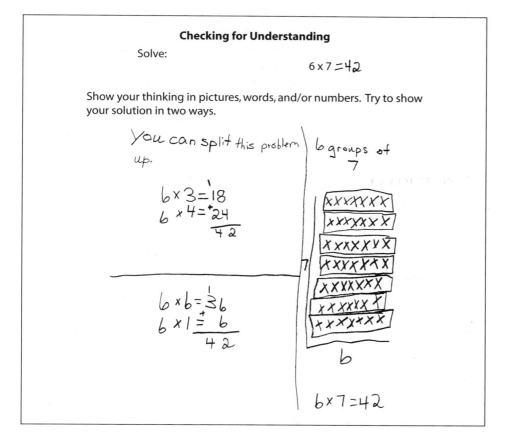

FIGURE 5–2 ◀

Rebecca's representation of 6 × 7.

FIGURE 5–3 ▶

Hayden's representation of 58 × 8.

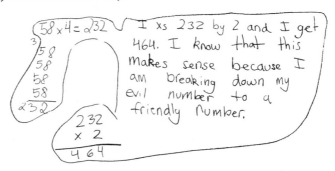

Checking for Understanding

Solve:

58 × 8

Show your thinking in pictures, words, and/or numbers. Try to show your solution in two ways.

TEACHER-TO-TEACHER TALK   Some of your fourth graders may have been exposed to the terms *factor*, *multiple*, and *product* prior to this unit. As you listen carefully, you may find that as the children try to apply the words, they often confuse one with another. It is not unusual to hear seventh graders, Algebra 1 students, and even adults do the same! These are difficult, but very important, words to learn and use correctly. This is one of those times when teaching by telling is appropriate. *Factor*, *product*, and *multiple* are labels for concepts. We can expect our children to explore the relationships between these concepts, but we will need to tell them the labels. We can model correct language usage and encourage children to do so as they talk and share. Post a multiplication number model with the factors and product labeled to provide students a visual reference.

$$
\begin{array}{r}
6 \quad \text{factor} \\
\times 7 \quad \text{factor} \\
\hline
42 \quad \text{product}
\end{array}
$$

Constructing sentences below the number model will help with the terminology as well. Have your students offer the sentences and then refine their use and understanding of these important words.

6 is a *factor* of 42.

7 is a *factor* of 42.

42 is the *product* of 6 and 7.

42 is a *multiple* of 6.

42 is a *multiple* of 7.

7, 14, 21, 35, and 42 are some *multiples* of 7.

6, 12, 18, 24, 30, 36, and 42 are some *multiples* of 6.

Adding *factor*, *multiple*, and *product* to your no-excuse spelling words will also reinforce their importance and usage.

Follow-Up Journal Write

Jacob had to multiply 3×55. Here is what he did:

Step 1: $3 \times 60 = 180$
Step 2: $3 \times 5 = 15$
Step 3: $180 - 15 = 165$
Step 4: $3 \times 55 = 165$

Multiply 4×39 using Jacob's method. Show the steps. Why does this method work?

One Hundred Hungry Ants

Duration: 2–4 class periods

One Hundred Hungry Ants, by Elinor J. Pinczes (1998), offers a context within which to investigate arrays and factors of specified numbers. This series of lessons, adapted from *Teaching Arithmetic: Lessons for Introducing Multiplication* (Burns 2001b), offers students the opportunity to:

- explore factors and factor pairs of specified numbers
- relate multiplication to rectangular arrays
- explore and articulate the connection between multiplication and division
- investigate, identify, and articulate the commutative property of multiplication

Materials

- *One Hundred Hungry Ants*, by Elinor J. Pinczes
- color tiles, 25–50 per pair of students
- chart paper
- newsprint, 1 piece per pair of students

In *One Hundred Hungry Ants*, one hundred ants are marching toward a picnic. The littlest ant suggests that the group march in varied numbers of lines and rows in hopes of getting to the picnic faster. The littlest ant organizes and reorganizes the one hundred ants into different marching formations as the story continues. But all this reorganizing is for naught—when the ants arrive at the picnic, they are too late for any food at all!

I begin the lesson with a read-aloud of *One Hundred Hungry Ants*. Many of the children are familiar with the book because many first and second grades use this piece of literature for their one hundred days of school celebration. Because the rhyme and illustrations of Pinczes's book are so engaging, children are happy to hear it again. Engaging the children in conversation as you read will direct their focus to the mathematics of the ant formations. Once the littlest ant suggests the first formation, ask the children what formation the littlest ant could suggest next: "Are there any other possibilities for marching formations? Why or why not? What could the formations be?"

As the students make suggestions, record their ideas on the board in words, pictures, and numbers. For example, the first formation of the ants would be recorded as follows:

make a chart ✓

definition of array

Words	Picture	Number Model
Two rows of fifty	....	$2 \times 50 = 100$

Recording the formations in this way will help children move from the words to the array to the symbolic representation of each ant array. Record each formation presented in the book either on the board or on chart paper. Volunteers can be asked to represent each formation as you facilitate the class conversation in order to direct and focus the class discussion.

Every class needs a Michael. As we were moving through the book and the arrays, Michael became increasingly concerned as he realized that he could not identify the array possibilities as quickly his classmates. Everything about Michael at that moment was screaming, "Slow down! Where are these numbers coming from?!"—his body language, his darting eyes, his furrowed forehead. This was certainly my clue to put the brakes on this conversation.

Michael wanted to know how his classmates were coming up with these arrays and their dimensions. "I don't even know how to begin!" Michael said with exasperation.

I asked the class, "Can anyone share how you think about a possible array for these one hundred ants?"

What I realized from that moment with Michael was that he was really concerned about the process. And for that, I was thrilled! He was less concerned with the numbers and more concerned with how he could think about the problem in order to come up with the numbers. The strategies offered by his classmates gave us all a chance to think about a systematic way of identifying possible arrays of one hundred. Hayden's strategy was to just start with one and go through the numbers in numerical order. "Can I make a one-by-something array?" he began. "You can always make a one-by-something array, so that works."

"Can I make a two-by-something array?" One hundred is even, so yes. A two-by-fifty will work.

"Can I make a three-by-something array?"

As a class, we spent some time talking about a 3-by-something array. "How can we start thinking about that array?" I asked. Some children went straight to the numbers; some wanted to draw arrays. Some went for the color tiles to manipulate their groups. In order to allow all the children ample time to explore this idea, I asked that they construct a number model to prove that we could or could not make a 3-by-something array.

Matthew and Michael used color tiles to investigate this problem. Even before all one hundred were laid out, Michael realized that he was not going to be able to make a 3-by-something array. There was going to be one tile left over. Michael wrote this number model to explain his thinking:

$$33 + 33 + 33 = 99 \qquad 99 + 1 = 100$$

When the children are asked to share their number models, the conversation can then be directed toward representations of one hundred in single number sentences. Michael's number sentences could be combined to create either of these number sentences:

$$33 + 33 + 33 + 1 = 100 \qquad or \qquad (3 \times 33) + 1 = 100$$

When we ask children to construct number sentences, it is equally important that we ask them to read and interpret them. Because this is the first time in the year that we have formally worked with parentheses, I take the time to discuss what they mean and what they tell us to do to offer the children another mathematical model that they can continue to apply in this particular activity and others like it.

Again Michael spoke up, "Do I have to do this with every single number from one to one hundred?" After all, recess was coming up. I repeated his question to the class.

Michael gave all of us the opportunity to slow down the class conversation and the task. Because of that, the lesson took on greater meaning and purpose. This was the fourth or fifth year that I had used *One Hundred Hungry Ants* with my class, and this particular lesson had gone so much better than previous ones. After working through the lesson several times, I now had greater clarity and purpose in my expectations and teaching. This was becoming a lesson rich in mathematical thinking and multiple written representations of that thinking—in words, in pictures, in numbers.

We agreed as a class to work only up through ten; the children were convinced that they could find all the arrays by the time they got to ten because of their informal knowledge constructed over the years about the number one hundred. Some children may be able to make that square root–square number connection between ten and one hundred; $10 \times 10 = 100$ or $\sqrt{100} = 10$. Posing the question "When does it make sense to stop finding new arrays when looking for the factor pairs of square numbers?" can offer an additional investigation for those ready for the challenge. Pose the investigation with another square number. Ask the children to represent the arrays and the number models to support their thinking. Down the road, students will uncover the realization that square numbers have an odd number of factors because the square root counts as a single factor.

want you as table group to come up w/ all arrays for 100 — words/pictures/#'s

"What about turnaround facts? What do we do about them?" was the next good question asked by Michael and Matthew. In our curriculum, 5×20 and 20×5 are referred to as *turnaround facts*. By this point in their mathematical career, fourth graders should be able to identify and articulate the commutativity of addition. It is important that we now offer our young mathematicians opportunities to think about, explore, and articulate the commutativity of multiplication. Rewriting Michael and Matthew's question as a number model can begin this conversation.

$$2 \times 50 = 50 \times 2$$

Ask, "Is this number sentence true or false?" and "How do you know?" to open up a discussion of commutativity. Encourage children to prove their convictions with numbers (calculations), pictures (arrays), and words.

You will want to determine prior to the lesson how you want the children to deal with turnaround facts. Because we talk about the turnaround facts in our investigation of one hundred, I inform the children that they are to include the turnaround facts on the charts that they will be asked to make for the next investigation. There is a correlation between the number of factor pairs (including turnaround facts) and the number of factors of a given number. I do not talk about this investigation with fourth graders, but it is something that they may investigate in the fifth and sixth grades.

By the end of the book, Michael announced that one hundred was such an "easy" number! When asked why it was an easy number, Michael and the rest of the class began to talk about the properties of one hundred:

- "One hundred is even, so we know it can be divided into two equal groups."
- "You can skip-count easily to one hundred by fives and tens."
- "One hundred ends in a zero, so we know five and ten go into it evenly."
- "One hundred is not odd; odd numbers would probably be harder to work with." (This statement was agreed upon with unanimous consent.)

And all of this from one picture book!

The lesson can now move to an investigation of other numbers. I ask partners to choose a number from one to fifty that interests them. They are to chart the arrays of that number in words, pictures, and number models just as we did with one hundred. In this activity, I ask my children to include the turnaround facts. Partners are also to include false starts—that is, the factors that do not work. The partners must also post summarizing statements at the bottom of their chart using the following heading: "What we know about _____." The children can then bullet their observations under the heading. Having access to color tiles or counters will help those children who wish to build the arrays before charting them. Have the children post their work when finished. (See Figure 5–4.)

[Handwritten margin notes: "Easy # 'why?'" and "Choose a # from 1-50 that interests you."]

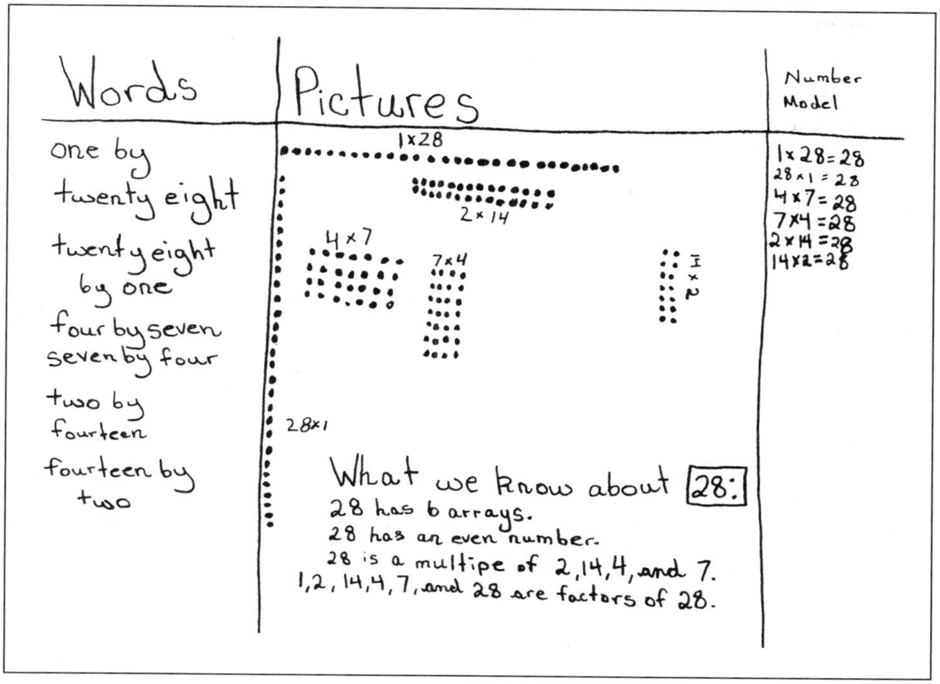

FIGURE 5–4 ◄

Sarah and Emma's representations of twenty-eight.

Words	Pictures	Number Model
one by twenty eight	1×28	1×28=28
twenty eight by one	2×14	28×1=28
four by seven	4×7	4×7=28
seven by four	7×4	7×4=28
two by fourteen	28×1	2×14=28
fourteen by two		14×2=28

What we know about 28:
28 has 6 arrays.
28 has an even number.
28 is a multipe of 2, 14, 4, and 7.
1, 2, 14, 4, 7, and 28 are factors of 28.

When you call the students together to process the activity, ask the following questions to focus the conversation and observations. When answering questions or making observations, children should be encouraged to use their own and classmates' investigated numbers to support their thinking and opinions.

- Why did you choose that number?
- What numbers had many arrays?
- What numbers had few arrays?
- What did you notice about even numbers and their arrays?
- What did you notice about odd numbers and their arrays?
- Do larger numbers always have more arrays? Why or why not?
- Do smaller numbers have fewer arrays? Why or why not?
- Are there numbers with an even number of arrays? An odd number? Why do you think that is?

The mathematics in this lesson is important. This lesson not only gives students the opportunity to investigate factors, products, and multiples but also sets the stage for future work with number theory. Children are intrigued by numbers. They are interested in their properties and why certain numbers can or cannot do certain things. James Hiebert and his colleagues (1997) speak to the importance of choosing appropriate tasks so that over time, students' experiences will add up to something meaningful.

factor
product
multiple

We need to be mindful of how our tasks are related and how they can be chained together to increase the opportunities for students to gradually construct understanding (31). The lessons developed from the context of *One Hundred Hungry Ants* can do just that.

Target 300

Duration: 1–2 class periods

Target 300 is a game from *Teaching Arithmetic: Lessons for Extending Multiplication* (Wickett and Burns 2001) that offers students opportunities to:

- practice basic multiplication facts
- multiply by ten and by multiples of ten
- apply number sense and reasoning skills while choosing numbers to multiply to reach the target number
- develop and apply mental multiplication routines within a problem-solving context

Materials

- *Target 300* directions (see Blackline Masters)
- 1 die
- number of players: 2

Recognizing and understanding what happens to a number when it is multiplied by ten or multiples of ten can have a significant impact on children's strategies of multiplication. Applying the pattern that emerges when multiplying by tens allows students to become more efficient when computing with multidigit numbers. Children need time and experience to help them make these big ideas of multiplication their own. *Target 300* can offer such experience as well as reinforcing thoughtfulness in problem solving and estimation. By the time we play *Target 300* in class, my fourth graders have had some experiences with multiplying by tens. I do not use this game as an introduction to the concept, but rather as an opportunity for the children to play around with randomly generated numbers and even some probability.

Because I like to introduce games with a partner's help, I ask the children to gather around a table at which I explain the game with the help of a student volunteer. I discuss the rules of *Target 300* with the children. I specifically instruct the students that each pair will share one die. I am also quite specific in my reasons for this. I explain to the class that I want to slow down the game to offer thinking and talking time for each player. It is equally important to slow down your explanation of the game. Giving the children the chance to discuss choices of factors in a structured setting will provide all the children access to the important mathematics of the game.

I show the students how to set up their score sheets in their math notebooks. Each student will need to set up his own score sheet. They will keep track of not only their rolls but their partner's as well. There are rarely any complaints about this practice. By this time in the year, your children should be accustomed to charting their thinking.

Once the children have set up score sheets in their math notebooks, I inform them of the factors they can choose from to multiply by the number rolled on the die. I post these choices on the board:

$$\times\ 10$$

$$\times\ 20$$

$$\times\ 30$$

$$\times\ 40$$

$$\times\ 50$$

I continue to remind the children of the goal of the game—to get as close to 300 as possible. They can get exactly 300, less than 300, or more than 300. I also inform the children that they will have six rolls and must use all six rolls. Having the children number their turns before they begin to play can help them visually and mathematically organize their choices, thinking, and calculating.

As I begin to model the game with my fourth-grade partner, children ask questions and note observations. We discuss multiplication strategies and choices as well as the probability of rolling certain numbers. Once I reach the fourth round, I ask the children what product I need to get close to 300 and how I can reach that product in two rolls. Children begin to play with their number sense, knowing that you can go over or below 300, but the player who is the closest wins. They contemplate their choices— and there may be quite a few! There have been years when this game modeling has taken up an entire math period because of the discussion accompanying the play of the game. Because the mathematics is rich and accessible, children are quickly engaged even while watching the game being played.

Once the game is finished, I write the following prompts on the bottom of my score sheet.

_____ *won.*

_____ *was* _____ *points away from 300.*

_____ *was* _____ *points away from 300.*

I ask the children to help me fill in the blanks, and then instruct each child to complete these sentences after each game. (See Figure 5–5.) After thinking about how much time I can allow for game playing—usually a full class period for multiple games—I decide the number of games the students can play. *Target 300* and *Target 600* can be revisited and replayed several times throughout the month as well as for months to come.

FIGURE 5–5   ▶

Kara and Camille's completed score sheet for *Target 300*.

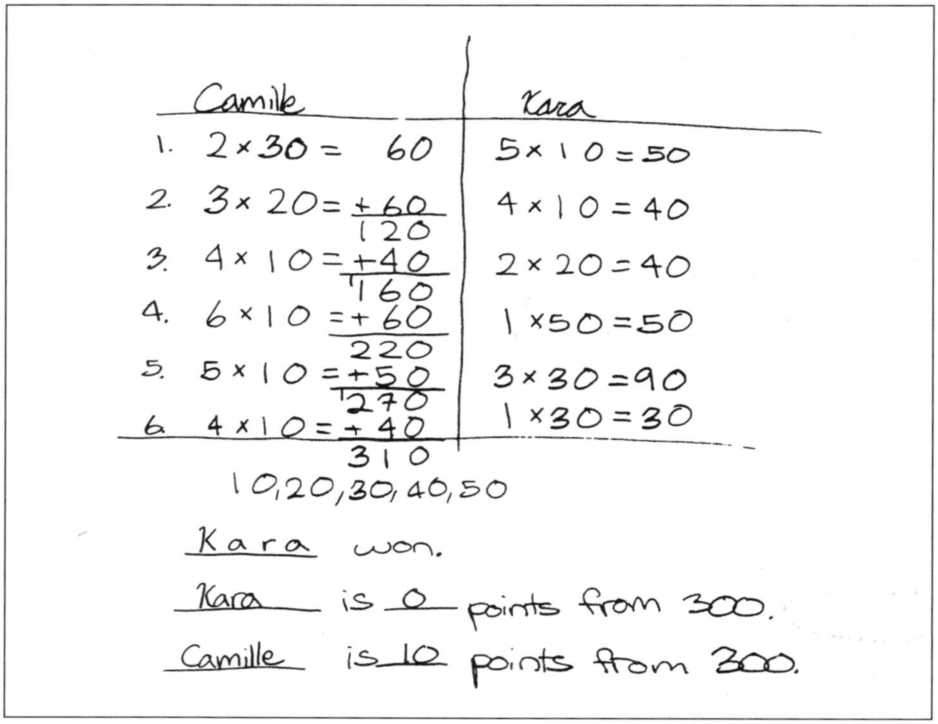

Camille	Kara
1. $2 \times 30 = 60$	$5 \times 10 = 50$
2. $3 \times 20 = +60$ / 120	$4 \times 10 = 40$
3. $4 \times 10 = +40$ / 160	$2 \times 20 = 40$
4. $6 \times 10 = +60$ / 220	$1 \times 50 = 50$
5. $5 \times 10 = +50$ / 270	$3 \times 30 = 90$
6. $4 \times 10 = +40$ / 310	$1 \times 30 = 30$

10, 20, 30, 40, 50

Kara won.

Kara is 0 points from 300.

Camille is 10 points from 300.

TEACHER-TO-TEACHER TALK   The multiplication facts have never been mastered by any fourth-grade class that I have ever taught. But every child must have accessibility to these facts. Yes, I send a parent newsletter home about how parents can help their children master these facts. Yes, I give weekly multiplication and division table quizzes. Yes, I remind the children frequently of the importance of knowing these facts. Yes, we review how to use our doubles to figure out our four times tables. Yes, I have multiplication flash cards and fact triangles available for children to practice with each other. Each child also has a multiplication table available to use at any time (except when completing quizzes or the unit exam). We fill them out in a whole-class lesson with lots of discussion, and when they're finished, I laminate them and punch holes in them so they can be housed in binders or trappers. We share personal stories about multiplication facts. I ask, "What is your hardest one? What is your easiest one? What is your favorite one?" I remind the children that once they know one fact, they also know its turnaround fact. Although I am forever expecting mastery of these facts, I would rather have a child grapple with the thinking and reasoning required by a problem than panic because she doesn't immediately know the answer to 8×7. Because I practice "full-immersion multiplication" (everything that can be multiplied in our world during that month is multiplied!), the children are well aware of the benefits of knowing their tables.

The children are also aware of my rule for not using the multiplication table during quizzes from the beginning of the multiplication unit. It is a fine line we walk. My suggestion to you is to find the shoe that fits and be consistent with your choice. If you wish to allow access to multiplication table aids, then so be it. But also decide the parameters of their usage—and make sure to inform students, parents, and even perhaps your principal of those parameters.

Extension

Students can move to playing *Target 600* once they have worked through several rounds of *Target 300*. *Target 600* encourages students to adjust their strategies as they multiply by the larger multiples of ten.

Follow-Up Journal Write

Evan's subtotal after two rounds of *Target 300* was 180. What could his rolls and multiplications have been to reach 180 in two rounds? Is there more than one possible answer to this question? How do you know?

Silent Multiplication

Duration: 1–2 class periods followed by shorter explorations several times a week

This lesson is adapted from *Teaching Arithmetic: Lessons for Extending Multiplication* (Wickett and Burns 2001, 37–55). This activity exposes patterns of factors and products that will support the children as they work to make sense of multidigit multiplication. Students develop strategies to solve increasingly complex multiplications by using what they know about simpler related problems. This activity offers students the opportunity to:

- practice basic multiplication facts
- explore the commutative, associative, and distributive properties of multiplication
- examine the effect on the product when one factor is halved or the other factor is doubled
- continue to explore the effects on the product when multiplying by ten and multiples of ten
- solve more complex problems by using what they know about simpler related problems
- continue to strengthen number sense, computation, and problem solving

Materials

- none

The beauty of this lesson is its adaptability. Initial lessons can focus on just one idea or procedure at a time. As silent multiplication routines continue throughout your unit, multiple concepts and procedures can then be applied to a longer, more complex string of multiplication problems. I am also very partial to this activity because of its use of silence—something that is certainly novel in my class! It is for that very reason that silent multiplication elicits significant focus and thought. It is the discussion following the activity, however, that is of critical importance as children work to make sense of the relationships between factors, products, and open number sentences as they calculate strings of multiplication problems mentally.

To begin this series of lessons, discuss with your students the rules for a silent lesson:

- A star drawn on the board signifies the beginning of the activity. Silence is required from everyone—including the teacher!
- When a problem is written on the board, students should indicate when they know the answer by putting their thumbs up.

After we discuss the rules of a silent lesson, I move right into such an activity by drawing a star on the board and waiting for silence. Choosing an initial problem that all children can solve will engage the group quickly. For example, your first problem could be:

$$1 \times 4$$

I wait for students to show their thumbs. I move around the room and hand the marker to a child with a thumb up. The child comes up to the board and completes the number sentence.

$$1 \times 4 = 4$$

Wait for students to show thumbs up in agreement with the answer. Then place another problem right below the first problem.

$$1 \times 4 = 4$$
$$2 \times 4$$

Again wait for children to give you a thumbs-up when they know the answer. Give the marker to another child to write the answer on the board.

$$1 \times 4 = 4$$
$$2 \times 4 = 8$$

Again, wait for a show of thumbs in agreement with the answer. Erase the star. Now the discussion can begin!

Quickly review the steps of the routine—the need to be silent, the need to show that you have an answer, as well as the need to show agreement, disagreement, or confusion with thumbs. I remind the children repeatedly of the need to think quietly and look for relationships from one problem to the next. It is also time to pull out my favorite directive: "Use what you know to figure out what you do not know."

Opening the class discussion with a question such as "How can the first problem help you solve the second one?" will keep the children focused on the relationship between the two problems, rather than on how easy or difficult they were to solve. The following questions can also keep the children focused on the relational thinking required by this lesson:

- How are these problems related?
- What is the same about these problems?
- What is different?
- What happened to the factors?
- What happened to the products?

As the children are talking among themselves, I draw another star on the board. I continue this practice with another string of problems, written one at a time:

$$3 \times 2 =$$
$$6 \times 2 =$$
$$12 \times 2 =$$
$$24 \times 2 =$$

Following the same procedure, I hand a marker to a volunteer with a thumb raised; that student writes an answer on the board. We move from one problem to the next. Remember to post one problem at a time. This slows down the lesson and offers the children more time to focus on that particular problem and its relationship to the prior one. Once again, these problems are easily accessible to the entire class and all children will be engaged by the thinking and mathematics required of the task.

Erase the star to once again begin a discussion using many of the same questions presented for processing the first string of problems. This time around, I record the relationships students offer. The process of recording not only gives focus to the discussion but also validates the observations of the children and helps them establish patterns for which to look when presented with new strings. Some of the observations may be:

- One factor is staying the same.
- When one factor doubles, so does the product.
- Each product is two times the one before.

Recording also gives you the opportunity to encourage the children to use more concise mathematical language. Terms such as *factor*, *product*, and *multiple* can be used to describe the noted patterns.

I then ask, "What could my next problem be?" Most children will chime in, "Forty-eight times two." Last year, however, Robert suggested that we could continue the string with "Two times twenty-four." Although I was prepared to spend a bit more time focusing on doubling a factor and the effect that had on the product, our class discussion moved to the awareness and use of the commutative property of multiplication. Looking at the relationship between 24 × 2 and 2 × 24 gave us time to talk about turnaround facts and how they affect multiplication. That year, some members of the class explained how they used turnaround facts to help them with recalling their basic facts. "I don't like seven times six, so I just make it six times seven!" one student explained.

The following sequence could then be used to continue to doubling pattern. Notice, however, that the factors are not doubled in the same predictable order as before:

$$2 \times 2 =$$
$$4 \times 2 =$$
$$4 \times 4 =$$
$$4 \times 8 =$$
$$8 \times 8 =$$
$$16 \times 8 =$$
$$16 \times 16 =$$

The big idea exposed by this string is that when one factor doubles, the product doubles. As you facilitate the class discussion about the patterns and relationships students notice in this string, be sure to include wait time in order to allow children to fully articulate their thoughts and insights. You may also need to remind the children to be patient with their classmates as others are sharing. We could easily point out to students how an action on one of the factors influences the action taken on the product. It is much more effective, however, to have the children explain this big idea to each other. This discussion can be quite powerful. As the discussion continues, encourage the children to speak to each other. If they are adding on to a classmate's observation, have them address that particular child as they speak.

TEACHER-TO-TEACHER TALK   You can probably tell by now that this silent multiplication routine is a favorite of mine. What I found the most challenging—and scary—when I began to implement silent multiplication in my classroom was the creation of the string of multiplication problems. Initially, I sat with paper and pencil and carefully crafted a series of problems. Sometimes I started out knowing the big idea I was after (halving one factor causes the product to be divided by two), and other times I just began a string and took it where it led me. I kept that paper handy as I went through the routine with my students. As I became more confident with my choice of starting problems and became more confident and competent in identifying the relationships myself, my need to handwrite the problems prior to class became less important.

I continue to be quite proud of myself when I develop meaningful strings on the spot. (When I do, I write them down and save them.) Crucial to the creation of problem strings is the relationship between the problems (Fosnot and Dolk 2001a, 98). Silent multiplication routines not only help our children construct relational thinking strategies but help us fine-tune ours as well! Although it seems simple, this silent multiplication routine can present and uncover meaningful, sophisticated mathematical ideas.

Other multiplication sequences can be explored in this format. Multiplication by tens can be added to the strings when you and your children are ready to do so.

$$4 \times 2$$
$$8 \times 2$$
$$8 \times 20$$
$$80 \times 20$$
$$160 \times 20$$
$$160 \times 40$$

Constructing a string with an odd number allows you to look at multiplication by fractions. By this time in the unit, your students should also be gaining proficiency in dividing factors and products by two.

$$5 \times 6$$
$$5 \times 12$$
$$2\frac{1}{2} \times 12$$
$$2\frac{1}{2} \times 120$$
$$2\frac{1}{2} \times 60$$

Silent multiplication routines push children to look at clusters of problems rather than problems in isolation, which may be a new experience for some. These routines also demonstrate the connectedness of mathematical procedures and concepts that we often omit from our instruction. *Teaching Arithmetic: Lessons for Extending Multiplication* (Wickett and Burns 2001, 37–55) contains helpful student vignettes and author commentary that offer additional insights about this activity.

Follow-Up Journal Write

How can knowing $6 \times 8 = 48$ help you solve $12 \times 8 = ?$ (See Figure 5–6 for one student's response.)

FIGURE 5–6 ▶

Deborah's journal response.

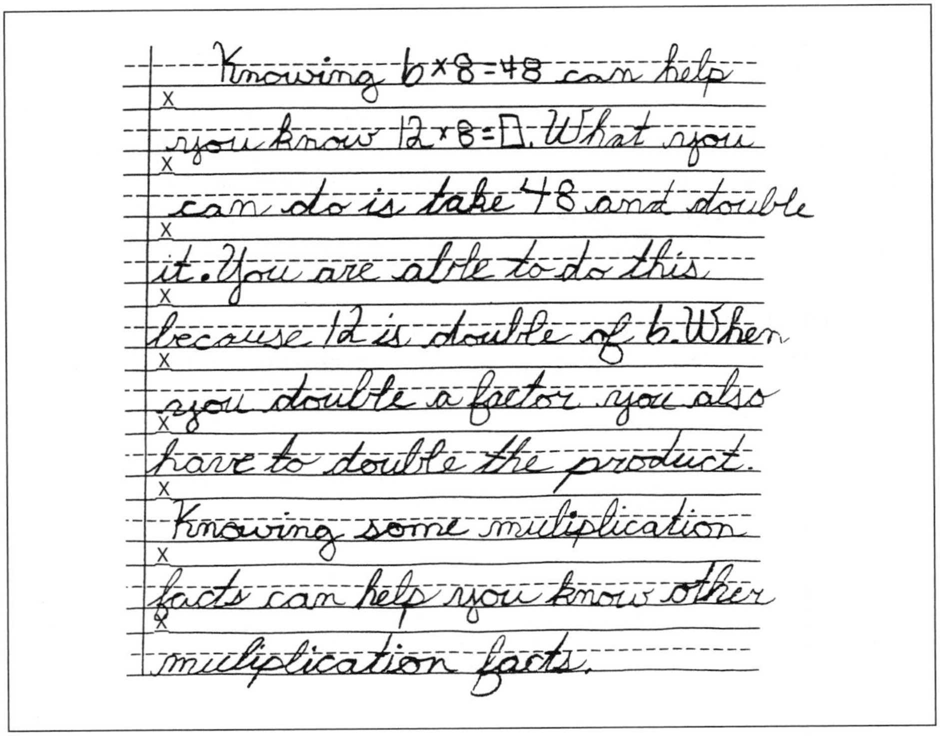

Knowing 6×8=48 can help you know 12×8=□. What you can do is take 48 and double it. You are able to do this because 12 is double of 6. When you double a factor you also have to double the product. Knowing some multiplication facts can help you know other multiplication facts.

Beans and Scoops

Duration: 3–4 class periods

This activity, adapted from *Teaching Arithmetic: Lessons for Extending Multiplication* (Wickett and Burns 2001), provides a context within which multidigit multiplication strategies can be explored by figuring out how many beans will fill a jar. This investigation offers students the opportunity to:

- apply and refine multidigit multiplication strategies
- continue to develop estimation skills and strategies
- gather and analyze data

Materials

- glass jars of varying sizes, at least 2
- bags of different-size beans (for example, kidney beans and white beans), at least 2
- coffee scoops of varying sizes, at least 2
- 1 paper plate per group of students
- optional: several sheets of chart paper

This activity provides students with a meaningful context for practicing multidigit multiplication. Because these lessons are presented in a problem-solving format, the multiplication has purpose. By determining how many scoopfuls of beans fill a jar, and how many beans fill a scoop, the class can apply multiplication strategies to figure out how many beans fill the jar. Several trials take place with different types of beans in order for strategies to be tested, refined, or even discarded for other more efficient strategies. It will be extremely helpful for you to work through this activity yourself before you present it to your class. You may wish to choose scoops or beans whose numbers will be more manageable. I have found that numbers differing in tens works best initially. A scoop that holds eighteen beans and a jar that holds sixteen scoops can be a little confusing in the first trial, so I begin with a scoop that holds twenty-three beans and a jar that holds sixteen scoops. You may wish to experiment with your scoops, jars, and beans until you find numbers that will better suit the desired mathematical objectives and outcomes.

I begin the lesson by showing the class a jar, a coffee scoop, and a bag of kidney beans. I explain that we are going to investigate how many beans we can fit in my jar by filling the jar with scoopfuls of beans. Then I ask, "How many beans do you think will fill the jar?" Children will offer responses but may quickly realize that answering the question is more complicated than they thought. Your students may realize that there are a few questions for which they need answers before they can set out to solve the problem. They may ask, "How many beans are in a scoop?" or "How many scoops fill the jar?" If these questions don't come up, you may want to ask the students if there is anything that they need to know before they can begin to answer the question.

The first question to investigate is how many scoops will fill the jar. Ask the students for estimates of how many scoops they think will fit into the jar. Write the estimates on the board. Place three scoops of beans into the jar. Make sure that your actions can be seen by all the children. I often cover my overhead with paper and do the pouring on the overhead. It is a little higher than a tabletop, and I can move it close to the children. Once the beans have been scooped into the jar and the children can see the level of beans in the jar, ask them if they wish to revise their estimates based on the information they now have. Ask the children to explain their estimates and why their new estimates make sense.

Continue using the same scoop to fill the jar to the top. Make sure to add a level scoopful of beans each time. You may wish to stop here and there to give students the chance to once again revise their estimates and explain why they wish to do so. This activity keeps students engaged because the visual representation of what is happening is often what they do not expect! The children may initially estimate that six scoops will fill the jar, when in fact it takes sixteen scoops! The children's curiosity will often carry them through the investigation.

Once the jar is filled, ask the students to now estimate the number of beans in the jar. Have the children share their estimates and reasoning with their neighbor before sharing out with the whole class. After the children have shared their estimates with the group, ask them what they need to know before they can proceed with the investigation. It now becomes necessary for the children to know how many beans are in a scoop.

Give each table group one level scoop of beans placed on a paper plate. Have each group count its beans, and record each count on the board. With the students, identify the mean, median, and mode of the collected data in order to decide on a number that best represents the number of beans in a typical scoop. If your children are unfamiliar with these statistical terms, it may be necessary to give a quick overview of how these landmarks can help you decide on an average number of beans in a scoop.

At this point in the investigation, to refocus students on the purpose of the activity, I ask them to refer to the original question: "What are we trying to find out?" Remind the children that they have gathered a lot of information up until this point, but now they need to decide what to do with that information in order to answer the question being asked. By this time in the lesson and unit of study, it should make sense to the children to multiply the number of beans in one scoop by the number of scoops to figure out how many beans are needed to fill the jar.

Modeling initial strategies on the board or chart paper can be helpful for the entire class. Processing your students' thinking, reasoning, and computing in this way can:

- give access to the mathematics of the problem
- validate children's thinking
- offer a paper-and-pencil format for solving the problem
- help the children apply the language of multiplication to the experience

Here was Jared's thinking as he explained it to the class:

16×23

I am going to start with 16 20s—and then I will deal with the 3 in the ones place later.

$20 + 20 + 20 + 20 + 20 + 20 + 20 + 20 + 20 + 20 = 200$ *(10 20s)*

$20 + 20 + 20 + 20 + 20 + 20 = 120$ *(6 20s)*

$200 + 120 = 320$ *That is 16 20s.*

So now I need 16 3s, or 3 16s, which is easier for me, to finish up the jar—

3 16s = 48

So 320 + 48 = 368!

Now I know that $16 \times 23 = 368$

As you can see, Jared loved repeated addition. What was so powerful in his explanation and discussion with his classmates was hearing him move from an additive procedure to one of multiplication. Jared's number sense was strong, and he often preferred to chunk numbers by tens. Having his work written down and then discussed gave him the opportunity to focus on the numbers and the efficiency of his thinking. When other students commented on something that Jared had done in his computation, I encouraged the children to carry on that discussion with Jared, not me! During Jared's presentation, we realized that just about everyone had used a variation of Jared's approach.

Once a thorough discussion of one approach is completed, other children can offer their approaches. Continue to compare and contrast strategies with one another. Share until you have several strategies posted, each labeled with the child's name for reference purposes. Then ask the children to solve the same bean problem with someone else's strategy. When the children share their work, ask them not to identify the author of the chosen strategy. Once a child's presentation is completed, the class can then try to identify the adopted strategy.

TEACHER-TO-TEACHER TALK I was apprehensive when I first began to encourage my fourth graders to construct personal strategies. I had no idea what the strategies would be. Where they would take the class? Would I be able to understand them? And what if they made no mathematical sense? These concerns kept me (and my students) mathematically hostage for too many years. Then there was a snowy day in mid-January. Half of my class was out of school that day because of the poor weather conditions. It seemed like a safe day to make that plunge into the unknown. Here's what I learned from that class:

- Listening intently is hard work.
- Asking for clarification is an art—it takes persistence, practice, and patience to learn when and how to question in order to make the child feel safe, validated, and mathematically confident.
- My children knew more about number sense and multiplication than I ever expected.
- Sometimes what we think we know and understand can prevent us from learning something new about how our children think about the mathematics of a problem.
- We need to help children identify and clarify their mathematical thinking.

James Hiebert and his coauthors (1997) describe the challenges of guiding mathematical activities when children construct, share, and defend their own strategies. How do we support our students as creative problem solvers and help them learn important mathematics? These authors advise us to accept two responsibilities: to select appropriate tasks and to provide our students with relevant information, realizing that both responsibilities require a deep knowledge of the subject and the students.

Current research continues to support the benefits of having children construct personal strategies. This can be a scary practice for all of us. I can remember going home with quite a headache after that snowy day in January when I took the first of many risks in my own classroom. But it was not a headache of frustration or fatigue. It was one brought on by thinking—plain and simple.

Lessons can continue following the same format but now using a different-size jar and/or different-size beans. You may also find in time that your children have moved beyond the need for the concrete context. They can then be asked to imagine a jar that holds fourteen scoops and a scoop that holds twenty-two beans, for example. Keeping the strategies of the first investigation posted may help students self-start or even try a new strategy. After the initial investigation, you can ask the children to demonstrate their computation using two strategies. The numbers and situations often affect which strategies children choose. Invented and chosen strategies enable children to be more flexible with the numbers involved in order to make the computation easier for them.

For multiplication, the ability to break numbers apart in flexible ways is even more important than in addition and subtraction (Van de Walle 2004, 214). Take a look at the following strategy for determining the number of beans in a jar. Hayden's ability and preference to distribute the 23 to the 10 and the 6 can easily be identified. She also breaks apart the 23 into smaller, more manageable numbers, as well. Notice that Hayden decomposes the 23 in two different ways: $20 + 3$ and $10 + 10 + 3$. Hayden has learned that for her, manipulating friendly numbers makes the computation more manageable. Both Jared and Hayden thought about *numbers*, not *digits*, as they applied number sense and understandings about multiplication to this calculation.

Although we need not label this strategy as one that applies the distributive property with the children, its application is apparent as children break numbers into manageable parts, multiply them, and then put them back together again to find the product. When the time is taken to assess Hayden's strategy, we can identify a fourth grader's ability to apply the distributive property.

$$16 \times 23$$

$$(\mathbf{10 + 6}) \times 23$$

$$(\mathbf{10} \times 23) \quad + \quad (\mathbf{6} \times 23)$$

$$10 \times \mathbf{20} = 200 \qquad 6 \times \mathbf{10} = 60$$

$$10 \times 3 = 30 \qquad 6 \times \mathbf{10} = 60$$

$$200 + 30 = \mathbf{230} \qquad 6 \times \mathbf{3} = 18$$

$$60 + 60 + 18 = \mathbf{138}$$

$$\mathbf{230} + \mathbf{138} = 368$$

$$16 \times 23 = 368$$

Children need many experiences to help them develop flexibility with numbers as well as their thinking about those numbers. Meaningful experiences and problems can offer those very opportunities. Problems that intrigue you will more than likely intrigue your students as well. It is always helpful to play around with a problem yourself before presenting it to the children. Can *you* solve it in two ways? Can *you* articulate your strategies? Where and what might the potential stumbling blocks be for the children as they work through this problem? What fragile understandings could be exposed? How can you question students to assess their understanding of multiplication as well as their chosen procedure? As you teach children to slow down, to look for relationships, and to make sense of the mathematics, you are equipping them with lifelong learning strategies. You are teaching them to think and act like mathematicians.

Story Problems

Duration: 1–2 class periods

In order to create multiplication story problems, children must have a conceptual understanding of the operation. This activity offers students the opportunity to:

- apply their conceptual and procedural understanding of multiplication
- clarify and deepen their understanding of multiplication
- apply their understanding of the language of multiplication
- create meaningful contexts

Materials
- 1 set of colored pencils or crayons per student

This activity begins with a prompt:

Write a story problem that includes a question that can be solved using multiplication.

Students are asked to create a story problem and find its solution. The solution should be represented on the back side of the paper with words as well as a number model. I also ask students to illustrate their problems.

Engaging children in the writing process can always be a challenge, especially when the prompt is as open-ended as this one. Scaffolding the writing process with several different types of prompts may be helpful at times. You may wish to initiate the writing process with a more specific prompt, such as:

Write a multiplication story problem that fits the following number model:

$13 \times 8 = \square$

Or you could agree as a class on a story problem context:

Write a multiplication story problem about our class of 25 fourth graders.

Writing story problems also presents the opportunity for children to revise and fine-tune their written language routines and practices. Asking the children to write rough drafts of their problems and solutions will allow you to conference with each child about not only the mathematics but also his word choice and the appropriateness of the question being asked. The use of technology can be meaningfully integrated with the writing of story problems. For this particular task, students can complete rough drafts by hand and final copies on the computer. Keyboarding and inserting clip art are the targeted technology skills. Figure 5–7 shows one student's story problem.

FIGURE 5–7 ▶

Grace's multiplication story problem and solution.

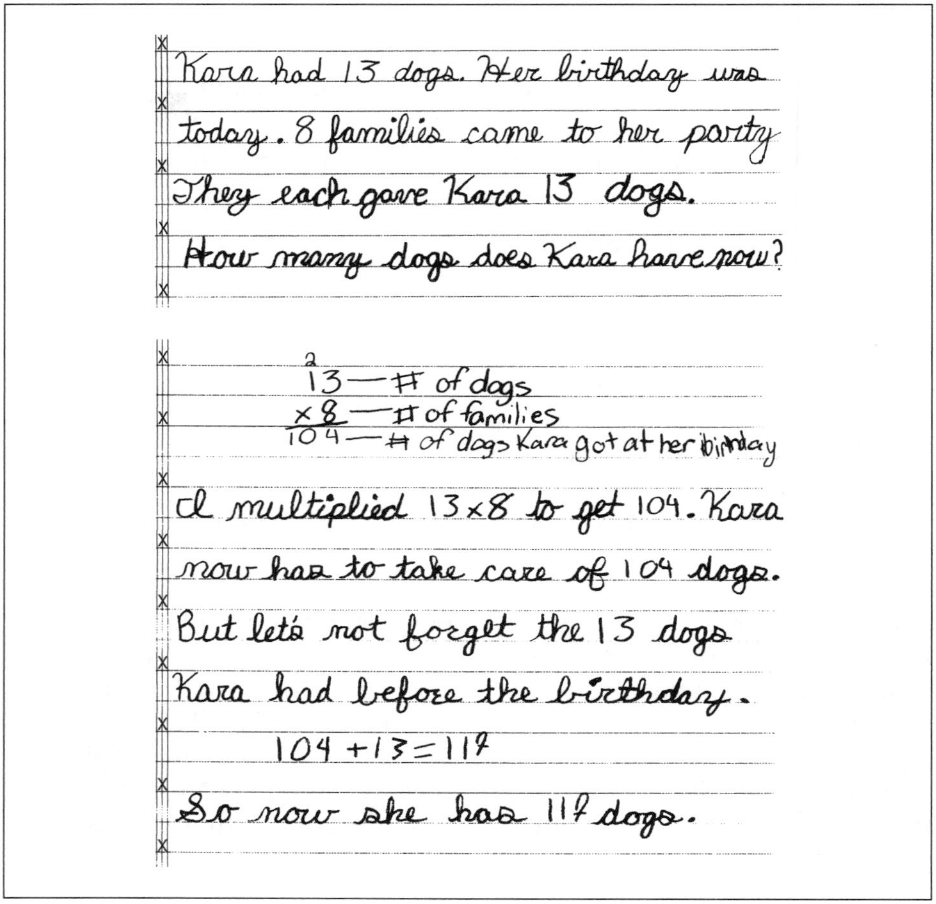

Kara had 13 dogs. Her birthday was today. 8 families came to her party. They each gave Kara 13 dogs. How many dogs does Kara have now?

$$\overset{2}{1}3 \text{ — \# of dogs}$$
$$\times 8 \text{ — \# of families}$$
$$104 \text{ — \# of dogs Kara got at her birthday}$$

I multiplied 13×8 to get 104. Kara now has to take care of 104 dogs. But let's not forget the 13 dogs Kara had before the birthday.

$$104 + 13 = 117$$

So now she has 117 dogs.

Games

Frequent practice is necessary to attain fluency and mastery of multiplication facts. Drill tends to be tedious and quickly loses its effectiveness. Multiplication games offer a context within which to practice and master the multiplication facts. The attitude of playfulness encouraged by games may very well be carried into other areas of the multiplication curriculum.

Rio

Rio is a multiplication game that is played by two children and offers students opportunities to practice and recall one multiplication table at a time.

Materials

- *Rio* directions (see Blackline Masters)
- 1 *Rio* game board (see Blackline Masters)
- 2 dice
- 5 two-color counters or 5 counters of one color per player
- number of players: 2

Ahead of time, create game boards for the tables you wish the children to practice using the template in the Blackline Masters. Each table game board should contain the products that result when multiplying the targeted number by the numbers two through twelve. There should be one free space on each board. Boards can be laminated for future and frequent use. I have three game boards for each of the factors four through nine. A sample game board is shown in Figure 5–8.

Rio			
12	18	24	30
36	42	Free Space	48
54	60	66	72

FIGURE 5–8 ◄

***Rio* game board for the multiples of six.**

Multiplication Bingo

This game is adapted from *Everyday Mathematics* (Everyday Learning Corporation 2002a). Although I do have a set of multiplication bingo boards that I have created and laminated (each board has a different configuration of products of the basic one through ten multiplication facts), the children much prefer to create their own boards from the products found on a multiplication matrix. *Multiplication Bingo* offers students opportunities to:

- practice and recall multiplication facts
- explore relationships between factors and products
- identify the frequency and probability of products that may occur with the factors two through ten

Materials

- *Multiplication Bingo* directions (see Blackline Masters)
- 1 multiplication matrix (for reference)
- 1 blank bingo board per player per game (see Blackline Masters)
- random number generators for the factors one through ten, such as 2 ten-sided dice; 1 deck of 1–10 number cards containing 4 of each number; or a set of flash cards containing 2 of each fact with factors from one through ten
- 1 colored pencil per player
- number of players: 2–3 or whole class

Because the students choose the products that will be placed on their bingo boards, they are more apt to focus on the relationship between the factors and the products they produce than on placements of unrelated factors and products. Some children may opt to complete their board with only even numbers because they think that even products will occur more frequently. Some children will omit prime numbers because they realize that these numbers are less apt to be called because of their limited factor possibilities. Some children will mix odd and even numbers, either equally or more of one than the other because of the frequency with which the children think they might occur. After each round, I ask two or three children to share their strategies for choosing products. The children make new boards for each round, and that in itself is a learning experience! Some children may begin to notice that some products have the possibility of being called more than others because of their number of factor pairs. Encourage them to act upon their observations by changing the rules of the game to include the use of duplicate products when filling in their game boards.

Follow-Up Journal Write

When completing his *Multiplication Bingo* board, Suren omitted the following numbers: 2, 3, 5, and 7. Why? Support your thinking with reasoning *and* number models.

Multiplication Bull's-Eye

This game, adapted from *Everyday Mathematics* (Everyday Learning Corporation 2002a), focuses on estimation skills within a multiplication context. *Multiplication Bull's-Eye* offers students opportunities to:

- practice estimation skills and procedures when multiplying two-digit factors
- apply number sense

Materials

- *Multiplication Bull's-Eye* directions (see Blackline Masters)
- 1 deck of 0–9 number cards, containing 4 of each number
- 1 die
- 1 calculator
- number of players: 2–3

Sample Round

1. Player 1 rolls a 4. The target range is between 3,001 and 5,000.

Number on Die	Range of Product
1	500 or less
2	501–1,000
3	1,001–3,000
4	3,001–5,000
5	5,001–7,000
6	More than 7,000

2. Player 1 turns over a 5, 4, 6, and 7. He uses estimation to form two numbers whose product falls between the range, for example: 54×76.

3. He finds the product on a calculator: $54 \times 76 = 4,104$. Since the product falls within the range, the player has hit the bull's-eye and scores 1 point.

Estimation strategies produce approximate results, and sometimes that is all that a problem requires, whether in math class or in a real-life context. Invented estimation strategies are as necessary and worthwhile as those the children create and apply for computations involving multiplication. A quick processing session following a few rounds of *Multiplication Bull's-Eye* will allow children to share their estimation strategies and perhaps adopt a new one or two. Shared strategies may include the following:

Front-End Estimation

54 × 76

50 × 70 = 3,500

Rounding

54 × 76

50 × 80 = 4,000

It is helpful to use the language of estimation as students share their strategies. Phrases like *about, almost, close to, a little more than,* and *a little less than* can help children identify the degree of an estimate's approximation.

Multiplication Tic-Tac-Toe

Multiplication Tic-Tac-Toe, which is adapted from *Nimble with Numbers* (Childs and Choate 1998), can be played with two different game boards. A board displaying products up to 36 can be used when the game is first introduced or for those children who may initially require a less intimidating factor list. A game board displaying products up to 81 can be used once the rules of the game have been mastered. *Multiplication Tic-Tac-Toe* offers students the opportunity to:

- practice and recall multiplication and related division facts
- move flexibly between multiplication and division in order to identify products, factors, divisors, or quotients

Materials
- *Multiplication Tic-Tac-Toe* directions (see Blackline Masters)
- 1 *Multiplication Tic-Tac-Toe* game board (see Blackline Masters)
- 13 colored counters or 1 colored pencil per player
- 2 large paper clips
- number of players: 2

Multiplication Tic-Tac-Toe can be played in class as well as assigned as homework. Playing math games at home can offer parents a window into your classroom as well as valuable information about how their children think about multiplication—and how well they know their times tables!

Calculation Routines and Practices

To develop and apply accurate and efficient computational strategies for multiplication, it is increasingly important for children to be able to break apart numbers in meaningful and flexible ways. Calculating with number sense should continue to be our primary goal in computation instruction. Meaningful and mathematically rich problems can offer opportunities for students to investigate multiplication and the procedural thinking that it requires. The numbers and context of a problem should determine the chosen calculation strategies when children are engaged in making sense of the mathematics.

Algorithms

A structured set of procedures that can be used across problems do have a place in a fourth-grade mathematics curriculum. Determining when and how to present and investigate algorithms is an important instructional decision. Algorithms are best introduced when students have a deep understanding of number relationships and of the operations required by the procedure. It is also important that children have had the opportunity to develop personal computational strategies from which procedural and conceptual comparisons and connections can be made when discussing and investigating other algorithms.

Arrays

Working with arrays gives children the opportunity to break down more difficult multiplications into simpler problems. Using an array model allows children to have a visual representation of important relationships found in and created by multiplication. Encouraging students to build large arrays by combining smaller arrays helps them visualize the problem. For example, 8×9 can be decomposed into smaller, more manageable multiplications such as 5×9 and 3×9. (See Figure 5–9.)

Arrays can be drawn on graph paper and then partitioned into smaller arrays. The children can color one of the arrays to identify the decomposition of the original array into two (or three) smaller ones and record the various combinations of arrays that can be used to cover an equivalent area. Recording how the smaller arrays relate to the larger array is important and scaffolds work in later years with the distributive property. It not only helps children identify equivalence but also offers a visual model of the taking apart and putting back together. If your children are not yet familiar with the use of parentheses, a mini-lesson on their usage will foster their application. Figure 5–10 shows one student's work with arrays.

FIGURE 5–9   ▶

FIGURE 5–9   ▶

An array of 8 × 9 broken into smaller arrays.

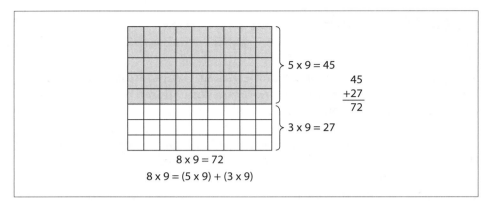

FIGURE 5–10   ▶

Kelsey's array and number models.

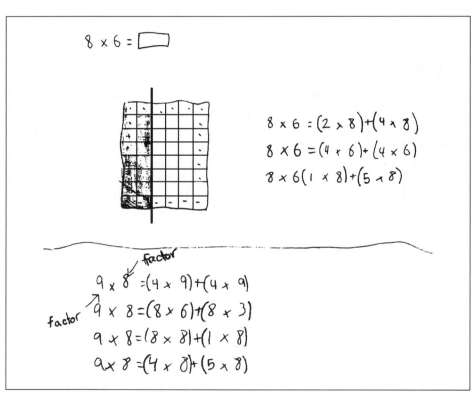

TEACHER-TO-TEACHER TALK   As my work with multiplication became more mindful and refined, I began to realize the underlying presence of the distributive property in just about every aspect of my thinking, teaching, and learning. Although I do not identify the property with my class as such, it is important for teachers to have a working understanding of what the distributive property actually represents. Maryann Wickett and Marilyn Burns describe it best in *Teaching Arithmetic: Lessons for Extending Multiplication, Grades 4–5:*

> The distributive property is a powerful tool for effectively and efficiently multiplying unwieldy numbers. The distributive property is a way to solve a multiplication

problem with large and complicated numbers by breaking it into two or more easier problems, doing these calculations, and then combining the partial products for a final answer. The property is often referred to as the distributive property of multiplication over addition and can be algebraically represented as $a(b + c) = ab + ac$. (2001, xiii)

The authors go on to say that lessons need not focus on learning the definition of the distributive property or its algebraic representation, but rather on its use to understand multidigit multiplication and to learn to compute efficiently.

Chunking

The chunking algorithm provides a concrete structure within which students apply the distributive property. It is a physical as well as conceptual framework within which the children can decompose numbers into smaller, more manageable parts in order to calculate partial products. For example:

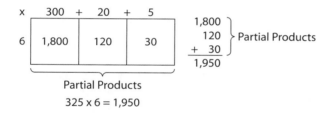

Here, 325 is decomposed into $300 + 20 + 5$. Each number is then multiplied by 6 to calculate the partial products. The partial products are then added to calculate the final product.

My students often refer to the grid used in this method as a *chunker*. The label works well. When children discuss strategies and use the *chunker* terminology, they have an immediate visual representation of the multiplication.

The chunking algorithm also works well with two-digit multiplication.

	x	30	+	6
70		2,100		420
+				
8		240		48

```
2,100
  420
  240
+  48
2,808
```

36 x 78 = 2,808

The number of partial products created by the chunking algorithm corresponds nicely with the total number of multiplications required by multidigit factors. Children will often look at a more complex multiplication problem consisting of two factors and assume that there are only two multiplications within the calculation. Fourth graders may procedurally equate 7×8 with the same number of multiplications as 76×84. Yes, the children are making an important generalization, but one that needs to be readjusted with the aid of the visual reference that chunking provides.

Partial Products

The partial products algorithm is also based on the distributive property of multiplication. As with the chunking procedure, factors are multiplied, taking into account the place value of each digit. The partial products are then recorded and added to compute the final product.

$$
\begin{array}{r}
385 \\
\times\ 7 \\
\hline
7 \times 300 = \quad 2{,}100 \\
7 \times 80 = \quad\ \ 560 \\
7 \times 5 = \quad +\ 35 \\
\hline
2{,}695
\end{array}
$$

As with the chunking algorithm, the factor 385 is broken down into hundreds, tens, and ones. Each value is then multiplied by the factor of 7. I encourage the children to begin their decomposing with the greatest place-value digit, moving from left to right through the calculation. This practice will help them keep better track of the place values as well as to construct a systematic written record of this procedure.

Once again, this big idea of taking apart numbers, operating on them, and then putting them back together is demonstrated by the partial products algorithm. If your students have worked through the chunking method as well as the partial products method of multiplication, asking them to compare and contrast the two procedures will help them identify and articulate their commonality, their benefits, and the application of the distributive property of multiplication.

The partial products algorithm also offers students another estimation strategy. This procedure encourages children to estimate the magnitude of a number without having to necessarily complete the procedure. When multiplying 385×7, we know that $300 \times 7 = 2{,}100$ and that $80 \times 7 = 560$. The product will therefore be in the 2,600 range because $2{,}100 + 500 = 2{,}600$.

As children practice and apply the partial products algorithm, they may begin to find the calculating tedious. Larger factors can begin to cause the children to question the efficiency of this procedure. Michael, my voice of reason, announced to the class one day, "Sure this works, but who wants to spend this much time doing multiplication?" This was actually a very good and appropriate observation! Michael's insights moved us to a discussion of the importance of efficiency in calculation and the presentation of the standard multiplication algorithm.

Standard Multiplication Algorithm

After you have laid a conceptual foundation throughout the study of multiplication with plenty of opportunity for the children to develop preferred and invented strategies, you can meaningfully introduce the standard multiplication algorithm. As with other algorithms, mathematical conversations need to occur as the procedure is introduced, practiced, and applied. Questions that push children to compare and contrast procedures, identify smaller problems within a larger one, and estimate will help them make sense of this traditional approach to multiplication.

TEACHER-TO-TEACHER TALK   There is a difference between proficiency and efficiency of calculation, which is interesting to contemplate—and even discuss with your class. A proficient calculation can serve us with the desired solution. Opportunities will undoubtedly present themselves, however, in which we'll need to assess the efficiency of a chosen calculation. Sometimes when my students are finding the calculating process tedious and inefficient, they ask, "Isn't there an easier way?" Introducing the standard algorithm can be an antidote. My curriculum's standards expect that students will work through the traditional algorithm. But what I always find so interesting is that when I present the standard algorithm toward the end of the unit, there is little need for drill. The children can often fit their conceptual understanding of multiplication into the standard algorithmic framework. What I also find interesting is when multiplication is required for a problem later on in the year, some children choose to use the standard algorithm and some do not. We need to be OK with that! The children who prefer it are very often those who have been working through this procedure with someone at home. These particular children are also usually the first ones to forget the algorithm a few months down the road. Because they learned the procedure as a series of steps instead of making sense of the actions involved in those steps, the process is difficult to re-create and is easily lost. When given a choice, many children will opt for the standard algorithm when factors are large and preferred strategies cumbersome. Just as they are able to choose an algorithm based on the numbers presented by the problem, they are able to choose an algorithm based on the efficiency of its completion.

Beginning with one-digit multipliers and then moving on to two-digit multipliers seems to be standard fare. Because of my concern with the preservation of place value, I ask the children to record each complete partial product, including the zeros.

$$
\begin{array}{r}
41 \\
\times\ 58 \\
\hline
328 \\
\underline{2{,}050} \\
2{,}378
\end{array}
\quad (205 \times \mathbf{10})
$$

Recurrent discussions about why it makes sense for that zero to placed in the second partial product helps keep the children focused on the multiplication by a ten that the second partial product represents.

Matthew preferred to refer to that elusive zero in the second partial product as an "added" zero. It was not until recently that I realized why that language concerned me. I rephrased Matthew's comment back to the class. "So if I *add* a zero to two hundred five, that leaves me with two hundred five because two hundred five plus zero equals two hundred five. Does this partial product represent two hundred five?" This question opened up a wonderful discussion about what that particular zero represented. It did *not* represent adding zero. It represented *multiplying by ten*. If we just added zero, the written representation would look something like this:

$$
\begin{array}{r}
41 \\
\times\ 58 \\
\hline
328 \\
205 \\
\hline
533
\end{array}
\qquad (205 + 0)
$$

Matthew's misconception provided an opportunity for meaningful discussion and thought about one simple zero, which, in reality, was not so simple! We all continued to remind each other why that zero had importance in partial products throughout the rest of the unit.

According to *Principles and Standards for School Mathematics*,

[S]tudents . . . should consolidate and practice a small number of computational algorithms for . . . multiplication . . . that they understand well and can use routinely. . . . Having access to more than one method . . . allows students to choose an approach that best fits the numbers in a particular problem. (NCTM 2000, 155)

Introducing, investigating, practicing, and applying several multiplication algorithms takes time, talk, and patience. It also requires the use of meaningful contexts in which the children have the opportunity to choose appropriate strategies. Having children share strategies and why it made sense to apply them in that particular context will offer opportunities to talk and think about the numbers, not just the procedure or the final product.

Mathematics Writing

When children write about a mathematical process, we have the opportunity to assess understanding, identify misconceptions, and assess their ability to apply new ideas and skills. Writing about procedures and the decisions that are made when working through a process requires specificity and attention to detail. As we assess children's writing, we need to look for the big ideas of multiplication.

- Are the students writing about groups of equal size?
- Are the students writing about breaking larger problems apart and putting them back together?
- Are students demonstrating their understanding of the commutativity of multiplication in their writing?
- Are students making connections between multiplication and addition? Multiplication and division?
- Are students creating and referring to mathematical models as they support their positions?
- Are students applying the language of multiplication? Are they weaving appropriate mathematical vocabulary throughout their writing?

Spending a class session or two to model a written response in a whole-class format continues to be a helpful routine. Choose an open-ended question that requires a calculation as well as conceptual understanding so you can model a fairly complex response with your class.

$$\square \times \triangle = 96$$

What might the missing numbers be? How many solutions can you find? Why do your number choices make sense?

Knowing where and how to start a written response can continue to be problematic for some fourth graders. Having a model from which to write can help anchor a child's thinking and subsequent writing. A question such as "What numbers work and why?" can provide the necessary scaffolding for a written response. Figure 5–11 shows how one class crafted a response to this question.

By this point in the year, strong introductory sentences should be a requirement. I remind the children that they are the experts when writing about their thinking. Encourage your students to be definitive in their opening statement. Some may continue to choose to open their response with "*I think* the two numbers could be . . ." The simple act of deleting *I think* will give greater clarity and conviction to the response.

Asking children to write about their procedures and thinking also offers us the opportunity to identify those children who can solve multiplication problems correctly, but with little mathematical comprehension. If a student writes a limited or superficial response, you can verify the student's mathematical understanding with a brief teacher-student conference. At that time, you can invite the child to elaborate on her writing and thinking. This practice also allows you to differentiate instruction for those children needing extra support in either writing or thinking about the mathematics.

$$\square \times \triangle = 96$$

There are many different solutions to this <u>open number sentence</u>. Since 96 is <u>even</u>, we know it is <u>divisible</u> by 2.

If $96 \div 2 = 48$, then $\square = 2$ and $\triangle = 48$

If 96 is <u>divisible</u> by 2, it could be <u>divisible</u> by 4.

If $96 \div 4 = 24$, then $\square = 4$ and $\triangle = 24$

We could try a double-digit number like 12.

If $96 \div 12 = 8$, then $\square = 8$ and $\triangle = 12$

We are dividing to find the missing <u>factors</u>. Since division is the opposite of multiplication, it makes sense to divide to help us to multiply.

Parent Communication

I have found over the years that more school-home communication transpires during our study of multiplication than in any other unit. In addition to the parent information form, a rather involved parent newsletter is sent home at the beginning of the unit. (See Figures 5–12 and 5–13.) This newsletter encompasses an overview as well as the mathematical and philosophical grounding of both the multiplication and division units. Each year I tweak and revise the letter, but the message remains the same. I want parents to be aware of my focus on the conceptual understanding of both operations and I ask for their support. I included two articles with the newsletter: one by Susan Jo Russell (2002) on developing computational fluency with whole numbers and one by Marilyn Burns (2003a) on the partial quotients algorithm for long division. A copy of this newsletter

FIGURE 5–12   ◀

Parent information form for January.

Parent Information and Involvement Form

From: Lainie Schuster
To: Parents of Fourth Graders
Re: Mathematics Curriculum
Month: January

During the next month, the major topic we will be studying is:

- multiplication

My goal in studying this topic is for the students to be able to:

- understand various symbolic representations of multiplication
- develop procedural mastery of single- and double-digit multiplication
- understand multiplication as equal groupings
- review strategies for multiplication fact recall
- apply multiplication models to problem-solving situations
- review and apply the use of parentheses in number sentences

Parents can help at home by:

- reviewing basic multiplication facts *nightly*
- encouraging children to assess the reasonableness of their products and solutions
- encouraging neat and orderly calculations on graph paper
- encouraging children to explain the *why* as well as the *how* as they complete calculations
- encouraging children to choose and explain their own strategies based on the context of the problem and how and why they work

---

is also forwarded to my principal. If she is going to receive phone calls about any math teaching of mine throughout the year, this is usually the time of year and unit in which she receives them! I want to have her on board and to understand my thinking and reasoning for teaching this unit as I do.

Each year I have a few students whose mastery of the basic multiplication facts is just not what it needs to be. I make a phone call to the parents to inform them of the situation and offer suggestions for home review. I also send home copies of game directions and game boards for games we've played in class that reinforce the application of the basic facts. This communication is important. Although we do spend time in class playing games that continue the review the basic facts, parents need to understand that in order for mathematical growth to continue, we need to move on to routines and practices that assume basic fact mastery.

FIGURE 5–13 ▶

Parent newsletter for multiplication unit.

January 23

Dear Parents of the Fourth Grade,

Happy New Year! We have already begun our work with multiplication in the fourth grade. Not only will we be covering the basics of single- and double-digit multiplication, but we will also be looking at inequalities, how parentheses work, beginning work with variables, and solving simple equations. We will then move on to long division and an algorithm that may look foreign to you. The *partial quotients* procedure is quickly becoming the algorithm of choice for many young mathematicians because it makes much more sense to the children. They can see where the numbers come from and are able to use friendlier numbers that are easier to manipulate. Please be assured that work is done with the standard long-division algorithm in the fifth grade when the children are better able to articulate and demonstrate their understanding of what it means to divide.

There will be a quiz every Friday as we move through the times tables. A set of multiplication and division facts will be given for each table. It is very important for the children to see that if they know their multiplication facts, they know their division facts as well. These pesky division facts require the reversibility of thought that is so crucial to pre-algebraic thinking. If $6 \times 8 = 48$, then $48 \div 6$ must be 8 because 8 6s can go into 48. Or what times 6 gives me 48? There are all sorts of methods and strategies for figuring out these division facts. It is very important for your children to make their *own* sense out of all of this. It is very easy for us to correct a child without paying much attention to her reasoning. It is very important that you hear your child's thinking as he is explaining a solution or a procedure to you. Ask for clarifications. Ask for examples. Ask for generalizations. Will this strategy always work? When will it not work? Is it efficient? Can she explain how and why it works?

We will then move on to a unit on long division. We cover only single-digit divisors in the fourth grade. We will spend a great deal of time with word problems and the interpretation of remainders. Remainders happen! Rarely are division problems in our everyday lives neat and clean. When do you throw a remainder away? When is the remainder the solution to the problem? When do you round the quotient up to the next whole number because of the remainder? When do you represent the remainder as a fraction or decimal?

What about teaching your children those little tricks that work so well for you? At this stage of mathematical development, I am almost more concerned with a child's understanding of how multiplication and division *work* than with correct solutions. When do you use multiplication? When do you use division? How is multiplication the inverse of division? Research supports that once conceptual understanding has been constructed by the child himself, calculation strategies and algorithms are then more easily developed and mastered.

Equipping students with quick tricks might given them the edge in mathematical competitions, but we fear it will also give them a misleading impression of the nature of mathematics and may even hinder their progress in subsequent

FIGURE 5–13   ◀

**Parent newsletter for
multiplication unit,
continued.**

courses. Mathematics is not a bag of tricks or even a list of formulas. It is a way of thinking, a thought process that we seek to cultivate in our students, no matter what their age. (Scavo and Conroy, "Conceptual Understanding and Computational Skill in School Mathematics," *Mathematics Teaching in the Middle School*, March–April 1996.)

I have attached two articles, including "Developing Computational Fluency with Whole Numbers." It articulates so well my concern with the necessity of conceptual development as well as procedural efficiency and proficiency as we work to develop mathematical thinkers. I have also included a piece written by Marilyn Burns about the beauty of the partial quotients algorithm for long division. Try this! It makes so much sense of the procedure. Keeping the dividend "whole" allows the children to focus on the concept of what it means to divide.

As always, I thank you for your continued support. If you have any concerns or comments as we move through these units, please do not hesitate to call. I love to talk math!

Conceptually yours,

Lainie Schuster

Lainie Schuster

Assessment

Just as well-designed lessons can provide us with valuable information about how our children think, reason, and calculate within the mathematical context of multiplication, well-designed assessments can inform us of the same. Assessment needs to inform teaching and support learning.

A question you must consider throughout the teaching and learning of multiplication is What do understanding and proficiency look like? Although it may look a little different in my classroom than yours, it continues to be important for each of us to be able to identify the essential understandings and proficiencies that our unit of study requires. It is equally important that we make those goals and expectations clear to our students. When we complete our initial *Checking for Multiplication Understanding* task at the beginning of the unit, I inform the children that they will be seeing similar prompts throughout the unit because I am interested in following the progression and application of their thinking, reasoning, and calculating. By this time in the year, journal writes have become important assessment tools. The children are well aware of the importance I place on thorough completion of journal responses and how I use them to assess their learning as well as my teaching.

Weekly multiplication-table quizzes are part of my assessment routine throughout this unit. Quizzes do not have to be standard fare, however. As with good problem-solving tasks, paper-and-pencil assessments can and should be mathematically meaningful and purposeful. Opening up a basic open number sentence, such as $6 \times 4 =$, can shift the assessment from one of isolated recall to one of reasoning. You may find some of the following suggestions helpful as you design multiplication-table assessments:

Include both the multiplication and related division facts:

$3 \times 5 = \square$ $15 \div 5 = \square$

$7 \times 3 = \square$ $21 \div 3 = \square$

$3 \times 9 = \square$ $27 \div 3 = \square$

Present the multiplication and division in a different representation than the week before:

$4 * 7 = \square$ $28/7 = \square$

$8 * 4 = \square$ $32/4 = \square$

$4 * 3 = \square$ $12/4 = \square$

Place the product or quotient on the left side of the equation:

$\square = 5 \times 9$ $\square = 45 \div 9$

$\square = 8 \times 5$ $\square = 40 \div 5$

$\square = 6 \times 5$ $\square = 30 \div 6$

Ask for an unknown factor, divisor, or dividend:

$7 \cdot \square = 42$ $42/\square = 7$

$\square \cdot 9 = 54$ $54/\square = 9$

$6 \cdot \square = 36$ $\square/6 = 6$

Pose an open-ended story problem task at the close of the quiz:

Write and solve a story problem with a product of 48.

Write a story problem with a factor of 9.

I give a unit exam at the end of my multiplication unit that follows the same protocol presented in the geometry unit. I carefully prepare a study sheet and distribute it to the children about one week before the exam. The sheet includes sample and practice problems as well as sample writing prompts. (See Figure 5–14.) Following the return of corrected exams, each child once again completes a test reflection. The completed tests and test reflections are filed in students' math portfolios.

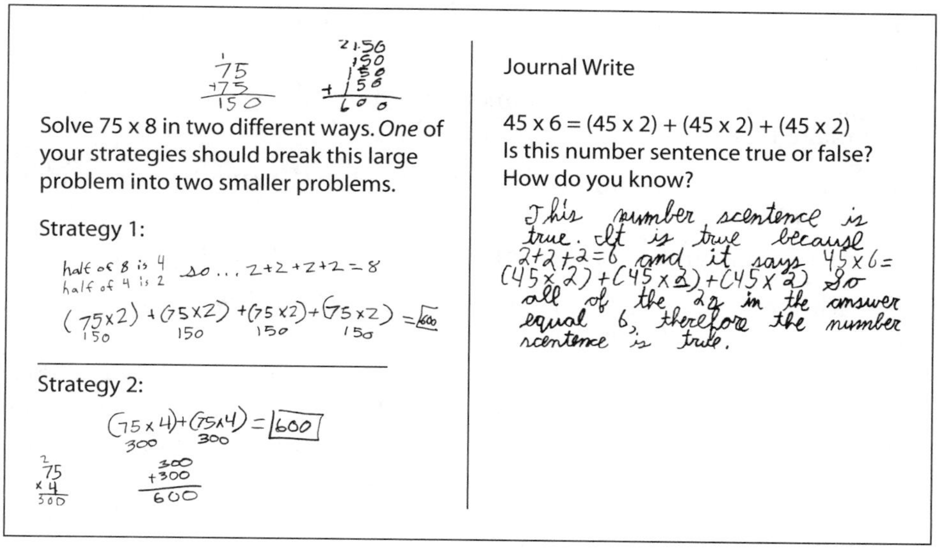

Solve 75 x 8 in two different ways. *One of your strategies should break this large problem into two smaller problems.*

Strategy 1:

half of 8 is 4
half of 4 is 2   so... 2+2+2+2 = 8

(75×2) + (75×2) + (75×2) + (75×2) = 600
  150   150   150   150

Strategy 2:

(75×4) + (75×4) = 600
  300   300

Journal Write

45 x 6 = (45 x 2) + (45 x 2) + (45 x 2)
Is this number sentence true or false?
How do you know?

This number sentence is true. It is true because 2+2+2=6 and it says 45×6= (45×2)+(45×2)+(45×2) so all of the 2s in the answer equal 6, therefore the number sentence is true.

FIGURE 5-14 ◄

Sample multiplication test items.

Fosnot and Dolk warn us about teaching directly to the standardized tests, which continues to be a concern in classrooms across the country:

> If we teach directly to standardized achievement tests, we may end up with children who can pass them but who know little mathematics. If we want to encourage mathematizing and the development of number relationships, we need to teach in a way that supports it. (2001a, 142)

Research is beginning to demonstrate, in fact, that if children are taught and assessed in ways that allow them to construct understanding and to make sense of the presented mathematics themselves, they perform better, even on standardized tests.

Resources

Math Matters (Chapin and Johnson 2006)—Chapter 2, "Computation" and Chapter 4, "Multiplication and Division"
Excellent descriptions of the mathematical properties and how they relate to multiplication.

About Teaching Mathematics (Burns 2007)
The "Multiplication" chapter offers activities rich in multiplicative reasoning and problem solving. Activities can be completed independently or in a menu format.

Teaching Arithmetic: Lessons for Introducing Multiplication (Burns 2001b)
Although recommended for younger children, activities can be easily adjusted to meet the needs of fourth graders—especially those who have not explored some of these tasks and concepts in the third grade.

Teaching Arithmetic: Lessons for Extending Multiplication (Wickett and Burns 2001)

Activities, student vignettes, assessment recommendations, and superb narration make this a must-have resource.

Hot Topics in Math: Multiplication and Division (Greenes, Dacey, and Spungin 2001b)

Creative and engaging problem-solving tasks in worksheet format.

Young Mathematicians at Work: Constructing Multiplication and Division (Fosnot and Dolk 2001a)

An overview of how children construct meaning and understanding within the contexts of multiplication and division. Includes student vignettes and excellent narration of topics such as the big ideas of multiplication, algorithms, mathematical models, and assessment.

Chapter 6

February

DIVISION

[Children's] formal instruction with division should begin with problem situations for them to solve. The situations can then be related to the standard symbolic representations. Also, children's understanding of division becomes more powerful when they begin to see the connection between sharing and grouping and between division and the other operations.

About Teaching Mathematics
Burns 2007, 245

The Learning Environment

Provide opportunities for children to identify and articulate connections between concepts, skills, and procedures.

Many fourth graders continue to perceive multiplication and division as isolated operations. We need to be deliberate with our instruction and facilitation of mathematical conversation as we help students uncover and make sense of connections between operations. Questions such as the following can help students connect what they already know to that which they are learning:

- How is this like . . . ?
- Where have we seen this before?
- How can you compare this with . . . ?
- How can knowing this help you understand . . . ?

Understanding is acquired and internalized when we can articulate how something is related or connected to other things that we know. According to Fosnot and Dolk (2001a), the connections children need to make between multiplication and division are not automatic. Carefully constructed problems and deliberate instruction can help make these connections visible and accessible to our students.

Continue to develop, apply, and strengthen talk moves.

By this time in the school year, students and teachers alike should be actively engaged in and committed to mathematical talk moves that support mathematical thinking and learning. Mathematical talk practices (see Chapter 2, page 27) can be used to assist and support students as they make connections between what they already know and what is being presented or explored. As connections are made, important mathematical ideas and generalizations are constructed that will become a foundation for their thinking about division.

The Mathematics and Its Language

Children continue to develop conceptual understanding of division.

Children's work with division should build upon their work with multiplication. Connections made between the two operations will help children uncover and build personal understandings of how and why division works.

By this time in the year, fourth graders are better able to recognize two types of division situations—those that require *sharing* as well as those that require *grouping*. The number sentence $20 \div 5 = 4$ can be modeled with both situations. Sharing contexts are those with which most children are familiar: *I have 20 jelly beans and 5 bags. How many jelly beans are in each bag?* The children are asked to *share* the twenty jelly beans among the five bags. A grouping context asks the children to take out *groups* of five from those same twenty jelly beans: *I have 20 jelly beans. Five jelly beans will be placed in each bag. How many bags of jelly beans can I make?* It is important for students to make sense of both situations and realize that both situations can be represented by the same number model. Mindfully scaffolded class conversations and problem-solving opportunities will help students differentiate between and think flexibly about these two division situations.

Children represent division symbolically in four ways:

$$20 \div 5 = 4 \qquad 20/5 = 4 \qquad 5\overline{)20}^{\;4} \qquad \frac{20}{5} = 4$$

Children can have difficulties reading and interpreting division number sentences. Because commutativity is not applicable to division ($a \div b \neq b \div a$), the order of the divisor and dividend does indeed matter in a division problem. Asking students to investigate the commutative property and whether it applies to division will help children assess the importance of reading a division number sentence. Offering students opportunities to see division problems in all four representations will strengthen the fluency of their mathematical reading and interpretation skills within a division context.

Children explore and articulate relationships among divisors, multiples, factors, and quotients.

As with the language of multiplication, the language of division becomes increasingly important as children continue to gain mathematical maturity. Identifying, discussing, and writing about *divisors*, *dividends*, *quotients*, *multiples*, and *factors* allows children to develop the language of division as they label, describe, and compare the components of a problem within a division context.

Children choose and carry out efficient computational strategies based on the task and the particular numbers involved.

It is helpful for children to have several options for completing division computations accurately and efficiently. It is important for children to use logical reasoning, their understanding of number, and mathematical properties to construct procedures to solve division problems. To do so, children also need to become proficient at dividing by ten and multiples of ten as well as manipulating their basic multiplication and division facts. Alternative and standard algorithms can be presented once children have had the opportunity to develop and investigate personal computational strategies.

TEACHER-TO-TEACHER TALK   I need to make a personal disclaimer here about algorithms, even though this section is more related to calculation routines and practices. I do not teach nor offer opportunities to investigate the traditional long-division algorithm in the fourth grade. I inform the parents early on in the unit of this practice in my parent newsletter as well as on the parent information form (see "Parent Communication" on page 219). The decision is deliberate, well thought out, based on wisdom gained through years of teaching fourth graders and observing the frustration that learning an algorithm based on a series of steps, rather than on understanding, can elicit. I have chosen to introduce only the partial quotients algorithm (see "Calculation Routines and Practices" on page 213) to my class once students have had experiences developing personal division strategies. Because the partial quotients algorithm is grounded in the conceptual understandings of division, the procedure is adopted quickly and enthusiastically by the children and they can make sense of how and why it works.

Children represent remainders in different ways, choosing a representation based on the context of the problem being solved.

Remainders happen! When students solve problems grounded in a meaningful context, remainders will be treated sensibly. If there are twenty-six children in a class and four children can be seated at a table, *seven* tables will be needed even though one table will not have four children. If Hayden has $26 in her pocketbook to buy pens at $4 each, she will be able to buy only *six* pens. Fourth graders need to encounter many problems in which the context affects the treatment of the remainder differently.

Children create and solve story problems based on division models.

Creating and solving division story problems gives students the opportunity to apply their understanding of division contexts. Children will be asked to apply not only their procedural understandings and proficiencies but their conceptual knowledge as well.

Investigations and Literature-Based Activities

Checking for Division Understanding

Duration: 2 class periods

This lesson sets the stage for work with division and gives students the opportunity to think about division. Because this task is similar to that given in the multiplication unit, it, too, can serve as an assessment model throughout the entire unit. The information gathered from these assessments can help guide, direct, and differentiate instruction. This lesson offers students the opportunity to:

- think about the meaning of division
- articulate understandings of what it means to divide
- make connections between division and multiplication
- represent division in pictures, drawings, numbers, and words

Materials
- several blank overhead transparencies
- 2–3 sheets of chart paper

This lesson is introduced in much the same way that *Checking for Multiplication Understanding* was introduced. The students will be accustomed to the format and will settle in quite quickly with the task. I begin by writing the problem $24 \div 6 =$ on the board. I ask the children to represent their thinking in pictures, symbols, and words as they solve the problem individually. I also ask the children to write a story problem that fits the number model at the bottom of their paper.

Strategies that demonstrate sound conceptual knowledge may include but are not limited to the following:

Showing division as the inverse of multiplication:

$24 \div 6 = \square$ *can be solved by asking* $6 \times \square = 24$

Showing division with a grouping representation—either six groups of four . . .

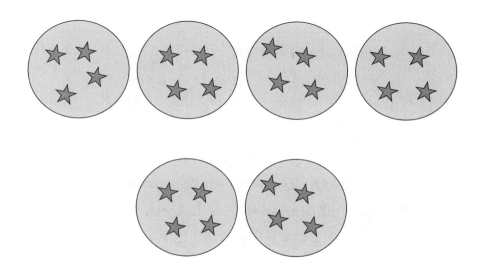

or six in each of four groups:

As you assess students' responses, keep in mind the number model, the grouping representation, and the story problem—are they all the same representations of 24 ÷ 6?

If you notice a discrepancy between representations, have an informal conversation with the child, or a small group of children, to draw out valuable insights. Do not be surprised if a discrepancy shows itself in a majority of your children's work—I see it every year in just about every child's paper! (See Figure 6–1 for a couple of examples.) As with all good assessments, the results of this task can help you develop and direct future instruction. When having conversations with children, it is helpful to keep your responses in question form.

- What does this number stand for?
- Where is this number in your drawing?
- Where is this number in your story problem?
- Could your story problem be represented with another number model? Are those number models the same or different? How do you know that?

I do not suggest that children make any corrections to their work. I want to listen to and assess what they know, what they think they know, and what they do not seem to know about division at this point in the unit.

FIGURE 6–1 ▶

Story problems misrepresenting 24 ÷ 6.

Write a story problem for 24 ÷ 6 = ④.

6 groups of 4 candy bars. Matt had He ate 3 groups, now he has 3 groups left and 12 candy bars

Write a story problem for 24 ÷ 6 = ☐.

I brought 26 donuts to school for my birthday. I gave out 6 before recess. How many donuts do I have now?

Indicating an understanding of the noncommutativity of division:

$$24 \div 6 \neq 6 \div 24$$

Showing division as repeated subtraction:

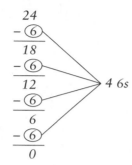

Using number sense and reasoning particular to the given numbers:

If 12 is half of 24, then 12 has two groups of 6. Therefore, 2 groups of 12 would have 4 groups of 6.

Making a real-world connection:

24 points in a football game can be divided into 4 touchdowns worth 6 points each with no extra points.

Writing story problems can be problematic for some students. Writing division story problems requires a beginning understanding of what it means to divide. Even though our students have been introduced to division in the third grade, understandings may be fragile. As the unit progresses, I expect that the students' story problems will increase in clarity and representational accuracy.

Before calling the class together to share ideas and strategies about division, I collect all the papers and take the time to look over each one. I choose several papers to copy on transparencies for the next day's lesson. I have found that reading story problems out loud is not as effective as reading the story problem with the aid of a written copy for all of the children to follow. The public sharing of children's work can be tricky. Some children are flattered, some are embarrassed, and for those children whose work is not shared, their feelings can be hurt. Because I carry out this assessment several times throughout the unit, I inform the children that they will all have a chance to share their work publicly *if* they wish to. I speak to those children whose work I want to share before each lesson and ask for their permission to do so. For this part of the lesson, I choose story problems that are representations of both sharing and grouping models of division that are clear and concise in their wording and representation of the division. Although I do not label sharing and grouping strategies as such, we do compare and contrast the language and processes of solving both types of problems. Figure 6–2 contains two story problems I chose to share with the class.

FIGURE 6–2   ▶

Sarah's sharing story
problem and Nolan's
grouping story problem.

Write a story problem for $24 \div 6 = \square$.

There are 24 marbels in all. I want to share them with 6 people (Including me). How many marbles did each person get?

A kid had 24 baseballs. He made groups up of 6 balls each. How many groups did he have?

I call the class together at the beginning of the second day's lesson to share strategies and story problems. The chart paper is up and the children are ready to share. Once again, I write $24 \div 6 = \square$ on the board and ask, "Who would like to share your strategy?" I record each volunteer's strategy on the chart paper, labeling it with the mathematician's name for future reference. We can compare, contrast, revise, or add on to strategies as we move through the representations.

Before story problems are shared, we take the time to discuss the importance of story problems in mathematics. Because the children have had frequent experiences throughout the year writing and solving story problems, they are very familiar with these tasks. It is at this point in the year that I begin to have conversations with the children about what I can learn about them as mathematicians through the writing and solving of story problems. I begin the ongoing conversations about multiple representations and how they help us develop mathematical understanding. Knowing that $24 \div 6 = 4$ is no longer enough. I now want to see that knowledge represented accurately in students' drawings and story problems. I want the children to make sense of this knowledge—in other words, to demonstrate their understanding of it. I inform the children that one number model is not enough to prove that they understand a problem or procedure. As they develop as mathematicians, they will need to offer mathematical proof of their understanding. The importance of making sense of the mathematics is made clear to the children as we once again revisit and reestablish standards and expectations.

Then I place a story problem on the overhead and ask the author to address the class as she reads the story problem out loud. If the comprehension of the story is not affected by a misspelled word or omitted punctuation, I try to stay away from a discussion of the mechanics of the author's writing because the focus needs to remain on the mathematics. The numbers and what they represent are identified within the context of each problem as is the original number sentence and how the story is a model of it.

As with the multiplication version of this lesson, this activity should be revisited several times within the unit to assess the progress and growth of each child's thinking and representation of division. Have fun with the numbers and the contexts of the problems. As the unit progresses, you may want to choose numbers that align with lesson objectives, such as divisors and dividends that result in quotients with remainders. You may wish to choose number models with double-digit divisors or triple-digit dividends. You may wish to pull student-generated nouns out of a hat and have everyone write story problems using those topics. Or you may wish to choose a context relevant to the goings-on of a class or school activity. My class greatly enjoys generating nouns from our current read-aloud book. When we began reading *Once Upon a Marigold* (Ferris 2002), the children generated a list of items for their story problems that could be found in Ed's cave. You will need to pay increased attention to children's ability to represent their number model with a mathematically relevant story as the unit progresses. Assessing the matchup of the numbers, contexts, and representations becomes increasingly important as understanding of division develops.

Follow-Up Journal Write

Patrick shared his favorite marbles with Tarun, Ryan, and Adam at recess. Each friend was given the same number of marbles. When Patrick got home from school, he found 7 marbles left in his pocket. How many marbles could each friend have received? How many marbles could Patrick have brought to school that day? How do you know your numbers make sense? (See Figure 6–3.)

TEACHER-TO-TEACHER TALK   Many colleagues and parents ask me what is the most difficult unit to teach in the fourth grade. I always respond with the same unit: division. I can do the math. But thinking about the math and about how to encourage and support my class to think deeply about it remain a challenge even after many years of teaching. Division is not intuitive or automatic. Jared could identify division as the inverse of multiplication, and he asked if that meant you took groups apart in division since you put them together in multiplication. Jared could also do the math. But I realized that Jared's mental picture of the math was fragile. He was trying to use what he knew about multiplication to understand division. He was getting there. But he needed more opportunities within meaningful contexts to make better sense of the math, to create stronger mental pictures of division contexts, to create, solve, and represent division story problems, and to talk about division and why and how it works. Yes, division is about groups; we ask how many groups of nine can be made from thirty-six candies or how many candies are in each group if we know there are nine groups. We ask our children to consider the whole, the number of groups that can be made from that whole, and the number in each group, keeping all of the information straight and all at the same time. No wonder division is difficult! It is a challenge to slow down our teaching when all that we feel is the pressure to speed it up. Our charge is to find and implement mathematically rich problems and tasks that require deep thinking about division. We need to listen to what our children are saying and read what they write. We need to hear what they understand and identify what they do not. We will not be able to do it all in the fourth grade. But we do need to make our fourth graders' time with us meaningful as they think, explain, justify, and demonstrate their conceptual and procedural understanding of division.

FIGURE 6–3   ▶

Kira's journal response.

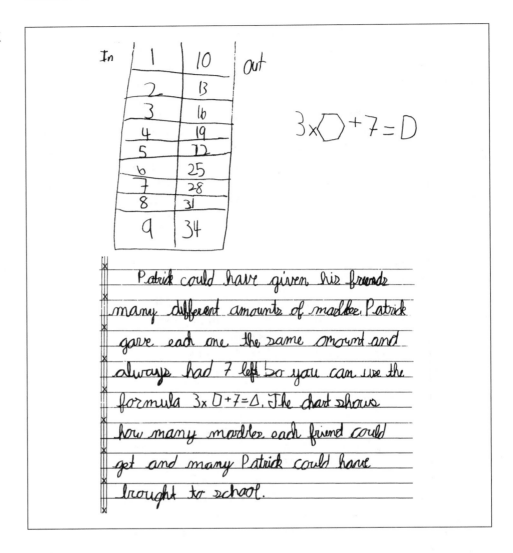

FIGURE 6–3   ▶

Kira's journal response.

Silent Division

Duration: 1–2 class periods, followed by shorter explorations several times a week

This lesson, adapted from *Teaching Arithmetic: Lessons for Extending Division, Grades 4–5* (Wickett and Burns 2003), exposes patterns of quotients when either the divisor or the dividend is changed in a related string of division number sentences. This lesson follows the same format as *Silent Multiplication* (see page 149). This lesson offers students opportunities to:

- explore and apply the language of division—*divisor*, *dividend*, and *quotient*—as patterns are identified and articulated

- develop strategies for solving increasingly complex problems by using what they know about simpler, related problems

- practice computational skills
- assess the reasonableness of answers
- develop and apply number sense in a division context

Materials

- optional: 1 piece of chart paper

If you are not familiar with the *Silent Multiplication* format, it may be helpful to review that lesson. The format and instructional routines of *Silent Multiplication* and *Silent Division* are similar. The beauty of both lessons is their adaptability. Initial lessons can focus on just one idea or procedure at a time, and later lessons can combine more complex ideas. The relationships and patterns presented and discussed in *Silent Division* may initially appear counterintuitive to the children, which is one more reason to incorporate both *Silent Multiplication* and *Silent Division* into a fourth-grade curriculum.

To begin this series of lessons, discuss with your students the rules for a silent lesson. Choose an initial problem that all children can solve to engage the group quickly. For example, your first problem could be:

$$8 \div 4$$

When the students have agreed on the answer, add another problem below the first one.

$$8 \div 4 = 2$$

$$80 \div 4$$

When you're processing these problems, take the time to discuss the terms *dividend*, *divisor*, and *quotient*. It may be helpful to label and display the components of a division problem on chart paper for the remainder of the unit. For example:

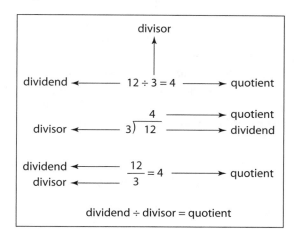

The next string of problems can continue to explore the effects of multiplying the dividend by ten while the divisor stays the same.

$$8 \div 2$$

$$80 \div 2$$

$$800 \div 2$$

$$8,000 \div 2$$

The process of editing, refining, and applying generalizations is hard work. The language of division is not easily accessible to many fourth graders. Because of this, I often ask the children to put their generalizations on paper after an initial discussion of the relationship(s) identified in a string of problems. Asking the children to work in pairs as they edit and revise their generalizations will help them fine-tune the language of their observations. As generalizations are shared, I write them on the board or chart paper. Children may wish to reference previous generalizations as they work to make sense of those that follow.

The next string of problems can build off the progression from the first string. For example, introduce a string of problems in which the dividend stays the same and the divisor is multiplied by ten from one problem to the next. I begin the string with the same pattern as the first string.

$$4 \div 4 = 1$$

$$40 \div 4 = 10$$

$$400 \div 4 = 100$$

$$4,000 \div 4 = 1,000$$

$$4,000 \div 40 = 100$$

$$4,000 \div 400 = 10$$

$$4,000 \div 4,000 = 1$$

As you move through the string, you may find students less confident and less willing to post quotients even though a predictable pattern is evident. The children are now being asked to manipulate both multiplication by ten and division by ten within the same problem. Once the discussion is opened, writing out the changes in each problem will support students' thinking about the calculation required by the string.

$$4 \div 4 = 1$$

$$40 \div 4 = 10 \quad (dividend \times 10) \div same\ divisor = (quotient \times 10)$$

$$400 \div 4 = 100 \quad (dividend \times 10) \div same\ divisor = (quotient \times 10)$$

$$4,000 \div 4 = 1,000 \quad (dividend \times 10) \div same\ divisor = (quotient \times 10)$$

$$4,000 \div 40 = 100 \quad dividend \div (divisor \times 10) = (quotient \div 10)$$

Craig could hardly contain himself when he noticed that the number of zeros in both the divisor and quotient added up to the number of zeros in the dividend. Although this is an important observation, it is equally important to discuss why this is so. Ask the children what they know about the relationship between multiplication and division to direct the conversation. Knowing that one is the inverse of the other will help the children begin to make sense of the inverse pattern of divisors and quotients.

As consensus begins to build about why the quotients decrease as the divisors increase, I ask the children to write down their generalizations once again with partners. Craig was especially proud of his work (see Figure 6–4.).

Initially, Craig was fine with just counting zeros. Persistence and mathematical curiosity, however, pushed him to move beyond the act of counting zeros to understanding why the number of zeros needed to be balanced between the problem's components. Craig said it best: when all is said and done, "the math still needs to work."

Silent Division can be revisited several times a week during this month of study. Even though children may be able to identify patterns more easily as they gain practice with the routine, the language and symbolic representation of what is happening may continue to be elusive for some. Strings of four or five problems will conserve precious class time yet continue to offer opportunities for the children to think about patterns in division.

The following series of problems could be used as you move through this unit of study. It is important to vary the representation of the division so that your students will become familiar and comfortable with all representations. Initially, it is easier for children to find patterns when the $\div$ symbol is used because the quotients are arranged in a list. As students become more comfortable with the activity, incorporate fractional notation as well as the / and $\overline{)\ }$.

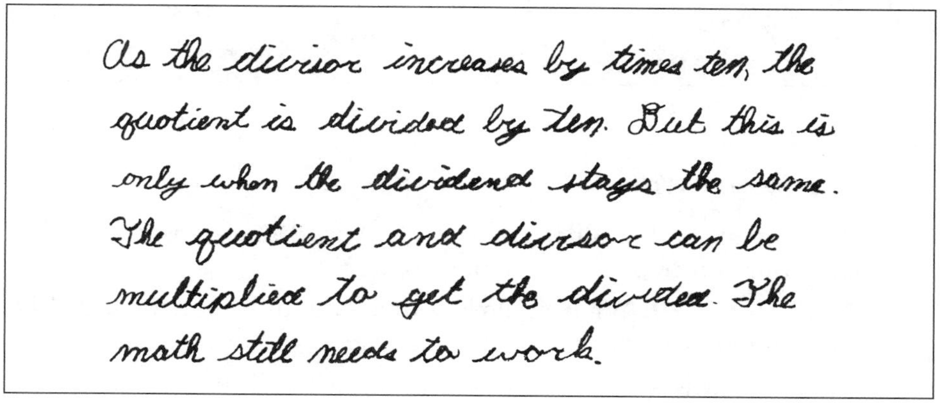

As the divisor increases by times ten, the quotient is divided by ten. But this is only when the dividend stays the same. The quotient and divisor can be multiplied to get the dividend. The math still needs to work.

FIGURE 6–4 ◀

Craig's division writing.

Multiplying the Dividend by Ten		Multiplying the Divisor by Ten
8/8 =	40/40 =	2,000 ÷ 2 =
80/8 =	400/40 =	2,000 ÷ 20 =
800/8 =	4,000/40 =	2,000 ÷ 200 =
8,000/8 =	40,000/40 =	2,000 ÷ 2,000 =

Multiplying the Dividend by Two	Multiply the Dividend by Ten and Doubling the Divisor
$\dfrac{20}{4} =$	48/8 =
$\dfrac{40}{4} =$	480/8 =
$\dfrac{80}{4} =$	480/16 =
$\dfrac{160}{4} =$	480/32 =

For more information on the *Silent Division* lesson, see *Teaching Arithmetic: Lessons for Extending Division* (Wickett and Burns 2003).

> **TEACHER-TO-TEACHER TALK**   My first initial strings of *Silent Division* are always a little messy. The children are often confused. The language I am asking them to use is new and not easily accessible. And writing generalizations can be a challenge. And then there's the math itself. But I am well aware of what lies ahead and more than willing to persevere. Dividing and multiplying by multiples of ten scaffold the understanding as well as the procedural proficiency of the partial quotients algorithm for long division. Making deliberate references to *Silent Division* (as well as *Target 300* and the chunking method of multiplication) as we work through the long-division procedure helps bring meaning to the process. Long division is no longer approached as a series of steps but rather as a string of problems that illustrate the relationship between and magnitude of the dividend and the divisor—all lessons learned from *Silent Division*!

Follow-Up Journal Write

- My quotient is 40. What could my dividend and divisor be? Why does your choice of numbers make sense?
- My divisor is 40. What could my dividend and quotient be? Why does your choice of numbers make sense?
- My dividend is 40. What could my divisor and quotient be? Why does your choice of numbers make sense?

Marshmallow Snowmen

Duration: 2–3 class periods

I adapted this lesson from one shared with me by Jamie Ramsdell, a colleague and wonderful friend. Children make snowmen out of marshmallows and gumdrops as they explore and devise personal strategies for division. This lesson offers students the opportunity to:

- explore division with single- and double-digit divisors with edible manipulatives
- reinforce the connection between multiplication and division
- practice estimation routines
- collect and represent data

Materials

- 1 10.5-ounce bag of miniature marshmallows (3 marshmallows per student)
- 1 13-ounce bag of gumdrops (1 gumdrop per student)
- 1 toothpick per student
- 1 *Questions for Snowmen* worksheet per student (see Blackline Masters)
- 1 sheet of 12-by-18-inch newsprint per pair of students
- 1 glue stick per pair of students
- 1 set of colored pencils or markers per pair of students
- 2 large paper plates or bowls per group of students
- 4 sheets of chart paper, each headed with one of the questions from the *Questions for Snowmen* worksheet
- optional: zip-top storage bags

February in New England can be cold and dreary. However, the activity of building marshmallow snowmen in math class adds a little excitement. This lesson sets up a context within which students can begin to create and manipulate strategies for multidigit division. Pairs of students will construct posters containing story problems and their solutions. When you conduct this investigation with your class, you may need to adjust your numbers and questions according to the data collected from and with your class. I also suggest playing around with the mathematics of the lesson prior to presenting it. Being able to quickly assess the reasonableness of students' solutions will help you move around to the groups who most need your assistance and direction.

Begin the lesson by showing the class a bag of marshmallows and a bag of gumdrops. Inform the children that they'll be making marshmallow snowmen. Explain that each snowman should be made with three marshmallows and one gumdrop hat, all held together with one tooth-pick. Demonstrate how to build a snowman for the class.

Then introduce the mathematical task to the class while handing out the *Questions for Snowmen* worksheets and newsprint. Ask each pair to fold its newsprint into fourths. They should solve one question from the worksheet in each quadrant of their poster. Review the expectations for completing the poster—each story problem will be represented by:

- an estimate,
- a number model,
- a calculation,
- a solution written in sentence form,
- a written explanation supporting the pair's choice of calculation strategy, and
- an illustration.

The story problems can be cut out and glued to the newsprint. Although the children are encouraged to illustrate their story problems, their first priority is to work through the mathematics of each problem. Illustrations can be added with colored pencils or markers once the mathematical and writing requirements of all the story problems are completed. (Cutout paper snowflakes make wonderful embellishments!)

I ask the children to read the story problems silently. As a whole class, we begin to discuss what we know, what we need to know, and how we can proceed with a bag of marshmallows and a bag of gumdrops. On the board, I create a class chart to keep track of what we know, think we know, and need to find out.

I know …	I think I know …	I need to find out …
Each snowman will have 3 marshmallows and 1 gumdrop.	There are more marshmallows in a bag than gumdrops.	How many marshmallows are in one bag?
We need three times more marshmallows than gumdrops because we need three marshmallows for each snowman, but only one gumdrop.	We will have to use division somewhere!	How many snowmen can be made from one bag of marshmallows?
		How many gumdrops are in one bag?
		Will there be enough gumdrop hats for all the snowmen that we can make from a bag of marshmallows?

We agree, as a class, that the number of marshmallows in the bag needs to be counted as well as the number of gumdrops. We also agree that once snowmen are made, they will not be eaten until the end of class. We agree, with some not-so-subtle guidance on my part, that each child can eat one snowman at the end of the lesson. The remaining snowmen can be sent home in zip-top storage bags at the end of the day. Before I open the bags of marshmallows and gumdrops and distribute them as well as toothpicks to each table group on paper plates, we also decide on how best to collect and organize the counts of marshmallows and gumdrops. By this time in the year, the children are accustomed to collecting data with a T-chart and it is often the preferred data-collection format. I write a T-chart on the board with the names of the children on one side and their marshmallow counts on the other. I make another T-chart for the gumdrops.

Marshmallows

Pair	Count
Emma and Hayden	32
Nick and Brad	26
Jared and Sarah	40
.	.
.	.
.	.
Total	352

Some pairs count marshmallows and others count gumdrops. Totals of both can then be calculated and the exploration can continue.

Creating a number bank on the board can remind students of the numbers needed for the exploration. We agree as a class what numbers and labels need to be included in the number bank:

Number Bank

25 = number of children in the class

352 = number of marshmallows in a bag

113 = number of gumdrops in a bag

3 = number of marshmallows in a snowman

1 = number of gumdrops per snowman

Once we agree that all the necessary numerical information has been collected and presented, the pairs begin to solve the story problems, paying close attention to what needs to be included on the poster when solving each problem.

Because a few instructional decisions will need to be made before you pull the class together to process, take inventory of the strategies the children are applying as well as their solutions as you move among the pairings. Are their strategies for Problems 2 and 3, in particular, varied or are there two or three strategies that seem to be favored by most groups? Do the solutions to Problems 2 and 3 cluster around one number, or do they represent a wider range? Are the children decomposing either the dividend or the divisor? Are the children using friendly multiplications or divisions? Are they multiplying or dividing by multiples of ten or doubling or halving? How are other operations applied in order to divide? How are the children keeping track of their work? Having this information available will help you direct the conversation and instruction. You may want to directly address symbolic misrepresentations (e.g., $75 \div 352$ instead of $352 \div 75$) or language misuse if you notice significant demonstrations of such. Students may ask whether they are looking for *groups of 75* or *75 groups*; if they don't, you might want to pose these questions! You might also want to scaffold part of the discussion in order to help the children make connections between similar strategies.

TEACHER-TO-TEACHER TALK   I call this "The Story of Jason," and we all have a similar story to tell. Jason did not like to solve problems. He did not like to share his thinking. And he did not like to work with his classmates. What he did like to do was compute with paper and pencil, following a memorized procedure. I hesitate to call these procedures learned, because there was little learning involved in his mastery. As the year progressed, I found out that Jason did "nightly math" with his parents at the kitchen table. He did his assigned homework first. Mom and Dad then proceeded to teach him the "right" way to do math. I didn't put all the pieces together until the day he wanted to share the traditional division algorithm with the class. "My dad taught me the right way," Jason announced to the class. "We do math every night and he shows me stuff."

Although I applauded Jason's dad for being so engaged in Jason's mathematical education, he was unable to see the effect this teaching by telling was having on Jason's in-class work and his conceptual development. Jason was losing ground fast in class. He was not able to keep up with the pace of the class and was having difficulties making connections between ideas and procedures. Jason was between a rock and a hard place. Was I right? Or was his dad right? And for this little boy, there was no gray area—ever.

So, what to do in this type of situation? I called Jason's home and his parents came in for a conference. I explained what I was seeing in class. I also explained the importance of having children make sense of the mathematics for themselves. I explained that yes, there are times for learned algorithms and procedures, but this was not one of them. Jason was having difficulties in class because he was so worried about forgetting the steps of the procedure that he forgot what the procedure was about in the first place. The relationship of the numbers meant nothing to him, but the mantra of *divide, multiply, subtract, and bring down* did. I shared examples of student work as I offered my abridged philosophy of teaching math and what I expected to see and hear from the children in terms of their work and thinking. I also shared *Math for Smarty Pants* (Burns 1982) with them. I openly celebrated their family math time around the kitchen table. I was hopeful that offering Jason's family this resource would help them choose more appropriate math activities that were better aligned with how and why we were thinking about the math in class.

In the end, I do not think Jason's parents stopped presenting procedures entirely, but I do think they were less heavy-handed about it. And they worked through some of the problems in *Math for Smarty Pants* as a family. Jason would occasionally bring in a completed problem and ask to share it with the class. He told me once that they worked on the *Ivan and the Grandmas* problem for three nights. And Jason's dad stopped by after school one day to ask me how I would solve that particular problem because he realized while working through the problem with Jason that there might be many ways to solve it!

We cannot change families like Jason's in one year. But we can begin and continue conversations about the importance of the mathematics we teach. Just as our children need to talk through their ideas and procedures in order to make them their own, there are times when we need to do the same.

Before we begin our class discussion, I ask the children to place their posters on the tabletops so the class can take a gallery walk to view everyone's work. As we begin our walk around the room, I remind the children to look for similarities and differences in strategies and solutions among the varied presentations. When children are aware of each other's work, they are more apt to compare their work with that of another child's as they are sharing.

Processing begins with a discussion about Problem 1: How many marshmallows will be needed for each class member to make one snowman? I capture children's thinking on chart paper as we move through the discussion. The children are accustomed to the routine of sharing strategies by this time in the year and are quick to volunteer. Because we have just completed our unit on multiplication, I do expect to see representations of multiplicative thinking. Volunteers read their solution sentences and number models and explain their strategies.

The discussion accompanying Problems 2 and 3 may take up an entire class session. As children describe their strategies, I record their procedures on the chart paper and label them with the names of the contributing mathematicians. Having posted strategies available will give the class the opportunity to compare and contrast strategies throughout the discussion. Once a strategy is offered, I ask if another pair of children has a similar strategy to share. As with the *Checking for Division Understanding* lesson, you may see examples of common strategies such as successive subtraction or making groups.

Robert and Kira were mathematically savvy and creative. Their number sense was as strong as their ability to connect new material with previously covered concepts and procedures. Everyone in class greatly anticipated their responses. When answering Problem 2, Robert and Kira applied a successive-subtraction strategy. They began with 352 and subtracted groups of 75. According to Robert and Kira, we could make four class sets of snowmen because we could take four 75s from 352. Their thinking was organized and well presented on paper. But they both commented that it would be easy to make mistakes with all that subtraction. Robert and Kira were subtracting in order to divide.

Emma and Vidya thought in terms of money. They knew that two groups of $0.75 would be $1.50. And two $1.50s would be $3.00. It would therefore take four groups of 75 to get to 352. Another group of 75 would put you over 352. According to Emma and Vidya, we could make four class sets of snowmen. Emma and Vidya were doubling and adding in order to divide.

Peter and Evan were determined to make the traditional long-division algorithm work. One of the boys had been shown this procedure at home and shared it with the other. They had difficulties from the get-go trying to determine which number went inside the "division house" (the dividend) and which stayed on the outside (the divisor). Even though they got lost in the process, they managed to come up with a correct answer because of the sense they were able to make out of the numbers. Evan knew that 352 was pretty close to 300. He also knew that two 75s was 150, so they needed four 75s to get to 300. And he knew they couldn't take anymore 75s out of the remaining 52. Peter and Evan eventually discarded the standard algorithm and relied on their number sense in order to divide.

Because of the meaning found in the context of the problems, not one child offered a solution of four remainder fifty-two. The entire class was quite willing to discard the remaining marshmallows from the solution and offer an answer of four. (Well, not exactly . . . all offered to eat the remainders!) I was flummoxed by this total consensus about the remainder. I wrote *4 R52* on the board. I asked the class, "Isn't this a solution to this problem?"

Michael shrugged his shoulders and gave me one of his looks. "That doesn't even make any sense." At this point, I was more than willing to leave this alone. I was delighted that the presence of leftover marshmallows meant little to the children. They acknowledged them but did not see them as influencing the answer to the question.

Question 3 presented a bigger challenge to some students. Given the numbers of my particular class, the children were to determine how many marshmallow snowmen could be made from the remaining fifty-two marshmallows. Robert and Kira's successive subtraction was more difficult now—there was a lot more to subtract in this problem than the last. Peter and Evan had long given up on the traditional long-division algorithm but were unsure how to start. Norah and Jared, however, offered a strategy of counting by groups of ten that many other pairs had carried out as well.

$$
\begin{array}{rl}
52 & \\
-30 & (10 \times 3) \\
\hline
22 & \\
-21 & (7 \times 3) \\
\hline
1 &
\end{array}
$$

17 *groups of 3*

Although Norah and Jared were subtracting out groups of three, their initial grouping of ten threes made the subtraction more manageable. Representing their work in a vertical format also made the remainder visible. But as in the previous problem, Norah and Jared did not concern themselves with the leftover marshmallow.

At some point in the conversation, you may need to ask: "Is there only one answer to these questions? Why or why not?" There is nothing wishy-washy about the answer to this question. We have finite quantities about which specific questions are being asked. We need to continue to acknowledge that there are, however, multiple procedures from which we can attain specific answers. Children, especially those who have had experience solving mathematically rich problems, will begin to identify the structures of problems for which there is one solution and of those for which there are several possible answers.

The lesson winds down with a discussion of Problem 4. When children share their strategies, they may also admit that they prefer using someone else's strategy at this point in the discussion. They may opt for a strategy that makes more sense to them or that is easier to manage. It is important for children to feel comfortable about trading in their strategy for another as they reason through problems. As they become more mathematically proficient, they need to be willing to let go of those ideas and procedures that do not make sense and adopt those that do.

This lesson can set the stage for the introduction of the partial quotients method of long division. Robert and Kira's successive-subtraction strategy offers a written representation similar to that of the partial quotients procedure, so I referred to it when introducing the algorithm. The partial quotients procedure is described in greater detail in the "Calculation Routines and Practices" section on page 213.

Follow-Up Journal Write

Choose a strategy that was presented in class and solve the following problem using that strategy. Explain why you chose this strategy.

$$117/9 = \square$$

Remainders of One

Duration: 3-4 class periods

A Remainder of One, by Elinor J. Pinczes (1995), offers a context within which to explore and discuss patterns of remainders of one up to dividends of twenty-five. This lesson offers students the opportunity to:

- investigate patterns of dividends with recurring remainders of one
- represent patterns with number models
- articulate conjectures and generalizations based on previously identified patterns

Materials

- *A Remainder of One*, by Elinor J. Pinczes
- 1 *Remainders of One* worksheet for each of the divisors two through six per student (see Blackline Masters)
- 1 sheet of newsprint, folded into sixths, per pair of students

Children are drawn to meaningful problems. Many problems in this month-to-month guide have real-life applications or applied contexts. In other words, the children have reason to solve them. Problems that ask children to explore numerical patterns present no worldly context but are equally intriguing and meaningful. It is important for children to have experiences solving these types of problems as well. This lesson exposes students to such problems.

A Remainder of One is the story of soldier Joe, a member of a squadron of twenty-five bug soldiers. The soldiers assemble in various lines to march past their queen—two lines of twelve, three lines of eight, then four lines of six—with Joe standing aside as the remainder of one, much to the chagrin of the queen. It is not until the soldiers march in five lines of five that the queen is pleased—and Joe is no longer the remainder of one.

I begin the lesson with a read-aloud of *A Remainder of One*. If you read *One Hundred Hungry Ants* (Pinczes 1998) while working through the multiplication unit, your children will undoubtedly recognize the author's voice in this book's rhyme. As I read the story, we talk about a squadron and what it means in this particular context. We examine how the squadron divides into equal lines in order to march—with the exception of poor Joe.

I ask, "Why is a squadron of twenty-five problematic?" to begin a class discussion about remainders. Because Michael and Matthew greatly enjoyed their work with the arrays in the *One Hundred Hungry Ants* lesson, they were already ahead of the class in this discussion one year. They announced to the class that there were only two ways the bugs could march without a remainder. The bugs could march in a 1-by-25 line or a 5-by-5 formation. Michael and Matthew also realized that there were many formations (that is, factor pairs) for twenty-four bugs, which was why Joe was always left out. As a class we reviewed all the ways we could make twenty-four with array dimensions:

1 × 24	*24 × 1*
2 × 12	*12 × 2*
3 × 8	*8 × 3*
4 × 6	*6 × 4*

Because of the children's previous work with arrays and multiplication, the discussion moves along quickly.

Next we talk about patterns and their importance in mathematics. There is something intriguing about patterns. I inform the children that they will be looking for patterns of number models with remainders of one.

I distribute *Remainders of One* worksheets to each child. (A template of the worksheet is included in the Blackline Masters. You will need to identify the divisor in the box for each worksheet.) Students work in pairs, but each student must complete the worksheets to document his thinking and work for each divisor. Each pair of children also receives a piece of newsprint folded into sixths. As students complete each divisor investigation, they record number models on the newsprint to aid in the identification of patterns. It can be helpful for the students to view the number models vertically as they work through the investigation. I have begun to offer this suggestion to the children prior to the exploration because of the time that the investigation takes from beginning to end. You can certainly choose to have the children determine their own recording format. For this particular investigation, I want students to spend more time thinking about and recording observations than deciding on a format with which to represent their work. As always, your goals for the lesson should determine your instructional decisions.

I instruct students to investigate the patterns of numbers in which remainders of one occur. The dividends on each worksheet are the same: 1–25. Children are asked to circle the dividends on each sheet that result in a reminder of one when divided by the number in the box at the top of the sheet.

Using the divisor of two as an example, I show the children how to represent the number models of each investigation on their posters:

Divisor of 2	Divisor of 3	Divisor of 4	Divisor of 5	Divisor of 6	Divisor of 7
1/2 = 0 R1					
3/2 = 1 R1					
5/2 = 2 R1					
7/2 = 3 R1					
9/2 = 4 R1					
11/2 = 5 R1					
13/2 = 6 R1					
15/2 = 7 R1					
17/2 = 8 R1					
19/2 = 9 R1					
21/2 = 10 R1					
23/2 = 11 R1					
25/2 = 12 R1					

As we model how to record data for a divisor of two together, I begin to push the students to offer a rule or number sentence that will help them determine what any dividend that will result in a remainder of one might be for that divisor. For example, for the divisor of two, the rule for any dividend could be:

$$Dividend = (multiple\ of\ 2) + 1$$

You can differentiate instruction by asking only certain pairs to represent rules in addition to writing their observations.

Following are some observations your students may make about the patterns in their posters.

Divisor of Two

- The dividends will all be *odd*. Numbers that are divisible by two are even, but in order to have a remainder of one, the dividend has to be one more than an even number, which will always make the dividend an odd number.
- The number model for any dividend with a divisor of two and a remainder of one will be dividend = (multiple of 2) + 1.

Divisor of Three

- The dividends will follow the pattern of *odd-even-odd-even.* . . . The pattern of multiples of three is also *odd-even-odd-even.* When adding one to each of the multiples, the same pattern will occur.
- The number model for any dividend with a divisor of three and a remainder of one will be dividend = (multiple of 3) + 1.

Divisor of Four

- The dividends will be all *odd.* All multiples of four are even because they are also multiples of two. In order to have a remainder of one, the dividend will be one more than an even number, which will always make the dividend an odd number.
- The number model for any dividend with a divisor of four and a remainder of one will be dividend = (multiple of 4) + 1.

Divisor of Five

- The dividends will follow the pattern of *odd-even-odd-even.* . . . The pattern of multiples of five is also *odd-even-odd-even.* When adding one to each of the multiples, the same pattern will occur.
- All dividends end in 1 or 6. All multiples of five have a 0 or a 5 in the ones place. In order to have a remainder of 1, the dividend will need to be one more than a multiple of five. The digit in the ones place will be either (0 + 1) or (5 + 1).
- The number model for any dividend with a divisor of five and a remainder of one will be dividend = (multiple of 5) + 1.

Divisor of Six

- The dividends will be *odd.* All multiples of six are even because they are also multiples of two. In order to have a remainder of one, the dividend will be one more than an even number, which will always make the dividend an odd number.
- The number model for any dividend with a divisor of six and a remainder of one will be dividend = (multiple of 6) + 1.

As a final task for the investigation, the children make conjectures about patterns of dividends with divisors of seven that have a remainder of one. Mathematical proof and reasoning are called upon as I ask all the children to support their conjectures about divisors of seven:

- What conjectures can you make about numbers that are divided by seven and have a remainder of one?
- Why do these conjectures make sense?

I ask the students to base their ideas on what they have already discovered about previous divisors and I do not provide them with a worksheet for this divisor. However, many students construct their own 1–25 grid or create a list of number models, following the same format they used for the divisors two through six. Some children proceed directly to a short listing of number models in which they can apply a previously identified pattern.

Other children initially present a symbolic representation of the pattern of dividends. The previously investigated patterns of dividends repeat between *odd* and *odd-even-odd-even* beginning with a divisor of two and ending with a divisor of six. Given this pattern, the pattern of dividends with a divisor of seven should be *odd-even-odd-even*. I remind those children who proceed directly to the symbolic representation that they will need to support their generalizations with mathematical models and reasoning.

This lesson offers students the opportunity to prove, justify, represent, and communicate patterns found and generalizations made about recurring remainders of one. The arithmetic is not complicated, but understanding how dividends and divisors relate to one another within the constraints of this lesson is.

Remainder Riddles

Duration: 1-2 class periods

Students create riddles based on clues about the divisor and the remainder of a division problem. *Remainder Riddles* can be presented as a follow-up activity to *Remainders of One* (see page 200). The format for this lesson is adapted from *Math and Literature, Grades 4–6* (Bresser 2004). This lesson offers students the opportunity to:

- build understanding of the meaning of remainders
- explore relationships between dividends, divisors, quotients, and remainders
- practice computational skills
- create and solve remainder riddles

Materials

- Remainder Riddle 1 reproduced on an overhead transparency or chart paper (see Blackline Masters)
- 1 copy of directions for *Remainder Riddles* per student (see Blackline Masters)
- optional: Remainder Riddles 2 and 3 reproduced on a transparency or chart paper (see Blackline Masters)

I use the riddle format in math frequently throughout the year. Riddles immediately engage children as well as invite thinking, reasoning, and conversation. And I enjoy creating them and solving them myself! I file away copies of all the riddles I have used for all the various units of the year for future reference and use. I have written many of them. The children have written many of them. Others have been collected from reference materials.

Prior to the lesson, reproduce the clues for Remainder Riddle 1 on an overhead transparency or chart paper. If you write the clues on chart paper, turn up the bottom edge to meet the top edge so that the children cannot see all of the clues at once. I began the lesson by telling the children that I was thinking of a mystery number between one and twenty-five. I explained I would present them with a series of clues that would help them guess my number. I instructed table groups to collaborate to solve the riddle as we worked through the set of clues.

Then I revealed only the first clue *When you divide my number by 1, the remainder is 0.*

"What do you know about my number so far?" I asked. Our work with *A Remainder of One* (Pinczes 1995) helped the children identify the role of the remainder, and they were eager to talk about the implications of this clue. I asked the table groups to decide what they knew from this first clue.

When I called for their attention, the children were convinced that we knew next to nothing from this first clue. Sarah was the first to announce that every number can be divided by one with a remainder of zero, so my mystery number could be any number from one to twenty-five. I asked the class what we should do. Michael said he wanted to see the next clue, so I uncovered it: *When you divide my number by 2, the remainder is 0.*

"Now what do you know?" I asked the class. Most hands went up without the need for table conversation. Once again, students made connections to our work with *A Remainder of One.* According to Nolan, all even numbers could be divided by two, so the mystery number had to be even.

I revealed the third clue: *When you divide my number by 3, the remainder is 1.*

"Now this is getting interesting!" piped up Robert. I asked the table groups to determine what we knew now from all three clues. I began recording assumptions on the board for reference as we moved through the remainder of the clues.

- The number is even.
- The number is not odd.
- The number is one more than a number that can be divided evenly by 3.
- The number cannot be divided evenly by 3.

Introducing the term *divisible* and how it can be used in this context will add yet another word to the children's developing division vocabulary. I asked the children if I could substitute the phrase "This number is not divisible by 3" for "The number cannot be divided evenly by 3." The class agreed. I added *divisible* to the word wall and the no-excuse spelling word list. I also spent a few minutes to identify the root word of *divisible* and the different ways it can be used in a sentence.

> Twenty-five is divisible by 6.
>
> Forty-one is not divisible by 5.
>
> Twenty-one is divisible by both 3 and 7.

The students noticed that the divisors in the clues went in order: one, two, then three. Jared speculated that the next clue would be about a divisor of four, and maybe the next one about a divisor of five. Michael also noticed that these clues were not all about remainders of one.

I presented the remaining clues to the children. I asked table groups to work together to determine my mystery number. I gave each group a sheet of paper on which to keep track of ideas. I reminded the groups to use indoor voices—and not to let the group beside them hear their thinking so as not to give away any of their astute mathematical observations!

After a short time, I called the class back together. I quickly reminded the children before we began the discussion that I did not want to know what the mystery number was yet. What I did want to know, however, was what they could tell me about my number. The class-generated list now looked like the following:

- It is even.
- It is a multiple of 3 + 1.
- It is not divisible by 3, 4, 6, or 7.
- It is divisible by 5.

Robert shared with the class that a number that is divisible by five and is even has to end in zero. I asked the class if we could then say that our mystery number was divisible by ten. Heads nodded. Asking the children why that would make sense helped them verbalize their informal understanding of the divisibility rules of five. I noticed that a few groups had actually written down some multiples of ten on their sheet of paper to help them analyze the other clues.

Our mystery number options were now narrowed down to ten and twenty. "Where do we go from here?" I asked the class. Many children wanted to go through the clues to identify which number fit the clues and which did not. I am always aware of the children who need a visual anchor from which to work while we are having a class discussion, so I suggested to the class that we represent each clue with a number model written on the board. Having these number models as a reference would support the reasoning and thinking of the class as we narrowed down the possibilities of the mystery number. The class decided that it was not necessary to move through every single clue for both possible numbers. Once we found a number sentence that was false, we could discard that number possibility. The list of number models for ten looked like the following:

$10 \div 1 = 10\ R0$ *true*

$10 \div 2 = 5\ R0$ *true*

$10 \div 3 = 3\ R1$ *true*

$10 \div 4 = 2\ R2$ *true*

$10 \div 5 = 2\ R0$ *true*

$10 \div 6 = 1\ R4$ *true*

$10 \div 7 = 1\ R3$ *true*

Once I wrote the last number sentence, the children cheered. Because the students were well acquainted with problems with multiple answers, Jared was leery of assuming that the only correct answer was ten. We followed the same recording format as we went through the clues for twenty.

$20 \div 1 = 20\ R0$ *true*

$20 \div 2 = 10\ R0$ *true*

$20 \div 3 = 3\ R1$ *false!*   ($20 \div 3 = 6\ R2$)

We could stop testing twenty after the third clue because the remainder did not fit the clue. Everyone was satisfied that we had found the one solution to the riddle.

At this point in the lesson, I wanted to draw students' attention to our class-generated list of what we knew about the mystery number. I asked the children how we could have used that list to test twenty without writing down the number models for twenty. Matthew noticed that twenty was divisible by four but our clues told us that the mystery number was not, so the mystery number could not have been twenty. This was an important lesson in itself for the children, reminding them that sometimes we overlook information that can make the mathematics a little easier. We now had proved that twenty could not be our mystery number in two ways.

At this point in the lesson, you will need to determine if your class would benefit from additional whole-group riddle solving (see Remainder Riddles 2 and 3 in the Blackline Masters) or if the students are ready to create remainder riddles for each other to solve on their own. You may wish to have table groups work on Remainder Riddles 2 and 3 and then quickly process the solutions as a whole group.

When you and the children are ready to proceed, distribute the directions for *Remainder Riddles*. Although this activity works well with pairs, I prefer to have the children work independently on their riddles. We do not spend much time working independently in class, and this presents a good opportunity to do so. The most difficult aspect of this task for some children is knowing how to start. For those children, you may want to suggest backward planning. Suggesting that the children first think of a mystery number and then work through writing the clues may help. Remind the children that they are to create riddles with only one answer. The writing of the riddles is only one part of the process, however. Once a riddle is written, the student must systematically test other numbers in order to confirm that her riddle has just one solution. The children are expected to write at least one riddle for a mystery number from one to twenty-five following the same format as the presented riddle(s). A model for the riddles is available on the *Remainder Riddles* directions sheet. Once that first riddle is completed, the children may then write additional riddles for mystery numbers from one to fifty. Having the children work independently will give you the opportunity to move around the room and talk to each child individually about the formation of his riddles. This individual conferencing will not only support the children as they write but also give you additional information about the thinking, reasoning, and language development of your students within this particular context.

Students should write only one riddle on a piece of paper, with the solution written on the back. Each child signs her name at the bottom of her riddle. The front pages of completed riddles can be copied and compiled into a class book. Number the riddles, create an answer key, and add it as the last page of the book. If you do not wish to compile a book, students may swap riddles with one another during a designated class time. This works equally well if time is unavailable to copy and compile a class book. If you choose to create a class compilation, you will need to check for duplicate riddles and make sure that each student has at least one riddle in the class collection.

Division Story Problems

Duration: 2–3 class periods

In order to construct division story problems, children must have a conceptual understanding of the operation. In this lesson, students solve a set of story problems and then create their own story problems that represent a specified number model. Not only does the context need to match the given division problem, but the interpretation of the remainder needs to be contextually relevant as well.

This activity offers students opportunities to:

- apply and deepen their conceptual and procedural understanding of division
- apply their understanding of how a remainder can influence the solution to a division problem
- apply their understanding of the language of division
- create meaningful contexts for division

Materials

- 1 copy of Take Me Out to the Ballgame! story problems per student (see Blackline Masters)
- 1 set of colored pencils per pair of students

The context of a division problem determines how the remainder influences the final solution. Students need to spend time exploring the effects of remainders on answers in various contexts. Creating story problem sequences can offer opportunities for our children to do just that.

The lesson begins with a reading and discussion of four division story problems that all take place at Fenway Park in Boston and that all can be represented by the number model $25 \div 4$. You may wish to change the context of these problems to fit your geographic area.

The context of these story problems is as important as their mathematics. Although each story can be represented by the same number model, they all result in different answers because of the influence of the context on the remainder.

I hand out the story problems and ask the children to read all four problems silently. When everyone is ready, I ask the children what they notice about all four problems. Most children will notice that the numbers in all the problems are the same. Each problem asks about the relationship found between twenty-five and four within a division context.

I focus the children on the first problem. "If the number model for this particular problem is twenty-five divided by four, is the answer then six remainder one?" I have the children talk to their neighbor about an answer that makes sense for this problem. We all agree that mathematically, $25 \div 4$ is, in fact, 6 R1. But is 6 R1 the answer to the question being asked? The focus of the lesson now moves from the mathematics to the language of the question.

One year, Kira announced that the class would need seven cars. I pushed Kira to address the fact that there was no 7 in our agreed-upon answer of 6 R1. Kira was easily able to use the context of the car problem to make sense of the need to round up the quotient to the nearest whole number regardless of the magnitude of the remainder. Kira said it did not matter if the remainder was one or three (and she reminded us that the largest remainder could only be three because of the size of the divisor); either way, the class would need another car for those extra children.

Each problem can be discussed with the focus on the effect of the remainder on the final answer to the problem. Each question requires a different interpretation of the remainder.

- Should the remainder cause the quotient to be rounded up to the next whole number (as in the car problem)?
- Should the remainder be ignored (as in the pennant problem)?
- Is the remainder the solution to the problem (as in the Fenway Frank problem)?
- Should the remainder be written as a fraction or a decimal (as in the baseball problem)?

As you are discussing each problem, record how the remainder influences the answer on the board for reference. Having the children word these responses will make the information more accessible to the class.

What Should We Do with the Remainder?
- The remainder "tells" us to round the quotient up to the next whole number.
- Ignore it.
- The remainder *is* the answer!
- Write the remainder as a decimal (or a fraction).

Once you have discussed the story problems, the children are ready to write their own story problem sequences. Have the children work in pairs to support their thinking and writing. This task will not be easy for some. The manipulation of the language, the mathematics, and the context can be challenging. I often ask my principal or our resource teacher to come in to help me conference with children during this lesson. It gives them a window into my classroom as well as the opportunity to work with children in a classroom setting, something I know they both enjoy!

I post the following five number models on the board:

$$30/4 = 8$$

$$30/4 = 7$$

$$30/4 = 2$$

$$30/4 = 7.50 \text{ or } 7\tfrac{1}{2}$$

I instruct the students to write a division story problem for each number sentence. If another adult is in the room, between us, we can conference with each pair of children about their completed stories.

At the close of a conference, I ask the pair to choose their favorite story problem. They rewrite that problem and illustrate it with colored pencils. These problems make a wonderful and informative bulletin board. I post the number models in the center of the bulletin board with the question "Can you match the problem with its number model?" underneath. This is a bulletin board presentation well worth showing off in a school hallway.

Games

As I seek out activities that support computational fluency, games continue to be a source of computational practice and the application of skills in a problem-solving context. Children often make fewer mistakes when playing games than when completing drill-and-practice worksheets. Partners pay close attention each other's computations and will often catch each other's errors. Because of the engaging context of well-selected games, more emphasis is placed on the mathematics and less on winning or losing. Games frequently become cooperative activities rather than ones promoting competition.

Leftovers with 25

Leftovers with 25 is a division game that is played by two children. It offers students opportunities to:

- practice division computation
- apply skills related to divisibility rules
- reason about the significance of and relationship among dividends, divisors, and resulting remainders
- continue to develop number sense and problem-solving skills

Materials

- *Leftovers with 25* directions (see Blackline Masters)
- number of players: 2

Prior to playing *Leftovers with 25*, it is helpful for children to have had some experience with thinking and reasoning about divisibility rules (see "Calculation Routines and Practices" on page 213). This background knowledge will help children choose divisors that produce the largest remainders possible.

Extension

When children have had experience and success with a start number of twenty-five, have them play with a start number of fifty and divisors from one to twenty. The goal of the game can also be changed; suggest that the children play games in which the player with the smaller sum of remainders wins.

Division Dash

Division Dash, a game adapted from *Everyday Mathematics* (Everyday Learning Corporation 2007a), requires the use of a calculator as a number generator. The game offers students opportunities to practice division computation.

Materials

- *Division Dash* directions (see Blackline Masters)
- 1 *Division Dash* score sheet (see Blackline Masters)
- 2 calculators with a square root key
- number of players: 2

Even though remainders are discarded in *Division Dash*, procedural efficiency is not compromised in any way. This is a favorite game in my class because the setup for the game is quick and easy and more time can be spent on dividing and scoring. The children also enjoy using the square root key on the calculator and the decimal numbers that it generates. Several years ago my class was intrigued by the pattern of square roots. We spent a little time in class discussing square roots and how they were calculated. Diana was beside herself when she realized that she could estimate the next square root in the sequence. For instance, look at the sequence listed in the following sample round. Diana was able to articulate that the square root of 67.53517602 would fall between eight and nine because $8 \times 8 = 64$ and $9 \times 9 = 81$. And 67.53517602 falls somewhere between 64 and 81. The square root of 67.53517602 is 8.217978828, so Diana was right! Many partners began to estimate the next square root in the sequence as part of their routine while playing *Division Dash*.

Sample Round

1. Enter 4561.

2. Press $\sqrt{}$ and get 67.53517602. The division problem is 60/2. Record the number sentence and result. Remainder is ignored. $60/2 = 30$

3. Press $\sqrt{}$ and get 8.217978828. The division problem is 82/8. Record the number sentence and result. $82/8 = 10$

4. Press $\sqrt{}$ and get 2.866701733. The division problem is 73/3. Record the number sentence and result. $73/3 = 24$

5. Press $\sqrt{}$ and get 1.693133702. The division problem is 70/2. Record the number sentence and result. $70/2 = 35$

6. Press $\sqrt{}$ and get 1.301204712. The division problem is 71/2. $71/2 = 35$

$$
\begin{array}{r}
30 \\
10 \\
24 \\
35 \\
+35 \\
\hline
134
\end{array}
$$

Games to Revisit

- *Rio*
- *Multiplication Bingo*
- *Multiplication Tic-Tac-Toe*
- *Target 300* (or *Target 600*)

Offering multiplication and division games in a menu format works well because of the familiarity and exposure that your children have had to these games. (See Chapter 5 and Chapter 6 for descriptions of these games.) Adding in other games with which the class is familiar will make the menu richer and offer the children even more options. The game directions in the Blackline Masters can be reproduced on card stock and placed at game stations. It may also be helpful to agree on a few class guidelines. In my room, each game must be played twice before moving on to another one. The children can also be asked to complete exit slips (see Blackline Masters) at the end of the menu session so you can monitor the games students have played.

Calculation Routines and Practices

Divisibility Rules

Exploring and applying divisibility rules help children make connections between multiples and divisibility. Numbers that are multiples of a number are also divisible by that number. For example, ten is a multiple of five. Ten is also divisible by five. It is important for children to know that when they divide a number by another number and there is no remainder, the first number is said to be divisible by the second.

Years ago, exploring and applying divisibility rules were rare activities in a fourth-grade curriculum. I like to think that our hard work of teaching for understanding has invited and engaged children to think about the structure of numbers. By fourth grade, many children have developed their own informal rules of divisibility for two, five, and ten. They know that a *double* is an even number and can be divided by two. They know that numbers that have a five or zero in the ones place can be divided by five with no remainders. They know that numbers that have a zero in the ones place can be divided by both five and ten—and two because even numbers can have a zero in the ones place as well. The divisibility rules for three and six are not as obvious to children as those for two, five, and ten, but they are equally useful. Asking children to investigate and articulate patterns found in listings of multiples of two, five, ten, and then three and six, can support the learning of divisibility rules as they emerge from the patterns. Following is a list of rules for two through ten. There is a divisibility test for seven. It is neither simple nor efficient and is not included. Divisibility by seven is best tested with a calculator.

- Divisibility by 2: The number is even.
- Divisibility by 3: The sum of the digits is divisible by three.
- Divisibility by 4: Either the last two digits are zeros or they form a number divisible by four.

- Divisibility by 5: The ones digit of the number is either zero or five.
- Divisibility by 6: The number is even *and* the sum of the digits is divisible by three. The number is divisible by both two *and* three.
- Divisibility by 8: Either the last three digits are zeros or they form a number divisible by eight.
- Divisibility by 9: The sum of the digits is divisible by nine.
- Divisibility by 10: The ones digit of the number is zero.

Although fourth graders will more than likely be able to articulate the divisibility rules for two, five, and ten, it will be necessary to offer and support the explanation of the rules for three and six. After exploring these rules, post them in your classroom or in the children's math notebooks to allow quick and easy access.

Our charge becomes one of making this knowledge accessible, applicable, and relevant to the problems our fourth graders are solving. We need to make connections between the problems we solve and the use of these rules deliberate and explicit.

- *You are solving 238 ÷ 5. Will there be a remainder?*
- *If we need to divide cookies into 6 batches with no leftovers, how many dozen cookies could we bake?*
- *What is wrong with this problem and its solution: 4,380 ÷ 6 = 724 R4?*
- *What four-digit number is divisible by 2, 5, and 10?*
- *What three-digit number is divisible by 3?*
- *What three-digit number is divisible by 2, 3, 6, and 10?*

Maryann Wickett and Marilyn Burns present three well-scaffolded lessons that explore divisibility rules in *Teaching Arithmetic: Lessons for Extending Division, Grades 4–5* (2003). The lessons include student vignettes, author commentary, and a discussion of the mathematics involved.

Partial Quotients Method of Long Division

Making sense of the process of long division is what leads to understanding. The partial quotients method of long division invites children to reason, estimate, calculate, and use common sense to move through the procedure. In this procedure, children will discover that the better their estimate, the fewer the steps and the greater the efficiency. I hesitate to label this computational method an *algorithm*. Although the partial quotients method is certainly a mathematical procedure, the multiplications and subsequent subtractions are determined by the individual mathematician. It is up to the child to decide which factors to choose given the magnitude of the dividend. As the children become more familiar with this procedure, they will often compare factors to see who was able to calculate the quotient in the fewest steps. Estimation skills are valued and fine-tuned as children work through long-division problems using this procedure.

The partial quotients method asks students to begin with estimation: How many 6s can we take out of 348?

$$6\overline{)348}$$

I remind the children that this method is meant to be friendly (and looks different from the way their parents learned to divide), so they should use friendly numbers. Jared suggested that we could take out ten sixes. If a child offers ten as an initial estimate, use it. It is important for children to be aware that any estimate is a right estimate, although some estimates will be more efficient than others. The children will very often come to this conclusion on their own as you work through more problems.

$$
\begin{array}{r|l}
6\,\overline{)348} & \\
-60 & 10 \\
\hline
288 &
\end{array}
$$

"Let's go back to that divisor of six. Now how many sixes can I take out of two hundred eighty-eight?" I asked. Jared offered ten once again. Now was the time to suggest that perhaps we could take out a few more. Sarah suggested that we could take out twenty sixes.

$$
\begin{array}{r|l}
6\,\overline{)348} & \\
-60 & 10 \\
\hline
288 & \\
-120 & 20 \\
\hline
168 &
\end{array}
$$

Because of the calculation we just made, Sarah quickly suggested that we take out twenty more sixes.

$$
\begin{array}{r|l}
6\,\overline{)348} & \\
-60 & 10 \\
\hline
288 & \\
-120 & 20 \\
\hline
168 & \\
-120 & 20 \\
\hline
48 &
\end{array}
$$

"Can I take out any more sixes?" I asked. Hayden suggested we could take out eight sixes and that our remainder would be zero.

```
6 )348
   -60  | 10
   288
  -120  | 20
   168
  -120  | 20
    48
   -48  | 8
     0
```

Next we talked about how to find the answer from the work we had done. Robert realized that the numbers listed down the side of the problem were the groups of 6 that we had taken out of 348. So, he said we just needed to "plus them!" Adding plus signs between each partial quotient may help the children make this connection.

```
        58 R0
6 )348
   -60  | 10
   288  | +
  -120  | 20
   168  | +
  -120  | 20
    48  | +
   -48  | 8
     0
```

As you solve additional problems, talk about remainders. Ask questions such as the following:

- How do we know we are finished with the calculation?
- Where does the remainder show up in the calculation?
- How big can my remainder be?

Using common language to talk through the calculation process allows children the opportunity to make connections that all will be able to identify and understand. I have found that the phrasing "How many thirty-fives can I take out of four hundred fifty-seven?" keeps the children focused on the act of "taking out" groups of thirty-five or partitioning the dividend into thirty-five groups. This phrasing also makes a nice connection to the successive-subtraction process that many children opt to use when first exploring long division. As a problem is solved, asking the children to share a story problem that fits that number model will keep the process grounded in context.

When working through the process with your class, be mindful of those children who make that first estimate as if they were applying the traditional long-division algorithm, something with which they may have had some experience in other classrooms or at home. They may be looking only at the first two digits of the dividend rather than keeping the dividend intact. This is another reason I am partial to this method (no pun intended)—there is no decomposition of the dividend, which contributes to strong place-value sense.

As students become more comfortable and competent with this procedure, they will quickly realize that better estimates make shorter calculations. Shorter calculations also offer less opportunity for subtraction errors. Another benefit of this procedure is the facility it allows and supports with single- and double-digit divisors. You may meet with some resistance from parents; if so, encourage them to take the time to learn this method with and from their children. They are often quite surprised at the sense that it makes—for them as well as for their children!

Paper-and-Pencil Practices

Although blank white paper or newsprint works well for charting work when solving problems, I continue to prefer that my children use graph paper when working through division procedures. Even with the partial quotients method of long division, lining up numbers continues to be important, as does the need to subtract efficiently. When working through this unit, many of my students ask if they can use their graph paper notebooks or loose pieces of graph paper to chart their thinking and calculations even before I get the chance to suggest it. I have several sizes of graph paper, ranging from quarter inch, to centimeter, to inch, available for use throughout the year. My children often write their calculations on graph paper and then mount the graph paper to newsprint for presentation.

Mathematics Writing

Much of the writing involved in this unit of study focuses on creating story problems. Students often find the solving of story problems challenging because they have difficulty defining the problem or identifying the important information and ignoring the unimportant. When students write their own word problems, they can better understand the connections that need to exist among the mathematics, the vocabulary, and the context of the problem from the author's perspective. Writing story problems offers students additional opportunities to deepen their conceptual and procedural understanding as well.

It is helpful to conduct a conversation about the components of a good story problem early in the unit. Compile a list with the children and then write it up as a checklist to be copied and posted in math notebooks for easy access and reference. The following is the list and subsequent check-list that my class compiled last year:

The Components of a Good Story Problem

- The choice of numbers make sense to the story.
- The story is easy to follow or to understand.
- There are not too many numbers or too much information in the story.
- There is a question at the end of the story.
- There is a beginning, a middle, and an end to the story.
- A thoughtful solution follows the story.
- The story is interesting.

Date: _____

Mathematician: _____

Story Problem Checklist

_____ My choice of numbers make sense to my story.

_____ My story is easy to follow and understand.

_____ There are not too many numbers or too much information in my story.

_____ There is a question at the end of my story.

_____ There is a beginning, a middle, and an end to my story.

_____ I have completed a thoughtful solution for my story.

_____ My story is interesting.

Comments from Mrs. Schuster:

When story problems are to be formally assessed, I ask that checklists be completed and attached to each child's story problem. A space at the end of the checklist is reserved for comments that I will write to the children.

Although I continue to be concerned about the mechanics of the children's writing, I am more concerned with the understanding and clarity or lack of such demonstrated by the story problem's context, vocabulary, numbers, and question. The following are possible story problem writing tasks:

- Provide students with a number model and ask them to write a story problem that fits that model.
- Provide a quotient (such as 15) and have students make up a story problem and corresponding solution that results in that answer.
- Provide a context within which the students have to create a division story problem.

Parent Communication

Even though I sent home a parent newsletter at the beginning of the multiplication unit (see Figure 5–13) that outlined the teaching and learning that would transpire in both the multiplication unit and the division unit, there are often phone calls, drop-in conferences, and notes from home communicating concern about my sole use of the partial quotients method of long division. I often make reference to the articles that were sent home with the newsletter as I speak with parents. Parents are also encouraged to engage their children in conversations about the partial quotients method—how and why it works. I encourage the children to teach their parents how to work through a division problem with this method. Students are reminded to allow their parents to choose their own friendly multiples with which to subtract from the dividend just as they do in class. I post a parent information form prior to the division unit that I also refer to when speaking with concerned parents. (See Figure 6–5.)

FIGURE 6–5 ◀

Parent information form for February.

Parent Information and Involvement Form

From: Lainie Schuster
To: Parents of Fourth Graders
Re: Mathematics Curriculum
Month: February

During the next month, the major topic we will be studying is:

- Division

My goal in studying this topic is for the students to be able to:

- understand various meanings of division
- develop fluency with single-digit long division (single-digit divisors)
- write and solve division story problems
- interpret remainders when solving division story problems

Parents can help at home by:

- learning the *partial quotients* procedure of long division*
- talking through procedures with their children
- refraining from sharing division tricks with children (What works for us may not work for them! It is more important for *them* to make sense of the mathematics.)
- asking children about the reasonableness of their answers—does the answer make sense?

*Many children will opt for this procedure of long division because it makes more sense of the numbers. A description of the process was included in an article by Marilyn Burns that I sent home last month with the parent newsletter. Please let me know if you would like another copy of the newsletter or article.

Parents may voice concerns about how their children will fare on the state-mandated test without exposure to the traditional long-division algorithm. If parents pose those concerns, invite them in for a conversation about the division tasks found on your particular state test. The following test items were obtained from the 2005 Grade 4 Massachusetts Comprehensive Assessment System math exam.

Example 1

What is the remainder for the division problem shown below?

$496 \div 6 = ?$

A. 0

B. 1

C. 3

D. 4

Example 2

One large bag of cookies contains the same number of cookies as 6 small boxes. Each small box contains an equal number of cookies. The boxes of cookies are shown below.

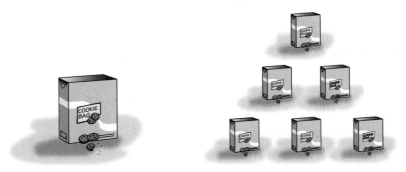

A large box of cookies contains 84 cookies. What is the total number of cookies that a small box contains?

A. 9

B. 11

C. 14

D. 20

Parents are often pleasantly surprised when they realize that these test items do not require the application of any particular procedure. Neither of these problems requires the use of the standard long-division algorithm—or any division algorithm, for that matter! Some students may use divisibility rules rather than a division algorithm to narrow down the options for Example 1. Others may use multiplication or repeated addition in lieu of division to determine the number of small boxes needed to equal the number of cookies in the large box in Example 2.

Assessment

If assessment has become embedded in your day-to-day routines, you may not need a division end-of-unit exam or formal assessment. Working within a problem-solving context allows and encourages us to design ongoing assessments that are focused on how the children are making sense of the mathematics. Checklists from story problems, anecdotal records from individual conferencing with students taken as they write and solve story problems, and observations made while children work through problems with one another all contribute to a formative assessment of mathematical progress during the unit.

As with the study of multiplication, we need to ask ourselves, "What do understanding and proficiency look like within a division context?" Examining and interpreting the evidence we collect from children's written, oral, and collaborative work become important as we make those generalizations about what determines and identifies the quality of mathematical reasoning for which we are looking. Mokros, Russell, and Economopoulos (1995) offer thoughtful criteria with which mathematical work can be assessed:

- To what extent is the student's use of mathematics [division] effective in helping him or her solve a problem?
- Does the student choose appropriate and flexible strategies for solving a problem?
- If the student uses algorithms or step-by-step procedures, can he or she explain why they work?
- Do the student's explanations, representations, or drawings of solutions clearly communicate his or her mathematical thinking?
- Is the student's work mathematically accurate?
- Is the student able to use "false starts" or mistakes in order to get on the right track?
- How does the student use tools or classroom reference materials to solve a problem? (98)

A solid understanding of our students' mathematical thinking not only will help us report to parents about the mathematical progress and achievements of their children but will also help direct and inform our teaching practices.

Resources

Math Matters (Chapin and Johnson 2006)—Chapter 2 "Computation" and Chapter 4 "Multiplication and Division"

Excellent description of mathematical properties and how they relate to division. Includes a description of the partial quotients procedure of long division.

About Teaching Mathematics (Burns 2007)

The "Division" and "Extending Multiplication and Division" chapters offer rich activities in a division context. Activities can be completed in whole-class investigations, independently, or in a menu format.

Teaching Arithmetic: Lessons for Extending Division (Wickett and Burns 2003)

Activities, student vignettes, assessment recommendations, and outstanding narration make this a must-have resource.

Hot Math Topics: Multiplication and Division (Greenes, Dacey, and Spungin 2001b)

Creative and engaging problem-solving tasks in a worksheet format.

Young Mathematicians at Work: Constructing Multiplication and Division (Fosnot and Dolk 2001a)

An overview of how children develop meaning and understanding within the contexts of multiplication and division. Student vignettes and excellent narration of topics such as the big ideas of division, algorithms, mathematical models, and assessment.

Resources for Parents

The I Hate Mathematics! Book (Burns 1975) and *Math for Smarty Pants* (Burns 1982)

Both books present engaging and reader-friendly math activities and explorations for children and their families.

"Marilyn Burns Demystifies Long Division" (Burns 2003)

Discusses and supports the use of the partial quotients procedure of long division.

Beyond Facts and Flashcards (Mokros 1996)

Offers parents a rich collection of games and activities that help children become successful math learners.

"Developing Computational Fluency with Whole Numbers" (Russell 2002)

Exceptionally defines and discusses computational fluency: what it is, what it looks like, and how it can be assessed.

Chapter 7

March

FRACTIONS

Fractional numbers are a rich part of mathematics. However, many students find them difficult to understand. To help students learn about and use fractions, it is important to introduce the multiple meanings of fraction and to emphasize sense making in all mathematical activities. Instruction in the early grades should focus on the part-whole interpretation of fraction but include all other interpretations as well. . . . Students should be encouraged to use models of fractional quantities . . . and to model equivalencies and operations before they are introduced to procedures and rules.

Math Matters
Chapin and Johnson 2006, 131

The Learning Environment

Acknowledge and celebrate effort.

Putting forth consistent effort in and out of class is a habit of mind that every child can develop. Our students need to realize that we value this approach to thinking and learning. Speaking openly and directly about the importance of effort, perseverance, and persistence in class discussions can help make our expectations explicit.

Do more math during the schoolday.

Children need to do math every day just as they need to read every day. In conjunction with implementing literacy initiatives, we need to bring more math into our schoolday. When children are lining up for recess, ask them to line up in an array—and let the remainders bring out the balls! When ages are given in reading texts or dates given in social studies lessons, have the children compare and contrast those ages and dates with their own. My personal favorite is the brownie lesson at lunch: The first graders always claim that someone got the "bigger half" of the brownie when brownies are shared, which is quite developmentally appropriate! I enlist the help of a few fourth graders to explain halves to those first graders. The first graders now become the experts about "bigger halves" and keep the other first graders in line with their choice of mathematical language when talking about fractional parts.

Slow down!

Children need time to accomplish learning. Our fast-paced world does not often value spending time exploring, thinking, and talking. And if done well, all of these take a great deal of time! Careful planning and identification of the goals and mathematics of a lesson will help you justify doing less rather than more. Instead of tackling two problems in a class period, investigating just one with greater depth will offer increased opportunities to slow down the pace of the class and allow more time for exploring, talking, and thinking hard about the mathematics.

The Mathematics and Its Language

Children name fractional parts of wholes and parts of sets.

As children work to make sense of fractional concepts, they need many opportunities in which to explore the relationship of the whole or set to its equal-size pieces. Making sense of fractions and fractional parts relies on students' understanding of the whole and the awareness that the whole can change from situation to situation. The whole matters!

Children investigate and apply the role of the numerator and the denominator.

In a given fraction model, it is important for our students to not only be able to identify the numerator but also articulate the information that the numerator gives us about that particular fraction. The same holds true for the denominator. Knowing that the denominator is the "bottom" number of a fraction is not enough. Understanding what the denominator (or numerator) represents in a fraction or fraction model helps our students attach meaning and purpose to the language of fractions.

Children explore multiple fraction models.

Fractions can be represented by area models, linear models, and set models. In order to develop and support the flexibility of thinking that work with fractions requires, it is important for students to investigate all three models.

Children explore and represent equivalence of fractions.

Equivalent fractions are ways of describing and representing the same value by using different-size fractional parts. Opportunities to visualize these relationships will help develop this understanding. Children need to see how one-fourth is related to two-eighths as they investigate how the *same* whole can be broken up into different amounts of equal-size pieces that have the same value. Too often we ask children to make that conceptual leap to the symbolic representation of equivalence without the necessary visual and physical scaffolding.

Children compare and order fractions.

When we ask children to compare fractions, we are asking them to apply ideas involving equivalence. When children are working to make sense of fractional concepts, they will order fractions according to their relative size, not by applying rules they have learned in other contexts. Children who have strong understandings about what fractions represent can reason their way through the process of comparing and ordering fractions.

Children apply their understanding of fractions to problem-solving situations.

Fourth graders need many opportunities to make sense of fractions, apply fractional language, and represent fractions with standard symbols. When students are solving fraction problems, it is important to encourage them to use models and materials (fraction strips, dot paper, rulers) that will support their thinking and sense making.

> **TEACHER-TO-TEACHER TALK**   Teaching and learning about fractions is hard work for everyone. For years, our fourth graders have been working to make sense of whole number concepts, operations, and procedures. Much of the work with fractions is counterintuitive to what children expect when compared with previous experiences with whole numbers. Because of that, children have to work hard and think hard to make sense of fractions.
>
> Fractions are relations and require relational thinking, which can also make work with fractions difficult. It is for this reason that I focus on only two big ideas of fraction instruction during this month of study: the part-whole relationships that fractions represent and equivalence.

Investigations, Games, and Literature-Based Activities

Fraction Kit Investigations

Duration: 4–5 class periods

Students make their own fraction kits by folding, cutting, and labeling different-colored construction paper strips. This activity offers children a *linear model* from which to work as they make sense of fractional concepts. Although many curricula promote the use of fraction strips, these activities are based on lessons from *About Teaching Mathematics* (Burns 2007). These lessons offer students opportunities to:

- construct and label equal-size parts of a whole
- explore how the whole determines the size and name of the parts
- represent and compare fractions
- explore equivalence of fractions with like and unlike denominators
- explore and articulate the relationships between the numerator and the denominator

Materials

- 1 set of 5 different-colored 3-by-18-inch construction paper strips per student. (Arrange pieces of 12-by-18-inch construction paper in alternating colors before cutting. Cut five sheets at the same time with a paper cutter, and you will have strips in sets of five colors. Ready-made fraction kits can also be purchased [Burns 2003b].)
- 1 marker per student (for labeling fraction kit pieces)
- 1 quart-size resealable food storage bag per student
- 1 fraction die with faces labeled $\frac{1}{2}$, $\frac{1}{4}$, $\frac{1}{8}$, $\frac{1}{8}$, $\frac{1}{16}$, and $\frac{1}{16}$ (also available with the ready-made fraction kits)

The directions for the following games can be presented in a whole-class format on an overhead or chart paper. They can also be reproduced for each pair of students.

- *Cover Up* directions (see Blackline Masters)
- *Uncover, Version 1* directions (see Blackline Masters)
- *Uncover, Version 2* directions (see Blackline Masters)

The teaching directions for completing fractions kits are available in two Math Solutions publications: *About Teaching Mathematics* (Burns 2007) and *Teaching Arithmetic: Lessons for Introducing Fractions* (Burns 2001a).

If the financial resources are available, ordering the ready-made Marilyn Burns Fraction Kit (2003b) is well worth the investment. The kit contains:

- precut fraction strips of varying colors, including strips for thirds, sixths, and twelfths (The students fold and cut the strips just as they would with teacher-made strips.)
- plastic zip-top bags for storage
- 2 sets of fraction dice (one set labeled $\frac{1}{2}$, $\frac{1}{4}$, $\frac{1}{8}$, $\frac{1}{8}$, $\frac{1}{16}$, and $\frac{1}{16}$ and the other set labeled $\frac{1}{2}$, $\frac{1}{3}$, $\frac{1}{4}$, $\frac{1}{6}$, $\frac{1}{12}$, $\frac{1}{12}$)
- magnetic fraction kit display for the board, which is wonderful to have
- *The Fraction Kit Guide* from the Marilyn Burns Fraction Kit (2003b)

Please note that creating fraction kits from construction paper is equally effective. If you are creating your own kits, be mindful that you will also need to create multiple sets of fraction dice. You can purchase blank dice from school equipment suppliers and mark the faces with the appropriate fractions.

A completed and labeled kit will look like the following:

TEACHER-TO-TEACHER TALK If you are looking to supplement your fractions curriculum with any activity, *Fraction Kit Investigations* is the one to use! The beauty of the fraction kit and the lessons presented is their ease of construction, presentation, and versatility. These lessons can be introduced in group sessions and then offered as free choice options or sent home as homework games to be played with families. I encourage my children to use their fractions kits at all times throughout the unit. They can use them on in-class work and homework. I even encourage them to use the kits on the unit exam! A few years ago as I was collecting scratch work from our math portion of our standardized tests, I noticed that several children had drawn fraction kits to help them work through the fraction questions.

I keep my magnetic fraction kit up on my whiteboard all year long. When having whole-class discussions, the students can come up to the board and manipulate the pieces to support their thinking or solutions.

What is so engaging about the construction and use of the fraction kit is that fractional relationships can be seen and touched. Encourage your children to talk to each other about the relationships they are seeing as they cut and construct their kits. Questions such as the following will help children focus on the relationships between the actual pieces of the kit as well as the numbers.

- What do you notice about halves and fourths? How are they related? What about fourths and eighths? Eighths and sixteenths?
- How are two, four, eight, and sixteen related? Where do we see that relationship in the fraction strips?
- How can you make sixteenths from fourths?
- How can you make eighths from halves?
- How can you make sixteenths from halves?

When students offer observations, ask them to show and tell using their fraction kits as mathematical proof. The numbers need to work, but so do the physical models!

Although more attention is paid to conversation and ideas as students are making their fraction kits you also need to address symbolic representation of fractions as the children label their fractional pieces. I ask that my fourth graders use a horizontal fraction bar. If your children are as accustomed to using graph paper as mine are, this will be easy for them when working with graph paper. The children can use the grid lines on the graph paper as the fraction bars, with the square above for the numerator and the one below for the denominator.

$$\frac{1}{4}$$

Follow-Up Journal Write

When Kira got home from school today and opened up her fraction kit, she realized that she had misplaced her eighths. She needs to make another set in order to complete her homework. Using her other fraction strips and what she knows about fractions, how can Kira make another set of eighths? What does she need to be mindful of as she creates this new set of eighths? How will she know if her newly made eighths are correct? (See Figure 7–1.)

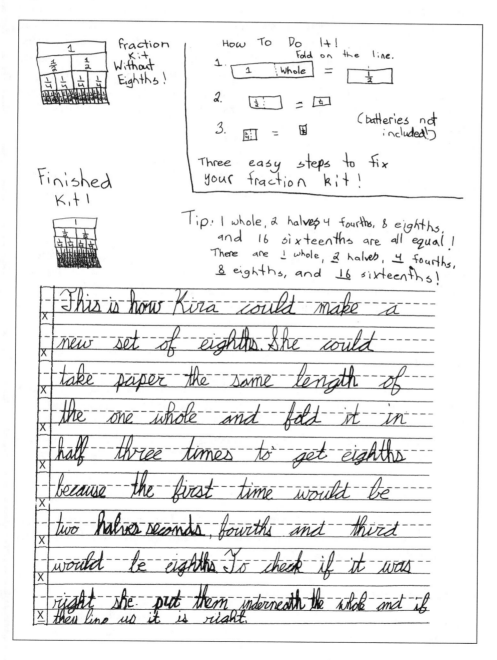

FIGURE 7–1 ◄

Norah's journal response.

Cover Up

With their newly constructed fraction kits, the children can now play the game of *Cover Up*. Playing *Cover Up* will help the children connect the use of fraction strips to representing and comparing fractions. Model the game with two students as a whole-group lesson. Allow plenty of time for the children to play multiple games. The more the children play, the more opportunity they will have to talk about the relationships that are made visible by the fractional pieces and the more quickly they will move to discussions about equivalence. After the third game, Jake asked me if he and his partner could change the rules of the game a bit. I asked him to tell me more. He and Diana wanted the winner to be the person to use the most pieces to cover the whole. If Jake rolled $\frac{1}{4}$, for example, he wanted to be able to substitute two $\frac{1}{8}$ pieces for the $\frac{1}{4}$ piece. Or if he rolled $\frac{1}{2}$, he might substitute eight $\frac{1}{16}$ pieces. I thought it was a wonderful rule revision and was happy to give their suggestion a thumbs-up. Some other pairs were ready for this new challenge and some were not. As I moved around the room, I checked in with each pair. If I felt they were ready for this new challenge, I asked them to ask Jake and Diana about their new rule to see if they, too, would be interested in adopting it. In this way I was able to differentiate the learning and challenge that this game could provide.

Follow-Up Journal Write

Emily had the following pieces on her whole strip: $\frac{1}{8}$, $\frac{1}{16}$, $\frac{1}{16}$, $\frac{1}{2}$, and $\frac{1}{8}$. Alexander had $\frac{1}{4}$, $\frac{1}{4}$, $\frac{1}{8}$, $\frac{1}{8}$, $\frac{1}{16}$, $\frac{1}{16}$, $\frac{1}{16}$, and $\frac{1}{16}$ on his. Emily claimed that she won the game. Alexander claimed that he, in fact, had won. Who won the game of *Cover Up*? How do you know? Use drawings, labels, and complete sentences to support your position.

Uncover, Version 1

Have two students model the game of *Uncover* for the class. Then have the students play in pairs. I often ask that the children choose partners other than those chosen for *Cover Up*. Allow yourself about fifteen minutes at the end of the period to process the game and to share experiences and strategies.

Follow-Up Journal Write

While playing *Uncover*, Nolan was left with $\frac{1}{4}$. He proceeded to uncover his board with three more rolls. What could those rolls have been? Why do your rolls make sense?

Uncover, Version 2

Because of the visual representation of the unit fraction strips, children are well aware of equivalence and how some fractions can be traded in for others. *Uncover, Version 2* offers children the opportunity to do just that. You can pull the class together to introduce the adjusted rules for *Uncover, Version 2*. More often than not, I prefer to have the rules available for pairs when they are ready for a new challenge after playing a few rounds of *Uncover, Version 1*. I ask partners to read over the new rules together and then proceed to play *Uncover, Version 2*.

Uncover, Version 2 gives children opportunities to manipulate equivalent fractions: to see them, to model them, and to exchange for them. Strategies are more important when playing *Uncover* than when playing *Cover Up*. The mathematics of the game becomes richer when those strategies are discussed and analyzed.

Follow-Up Journal Write

When playing *Uncover, Version 2* (when you can remove fractions equivalent to the roll), Sarah quickly traded in her $\frac{1}{2}$ piece for 8 $\frac{1}{16}$ pieces. On her next turn, Sarah traded in her other $\frac{1}{2}$ piece for 8 more $\frac{1}{16}$ pieces. Why does Sarah's decision make sense?

Cover the Whole

Addition fractions strings are created as children cover their whole strips in five different ways. The students are asked to record number sentences for each string of fractions used to cover one whole. Once strings are recorded, the class can discuss how to shorten a sentence by combining fractions with like denominators.

For example, Matthew covered his whole and recorded his number sentence:

$\frac{1}{4}$	$\frac{1}{4}$	$\frac{1}{8}$	$\frac{1}{8}$	$\frac{1}{8}$	$\frac{1}{16}$	$\frac{1}{16}$

$$\frac{1}{4} + \frac{1}{4} + \frac{1}{8} + \frac{1}{8} + \frac{1}{8} + \frac{1}{16} + \frac{1}{16} = 1$$

I recorded Matthew's number sentence on the board. "That's a lot of fractions!" commented Sarah. "Do we have to write them all down?" Sarah's question led the class into an important discussion about efficiency. Ask the class if there is a more efficient way to record a string to encourage the class to think about combining fractions with like denominators. Once like fractions are combined, Matthew's string becomes more efficient and shorter.

$$\frac{2}{4} + \frac{3}{8} + \frac{2}{16} = 1$$

I have no difficulty leaving $\frac{2}{4}$ as $\frac{2}{4}$ because the objective of this lesson is one of comparing and combining fractions, not one of simplifying fractions.

Some children may ask, however, if they can change $\frac{2}{4}$ into $\frac{1}{2}$. Once again, the objective of your lesson will direct your instruction and focus if students ask this question. Each year in my class someone asks about this. I want the children to represent what they are *seeing* covering the whole. Yes, two-fourths is equivalent to one-half, but there are two fourths on Matthew's whole and I ask that we stick to that representation. I let them know that I want their sentence to represent their particular model. It is also important to realize that later on in a child's mathematical career, keeping a fraction such as $\frac{2}{4}$ in this unsimplified form might be preferred when completing computational and probability tasks.

I then ask the children to work independently to combine fractions with like denominators as they make their sentences shorter and more efficient. I remind them that their number sentences need to model the visual representation of their string of fractional pieces. I suggest that they ask themselves, "Am I recording what I am seeing?" as they write their number sentences.

Dot Paper Fractions

Duration: 4–5 class periods

This series of lessons offers children an *area model* from which to work as they make sense of fractional concepts. These lessons also revisit and review concepts and routines related to area. These problem-solving activities, adapted from *Different Shapes, Equal Pieces* (Tierney et al. 2004), offer students the opportunity to:

- construct and label equal-size parts of a whole
- explore how the whole determines the size and name of the parts
- explore the idea that equivalent fractions have the same area
- understand that equivalent fractions are not necessarily congruent when working with an area model
- represent and compare fractions
- explore and articulate the relationships between the numerator and the denominator

Materials

- several overhead transparencies of large dot paper square (see Blackline Masters) (If you are projecting on a whiteboard, one transparency can be used for multiple examples. Write on the projected image on the whiteboard, then erase for the next example.)
- 3 sheets of small dot paper squares per student (see Blackline Masters)
- a variety of colored pencils per student
- 1 *Fabulous Fourths* worksheet per student (see Blackline Masters)

- 1 *Awesome Eighths* worksheet per student (see Blackline Masters)
- 1 overhead transparency of *Combining Fractions* worksheet (see Blackline Masters)
- 1 *Combining Fractions* worksheet per student
- 1 copy of *Getting to One Whole* directions per pair of students (see Blackline Masters)
- 1 *Getting to One Whole, Version 1* record sheet per student (see Blackline Masters)
- 1 *Getting to One Whole, Version 2* record sheet per student (see Blackline Masters)
- optional: 1 sheet of dot paper rectangles per student for work with thirds, sixths, and twelfths (see Blackline Masters)

Much of these lessons are introduced with an overhead projector. As with the fraction kit, the visual representation of the fractions is what supports and directs the instruction.

The series of lessons is introduced with a transparency of the large dot paper square. The outside border of the square, which will become the whole, is outlined.

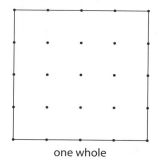

one whole

Connecting the dots to make a square of 1 square unit can open up a conversation about area and what that one square represents.

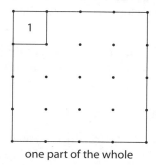

one part of the whole

Dividing the dot paper square in half on the diagonal can offer opportunities for conversation about halves but also about how to measure the area of each half.

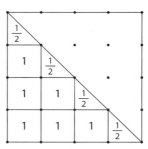

half of the whole,
measuring 8 square units

Counting as you partition off the units on the overhead will help the children visualize the area and measure of the half. Ask, "If half of this square is eight, what does this tell us about the whole?" to focus the conversation not only on the visual representation of the half but on the numerical relationship of the half to the whole as well. The children may quickly offer the opinion that the whole must be 16 units if the half is 8. Do not stop there, however. Ask a child to prove that the whole is 16 units on the overhead. Numbering the units as they are drawn also serves as proof that the whole is made up of 16 units. The talking, partitioning, counting, and labeling all reinforce and preserve the whole square.

Present the class with another blank large dot square. Ask the children if there is another way to divide this square in half. Children may offer the following possibilities:

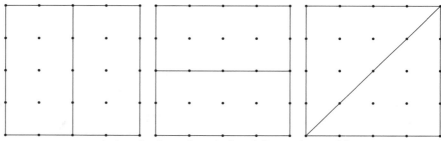

congruent halves (horizontal, vertical, and diagonal cuts of the square)

Ask students to prove that they have created halves by partitioning, counting, or labeling. I make an effort to continue to make reference to the whole throughout the discussion with questions such as:

- How do we know this is a half?
- What is the numerical relationship between the half and the whole?
- If you tell me that a half is 10 units, what do I know about the whole?
- If you tell me that the whole is 24 units, what do I know about the half?

- What if the dimensions of my square were 5 units by 5 units? What can you tell me about the whole? What can you tell me about the half?

Very little prompting is necessary to move students to thinking about more interesting halves. If an "unusual" half is not presented by the children, I draw one such as the following:

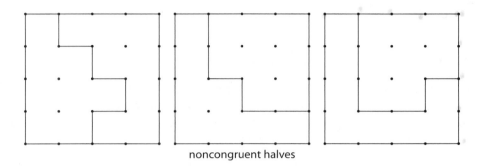

noncongruent halves

The skeptics in your class may argue that these do not "look" like halves. I love that supposition. And if someone in the class does not offer this idea, I do. Recording what the students already know about halves on the board will give them talking points about the equivalence of noncongruent halves. The class will quickly agree that if the whole is 16 units, then the area of a half must be 8 units. So we count and label the units of an irregular half and, in doing so, prove that it is a half.

This becomes a meaningful opportunity to discuss the term *congruent*. Some children may remember the term from their study of geometry, but its meaning and relevance to this particular lesson will need to be discussed. In this lesson, halves must be equal in area, not necessarily in shape. Therefore, noncongruent shapes must be equal in area. This may be an intriguing as well as counterintuitive concept for some children, so you'll need to devote some time to its development.

Hand out sheets of small dot paper squares to the children and instruct them to create as many different ways as they can to divide the squares into halves. Ask them to partition and then number each unit of one of the halves of each square as mathematical proof. Also ask them to color in the unnumbered half with a colored pencil. There are two rules about making halves and other fractional parts that will hold for following investigations and will need to be shared with the class.

- Each fractional part must be contiguous; pieces of the whole cannot be disconnected.
- Each solution must use the entire area of the whole.

Although the children are working independently, encourage discussion and sharing of solutions and strategies among table groups. In many ways, this lesson takes on a life of its own and the children become their own best teachers.

At first, a lesson about halves may appear to be too elementary for fourth graders. It is the shift in thinking, however, from a linear model to one of area that is of importance in this initial lesson. The partitioning, counting, labeling, and coloring slow down the lesson, which allows you to have meaningful conversations with individual students or table groups about congruency, noncongruency, and what constitutes equivalence within an area context as you move around the room.

Fabulous Fourths and Awesome Eighths

This lesson can be introduced with a review of the previous day's work. Take time to discuss the area model and what constitutes equivalence. Take additional time to focus on the continued importance of the whole and how the numbers connect to the model of halves.

TEACHER-TO-TEACHER TALK   Understanding fractional concepts within an area context can be problematic for some children. When working through the fraction kit activities, the whole is labeled and visualized as a quantity of one. The area model asks the children to think of the whole in terms of its area, which could be any sum of its collective parts. In this scenario, the whole is 16 units. Some children may have difficulty making that shift in their thinking. Students often comment, "I thought the whole was one," in initial lessons.

The idea that noncongruent shapes having the same area can represent equal parts of the whole can also be problematic for some. Again, flexibility in thinking and understanding is required. We need to carefully scaffold class conversations and activities, and purposefully choose denominators in these activities as we work to help children make meaningful comparisons between the two models. Asking children to make connections between the two models will help them move flexibly between one and the other. Understanding will be evident when knowledge can be transferred from the use of one model to another.

Ask a question such as "If the whole is sixteen units and the half is eight units, what can you tell me about fourths?" to set up the next exploration, in which the students will divide dot paper squares into four equal pieces and then eight. It is important to guide and direct your students as they make connections between what they already know about fractions and what they now are being asked to investigate.

Having a dot paper transparency available to model fourths will not only help the students who need the visual reference but also offer all the children a physical model upon which to ground their thinking and conversation. With the aid of the overhead, ask the children to offer a way to divide a square into fourths. As students suggest possibilities, have them justify how they know that their divisions have produced fourths by asking the following questions:

- How do you know these are fourths?
- Are the divisions "fair"? How do you know? In this model, what constitutes a fair share?
- Do all the fourths have to be congruent (same shape and size)? Why or why not?
- Can you use any of your patterns for halves to help you create fourths?

Students will quickly identify and offer the more common ways to divide the square into fourths. It will be necessary for them to dig deeper into the mathematics of area and number, however, as they work to create more irregular divisions. You will need to have many conversations about why fourths are fourths within an area model. Because the children have had experience with the fraction kit, they may continue to think linearly, meaning that fractions are equal parts of a whole and are equal in shape and size. Moving flexibly from one model to another and knowing how to differentiate one from the other are important (and difficult!) as children work to make sense of varying models of fractions.

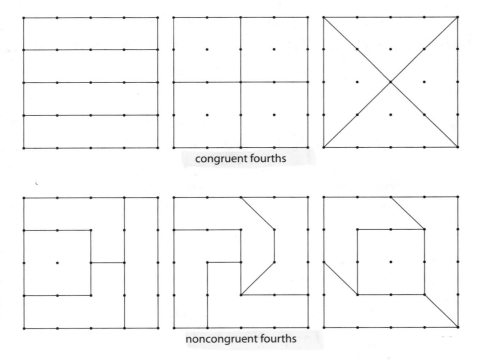

congruent fourths

noncongruent fourths

Hand out sheets of small dot paper squares to students and ask them to generate as many ways as they can to divide the whole into fourths. As the children create a set of fourths, they must prove that they are fourths by counting and labeling the unit squares of one fourth. They use a colored pencil to shade in each of their fourths.

As children independently complete six or so Fabulous Fourths, they can move on to drawing eighths. I ask that each child conferences with me before he moves on so that we can discuss what will constitute eighths within this model. Individual conferencing gives me a chance to listen to each child's insights, understandings, and possible misconceptions. I remind the children to use what they know about fourths to help them think about eighths. For some, this may be nothing more than a reminder. For others, more direct conversation and instruction may be needed. Asking those particular children to reconstruct a favorite pattern of fourths first and then to work within those divisions to create eighths will offer them the needed visual and physical grounding. Awesome eights can be completed on the remaining dot paper squares.

Although the children are working independently, there is always much talk that accompanies these activities. I encourage the children to stop and compare patterns and divisions with each other. I am delighted when I hear children asking each other for proof of their divisions. Hearing "Are you sure these are fourths?" warms my heart. Encourage the children to prove to each other that their divisions are fourths (or eighths). Jacob and Jamie, two out-of-the-box thinkers, chose to work together each day on their divisions. They were equally creative and equally entertained by each other's work.

After the children have completed their page of fourths and eighths, I ask them to complete a *Fabulous Fourths* worksheet and an *Awesome Eighths* worksheet. These sheets ask students to include written proof of the accuracy of their divisions. This task can be easily used as an assessment with attention paid to the following criteria:

- How do the students prove their divisions?
- Are they focusing on the area of the pieces rather than the shape?
- Are they focusing on the area of the whole?
- Do they make the numbers work? Do they articulate the connection of the number of units in the whole to the number of units in the fourth (or eighth)?
- Can you follow their reasoning?
- Are they transferring their use of language and understanding from their work with fourths to their work with eighths?

Figures 7–2 and 7–3 show how two students computed their worksheets.

Combining Fractions

Students will now find ways to divide a whole into a combination of halves, fourths, and eighths. I start the lesson with an overhead transparency of the *Combining Fractions* worksheet. I open the initial class

Draw one of your most interesting fourths.

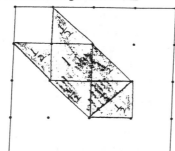

What makes this piece $\frac{1}{4}$? Explain in words and/or diagrams how you know.

My peice is $\frac{1}{4}$ because it has 6 $\frac{1}{2}$s which is equivelent to 3 squares plus the one unit in the middle equals 4. 4 squares is equivelent to $\frac{1}{4}$. ~~because~~ There are 16 squares and $4 \times 4 = 16$ which makes 4 squares equivelent to $\frac{1}{4}$.

FIGURE 7–2 ◄

Kathleen's proof of her favorite fourth.

Draw one of your most interesting eighths.

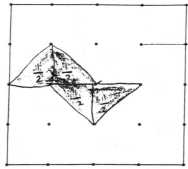

What makes this piece $\frac{1}{8}$? Explain in words and/or diagrams how you know.

This piece is equivalent to $\frac{1}{8}$ because $\frac{1}{2} + \frac{1}{2} = 1$ unit. I have 2 sets of units (four halves) so if I were to divide the whole (16) by 2 I would get 8. This means that $\frac{1}{8}$ is equivalent to 2 Squares or 4 halves in this case.

FIGURE 7–3 ◄

Harry's proof of his awesome eighth.

discussion with a question such as "What do you notice about the whole?" to offer the children some familiarity with the task. Some children will quickly identify the whole as being the same size as the whole they have been using with the prior activities. I have learned over and over again to never accept an assumption by a few children as conviction for the rest! Asking someone to come up to the overhead and prove that assumption will help convince the less vocal skeptics.

After the whole-class discussion and modeling, I hand out the work-sheets and ask the children to combine halves, fourths, and eighths into one design. They can look back at previous divisions that they have made and proved to help get started on this task. Remind the children that they need to be able to prove what each section represents with words and numbers.

Jacob had some difficulty combining his pieces into one whole. He pre-ferred to partition the fractional parts first and then go back to try to prove their fractional relationship to the whole. This became frustrating for Jake; his routine was one of partitioning, then erasing, partitioning, then erasing some more. Up until this point, this series of activities had been engaging and successful for him. Needless to say, I did not want to see this positive experience quickly go sour. I turned over the dot paper and asked him to talk about the numbers. What constituted one whole? How many units would be one-half and why? How many units would be one-fourth and why? How many units would be one-eighth and why? We kept track of our thinking and charted the fractional parts and the num-ber of units they would each need to be. This chart scaffolded Jacob's thinking as he began to work once again. He was able to move from a trial-and-error approach to one based on logic and reasoning.

When the children have completed their designs and are happy with their divisions, they should write their design as an addition string. If like fractions can be combined, they should rewrite their sentence in much the same way as when completing their work with the fraction kit. This final written representation helps the children make important connections be-tween their work with dot paper fractions and the work done with the fraction kit. (See Figure 7–4.)

FIGURE 7–4   ▶

Abby's design and addition string.

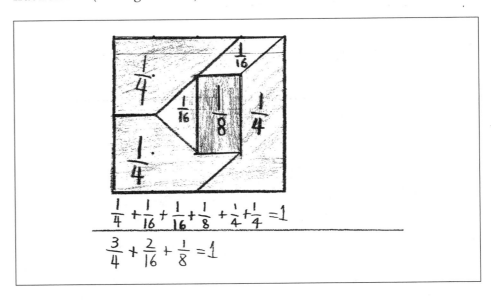

Follow-Up Journal Write

The following is Nolan's addition string for one whole:

$$\tfrac{1}{4} + \tfrac{1}{8} + \tfrac{1}{2} + \tfrac{1}{8} = 1$$

What could his design look like? Why would this design make sense?

Getting to One Whole

This game is played with dot paper squares and the fraction dice created for use with the fraction kit. Because the dice include sixteenths, you may need to have a discussion about sixteenths in relationship to this particular model. The children take turns rolling a die and coloring in fractional parts on their wholes. The first to color in one whole wins the round. Addition strings are recorded following each game. For those ready for the challenge, a version of this game can be played with a whole of 32 units, which requires students to rethink the area of halves, fourths, eighths, and sixteenths.

Additional activities requiring the discussion, creation, and manipulation of thirds, sixths, and twelfths can be constructed following the same protocol as the work completed with halves, fourths, and eighths. A 6-by-4 rectangle can be used as the whole (see dot paper rectangles).

Everyday Data, Everyday Fractions

Duration: 1 class period, followed by shorter explorations throughout the unit

Data generated from class graphs supply the numbers and part-whole relationships for class discussions of and about *set models*. Several class graphs can be analyzed and discussed in one class period. Another option is to collect data throughout the unit and take time to discuss and analyze the collected data when time allows. This lesson offers students opportunities to:

- explore how the whole determines the size and name of the parts
- identify and articulate the role of the numerator and the denominator of a given fraction for a particular set

Materials

- several class graphs posted on sheets of chart paper

Using data collected from class graphs can offer opportunities for children to explore set models in which the whole is understood to be a set of objects. In this lesson, the whole is the total number of students being polled. Initially, the denominators of these fractions may be a little messy or unfamiliar to the children. Data may be reported as twenty-fourths or twenty-eighths or even thirtieths. It is also important for the children to realize that with this particular model, the whole may vary from day to day, depending on the attendance of the class!

Prior to math class, post a graph on chart paper on which the children will record their personal data. The following is a listing of data-collection possibilities and good questions to ask.

Dog Days! Do you own a dog? Sign your name.	
Yes	No

Good Questions to Ask

- What is the whole?
- What fraction of the class does not have a dog? Is this more or less than half (or a fourth or a third) of the class? How do you know?
- What fraction of the class has one dog? Is this more or less than half (or a fourth or a third) of the class? How do you know?
- What fraction of the class has more than one dog? Is this more or less than half (or a fourth or a third) of the class? How do you know?
- What do these data tell us about our class?

Syllables How many syllables are in your first name? Write your name in the correct column.			
1	2	3	4

*[Handwritten margin note: * whole is # students being polled * whole may vary from day to day]*

Good Questions to Ask

- What is the whole?
- What fraction of the students have one syllable in their name? Two? Three? Four?
- What fraction of the students have fewer than three syllables in their name? Why does your answer make sense?
- Where does the majority of the class fall in this graph? What fractional part do you consider to be a "majority"? How does your answer support your opinion of what the majority is?
- What do these data tell us about our class?

First and Last Names Make a Tally (卌 II)		
My last name is longer.	My names are the same.	My last name is shorter.

Good Questions to Ask

- What is the whole?
- What fraction of the students have a last name that is longer? Is this more or less than half (or one-fourth or one-third) of the class? How do you know?
- What fraction of the students have a last name that is shorter? Is this more or less than half (or one-fourth or one-third) of the class? How do you know?
- What fraction of the students have a last name that is the same length? Is this more or less than half (or one-fourth or one-third) of the class? How do you know?
- Why do your fractions make sense?
- What do these data tell us about our class?

Letters in Last Names Color in a Square									
2									
3									
4									
5									

Good Questions to Ask

- What is the whole?
- What fraction of the students have a last name with more than five letters? Why does this fraction make sense?
- What fraction of the students have a last name with more than seven letters?
- What fraction of the students have a last name with fewer than seven letters? Why does your answer make sense?
- What do these data tell us about our class?

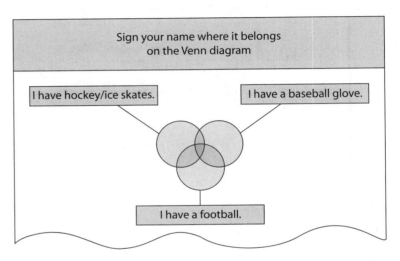

Good Questions to Ask

- What is the whole?
- What fraction of the class owns a baseball glove? What does that tell you about the class?
- What fraction of the class owns a football? What does that tell you about the class?
- What fraction of the class owns hockey or ice skates? What does that tell you about the class?
- Where do you see the fractional parts on the Venn diagram?
- What fraction of the class owns a baseball glove and a football? Why does your fraction make sense?
- What fraction of the class owns a football and hockey or ice skates? Why does your fraction make sense?
- What fraction of the class owns a baseball glove and hockey or ice skates? Why does your fraction make sense?
- What do these data tell us about our class?

Developing and securing understandings of fractional concepts represented by a set model are not the only benefits of these graphing activities.

Fourth graders are engaged by polls of all kinds and are fascinated by the stories that the data can tell them about their class. These lessons also provide opportunities to introduce one-half as a benchmark with which to compare fractions as well as meaningful contexts in which children can collect and interpret data.

TEACHER-TO-TEACHER TALK　Talking, thinking, and writing about numerators and denominators help children make sense of the relationships that fractions represent. I have realized over and over again that a child's ability to *identify* a denominator or a numerator has little to do with her *understanding* of what those fractional components represent—and they represent something different in every fraction, depending on the whole. I will often begin class with a fraction talk. I place an unfamiliar fraction on the board, such as $\frac{9}{13}$. I then ask the children to tell me everything they know about this fraction. When the children tell me something about the number of pieces in the whole, I push them to use the word *denominator* in their explanation. Or if they want to talk about the number of pieces being counted, I ask them to work with the word *numerator*. I also ask the children to explain how these two concepts are related in this particular fraction. Can knowing about the numerator and denominator help us compare this fraction with a benchmark of one-half? Or a benchmark of one? One year a fourth grader announced to the class that there was no such thing as thirteenths. His reasoning was that denominators could not be odd numbers. As ridiculous as this initially sounded, I began to wonder how many other children had that same thought. So fraction talks are routine in my classroom now. I also try to use the particular fraction from the talk whenever possible throughout the remainder of the schoolday. I enlist the help of the children to find interesting fractions that have some relevance to our schoolday that we can use for fraction talks.

Only One

Duration: 1–3 class periods

Only One, by Marc Harshman (1993), provides a context within which to identify fractional parts of a set. This lesson offers students opportunities to:

- explore how the whole determines the size and name of the parts
- identify and articulate the role of the numerator and the denominator of a given fraction for a particular set
- make real-world connections with sets of objects and their fractional parts
- create and represent sets and fractional parts of that set

Materials

- *Only One*, by Marc Harshman (1993)
- 1 set of colored pencils per student group

In *Only One*, Marc Harshman identifies the organizing principle of sets of familiar objects. For example:

There may be 9 players,

But there is only one team. (16)

There may be 8 horses,

But there is only one merry-go-round. (18)

The book's illustrations depict the set and its collective members. In this lesson, students listen to a read-aloud of the book and then use colored pencils to illustrate a set of objects and identify its organizing principle, mirroring Harshman's language and style. They then identify one member of that set as a unit fraction—a fraction with a numerator of one. Children will often use unit fractions as benchmarks when comparing other fractions with the same denominator. I find it helpful to use the term *unit fraction* with my class, especially when completing work with number lines. Identifying the unit fraction often helps them estimate and identify locations of other fractions with the same denominator on a number line.

A collection of these finished sets makes for a lovely bulletin board or collated class book. Some children may find it difficult to initially think up a set. But once the class gets into this activity, ideas for other sets just seem to flow. As students come up with new ideas, I keep a running list of unused sets on the board for those children who are finding it difficult to self-start. Colored pencils are my favorite medium for just about everything in math class, but watercolors make a beautiful alternative if you wish to involve your art department. (See Figure 7–5.)

FIGURE 7–5 ▶

Vidya's representation of $\frac{1}{100}$.

You will need to decide when to present this activity to the class and if you wish to offer additional written tasks. If you present it at the beginning of the unit, you may wish to focus only on the use of unit fractions. If you teach it toward the end of the unit, you may want your students to identify the unit fractions and also write three other sentences identifying other parts of the group.

Put in Order

Duration: 1 class period, followed by repeated experiences throughout the unit and school year

This lesson provides students experience with comparing and ordering fractions. This activity, adapted from *Teaching Arithmetic: Lessons for Introducing Fractions* (Burns 2001a), offers students the opportunity to:

- compare and order fractions with like and unlike denominators
- establish the use of benchmarks such as zero, one-half, and one whole when comparing fractions
- apply and articulate mathematical and fractional reasoning
- develop strategies for comparing and ordering fractions based on the fractions being considered

Materials
- several sets of 4-by-6-inch index cards with a fraction written on each large enough for all students in the room to see

   Sample sets:

   Set 1: $\frac{1}{8}, \frac{3}{8}, \frac{5}{8}, \frac{1}{4}, \frac{2}{4}, \frac{1}{2}, \frac{3}{4}, \frac{7}{8}, \frac{1}{1}$

   Set 2: $\frac{1}{16}, \frac{3}{16}, \frac{1}{4}, \frac{1}{2}, \frac{7}{16}, \frac{8}{16}, \frac{6}{8}, \frac{3}{4}, \frac{5}{8}, \frac{15}{16}, \frac{1}{1}, \frac{9}{8}$

   Set 3: $\frac{1}{8}, \frac{1}{6}, \frac{1}{4}, \frac{1}{3}, \frac{1}{2}, \frac{2}{3}, \frac{3}{4}, \frac{15}{16}, \frac{8}{8}, \frac{17}{16}, \frac{4}{3}$

- optional: fraction kits

The teaching directions for *Put in Order* are available in two Math Solutions publications: *About Teaching Mathematics* (Burns 2007) and *Teaching Arithmetic: Lessons for Introducing Fractions* (Burns 2001a).

Clear off the chalk tray so that the cards can be placed on the tray for the entire class to see. I walk around the room with the cards fanned out facedown in my hand and ask a volunteer to choose a card. The volunteer walks to the chalk tray and places the card in the appropriate spot based on its magnitude. I remind the children that placing the card in the appropriate spot is not enough! They need to explain their reasoning for doing so. They may also make adjustments in the placement of other cards if some need to be moved down or apart in order to fit in their card.

As with so many good math activities, the beauty of this activity is the simplicity of its presentation and the opportunity it offers for all of us to practice talk moves. Because this lesson relies heavily on oral communication, it may be necessary to once again establish listening expectations—this is, after all, fourth grade! You may want to quickly discuss how children can respectfully disagree with placements and the importance of wait time to allow children who have made an error to rethink their placement up at the board.

There have been several times over the years when my class has placed a complete set of cards with one in an incorrect spot and no one has caught the mistake. When the task is completed, I tell the children that I do not agree with the placement of all of the cards and that I am bothered by one card's placement. I often ask the children to talk with a neighbor about where the error might be. As we work through correcting this wrong placement, I am careful to ask for reasoning as well as a visual justification. Many times the children will reach for their fraction kits if we are working through Set 1 or Set 2.

Nick devised a method that quickly became known as Nick's Way because of the clarity with which he explained his thinking. The problem arose with the placement of the $\frac{3}{4}$ and $\frac{15}{16}$ cards in Set 2. Sarah had placed them on top of each other because she believed that they were equivalent. According to Sarah, both numerators were one digit away from their denominators, so the fractions were therefore of equal value. I was actually quite surprised that no one took exception with Sarah's justification, but I let it go until the end of the task. When I asked the class to regroup and look at the order of the fractions, Nick realized that three-fourths and fifteen-sixteenths were not equivalent. Nick reasoned that you needed one-fourth to get from three-fourths to one whole and that you needed only one-sixteenth to get from fifteen-sixteenths to one whole. Because one-sixteenth was much smaller than one-fourth, fifteen-sixteenths was closer to the whole and therefore larger. It was the first time that someone in the class had used one whole as a benchmark, and I was thrilled! What still amazes me is how easily children can manipulate fractions without having to even think about common denominators, the method with which I was expected to compare everything when in the upper-elementary grades. Even on the unit exam, some of the children referred to Nick's Way as they compared fractions. Nick was also able to extend his method to include fractions other than unit fractions because he could understand and articulate how the size of the denominator as well as the relationship of the numerator to the particular denominator determined magnitude and its distance from one.

Calculation Routines and Practices

Because fractions represent relationships, children need the time to explore, articulate, question, manipulate, and represent those relationships. As children begin to make sense of fractional concepts, they begin to informally combine and compare fractional parts with reasoning, not with memorized procedures and rules. In *Teaching Arithmetic: Lessons for Introducing Fractions*, Marilyn Burns writes:

> I teach fractions through a think-and-reason approach, not through a memorize-and-practice approach. When learning and practicing procedures becomes the focus, the main goal of instruction—making sense of mathematics—too often takes a back seat. (2001a)

The representation of fractions with standard notation and pictures or diagrams takes on greater importance than calculation routines and practices in this unit of study. Although the children write addition strings as they play *Cover the Whole*, the focus remains on the process of making sense of those combinations of fractional parts rather than on the procedure of addition.

Equivalence

Once visual representations and models of equivalent fractions have been explored and discussed, numerical representations and manipulations can then be introduced. One of my biggest challenges each year is to make sure that I do not slip into presenting those procedures of manipulating fractions with which I was taught so many years ago. Diana announced to the class one day that her sister told her to just multiply the numerator and the denominator by the same number to find an equivalent fraction. Instead of dismissing this suggestion, I had the class work through the reasoning behind this procedure.

If we want to find a fraction equivalent to three-fourths, for example, we can certainly multiply both the numerator and the denominator by the same number. The question then becomes Why does that work?

$$\frac{3}{4} \times \frac{2}{2} = \frac{6}{8}$$

When both factors are written as a fraction, the children can quickly see that, in fact, you are multiplying the fraction by one. You can then ask the children what they know about any number being multiplied by one. By this time in the year, your students should be able to articulate that multiplying a number by one produces a product *equal* to the given number, otherwise known as the *identity property of multiplication*.

Taking time to discuss the word *equivalent* can prove interesting in a fourth-grade math class. Fourth graders are certainly capable of having such a conversation, especially after working with the fraction kits and dot paper fractions. Begin by placing two equalities on the board and posing the following question:

Which number sentence represents equivalence?

$$\frac{3}{4} = \frac{3}{4} \qquad \frac{3}{4} = \frac{6}{8}$$

Each year in my class, the children are able to articulate equivalence as "a different representation of the same value." Rebecca took the discussion even further and made a distinction between *equality* and *equivalence*. She felt that three-fourths and three-fourths were equal—same value, same representation. Three-fourths and six-eighths, on the other hand, were equivalent—same value, but different representation. Rebecca also felt that we used the term *equal* a little loosely; it could represent both equality and equivalence. *Equivalence*, however, represented equality in value but did not necessarily mean that both sides of the equals sign had to *look* the same. Rebecca's insights opened the door for future discussions about fraction and decimal equivalence. When we moved to decimals, the class was able to pick up this conversation once again as we worked with equivalencies such as 0.5 and $\frac{1}{2}$.

Benchmarks

The use of benchmarks, or reference points, such as zero, one-half, and one can help children identify or compare the relative sizes of fractions. Identifying and using benchmarks also help children move to a number line model as they compare and contrast the magnitude of fractions. Fraction kits and dot paper fractions help children see fractional parts of a whole. The number line, on the other hand, gives children the opportunity to make sense of fractions and their order when they fall between whole numbers. A number line also offers yet another model to refer to when exploring and discussing equivalence.

I had the Set 2 fraction cards from *Put in Order* on my desk. I placed the three-sixteenths card on the chalk tray. "Where does this fraction fall? Between zero and one-half or between one-half and one?" I asked.

Nick explained that with sixteenths, one-half would be eight-sixteenths because eight was half of sixteen. He was able to reason that three-sixteenths was actually much less than one-half, maybe even closer to zero. "Half of eight-sixteenths would be four-sixteenths. Hey, that's half of a half! Four is one-fourth of sixteen, so four-sixteenths must be one-fourth. And three-sixteenths is even less than that. So I would say that three-sixteenths is really close to one-fourth—one-sixteenth less than one-fourth—but I would say three-sixteenths is closer to zero than to one-half."

We then went through each of the cards from Set 2 and completed the following chart. Students placed each fraction and gave their explanation and reasoning for the placement.

A new conversation developed when we came upon the $\frac{9}{8}$ card. Where would that go? The class agreed that another column should be added to

Between 0 and $\frac{1}{2}$	Between $\frac{1}{2}$ and 1
$\frac{1}{16}$	$\frac{6}{8}$
$\frac{3}{16}$	$\frac{3}{4}$
$\frac{1}{4}$	$\frac{5}{8}$
$\frac{1}{2}$	
	$\frac{15}{16}$
	$\frac{16}{16}$
$\frac{7}{16}$	
$\frac{8}{16}$	

our collection of benchmarks. The children wanted to make a new column labeled "Greater than 1." The $\frac{9}{8}$ card would go into that column because it was one-eighth more than one whole.

Now that each fraction of this set had been compared with the benchmarks zero, one-half, and one, the class was ready to compare one with another using a number line model. Draw a number line on the board with the benchmarks labeled and have students add a point for each fraction.

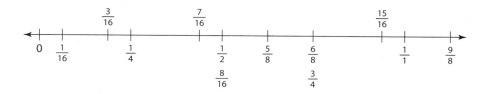

As children identify a location for each fraction, asked them to explain their reasoning for the placement. Each year I am surprised at how readily the children use their understanding of benchmarks to place and compare other fractions. Many will make the connection between this activity and *Put in Order*; the only differences are the use of the number line and the focus on the benchmarks. The order of the sets should be the same!

What began as a discussion about the use of benchmarks can now move to one of additional strategies that can be used to compare fractions. Building an ongoing list of strategies with your class for comparing fractions can serve as a reference and provide additional opportunities for children to articulate their reasoning. Because these strategies are constructed and generated by the students themselves, the application of these strategies should be student generated as well. The following are some strategies collected from previous classes:

- If the denominators are the same, just compare the numerators.
- To find $\frac{1}{2}$, just divide the denominator by 2 to get your numerator.
- If the numerators are the same, compare the denominators. Remember that the bigger the denominator, the smaller the piece.
- A numerator that is only 1 away from the denominator is often closer to 1 whole—except for $\frac{1}{2}$. $\frac{1}{2}$ is $\frac{1}{2}$! The bigger the denominator, the closer the fraction will be to 1. For example, $\frac{15}{16}$ is closer to 1 than $\frac{2}{3}$. $\frac{15}{16}$ is $\frac{1}{16}$ away from 1 and $\frac{2}{3}$ is $\frac{1}{3}$ away from 1. And $\frac{1}{16}$ is much smaller than $\frac{1}{3}$.
- If you are comparing two fractions with two different denominators, try to determine if one is greater than $\frac{1}{2}$ or less than $\frac{1}{2}$.
- Use your fraction kit if you get really stuck!

Mathematics Writing

Mathematicians write about their ideas. They communicate their approaches to problems, insights, and false starts. Our fourth-grade mathematicians need to do the same. The study of fractions offers multiple opportunities for children to make their conceptual and relational thinking visible. Some of the year's most valuable writing can happen in this unit if our commitment is to facilitate and support sense making of the concepts and relationships presented in the lessons.

Because multiple models are used to present the concept of equivalence, children will need multiple opportunities to write about it—how they see it, how the pieces work, how the numbers work, and how equivalence can be demonstrated with one model and then connected to a demonstration with another. In addition to the frequent follow-up journal writes that I assign to my class, most paper-and-pencil tasks also include a writing component. For example, I created a homework assignment containing dot paper squares divided in various ways. The children must circle the dot paper wholes that are divided into halves. The assignment concludes with the following question:

> *Choose one design that does* not *represent* $\frac{1}{2}$. *Prove your choice with words and drawings. How could you alter the division to make halves?*

Counterexamples can be very helpful as children work their way to understanding. Thinking and writing about counterexamples require a flexibility of thinking and fluency with language and concepts that offering a mere description does not. It requires being cognizant not only of what something is but also of what it is not!

Keeping a list of no-excuse spelling words posted in journals and on the word wall will again make everyone's life a little easier. Students will need to use words such as *denominator*, *numerator*, *equivalent*, and *congruent* as they write. We want our children to use these mathematical terms often and appropriately.

Parent Communication

Parents' expectations about any unit in mathematics are often based on their own experiences. Because this unit does not resemble the traditional approach to teaching and learning fractions, you need to initiate parent communication early on in the unit. A parent information form can help parents identify the mathematical objectives of the unit, which, in reality, are much the same as their own were when learning about fractions. (See Figure 7–6.) If you stress the importance of conceptual understanding and

FIGURE 7–6 ◄

Parent information form for March.

Parent Information and Involvement Form

From: Lainie Schuster
To: Parents of Fourth Graders
Re: Mathematics Curriculum
Month: March

During the next month, the major topic we will be studying is:

- fractions

My goal in studying this topic is for the students to be able to:

- understand that equal fractions of a whole have the same area
- understand that equal parts of shapes are not necessarily congruent
- understand that cutting and pasting shapes conserves their area
- be familiar with relationships among halves, fourths, and eighths

Parents can help at home by:

- identifying uses of fractions in real-world contexts (Cooking is a great one!)
- listening to children's reasoning and sense making
- refraining from sharing "tricks" with children about manipulating fractions (We do not reduce or simplify fractions in grade 4! It is more important for your child to *reason* about fractional concepts as she constructs foundational understandings about fractions and how they work.)
- reviewing multiplication facts—the ability to manipulate and make connections between fractional concepts relies on the mastery of these facts

---

communication, parents are likely to enjoy working with their children at home, knowing that they are supporting the curriculum as well as their children's learning.

I post many of the coloring activities that we do with dot paper fractions with descriptions of the tasks on hallway bulletin boards. Most parents take the time to study these papers and the activities while waiting in the hallway for their children. Although they are interested in their own child's work, they are equally intrigued by the varied methods other children employed to complete the tasks.

Students need time to work with concrete models in order to make sense of fractional concepts. You can assign the games of *Cover Up*, *Uncover*, and *Getting to One* as homework to engage families in meaningful conversation about these important concepts. The children can use this time to share their fraction kits with their parents or how dot paper squares work as they represent and manipulate fractions. You can send home copies of game directions in addition to a fraction spinner (see Blackline Masters) in lieu of dice.

Assessment

In *Understanding by Design* (2005), Grant Wiggins and Jay McTighe state that students who *really* understand an idea can:

- explain
- interpret
- apply
- reflect

These facets of understanding can and should direct our teaching and the design of our lessons and assessments. As we review student work and process mathematical talk, we should be asking ourselves:

- How is this child *explaining* what he knows? Is this child thoughtful? Is this child making meaningful connections? Is this child justifying his position or opinion with sound argument or evidence?
- How is this child *interpreting* what she knows? Is this child interpreting the problem with meaning? Is this child able to make sense of her solution?
- How is this child *applying* what he knows? Is this child applying what he knows in authentic or messy problem-solving situations? Is this child able to apply what he knows to a novel problem-solving situation? Is this child able to self-correct as he solves problems?

- How is this child *reflecting* on what she knows? Is this child able to self-assess and effectively self-regulate as she solves problems? Is she able to recognize her mathematical strengths and needs? Is she able to accept feedback?

These facets of understanding can be applied when assessing journal writes, small-group conversation, whole-class discussion, open-response questions, quizzes, and tests. When assessing as you teach becomes part of your teaching routine, you will be able to identify and celebrate those moments when you realize your children get this work with fractions. Sean announced to the class one day that he felt much more comfortable adding halves and fourths now that he *knew* what a half and a fourth were. That was one of those moments!

I give a unit test upon completion of our work with fractions. Over the years, however, I have found myself straying more and more from a traditional testing format. I now ask the children to choose one of three tasks as their summative assessment. As always, study sheets are given out several days prior to the exam to help the children review the important concepts we covered throughout the month. An explanation of the testing process is also spelled out for the children (and their parents) on the front page of the study sheet.

Here are two of the possible questions on last year's exam:

1. *Combine halves, fourths, eighths, and sixteenths to cover the whole.*

   - *Label your fractional parts.*
   - *Create a number sentence to represent your drawing.*

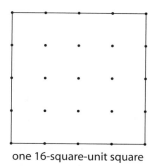

one 16-square-unit square

- *Re-create your design on the following whole.*
- *Label your fractional parts.*
- *Create a number sentence to represent your drawing. (Your number sentence should be the same as the number sentence above!)*

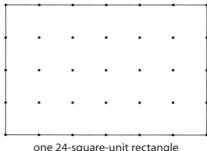

one 24-square-unit rectangle

Explain: How did you go about re-creating your design on the second whole? Describe your thinking. What did you need to know about the wholes? How did the whole affect the area of each fractional part? What was difficult about this task? What was easy? Use diagrams and words to explain your thinking.

2. *With your fraction kit, complete the following set of true-or-false problems.*

$\frac{1}{4} + \frac{2}{8} + \frac{1}{16} = 1$ *true or false*

$\frac{3}{4} + \frac{1}{16} + \frac{1}{16} = 1$ *true or false*

$\frac{1}{4} + \frac{1}{2} = \frac{3}{4}$ *true or false*

$\frac{1}{2} + \frac{4}{16} = \frac{3}{4}$ *true or false*

$\frac{1}{16} + \frac{1}{4} + \frac{1}{8} + \frac{1}{2} = 1$ *true or false*

$\frac{5}{8} + \frac{1}{16} = 1$ *true or false*

$\frac{1}{4} + \frac{5}{8} + \frac{1}{8} = 1$ *true or false*

$\frac{2}{4} + \frac{7}{16} = 1$ *true or false*

Explain: Choose one false number sentence. Circle it. Why is it false? How could you make it true? What was hard about this? What was easy? Use diagrams and words to explain your thinking.

Giving children a choice of test questions gives them ownership and control of their learning and understanding. They must first analyze each question, which is an assessment in itself. Students need to ask themselves, "Do I have the understanding to answer this question thoroughly?" when reading each question as they decide which one to answer. You may wish to start with two options as children learn to choose with purpose and you learn to scaffold their thinking about thinking.

Resources

Math Matters (Chapin and Johnson 2006)—Chapter 5, "Fractions"
Excellent descriptions of the multiple meanings of fractions with emphasis on conceptual development of the part-whole interpretation of fractions and equivalence in elementary school instruction.

About Teaching Mathematics (Burns 2007)
The "Fractions" chapter offers rich activities and whole-class lessons. The creation of the fraction kit is presented in detail.

Teaching Arithmetic: Lessons for Introducing Fractions (Burns 2001a)
An outstanding resource with lessons, student vignettes, narration by the author, and assessment recommendations. The fraction kit is presented in detail. A must-have resource.

Seeing Fractions (Corwin, Russell, and Tierney 1991)
A resource that set the stage for the unit *Different Shapes, Equal Pieces* from the Investigations in Number, Data, and Space curriculum. Narration, lessons, and assessments are offered for area models of fractions. Comprehensive and informative.

Young Mathematicians at Work: Constructing Fractions, Decimals, and Percents (Fosnot and Dolk 2002)
An overview of how children construct meaning and understanding within the contexts of fractions, decimals, and percents. Student vignettes and excellent narration of topics such as the big ideas of rational numbers, mathematical models, and assessment.

Math and Literature, Grades 4–6 (Bresser 2004)
A compilation of children's literature for varied mathematical topics. Several lessons and student vignettes are included for the study of fractions.

The Marilyn Burns Fraction Kit, Grades 4–6 (Burns 2003b)
The entire fraction kit for a class of thirty (including thirty sets of eight colored strips, beginner fraction dice, advanced fraction dice, and teacher set of magnetic strips) can be purchased as well as individual components.

Chapter 8

April

DECIMALS

In the rush to build students' skills, teachers often stress decimal operations and teach them as isolated procedures. They spend little time on decimal concepts and relationships. . . . Thus, teachers of middle school students often discover that students lack a fundamental understanding of decimal numbers. . . . Instruction needs to focus on helping students connect notation and quantity, make generalizations about the results of operations on decimal numbers, and relate decimals and fractions.

Math Matters
Chapin and Johnson 2006, 147

The Learning Environment

Continue to strive for understanding.

Understanding has come to be defined as the ability to see how something is related or connected to other things that we already know. The more relationships we can establish, identify, and articulate, the better we understand (Hiebert et al. 1997). There are many connections to be made between fractions and decimals. These connections will also support future explorations and understandings of percents. Although sense making needs to be internal and personal, it is our responsibility as teachers to scaffold lessons and learning in such a way that these connections and relationships are visible, tangible, and accessible to our students.

Support and offer opportunities for reflection.

The process of reflection provides continued opportunities for understanding. As we ask children to think consciously about their experiences, we are asking them to "turn ideas over in their heads, to think about things from different points of view, to step back and look at things again, and to consciously think about what they are doing and why they are doing it" (Hiebert et al. 1997, 5). Assessing new ideas and rethinking old ones can help establish new relationships and further understanding. Questions such as the following can promote and support reflective thinking:

- Why do you think that?
- How did you know to try that strategy?
- How is your solution like another student's?
- When will this strategy not work?
- Where did you make your mistake?
- What would you do differently if you were to do this again?
- Why does another student's strategy make sense?

TEACHER-TO-TEACHER TALK   When and where your decimal unit falls in the school year may be dictated by your adopted curriculum or state standards. The units in this book are not hierarchical and can easily be switched one with another. Several years ago I moved my decimal unit to follow our unit on fractions, which was not in the suggested scope and sequence of my prescribed curriculum. Once I did so, I wondered why I had not made this shift earlier, given the pedagogical and contextual sense that it made for both the children and me. The children expected and anticipated the deliberateness of my instruction. When they would use the fraction $\frac{1}{2}$, I would pause and they would respond, "Five-tenths." When they would use the decimal 0.75,

I would pause and they would respond "Three-fourths." Because the students were so accustomed to supporting their work with models when working with fractions, this same routine was easily established when working with decimals. Students often asked, "Can I draw you the answer?" during both units! If your decimal unit does not follow your fractions unit for whatever reason, it will be helpful to remind your children of the routines followed when working with fractions as you begin your work with decimals. Be deliberate in your expectations and in the need for the children to connect their work with fractions to their work with decimals.

The Mathematics and Its Language

Children develop a beginning understanding of decimal numbers and explore their relationships to fractions.

Decimal numbers are another way of writing and representing fractions. For many of us—children and adults—the world of decimals and world of fractions are separate and distinct because of differences in symbolic notation. A goal of instruction in this unit of study is to help students see that both notations and systems represent similar concepts.

Children represent decimal numbers with models and symbolic form.

Models involving hundreds grids, decimal cards, base-ten blocks, or linear measures can help children make connections between decimal places, powers of ten, and fractions. Models can also develop understanding and support correct use of decimal notation.

Children explore and represent equivalence of decimal numbers.

Models and drawings can help children explore the equivalence of decimal numbers. As with whole numbers, it is helpful for children to understand the importance of comparing like place values of decimal numbers—that is, comparing tenths to tenths and hundredths to hundredths. Affixing zeros to the right of a decimal number does not change its value. With the help of hundreds grids or decimal cards, children can *see* that 0.5 and 0.50 are representations of the same value. Each tenth in 0.5 has been divided into ten equal pieces, which also represents 0.50.

Children compare and order decimal numbers.

As children develop number sense about decimal numbers, they need to have time and opportunities to compare and order decimal numbers. When ordering and comparing decimals, students must understand the meaning of such numbers. Children need to understand that it is the place value of the digits to the right of the decimal point that determines the magnitude of the decimal number, not the face value of the digits alone. For example, some children may assume that 0.32 is greater than 0.4 because 32 is greater than 4.

Children develop benchmarks for decimal numbers by exploring their relationship to equivalent benchmark fractions.

Benchmarks are familiar numbers that mathematicians work with daily. Investigating and identifying benchmarks for equivalent fractions and decimals are useful when estimating and comparing decimals. It is also important for our young mathematicians to be able to convert back and forth between decimal benchmarks and their fraction equivalents.

Children use visual models, benchmarks, and equivalent forms to add and subtract decimal numbers.

As children begin to better understand the importance of place value when manipulating decimal numbers, they can and will begin to informally add or subtract decimal numbers. The logic of the addition and subtraction procedures will then be grounded in students' experiences and understandings not only of decimal numbers but of whole numbers as well. Addition and subtraction of decimals are based on the concept of adding or subtracting numbers in like place-value positions. Children should be encouraged to develop and apply estimation strategies as they check for the reasonableness of their calculations.

Children apply their understanding of decimal numbers to problem-solving situations.

Well-scaffolded opportunities are needed to support children as they explore, investigate, and make sense of situations involving decimal numbers. Students should be encouraged to use problem contexts, models, drawings, patterns, or estimation as they reason about problems involving decimal numbers.

TEACHER-TO-TEACHER TALK   Many children assume that anything less than one is negative. This misconception can apply to work with fractions and decimals. You may hear children say that if they divide three by four, they will get a negative number. This is an important misconception to unravel. Decimal numbers present a new notation, which can be confusing in itself. When children look at 0.3, they may assume that the .3 is less than 0 on a number line. I find a number line model to be extremely helpful in this teachable moment. Mathematical talk becomes not only important but imperative. It is through conversation that these misconceptions reveal themselves.

Our questions are equally important. We need to be mindful as we direct conversations if and when misconceptions arise. We must be equally mindful as we pose questions to help our children reconstruct their understanding of decimal notation and place value. Questions such as the following can help your children make sense of decimal numbers:

- Why do you think so?
- Can you show this to me in a drawing or on a number line?
- What do you know about negative numbers? Where do they fall on a number line?
- Can you have 0.5 of a brownie? How would that work?

Depending on where this conversation takes you with your class, a discussion of negative decimal numbers may be interesting for some. Using an extended number line model, children can distinguish −0.5 from 0.5, and 0.5 from 1.5. It is equally important for children to understand that there are decimal numbers greater than 1 and less than −1! Just be aware of the potential looks of horror from a few as they ask, "Are there negative fractions, too?"

Investigations and Literature-Based Activities

Exploring Tenths and Hundredths

Duration: 3–5 class periods

In these lessons, children are introduced to tenths and hundredths using grid models, Decimal Squares, and base-ten blocks. Students explore and discuss decimal place values. These lessons offer students the opportunity to:

- extend knowledge of place value of whole numbers to decimal numbers
- explore decimal representations of fractions with models and decimal notation
- explore place-value interpretation of tenths and hundredths
- explore the part-whole relationship of decimals
- make connections between decimals and fractions
- practice reading, writing, and representing decimal numbers

Materials

- 1 brainstorming web per student (see Blackline Masters)
- 1 overhead transparency of each place-value progression grid—whole, tenths, hundredths, and thousandths (see Blackline Masters)
- several sets of Decimal Squares (see the "Resources" section for information about this commercial product specifically designed for decimal numbers)

- 1 set of Decimal Squares for the overhead
- 2–3 sheets of chart paper
- 1 red marker
- 1 green marker
- 1 copy of *Decimal Bingo* directions per student (see Blackline Masters)
- 1 place-value chart per student (see Blackline Masters)
- 1 sheet of tenths grids and 1 sheet of hundredths grids per student (see Blackline Masters)
- colored pencils, one color per student
- base-ten blocks (flats, longs, and units), enough for class demonstrations
- optional: 1 yellow marker

Many fourth graders bring everyday experiences to their study of decimal numbers. Dealing with money, batting averages, and measurement may have offered opportunities for your students to informally manipulate decimal numbers. Gathering information about what your students know, do not know, and need to know about decimal numbers is important as you develop and scaffold lessons and instruction. Having the children fill out webs about decimal numbers will give them the opportunity to brainstorm what they already know (or think they know) about decimals. Brainstorming can be carried out in a whole-class format or in small groups; either way, each student fills out his own web. For this unit, I like students to complete the initial web in one color. As new ideas are investigated and formulated, students add them to the web in another color to designate new understandings. (See Figure 8–1.)

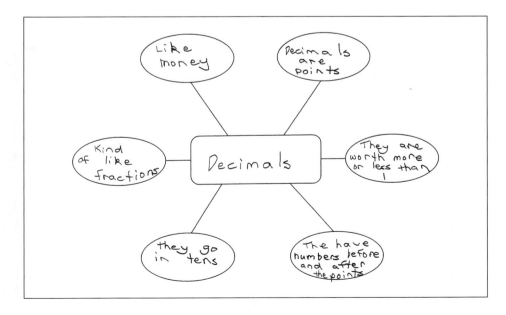

FIGURE 8–1 ◀

Initial decimal numbers web.

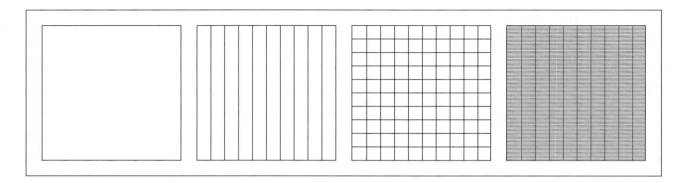

FIGURE 8–2   ▲

Four squares in progression—one whole, ten tenths, one hundred hundredths, and one thousand thousandths.

This investigation begins as a class discussion centered on the overhead transparencies of one whole, ten tenths, one hundred hundredths, and one thousand thousandths. (See Figure 8–2.)

Overlaying the transparencies on top of each other will help the children visualize what happens each time we move one place to the right of the decimal point. The transparencies present a powerful visual image of how each decimal place to the right is ten times smaller than the one to its left. Much conversation needs to accompany each overlay. Questions such as the following can support students' beginning understandings of the powers of ten in our decimal number system.

- What does this model represent? *One whole.*
- Where have we seen this model before? *In our work with fractions.*
- [Overlay the tenths on top of the whole.] What have I created now? *Tenths.*
- How do we know these are tenths? *Ten of them make up one whole.*
- How many tenths make up one whole? Why does this make sense?
- How much smaller is one-tenth than one whole? *Ten times smaller.*
- Could I make hundredths from this model? *Each tenth can be cut into ten pieces.*
- [Overlay the hundredths on top of the whole and the tenths.] How do we know these are hundredths? *One hundred of them make up one whole.*
- How many hundredths make up one whole? Why does this make sense?
- How much smaller is one-hundredth than one-tenth? *Ten times smaller.*
- What if I took each hundredth and cut it up into ten pieces? What would I have then? *Thousandths.*
- How many thousandths make up one whole? Why does that make sense?
- How much smaller is one-thousandth than one-hundredth? *Ten times smaller.*
- To make a ten, I need ten ones. To make a hundred, I need ten tens. How can you explain the movement to the right of the decimal point using this same logic and language?

The visual image of moving to the right of the decimal point is as meaningful as it is intriguing to the children. Too often place-value charts and terminology are introduced without the visual grounding that these overlays offer. As the children move on to the thousandths, they can begin to see how the relative magnitude of each place value progresses. There is often much talk as the children speculate about how small ten thousandths would be—and even hundred thousandths!

These conversations also present the opportunity to discuss the root of *decimal* and why our number system can be described as a *deci*mal number system. As we move to the left and to the right of the decimal point, place values increase or decrease by powers of ten. Many fourth graders will continue to refer to the various place values as "adding a zero" or "subtracting a zero." Be vigilant in your correction of this language. We are not *adding* zeros; we are *multiplying* or *dividing* by ten. Although this can be a difficult concept for many fourth graders, they must grapple with it and eventually make sense of it.

Decimal Squares Model

Many curricula introduce decimal concepts with tenths and hundredths grids. Although I, too, use tenths and hundredths grids, I prefer to start with a hands-on introduction to a concept. The use of Decimal Squares offers such an experience. Decimal Squares are a commercial product specifically designed for the study and exploration of decimal numbers. The Decimal Squares manipulative models are a collection of fifty-seven color-coded cards: tenths (red), hundredths (green), and thousandths (yellow). The cards can provide students with an intuitive understanding of decimal relations and operations before the use of symbols. A teacher's guide (Bennett 1992) is available if an entire kit is purchased that contains activities, games, and sample lessons that can accompany and support the use of these tenths, hundredths, and thousandths grid cards. Sets of overhead cards are also available.

The reading and writing of tenths and hundredths can be introduced with the aid of Decimal Squares. Beginning with the tenths (red cards), distribute random squares to table groupings. Ask partners to list all their observations about these cards. (See Figure 8–3.)

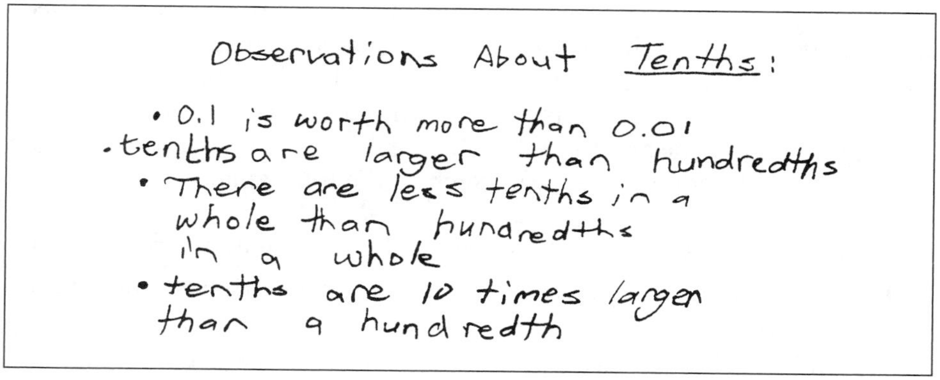

Observations About <u>Tenths</u>:

- 0.1 is worth more than 0.01
- tenths are larger than hundredths
- There are less tenths in a whole than hundredths in a whole
- tenths are 10 times larger than a hundredth

FIGURE 8–3 ◀

Paige's observations about tenths.

FIGURE 8–4 ▶

Paige's observations about hundredths.

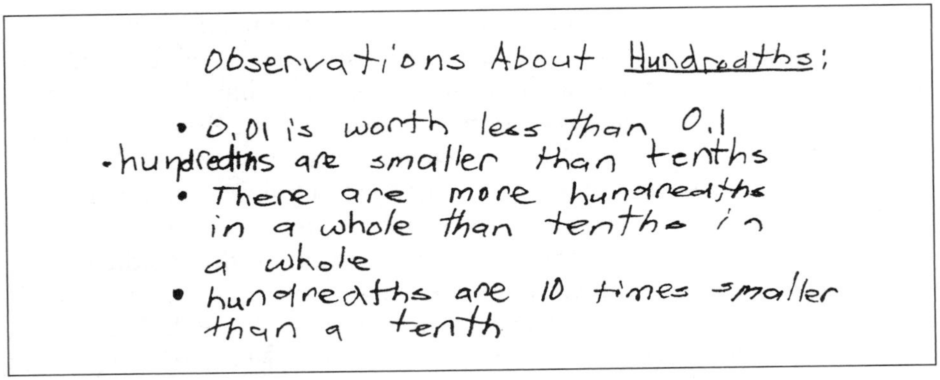

Observations About <u>Hundredths</u>:

• 0.01 is worth less than 0.1
• hundredths are smaller than tenths
• There are more hundredths in a whole than tenths in a whole
• hundredths are 10 times smaller than a tenth

Post a piece of chart paper on the board and record the observations using a red marker to identify the red squares. Together, the class discusses and adds to the observations. Making connections to familiar fractional concepts will help children begin to identify the similarity in concepts and language between these two different representations. Michael often referred to his square of nine-tenths as a square with "nine out of ten" pieces colored in. I asked Michael, "Could I write this as nine-tenths?"

"Hmmm . . . yeah, I guess. That is what nine over ten means, doesn't it?" Michael responded. I began to place tenths squares on the overhead and ask for labels for each square. Next to each card, I wrote the fractional notation. I would introduce the decimal notation in the next day's lesson. This familiar notation allowed the children to make sense of the quantities that the tenths squares represented based upon prior experience and knowledge.

Then I repeat this activity with the hundredths squares (green cards). I post observations with a green marker on a piece of chart paper. (See Figure 8–4.) Hundredths squares are placed on the overhead and students name each square with fractional language. Be sure to focus on the denominators of the hundredths squares because the whole is now divided into one hundred parts.

You'll need to decide whether to proceed with the thousandths squares. Once understandings about tenths, hundredths, and their respective place values and meanings have been developed, I find little need to proceed with the thousandths. The children are now able to make sense of place values that extend to the right of the hundredths place and transfer their knowledge of decimal numbers beyond what they have experienced.

Big ideas about decimal numbers will emerge from discussions about the tenths and hundredths squares, such as the following:

- Decimals represent a part-to-whole relationship, just as fractions do.
- Tenths are divided into ten equal parts. One-tenth has a denominator of ten.
- Hundredths are divided into one hundred equal parts. One-hundredth has a denominator of one hundred.

- Each tenth can be divided into ten equal parts. Those new parts are hundredths.
- Each hundredth can be divided into ten equal parts. Those new parts are thousandths.
- A square with four-tenths shaded in represents four out of ten.
- A square with thirty-five–hundredths shaded in represents thirty-five out of one hundred.
- Ten-hundredths is equivalent to one-tenth because the same amount is shaded in. They have the same value but different representations.

Because decimal notation has not yet been introduced, the focus can remain on the language of decimals, not the notation. Conceptual understanding is easy to assess because language is necessary to explain the model.

Decimal

Decimal Bingo can be played as a follow-up activity to reinforce the reading and interpretation of the Decimal Squares included in a set. The most important rule of the game is that children may have equivalent representations, but *not* duplicates. If they have duplicate cards, they should trade with a neighbor or exchange cards with the teacher. When a student has a bingo, he must read off his Decimal Squares. "I have four-tenths; forty-hundredths, which is equivalent to four-tenths; and fifty-five–hundredths." The naming of the Decimal Squares may take a little time, but is well worth the time and effort.

Introducing Decimal Number Notation

Place a blank transparency of a tenth grid on the overhead. Begin the lesson by asking for a volunteer to come up to the transparency and shade in six-tenths of the square. Ask the students if they agree with the shading. Write the fractional notation next to the decimal square: $\frac{6}{10}$. Ask if anyone knows how to write this fraction in decimal notation. Some children may be familiar with the decimal point and decimal notation, but some may not. If no one offers the decimal equivalent, write 0.6 next to the decimal square. Although this decimal can be named as "point six," I ask the children to use its full name, "six-tenths." I also ask that a zero be placed in the ones place to designate that this number has no whole numbers because it is less than one whole. Repeat this process with several more tenths. Write the notations as equations ($\frac{7}{10} = 0.7$) to set the stage for future conversations about equivalence and fraction-decimal connections.

Building a place-value chart at this point in instruction will help ground beginning understandings of decimal place values and notation with a visual model. As I create the place-value chart with the class on chart paper, I have the students fill in their own at their seats. This class-generated place-value chart remains posted throughout the unit for frequent and easy reference. I also encourage the children to consult their own charts whenever necessary or helpful. We need to be mindful that fourth graders are not always sure when to use reference materials. "Use your tools!" is a mantra often heard in my classroom. This place-value chart can be an important tool as our students develop understandings that will carry them through later years of mathematical study.

Initial focus on the placement of the decimal point in this chart will give the children a visual model of extending place values to the left and to the right of the decimal point. Before tackling the decimal place values, it is helpful to label the place values to the left of the decimal point as a review of whole number place value. The ten-makes-one rule applies indefinitely to place values to the left as well as to the right of the decimal point, and the children should be familiar with it from their study of whole numbers. After children discuss place-value relationships to the left of the decimal point, they can apply generalizations and understandings to the place values to the right of the decimal point. Refer to the overhead overlays presented earlier in this unit to support this representation of the mirrored progression from one side of the decimal point to the other. The goal of this discussion is to help students see, make sense of, and articulate the ten-to-one relationship that extends indefinitely in both directions on a place-value chart. (See Figure 8–5.)

This discussion needs to be a give-and-take of ideas and student-constructed conjectures monitored by teacher guidance and direction. The engagement of the students may surprise you. As we encourage and support our children in the process of connecting previous knowledge and understandings about place value to new generalizations and connections, we

FIGURE 8–5 ▶

Completed place-value chart.

hundreds	tens	ones	Decimal Point	tenths (1/10)	hundredths (1/100)	thousandths (1/1000)
		0	.	8		
		1	.	1		
	1	2	.	5		
		0	.	4	2	
		0	.	0	4	
1	4	6	.	7		
	8	8	.	8		
	8	8	.	0	8	
	8	8	.	8	8	
		0	.	9		

are teaching our children to think, reflect, and understand. As mentioned in the opening quote of this chapter, many difficulties that middle school students encounter when manipulating decimals can be attributed to early misunderstandings about decimal place value, relationships, and concepts. What we do in the fourth grade matters!

As decimal cards are presented on the overhead, the students represent the value of the card in numbers on their place-value charts. By placing a 0 on the ones place and a 4 in the tenths place, students will see how a decimal number such as 0.4 is built symbolically. It is also important to encourage the children to use place-value names when identifying and naming decimals. Naming a decimal as "point four" requires less understanding of place value than naming the number "four tenths."

Some children may begin to ask questions about equivalency as decimal cards are presented and represented numerically. Matthew noticed that 0.5 had the same amount of area colored in as 0.50. Posing a question back to the children such as, "Does that make sense?" or "Why do you think that is?" can support beginning conversations and understandings about decimal equivalence. After several decimal cards are presented and notated, the shift can be made to ask the children to represent decimal numbers without the physical model of a decimal card.

Students may have difficulties trying to make sense of the decimal amounts when reading decimal numbers without a physical model. We read 1.46 as "one *and* forty-six–hundredths." The difficulty arises when children see the 46 and want to read it as they would a whole number. Hundred*ths* being two places to the right of the decimal point creates a disconnect with previous knowledge of hundred*s* being three places to the left of the decimal point. Referring to the place-value chart may help children move beyond this mismatch of face value and place value.

One class period is not enough time to devote to identifying, describing, and writing decimal numbers. Coloring activities with tenths and hundredths grids can support these new skills. Focusing on tenths and then moving to hundredths will offer a progression from one place value to the next, which will support the development of expanded-notation understandings (see "Calculation Routines and Practices" on page 279). Using place-value labels also reinforces the connection decimals have with fractions. I tend to focus on tenths and hundredths in my class, but we talk about thousandths and ten thousandths as well. Asking the children to generalize about thousandths and ten thousandths from what they have learned about tenths and hundredths will help those children who are ready and curious to think beyond the task at hand. Figures 8–6 and 8–7 on the next page show two worksheets I use for more practice in naming and representing decimals.

Follow-Up Journal Write

Diana says that 0.5 is greater than $\frac{1}{2}$. Michael says that 0.5 is equal to $\frac{1}{2}$. With whom do you agree? Why? Use drawings or diagrams to support your answer. (Have blank tenths grids available for students to use.)

FIGURE 8–6 ▶

A sample student
worksheet for naming
and representing
decimal numbers.

Decimals! Decimals! And More Decimals!

- Color in the decimal cards to match the words.
- Write the decimal number.
- Complete the expanded notation.

six-tenths

0.6 $0 + \frac{6}{10}$

one and two-tenths

1.2 $1 + \frac{2}{10}$

two and eighty-hundredths

2.80 $2 + \frac{8}{10} + \frac{0}{100}$

FIGURE 8–7 ▶

Another sample student
worksheet for naming
and representing
decimal numbers.

Other Names for Decimal Numbers

Decimal Number	Fraction or Mixed Number	Word Name
1.6	$1\frac{6}{10}$	one and six tenths
0.13	$\frac{13}{100}$	thirteen hundredths
2.05	$2\frac{5}{100}$	two and five hundredths
0.01	$\frac{1}{100}$	one hundredths
3.9	$3\frac{9}{10}$	three and nine tenths
3.90	$3\frac{90}{100}$	three and ninety hundredths
12.15	$12\frac{15}{100}$	twelve and fifteen hundredths
4.0	$4\frac{0}{10}$	four
50.1	$50\frac{1}{10}$	fifty and one tenth
6.66	$6\frac{66}{100}$	six and sixty-six hundredths

Base-Ten Blocks Model

Base-ten blocks offer another model from which to build, name, and decompose decimal numbers. When a flat is assigned a value of one, the long then has a value of one-tenth, and a unit cube has a value of one-hundredth.

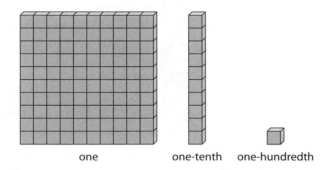

one   one-tenth   one-hundredth

The use of the blocks not only supports decimal notation but offers another visual model of how decimal numbers are built. You can also investigate decimal numbers greater than one. Ask children to identify decimal numbers from models you display and to build models when given a number. Modeling and naming decimal numbers greater than one can introduce or reinforce the concept that decimal numbers can be greater than one, much like mixed numbers.

Modeling decimal numbers with base-ten blocks can also scaffold the thinking necessary for later work with addition and subtraction of decimals. Combining models will offer the children experience in regrouping and trading in ten for one as with whole numbers. (See Figure 8–8.)

Manipulation with the blocks will further reinforce the process of adding like units: ones added to ones and tenths to tenths. This process can be connected to students' understandings of adding and subtracting with whole numbers.

The decomposition of decimal numbers can be physically modeled with base-ten blocks, which is another benefit of their usage. Having a visual model of 1.04 as $1 + \frac{0}{10} + \frac{4}{100}$ can also develop decimal number sense and place-value understandings. In the "Calculation Routines and Practices" section, I discuss using this expanded notation with decimal numbers.

Too often decimal concepts are presented to children using symbols and notation without the aid of visual and physical models. These physical and visual models not only help students build decimal numbers with meaning but also represent the multiplicative relationships between place values evident in our base-ten number system. I remind the children as we move through these initial exercises that we are exploring the same place-value concepts that they visited in first, second, and third grades. The rules have now changed some because the representation of one has changed. Although the values of all the blocks change according to the value of one, the multiplicative relationship between adjacent places remains the same. This is not just a big idea in our place-value system—it is a huge one!

FIGURE 8–8 ▶

Addition with base-ten blocks.

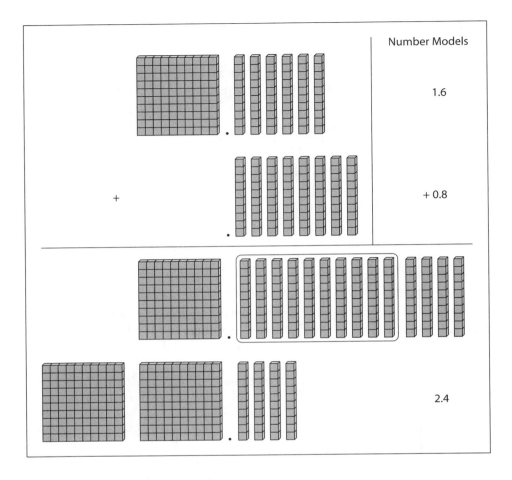

Follow-Up Journal Write

Who is the outlaw (something that does not belong) in this set of numbers? Why does your choice make sense? Can you find another outlaw? Explain your reasoning.

$$\frac{1}{2} \qquad 0.6 \qquad 0.5$$

TEACHER-TO-TEACHER TALK ·As we embrace a philosophy and a pedagogy that support problem solving, personal construction of knowledge, and making sense of mathematics, we will forever wrestle with the issue of when it is appropriate or even necessary to teach by telling. I seem to ask this question more when teaching decimals than other units. The process of making personal meaning is a tricky one that requires mindful instructional decisions and understanding of what is being taught and learned. There are days when the math notebooks come out, I am up at the board, and the children are writing and raising their hands. As we work to represent decimal numbers symbolically, I find that I am more directive in my teaching and delivery. "Be careful where you place the decimal point." "Don't forget the decimal point!" "Remember, those are hundredths, not tenths." "Who can read this decimal number for me?" The presented mathematics involves relationships, concepts, and procedures rooted in logic. It is necessary for children to make sense of these ideas for themselves in order to gain understanding. The terminology and symbolism that we use to represent those ideas, however, are social conventions and very often not rooted in logic. And although place value is rooted in the logic of our base-ten number system, each year I find it necessary to spend time directly focusing on the nuts-and-bolts of representing these decimal numbers. Base-ten blocks and Decimal Squares are never far away as I work with the children to represent decimal numbers accurately, but so are my reminders and direction. After such a lesson, I often ask the students what they noticed about my teaching that day. Invariably they will respond, "You talked a lot and we wrote a lot today!" I then offer the reasoning for my approach and the importance of being able to represent decimal numbers appropriately and accurately. I remind the children that there is a big difference between a batting average of .205 and .250 and I would certainly rather have $55.00 than $0.55! As informed and competent mathematicians, our students need to know how to represent, as well as articulate, those differences.

Place-Value Riddles

Duration: 1–2 class periods

Place-Value Riddles provides additional practice in naming decimal numbers as children apply and cement place-value understandings. This lesson offers students the opportunity to:

- extend knowledge of place value of whole numbers to decimal numbers
- read, build, and symbolically represent decimal numbers

Materials

- overhead transparency or chart containing a sample place-value riddle (see Blackline Masters)
- 1 set of place-value riddles per pair of students or 5 different-colored pieces of card stock and five envelopes if you are going to make clue strips for the riddles (see Blackline Masters)
- optional: 1 place-value chart per student (see Blackline Masters)

Children love riddles—and fourth graders are no exceptions! In this lesson, the riddles can motivate and encourage children to think flexibly about decimal numbers in nontraditional ways. Allow students to use place-value charts to support them as they compare, contrast, and compute while moving from one place-value position to another. Creating additional riddles of your own will offer additional opportunities for children to work with the vocabulary, concepts, and procedures required with decimal numbers. This activity can also be a time to revisit previously covered concepts as you refer to sums, products, multiples, or consecutive numbers, just to name a few.

Introduce the first riddle in a whole-class format to model riddle-solving procedures. Then have the children break up into pairs to work through the remaining riddles so all the students get a chance to talk and think through the clues with a partner. Ask students to keep a record of their solutions and thinking in their math notebooks. If pairs need help, I ask that they confer with another pair before they ask for my assistance.

Riddles can be reproduced as packets or each riddle can be reproduced on card stock (use a different color for each riddle), cut up into individual clue strips, and packaged as sets of clues in envelopes. The benefit of this packaging technique is that the children can view one clue at a time. They can also determine which clues their solution has met and which clues need to be addressed by sorting the strips into two piles. There is something about the physical manipulation of clue strips that makes solving the riddles more manageable for some. You can then use the clues from year to year—just make sure no clues are missing!

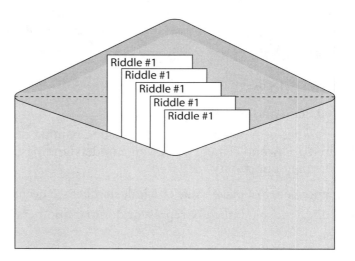

Processing and solving the first riddle in a whole-class format will allow you to once again revisit problem-solving strategies and procedures. Post the riddle on chart paper or an overhead. It will be helpful to be able to refer to previous clues as more information is gathered. You may wish to uncover one clue at a time to keep the children focused on the clue at hand.

The mystery number has no repeated digits.

The mystery number falls between 6 and 7.

All the digits are even.

The digit in the ones place is three times the number in the hundredths place.

The digit in the tenths place is two times the number in the hundredths place.

As you move through the clues, pose the following types of questions to keep the discussion focused on the process of solving the riddle and not exclusively on the solution. Inform the children that it is not necessary to review the clues in any specific order.

- What can you tell me about the mystery number by looking at the boxes for the missing digits?
- What do you know about the missing number from looking at the first clue? Are there several digit possibilities? How do you know?
- Can you exclude any numbers for any digits from this first clue? Why?
- Does the second clue give you more information? Does it support your proposed digit(s) from the first clue? Do you need to change your digit choices from the first clue? Why?

Continue to move through the clues until you have discussed them all. Once a solution is agreed upon, review each clue once again with the class to determine whether the proposed solution fits the constraints of the riddle.

You will need to decide how many riddles each pair will be expected to complete. Your decision will be determined by the strengths and needs of your particular group of students. Some years I ask all groups to complete all of the puzzles. Other years I require specific riddles for specific pairs. Additional riddles can then be chosen a la carte with time permitting. As you circulate, assess each pair's understanding of decimals. This will not be a quiet lesson—nor should it be! It is through conversation that understandings will become apparent and fluent, both to you and to the children.

Call the students back together once again after they've had time to work on the puzzles to allow them the time and opportunity to share solutions and strategies. You may wish to process each riddle, or perhaps choose two or three to discuss in depth while keeping the focus on the process and thinking necessary to solve each riddle.

Follow-Up Journal Write

The mystery number is 0.319. Develop a series of place-value clues that will identify this decimal number. (See Figure 8–9 on the next page.)

Put in Order: The Sequel

Duration: 1 class period, followed by repeated experiences throughout the unit and school year

The decimal version of *Put in Order* follows the same routine as that of the fraction version (see Chapter 7, page 247). This lesson provides students experience with comparing and ordering decimal numbers. Fraction cards can also be added into later sets to give students opportunities to think flexibly about moving from one representation to the other. This lesson offers students opportunities to:

- compare and order decimal numbers
- apply the use of familiar fraction benchmarks such as one-fourth, one-half, and three-fourths when comparing decimal numbers

FIGURE 8–9   ▶

Harry's set of clues
for 0.319.

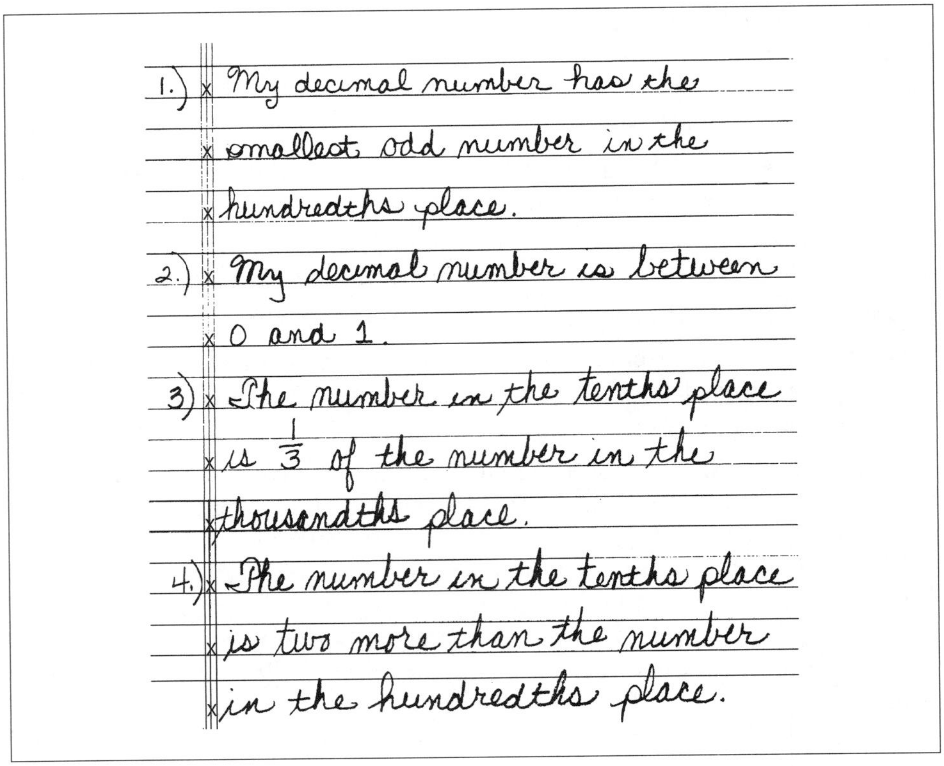

1.) My decimal number has the smallest odd number in the hundredths place.

2.) My decimal number is between 0 and 1.

3) The number in the tenths place is $\frac{1}{3}$ of the number in the thousandths place.

4.) The number in the tenths place is two more than the number in the hundredths place.

- apply and articulate place-value reasoning
- develop strategies for comparing and ordering decimal numbers based on the particular decimal numbers being considered
- think about decimals in terms of familiar fraction equivalents

Materials
- several sets of 4-by-6-inch index cards with a decimal number written on each large enough for all students in the room to see

  Sample sets
  Set 1: 0.1, 0.25, 0.3, 0.45, 0.5, 0.63, 0.75, 0.80, 0.99, 1.0
  Set 2: 0.04, 0.10, 0.11, 0.2, 0.21, 0.5, 0.51, 0.6, 0.75, 0.79, 0.8, 0.90
  Set 3: 0.02, 0.22, $\frac{1}{4}$, 0.380, 0.384, 0.44, $\frac{1}{2}$, 0.51, 0.625, 0.7, $\frac{3}{4}$, 0.78, 0.884, 0.9, 1.125, 1.3, 1.45, $1\frac{1}{2}$

If your students have previously played the fraction version of *Put in Order*, they will quickly fall into the routine of volunteering to choose cards and place them in order along the chalk tray. Because my children are familiar with this activity, they automatically explain their reasoning for card placements. Careful direction and guidance of the conversation can offer the children opportunities to make important connections between what they are learning about decimals and what they already know about fractions. You may find that some children immediately refer to familiar fractional benchmarks or equivalents as they make placements. Some children may prefer to convert tenths to hundredths in order to compare numbers with like place-value positions. Allowing enough time for a child to think and talk through his placement is crucial. Remind students that they need to be patient with each other.

Set 3 always raises a few eyebrows because I don't tell the children that fractions are included. The students are a bit surprised when the fractions show up but are usually quite comfortable in making placements and providing supporting arguements.

Often the children will ask to place a tick mark on the board to represent one-half before they begin to place the cards. Jane claimed that she needed that reference point to make placements because she compared everything less than one with one-half. Ask, "Is there another friendly fraction between zero and one that we could use also use as a benchmark?" to open up a discussion of using one-fourth and three-fourths as benchmarks. Some students may find a money reference handy here as they think in terms of hundredths—$0.25, $0.50, and $0.75.

Even though we do not formally investigate thousandths in my class, they are included in Set 3. Children feel mathematically powerful when they can make independent generalizations based on previous knowledge and understandings. They are learning to use what they already know to help them make mathematically sound decisions and judgments about what they do not. I occasionally include a number like 0.25146 in a set of cards, and the children clamor to have the opportunity to place it in the progression! They know exactly where it falls and why.

Follow-Up Journal Write

Four fourth graders are needed to make a team for a 200-yard relay race. Each fourth grader will run 50 yards. Out of the following list of children, who would be on your team and why?

Runner	Time for 50 yards (seconds)
Diana	8.9
Rebecca	8.5
Jared	7.04
Hilary	6.3
Chris	7.9
Patrick	7.0
Kathleen	7.75
Nolan	6.39

Games

Because a formal study of decimal numbers may be relatively new for many fourth graders, games can offer reflective opportunities for children as they wrestle with new and emerging ideas and understandings. Group processing, both during and after play, will help the children formulate and articulate connections between the concepts, procedures, and strategies applied. Listen carefully to students as they play and make sense of the games to determine how to direct your conversations and follow-up instruction.

The Place-Value Game

The Place-Value Game, adapted from *About Teaching Mathematics* (Burns 2007), requires the application of place-value understandings in order to make the largest (or smallest) number possible from numbers randomly generated from zero to nine. The game offers students opportunities to:

- apply decimal place-value understandings
- read, write, and compare decimal numbers
- create decimal numbers based on the probability of used and unused number choices

Materials

- *The Place-Value Game* directions (see Blackline Masters)
- 1 random number generator, such as a 1–6 die, a 0–9 spinner, or a set of number cards labeled 0–9
- number of players: 2–4

Players take turns generating numbers by rolling the die, spinning the spinner, or flipping cards from a deck. Each time a number comes up, every player writes it in one space on her record sheet. The players also have the option of discarding the number. Once a number is placed in a position or discarded, it cannot be changed. The winner is the player with the largest number and must be able to read it. The rules can also be adjusted to allow for the smallest number to win.

Follow-Up Journal Write

Kira and Jane are playing a round of *The Place-Value Game* with one die. Here are their record sheets:

| Kira | 5 2 3 . __ 4 | Discard 1 |
| Jane | 5 _ 1 . 3 4 | Discard 2 |

Kira claims that there is no need to roll the die for the final roll. Jane has won. Do you agree with Kira? Why or why not?

The Greatest Wins

The Greatest Wins is a variation of *The Place-Value Game* and is adapted from *Teaching Arithmetic: Lessons for Decimals and Percents* (De Francisco and Burns 2002). This game offers students opportunities to:

- apply decimal place-value understandings
- read, write, and compare decimal numbers

Materials
- *The Greatest Wins* directions (see Blackline Masters)
- 1 die
- number of players: 2–4

The children play ten rounds as they take turns rolling the die and creating numbers. The game can be extended by adding a third place for thousandths. Students can also play for the smallest decimal number of each round.

Calculation Routines and Practices

The Use of Expanded Notation

The routine and practice of representing decimal numbers with expanded notation can prove to be helpful as children work to make sense of place value, the decimal-fraction connection, and the logic of adding and subtracting decimal numbers.

Although 0.25 is read "twenty-five–hundredths," it is important for our students to be aware of other numerical representations of the same decimal number. The decimal 0.25 can be represented as $\frac{25}{100}$. But it can also be represented as $0 + \frac{2}{10} + \frac{5}{100}$. Name collection boxes (Everyday Learning Corporation 2007a) are graphic organizers used to collect and represent equivalent names for numbers. The use of name collection boxes can provide a context within which the children can rename decimal numbers not only with the use of expanded notation but with other equivalent labels, models, and representations as well.

0.25	$\frac{1}{4}$ of a dollar
twenty-five–hundredths	$\frac{1}{4}$
$0 + \frac{2}{10} + \frac{5}{100}$	25 cents

It is also important for children to move flexibly from an expanded-notation representation to a decimal number. For example:

$$10 + 3 + \frac{4}{10} + \frac{3}{100} = \square$$

or

$$\triangle = 0 + \frac{0}{10} + \frac{3}{100} + \frac{4}{100}$$

Physical models such as Decimal Squares and base-ten blocks can also support the place-value understanding and flexibility that is required when we represent decimal numbers in this form. Questions such as the following can guide instruction when renaming 0.45, for example. Make sure each child has a shaded-in hundredths grid in front of him to represent 0.45. Place a 0.45 Decimal Square on the overhead, or place four longs (representing tenths) and five units (representing hundredths) at each student table.

- What does this Decimal Square represent?
- How can it be written in expanded notation?
- Where are the four tenths in the model? Show me.
- Where are the five hundredths? Show me.
- Where are the forty-five hundredths?

Representations of equivalent decimal numbers can also be reinforced with expanded notation.

- *Why does 0.4 = 0.40? How do you know? Where is the equivalent value? Show your answer on a Decimal Square or with base-ten blocks.*
- *In this decimal number, why does the 0 in the hundredths place not affect its value? What does that 0 tell you?*
- *Is this statement true or false: 0.4 = 0.04? What is significant about the zeros in these decimal numbers?*

Expanded notation will also scaffold the logic needed when adding and subtracting decimals. Because of their fluency with whole numbers, fourth graders will realize the importance of adding like place-value positions: tenths with tenths, hundredths with hundredths. Experiences with expanded notation will help children develop flexibility with decomposing decimal numbers as they prepare to add or subtract.

Worksheets can be used selectively to reinforce the use and practice of representing decimal numbers with expanded notation. Tasks should ask the children to move from one representation to another—and then back again.

Addition and Subtraction of Decimal Numbers

The *Decimal Square Blackjack* game (see Blackline Masters for directions) offers an opportunity for children to investigate the addition and subtraction of decimal numbers in a game format. Much of the calculation is done mentally and relies heavily on decimal number sense and place-value understandings. If your curriculum requires paper-and-pencil proficiency with addition and subtraction of decimal numbers in the fourth grade, you may wish to refrain from that instruction until after the game is played. The flexibility of thinking and conceptual fluency that this game requires will prepare students for paper-and-pencil tasks.

Decimal Square Blackjack

Disclaimer: This game is loud and loads of fun! The goal of the game, adapted from *Decimal Squares* (Bennett 1992), is to reach one whole with tenths and hundredths Decimal Squares. This game can be played with candies but can just as easily be played with counting chips of any kind. It works well to rearrange the desks or tables in a semicircle prior to playing and have the teacher act as the dealer.

Addition and Subtraction with Estimation and Paper and Pencil

In the past, addition and subtraction of decimals were dominated by one rule: line up the decimal points. Our students may in fact do just that, but if we have spent time investigating and exploring place value, expanded notation, and informal manipulation of decimal numbers, the process of adding and subtracting decimal numbers will be carried out with number sense and not merely with the application of a memorized rule. As students become more efficient with the adding and subtracting of decimal numbers, they may articulate and apply the practice of lining up the decimal points for themselves. The big difference is that this rule is now rooted in logic and self-constructed understanding.

Estimation strategies should be developed and encouraged early on in computation practice. If students are asked to compute a sum of 7.3 and 0.84, first have them estimate the sum using number sense and their understanding of place value: "Since seven and three-tenths is close to seven and eighty-four–hundredths is close to one, my sum should be close to eight."

Estimating the sum prior to calculation will allow the children to check the reasonableness of their solutions. If students inadvertently line up the digits without paying attention to the place values of the digits, they will quickly realize that their solution is not even close to their estimate. This practice allows the children to self-correct or seek additional help.

Estimation routines also offer children practice with rounding decimal numbers in order to make them friendlier and easier to manage mentally.

Using graph paper will help students with the visual organization of written calculation tasks. I ask students to give the decimal point its own box because it is that important! You may find that less time is necessary to introduce and carry out a lesson based on paper-and-pencil computation routines and practices when the conceptual groundwork has been laid and nurtured.

Follow-Up Journal Write

Mac, Quentin, and Griffin are playing a game of *Decimal Square Blackjack*. Here are their hands:

> Mac: 0.5, 0.25, 0.35
> Quentin: 0.4, 0.15, 0.1
> Griffin: 0.8, 0.15, 0.2

If no one folds and one more card is handed out, who can win with a sum of 1.0? What decimal square would produce that sum? Explain your thinking.

Mathematics Writing

Writing about mathematical concepts is always important. When asked to explain a concept or idea, students are actively engaged in their learning. Understandings become evident and misunderstandings reveal themselves. You can use writing to assess students and modify your instruction. Even at this time in the year, it's beneficial to have a discussion prior to the writing to scaffold students' thinking and offer access to the mathematical reasoning required of the task. Questions such as the following may help your children draw upon the tools used in class to explore and demonstrate concepts as well as improve the writing process itself.

- Would it help to model the numbers with a drawing or diagram?
- Would it help to illustrate your thinking with a drawing or diagram?
- Would the use of expanded notation help you support your thinking?
- Can you connect this idea to another studied in an earlier unit?

As the year progresses, so too should the depth and proof of the children's writing and thinking. You need to make known your expectations as well as your assessment criteria. I have found over the years that a single discussion about expectations is often not enough. Writing about mathematics may continue to be a rather new experience for our children and we need to offer continued support and feedback throughout the year. Writing Focus Areas (see Chapter 2's "Mathematics Writing" section on page 48), checklists, or rubrics can be used to identify what is expected in assigned writing. These guidelines can also keep the children focused on the mathematics as well as the writing process for a particular assignment.

At this time in the school year, the class can formulate and apply self-assessment routines and practices. By April, your fourth graders will have had ample writing experiences and should now be able to value and articulate the merits of mathematical writing. Developing a set of self-assessment criteria with your children will support and facilitate reflective practices and habits of mind. Developing a set of standards with your children will allow you the opportunity to make your expectations and what they value about writing known. The following is a possible set of expectations:

What Good Mathematical Writing Looks Like in Mrs. Schuster's Class

1. It is easy to read.

2. It answers the question being asked.

3. It includes appropriate mathematical vocabulary.

4. It includes drawings, diagrams, or charts to support our thinking.

5. When we describe how we did something or why we think something, we include our reasoning.

6. Our writing is detailed and makes sense to the reader.

7. It is OK if you are not sure of a definition or a way of solving a problem. You can let the reader know that you are making a conjecture!

8. It is also OK to realize halfway through the writing that you made a mistake! Say so and explain how you know that you made a mistake.

Post this list in the classroom and in students' math notebooks to support the writing process. It will help students access their mathematical reasoning and representations as well as scaffold the revision process. Learning to improve one's writing process and skills requires monitoring, mentoring, and support. It requires knowing not only what to write but also how best to communicate one's ideas.

TEACHER-TO-TEACHER TALK   Each year, a colleague or two ask me why I don't create this class list of writing expectations earlier in the school year. And of course, I have my reasons! The teaching of writing in the fourth grade is a huge undertaking across all disciplines. Students are completing reading logs, learning to write five-paragraph essays in language arts, creating summarizers in social studies, and writing reports about pollution and endangered animals in science. Mathematical writing may be new to many of them. It may take several months for the children to settle in to the routines of writing in math class. By March, fourth graders have come to expect classwork and homework requiring mathematical writing. The once frequent questions, like "Is this in pencil?" "Do I need complete sentences?" "Can I bullet my ideas?" and "Can I use colored pencils?" are now seldom heard because the children have become accustomed to various tasks, prompts, and forms of feedback. Now that the children have several months of writing experiences upon which to draw, we can establish and agree on norms and expectations. Although good writing is good writing, proof, support, and reasoning lay the foundation of good writing in mathematics. As more and more state-mandated tests include increasing numbers of open-response questions, defining and developing sound mathematical writing practices and routines for and with our children will be of greater benefit.

Parent Communication

As with previous units of study, a parent information form can be created and distributed to help parents support their children at home. If completing a parent information form for each unit has become part of your teaching repertoire, you may find parents waiting or even asking for this information. This is a good thing! When parents are interested and engaged in what is going on in math class, everyone benefits. Figure 8–10 is a sample information form for April.

Because the end of the school year is fast approaching, it may be helpful to begin to develop plans for end-of-year reporting to parents. Although report cards are frequently the vehicle for reporting a child's progress over the year, many schools are beginning to implement student-led parent conferences with which to illustrate a child's growth and progress throughout a school year. Observing the progress made through their children's eyes is truly a gift to parents.

Children need to be actively involved in the selection of work that will be shared at conferences. This process takes time. I usually allow a full class period to introduce the process and offer children the time to complete the selection process. Setting up guidelines from which to work will help the children choose strong pieces from their portfolios. You may wish to suggest that the children choose three pieces of work, each representing one of the following five categories:

- the child's best work
- a favorite investigation
- a favorite journal response
- a paper in which a mistake was made and insights were gained
- a paper that clearly explains mathematical thinking

FIGURE 8–10   ◀

Parent information
form for April.

Parent Information and Involvement Form

From: Lainie Schuster
To: Parents of Fourth Graders
Re: Mathematics Curriculum
Month: April

During the next month, the major topics we will be studying are:

- decimals
- money: writing checks, balancing checkbooks, electronic banking

My goal in studying these topics is for the students to be able to:

- model, read, and represent decimal numbers
- develop place value understandings about decimal numbers and how they compare with what the children already know about whole numbers
- explore the relationship between fractions and decimals
- add and subtract decimal numbers with logic and reasoning
- apply decimal understandings to real-life contexts (money, finances)
- apply decimal understandings to problem-solving tasks and situations

Parents can help at home by:

- identifying uses of decimal notation in real-life contexts
- listening to the *whys*: Why is 0.5 greater than 0.25? Why is $\frac{1}{2} = 0.5$?
- listening to children's reasoning and sense making
- sharing appropriate information about household finances: Do you use a checkbook? Do you pay bills online? How do you manage a debit card?
- not pushing children to formally add and subtract decimals; instead, ask for estimates of sums and differences and then ask them why their estimates make sense

In order to make the best use of class time, I ask the children to complete a written reflection on only one chosen piece of work. The other two pieces are shared, but only one piece is evaluated in depth by the child. As the children work independently to respond to the prompts in Figure 8–11 (see the next page), I am able to individually conference with them as they reflect, write, and assess.

Sessions in which children share their work with parents do not necessarily have to be conducted in school. If student-led conferences are not part of your assessment practices, sending home this collection of student work can be just as effective. See the "Parent Communication" section in Chapter 10 (page 359) for a more detailed discussion about sharing student work with parents at home.

FIGURE 8–11   ▶

Student-led conference reflection.

Student-Led Conference Reflection

I selected this piece of work because I am really proud of:

I would like you to notice:

What I learned in the process of completing this piece of work:
  About the mathematics:

  About myself as a learner of mathematics:

If I did this again, here's what I would do differently:

Assessment

T. S. Eliot (1964) once wrote of April as "the cruellest month" (51), but I am not sure that he was making reference to that time of year in which many of our state-mandated tests fall! Come April, many of us find our daily schedules and curricular focus dismantled by testing demands. Our study of decimals may be interrupted by school and district decisions and policies over which we have no control.

There are several schools of thought as to how best to prepare our children for these inevitable assessments. Please be aware, however, that there is considerable research to support the testing success that children who have learned conceptual ideas by doing mathematics in a relational manner can have (Van de Walle 2004). Mindful and well-spaced calculation review and practice throughout the year can certainly support procedural concepts and skills. Teaching children how to be test savvy with test-taking strategies is another worthwhile practice. It is best to introduce and discuss test-taking strategies shortly before the testing dates. Such strategies may include:

- careful reading of the question to identify what is being asked
- estimating an answer first before spending time with computation in order to eliminate some multiple-choice responses
- working backward from a possible answer

Van de Walle reminds us that successful test-taking strategies require good concepts, skills, and number sense. Without sound understanding from which to work, test-taking strategies will do little good!

Resources

Math Matters (Chapin and Johnson 2006)—Chapter 6, "Decimals"

In-depth discussion of decimal concepts, the importance of place value, and the value of working from models.

About Teaching Mathematics (Burns 2007)

The chapter on decimals offers whole-class lessons as well as independent (menu) activities.

Elementary and Middle School Mathematics (Van de Walle 2004)—Chapter 17, "Decimal and Percent Concepts and Decimal Computation"

A strong chapter discussing the big ideas of teaching and learning about decimal numbers, the importance of place value, and making the fraction-decimal connection.

Logic Number Problems for Grades 4–8 (Sherard 1998)

Presents whole number logic puzzles that can easily be adapted for use with decimal numbers by inserting decimal points and changing place-value labels.

Decimal Squares: Step by Step Teacher's Guide (Bennett 1992)

A program of manipulative models, activities, and games that supports the teaching of decimal concepts from readiness to abstract levels, including teaching notes, Blacklines, and directions for games.

Chapter 9

May

ALGEBRAIC THINKING AND DATA COLLECTION AND ANALYSIS

If students have had algebraic experiences before they encounter algebra as a course in middle or high school, they will more easily make the transition from reasoning about number to reasoning about symbols and relationships. In the early elementary grades, studying patterns is the most prominent algebraic experience; patterns are the basis for reasoning about regularity and consistency. As students move into the upper elementary grades and middle grades, they need to generalize these patterns and express the relationships in a variety of ways. Students learn to use language, tables, and graphs to represent relationships and to formalize them using function rules and equations.

Math Matters
Chapin and Johnson 2006, 219

The Learning Environment

Support and celebrate the having of wonderful ideas.

According to Eleanor Duckworth (1987), the having of wonderful ideas is the essence of intellectual development. Our willingness to accept children's ideas and the provision of an environment that can initiate such ideas give our children reasons and occasions for having them! It is *by* thinking that children get better *at* thinking. Our children have now spent the better part of a school year thinking, investigating, collaborating, and creating in many areas of mathematics. As your children explore, articulate, and represent patterns and data, you should elicit, support, and act upon their wonderful ideas. Allow their questions and insights to drive the instruction whenever you can. Then take the time to be amazed by and delighted with their wonderful ideas.

Continue to develop and enjoy your classroom culture.

When tasks are treated as genuine mathematical problems and our children are treated as genuine mathematicians, meaningful teaching and learning occur. An environment that focuses on reflection and communication about mathematical activities and ideas stimulates and supports all those who are a part of it. By this time in the year, our children are thinking and writing with greater clarity and are more willing and able to dig deeper into the mathematics. Celebrate and enjoy the competence, confidence, and playfulness that a productive and successful culture can provide.

The Mathematics and Its Language

Children engage in explorations that support algebraic thinking.

Fourth graders can be introduced to algebra as a *way of thinking*. When we ask children to predict, continue, and articulate patterns, functions, and generalizations, we are asking them to think algebraically. Such habits of mind will provide fertile ground as our children move into the middle grades and beyond, when the study of algebra becomes more formalized. Tasks that support algebraic thinking can also support, enhance, and extend children's arithmetic skills and learning.

Children continue their study of the use and meaning of variables.

Variables are letters, symbols, or other placeholders ($\square$ or $\triangle$) that stand for unknown values in mathematical expressions or equations. In the process of learning how to work with variables, students need to learn how values are represented symbolically with letters or shapes. Once students have made sense of the symbols, they then need to make sense of the different meanings for letters or shapes in equations, inequalities, formulas, and functions (Chapin and Johnson 2006).

Children investigate and represent growing patterns.

In the earlier grades, children were introduced to *repeating* patterns (a pattern with a core that repeats over and over). Explorations of *growth* patterns now require students to identify what comes next in a sequence and to generalize a rule that can predict how the particular pattern is growing. Growth patterns can be represented with models as well as pictures, T-charts, words, and graphs. Each pattern tells a story, as do its various representations. The connections between representations need to be deliberate, visual, and accessible.

Children investigate, articulate, and represent the relationship of equality.

Equality is symbolized by the equals sign, but its *meaning* can continue to be elusive for many fourth graders. Equality can be modeled by thinking of a level balance scale. Many fourth graders continue to interpret the equals sign as an *operational* symbol that tells them to do something. It is, in fact, a *relational* symbol representing a relationship of equal value between the two sides of an equation. We need to include alternative routines, such as placing the equals sign at the front end of an equation ($8 = 3 + 5$), and discussions about the meaning of equality in our instruction to help children continue to make sense of this symbol.

Children collect, interpret, and represent real-world data.

Data can be gathered, organized, and examined in order to answer questions about populations from which the data come. Statistical landmarks such as sample size, range, mode, and median can help our students describe and make sense of the data as can their developing proficiency with graphing and generalizing. It is important for children to formulate their own questions as they work to make sense of the data-collection process. The data collection, organization, and subsequent analysis then have purpose and meaning.

Investigations, Games, and Literature-Based Activities

TEACHER-TO-TEACHER TALK   For this unit of study, it might be helpful to refer to the "Calculation Routines and Practices" section (page 331) before studying and implementing any of the following lessons. Lessons that promote, develop, and support algebraic thinking can offer continued opportunities for calculation practice and numerical reasoning. I have presented an overview of the arithmetic practices often found in standard fourth-grade curricula that can be explored in May. You may wish to thread these arithmetic practices throughout the lessons when appropriate. For example, I often introduce work with parentheses and substitution when working with functions. I refer to true and false mathematical statements throughout the month. I use variables whenever appropriate in discussions and tasks. If this line of thinking and lesson planning intrigues you, you can begin to include some of these practices in other units of study throughout the year in years to come. You may wish to check out some of the references listed at the end of the chapter to help supplement yearlong work with algebraic thinking routines and practices.

Graphing Tic-Tac-Toe: An Exploration of Coordinate Grids

Duration: 1–2 class periods

This graphing version of tic-tac-toe, adapted from *Lessons for Algebraic Thinking, Grades 3–5* (Wickett, Kharas, and Burns 2002), requires students to plot points on a coordinate grid. This game offers students the opportunity to:

- practice plotting ordered pairs on a coordinate graph within a problem-solving context
- articulate and reinforce the standard language and notation of graphing

Materials

- 1 overhead transparency of centimeter grid paper (see Blackline Masters) or piece of chart paper with a grid drawn on it
- 1 overhead transparency of *Graphing Tic-Tac-Toe* one-quadrant grids sheet (see Blackline Masters)
- 2–3 *Graphing Tic-Tac-Toe* one-quadrant grids sheets per pair of students
- *The Fly on the Ceiling*, by Julie Glass (1998)
- optional: 2–3 *Graphing Tic-Tac-Toe* four-quadrant grids sheets per pair of students (see Blackline Masters)

This version of tic-tac-toe engages students' interest, making it an ideal activity to introduce or provide practice with plotting points on a coordinate graph. Although I make game boards available to the students for their tic-tac-toe games, I introduce the lesson in a whole-class format with a blank centimeter grid transparency or piece of chart paper on which I've drawn a blank grid. I want the children to understand the underlying structure of graphing and not simply the process of plotting points. When the children are initially involved in the construction and discussion of a coordinate grid, they can begin to make sense of the system, its labels, and the numbers along each axis.

Begin by showing the class a blank grid and asking, "What do we know about using grid paper?" This allows the children to share their prior knowledge of mathematical representation and graphing. Some children may say that they do everything on grid paper, from multiplying to scratch work. Direct the conversation to the use of grid paper for graphing. Have a quick discussion of bar graphs and line plots, focusing on how we use the paper and its grid lines to help us represent the data.

The difficulty in moving from bar graphs to coordinate graphs is understanding where, how, and why to number the axes. It is important to have our children construct their own graphs and axes. If they do not, they won't understand where to place the numbers along each axis or why this numbering system makes sense. Although I do have the children use prepared game boards for the follow-up activity, the initial instruction revolves around the creation of the coordinate grid. I place a point on an intersection somewhere in the middle of my blank grid and ask, "What can you tell me about this point?" This question is usually met by some silence, which is my intent! We actually know nothing about this point—its location or what it represents.

I now introduce the coordinate graphing system to the class with this lone point and the axes constructed around it. (See Figure 9–1.)

It's important to include the intersecting lines at the origin (0, 0) of this graph in this introduction. This representation allows the children to think beyond Quadrant I and realize that perhaps points can be located in surrounding quadrants. Although I do not introduce this idea at this particular time, if students bring it up, I'm happy to have a short discussion about it.

"What can you tell me about this point now?" I ask. Hayden announced to the class that the point fell in between those two lines but that

FIGURE 9–1 ▶

A coordinate graphing system.

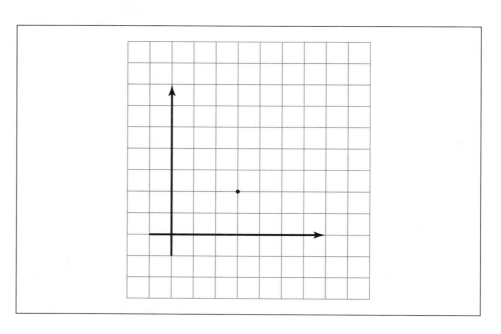

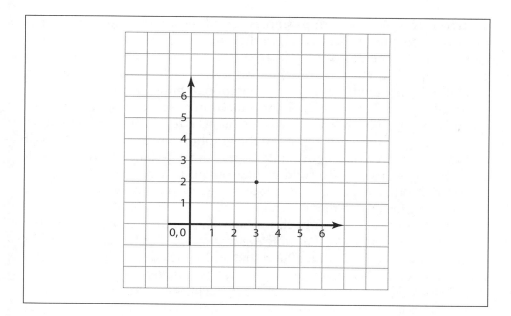

FIGURE 9–2   ◀

A labeled coordinate grid.

it "still [didn't] have a home." As I placed tick marks along the x-axis, I asked the class if this might help give that point a "home." The class agreed to number the x-axis in intervals of one as well as the y-axis. "Hey look! Two number lines!" Hayden responded. (See Figure 9–2.)

Encouraging the children to identify the axes as number lines will help those who are interested to later move their *Tic-Tac-Toe* games into Quadrants II, III, and IV.

We continued to discuss the coordinate graphing system. I introduced the term *origin* and pointed out its location on the graph. We also talked about the labels of the axes. Because my children are accustomed to the labels of □ and △ to identify the x and y values of in-and-out tables, I initially label the x-axis with a □ and the y-axis with a △.

I asked, "Where have we seen these labels before?" to help the children make connections between their previous work with in-and-out tables and our present work with the coordinate grid. I then introduced the x and y labels and placed them on the axes as well. By the end of the unit, most children abandon the □ and △ labels for the more sophisticated x and y. According to Robert, the use of the x and y labels makes the students "look smarter."

Next I asked, "What can you tell me now about this point?" to redirect the focus of the lesson back to the location of points on a coordinate grid. I informed the children that we were first going to determine how far over we needed to go on the x-axis as we labeled the location of this point. Sarah was quick to respond that we had to go over four and then up six to find the "home" of the point. I wrote Sarah's words on the board: *go over four and then up six*. I explained that mathematicians label this point's home with an *ordered pair* of (4, 6) and that we would do the same.

Taking the time to discuss the meaning of (4, 6) and the conventions of writing an ordered pair will help establish symbolic expectations. Each ordered pair is written with parentheses, and the *x* and *y* values are separated by a comma. I listed several other ordered pairs on the board and had children come up to the grid to plot the points. I also plotted some points and asked students for their respective ordered pairs to develop flexibility in moving from one representation to another.

Graphing Tic-Tac-Toe can be introduced in a whole-class format with you playing against the class when you feel that your children have obtained an initial understanding of the graphing process. This version of tic-tac-toe is played on a coordinate graph with a T-chart identifying each player's ordered pairs. Two children play on one board, taking turns as the recorder of ordered pairs. I introduce the game on the overhead with a copy of the game board that the children will be using. (See Figure 9–3.)

An in-depth discussion and a classroom vignette of *Graphing Tic-Tac-Toe* can be found in *Lessons for Teaching Algebraic Thinking, Grades 3–5* (Wickett, Kharas, and Burns 2002). That resource also includes a follow-up lesson titled *Four Points: Investigating Patterns in Coordinates*, which engages students in looking for patterns of ordered pairs in lines found in winning games.

The children break up into pairs and play several rounds of *Graphing Tic-Tac-Toe*. As you circulate around the room, you will become aware of children who have mastered the graphing and recording process. I present them with the ordered pair (3, –2) and ask them where that point might "live" on their graph. The children are quick to begin to move over three on the *x*-axis and then speculate as to where the –2 would be on the *y*-axis. Rebecca and Deborah were quite certain that the point was somewhere beyond the boundaries of their Quadrant I grid. "Can we extend these number lines?" Deborah asked as she continued the *y*-axis below (0, 0). Deborah continued her reasoning aloud. "Since the numbers above (zero, zero) are positive, then maybe we can continue with negative numbers below (zero, zero)." Deborah acted upon her instincts and did not wait for

FIGURE 9–3 ▶

One pair's completed *Graphing Tic-Tac-Toe* **board and T-chart.**

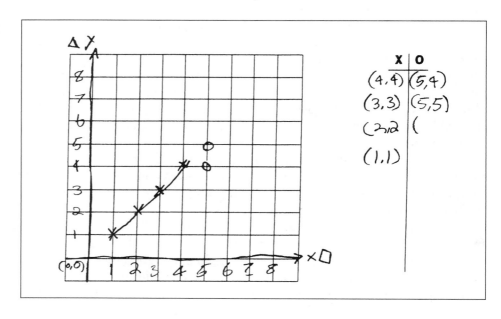

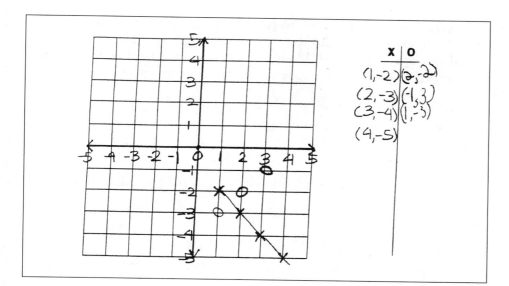

FIGURE 9–4 ◄

Rebecca and Deborah's completed game board extending into all four quadrants.

my reply. She continued both the *x*-axis and *y*-axis into their respective negative directions. (See Figure 9–4.)

It will be helpful to determine how you plan to differentiate the instruction for the two versions of this game. There are times when I work with small groups of six to eight children and times when I work with pairs. Some years, an entire class is ready to move into the use of negative numbers, and some years, only a few are ready and able. Identifying the strengths and needs of your students as well as the purpose of the lesson will help you make thoughtful decisions about differentiating instruction.

Read *The Fly on the Ceiling* (Glass 1998) aloud to bring closure to the lesson and reinforce the time spent plotting ordered pairs on a coordinate graph. Your students will be engaged and entertained by the story of Rene Descartes and his resolution to the dilemma of one very messy house.

Follow-Up Journal Write

Without graphing the following points, what can you tell me about the picture that they make? Why does your thinking make sense?

(3, 2)

(4, 2)

(5, 2)

(6, 2)

Ins and Outs: Functions

Duration: 2–3 class periods, followed by shorter explorations throughout the unit

Students' observations of patterns that define how quantities in tables of values (T-charts) are related provide them with beginning experiences with functions. Functions allow us to identify, generalize, and represent relationships between variables. Functions model change and can be represented in ways that help children understand and articulate that change. This series of lessons offers students the opportunity to:

- examine, record, and extend a growth pattern
- investigate the T-chart as a representation of change
- describe and represent a function with a rule and an algebraic equation
- practice and apply calculation skills in a problem-solving context

Materials

- *Two of Everything*, by Lily Toy Hong (1993)
- 1 copy of Magic Pot Task, Version 1 or Version 2 per pair of students (see Blackline Masters)
- several blank transparencies

Chances are your fourth graders have had some experiences with in-and-out tables in previous grades. T-charts representing growth patterns can be drawn horizontally or vertically, as shown:

In (□)	0	2	4	6	10
Out (△)	3	5	7	9	13

In □	*Out* △
0	3
2	5
4	7
6	9
10	13

$$Out = In + 3$$
$$△ = □ + 3$$

Presenting values in both horizontal and vertical formats offers opportunities for children to think flexibly as they move from one representation to another. Each set of ins and outs has a rule associating each in value with exactly one out value, as illustrated by the equations above. Although I do not refer to ins and outs directly as *functions* with my fourth graders, they are aware that a relationship or rule pairs every in value with exactly one out value.

I began the lesson by reading aloud the Chinese folktale *Two of Everything*, by Lily Toy Hong (1993). The children were delighted with the escapades of Mr. and Mrs. Haktak and their magic pot. I asked the class to describe the magic pot to set the stage for our work with ins and outs. As the children described the doubling process, I wrote their ideas on the board.

Put in 1 coin purse—get out 2!

Drop in 1 hair pin—get out 2!

One Mrs. Haktak falls in—get out 2!

I reminded the children that all this writing was a little cumbersome. Because my children had had previous experiences with ins and outs, they immediately suggested representing this information in a T-chart. You may be pleasantly surprised at the ease with which your children move to charting mathematical language by this time in the school year. I reminded the children of the importance of efficiency. A T-chart would allow us to examine the mathematics of the story with greater efficiency and clarity.

In □	Out △

After constructing the T-chart on the board, I referred to the language on the board describing the actions of the Haktaks. "When Mr. Haktak puts in one coin purse, two come out." As the children retold the story, they agreed that this was a doubling magic pot. I posed other in values for the class within the context of the story, such as:

- What if Mr. Haktak put two carrots into the pot? What would come out?

- What if Mrs. Haktak put three socks into the pot? What would come out?

- What if Mrs. Haktak put four eggs in the pot? What would come out?

- What if Mr. Haktak put five seeds in the pot? What would come out?

As the students responded to my questions, I continued to add values to the in-and-out table.

In □	Out △
1	2
2	4
3	6
4	8
5	10

Once these first five values were posted in the table, I asked my favorite question: "What do you notice?" Michael noticed that the out values increased by two each time. Alison noticed that as the in values went up by one, the out values went up by two. Robert reminded us that we were all doing too much work; all we really had to do was take the in value and multiply it by two to get the out value.

Although the mathematics of the conversation may appear simplistic, the relational ideas with which the children were working are not. Michael and Alison were looking at the *iterative* relationship of the values—identifying how a value determines the one that follows it. Robert was looking at the *explicit* relationship—identifying the rule with which we could determine an out value for any given in value. Michael and Alison were looking vertically to identify the doubling relationship, whereas Robert was looking horizontally. Our fourth graders need experiences that can offer contexts in which to do both. They need to identify and articulate how the pattern is growing from one stage to the next. Although some children may be more ready than others to identify and articulate a rule to generalize the growth for any stage, we need to continue to offer experiences that will help our children develop these algebraic habits of mind. One such support can be the use of a written prompt like "To find the number of items found in the pot, you. . ." Offering language that will scaffold the rule can give them access to the relational thinking required by the task.

I asked Michael, Alison, and Robert to repeat their observations so I could write them on the board. The conversation of efficiency once again began. The class agreed that although Michael and Alison's observations were certainly correct, Robert's was the easiest one to write mathematically. I asked the children to talk with their neighbor about the different ways we could write Robert's rule. The class generated the following list as well as identified the commutativity of the equations.

$Out = 2 \times In$

$Out = In \times 2$

$\triangle = 2 \times \square$

$\triangle = \square \times 2$

I then suggested ten as my next in value. "What if Mr. Haktak put ten goldfish in the pot?" The class responded in unison that Mr. Haktak would be able to get twenty fish out of the pot. Moving to the tenth stage encouraged the children to apply the explicit rule of Out = 2 × In rather than think iteratively.

In $\square$	Out $\triangle$
1	2
2	4
3	6
4	8
5	10
.	.
.	.
.	.
10	20

To increase their awareness of the efficiency of the explicit rule, I asked the children if it was necessary to include all the values between five and ten. They agreed that we did not need those middle values, but we could put them in if we wanted or needed to. This is an important point to make with your class in order to support those children who may continue to need the iterative scaffolding in order to determine a table value. Questions such as "What if Mrs. Haktak pulled out fourteen heads of lettuce? How many did she drop in?" will offer additional opportunities for the children to think flexibly.

Next we discussed how many items Mr. Haktak would pull out if he dropped twenty of those items in the pot. We added *20* to the In column and *40* to the Out column. You will need to decide whether or not to talk about an in value of one hundred. Because one hundred is a friendly number for most fourth graders, I include it as the next in value and continue to do so with other functions.

I asked the children to get out their math notebooks and pair up with someone at their table. I presented the class with another magic pot scenario. As I constructed the T-chart, I asked the students to think quietly about what the magic pot might be doing.

In □	Out △
1	5

I stopped after the first set of values and asked the students what they could tell me so far about my pattern. It is important for the children to realize that one set of values is not enough information to make a decision about a rule or relationship between values. Jackson announced that the rule could be "plus four." "Could it be anything else?" I asked, knowing that a "times five" rule was also a possibility at this point.

"Oh yeah," commented Vidya. "It could also be a 'times five' rule. Hey, could it be either?" I informed the class that only one rule can apply to a set of ins and outs, but I would put in the next set of values and then we could decide which one was correct.

In □	Out △
1	5
2	6

"Well, it's not times five," Robert announced.

"How do you know?" I asked.

Robert explained that a "times five" rule with an in value of two would result in an out value of ten. "And last time I checked, six is not equal to ten!" Robert continued, to the delight of his classmates.

"How about another in value?" asked Jackson. I asked the class to discuss with a neighbor why seeing another set of values would be helpful. They had important discussions about the need to double-check predictions with additional in values.

The lesson continued as I recorded additional in values that supported a rule of Out = In + 4. The T-chart was formatted in the same way as the initial T-chart.

In □	Out △
1	5
2	6
3	7
4	?
5	?
.	.
.	.
.	.
10	?
.	.
.	.
.	.
100	?

I instructed the children to complete the T-chart in their notebooks and then discuss the rule with a neighbor. I asked them to write their rule *in words* and then work together to rewrite it *as an equation.* (See Figure 9–5.)

As mentioned previously, it is not the mathematics that makes this task challenging, but rather the generalization from the values, to the words, and then to the rule. There are important connections to be made as the children write out the relationship in words and then move to symbols. Their words ground the rule in meaning. When + *4* shows up in a rule, I ask the children to show me the + *4* in their T-chart and in their words.

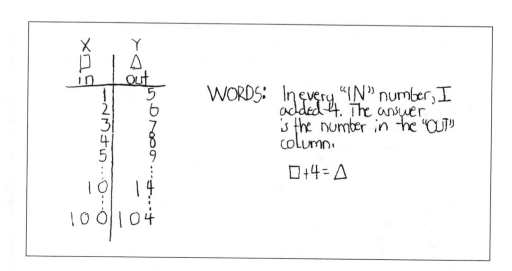

FIGURE 9–5 ◀

Nolan and Jackson's T-chart and rule ($y = x + 4$).

The task of moving from words to the symbolic representation of a rule can set the stage nicely for a discussion about the term *equation*. Teachers and students alike often use the term freely without an understanding of the sense that the word itself actually makes. An equation contains an equals sign. Therefore, a number sentence must contain an equals sign in order to be called an equation. The root word of *equation* is *equate* or *equal*. Therefore, any number sentence containing an equals sign is an equation. An *inequality* contains a greater than, less than, or not equal to ($\neq$) sign. An *expression*, on the other hand, is a numerical phrase without a relational symbol such as $=$, $<$, $>$, or $\neq$. Equations and inequalities can be true, false, or open and are discussed in further detail in the "Calculation Routines and Practices" section on page 331. We can certainly continue to refer to equations and inequalities as number sentences, but an understanding and usage of these terms will familiarize students with the algebraic terminology they will be expected to use in the middle grades.

Equations	*Inequalities*	*Expressions*
$4 + 13 = 17$	$14 < 5 \times 5$	$24 + 3$
$2 + (4 \times 3) = 14$	$24 > 20 + 1$	$14 - \triangle$
$20 = \square + 13$	$21 \neq 25 - 5$	$6 + (7 \times 4)$

Then I pass out directions for the Magic Pot Task, Version 1, which instructs students to create their own magic pot pattern with a partner. When children complete one set of ins and outs, I have them complete another. You may wish to differentiate the task in order to support struggling learners. Some children may not be ready to make that cognitive leap from iterative thinking (using the previous stage to predict the following) to explicit generalization (identifying a rule that will work with any stage). You can give those children the Magic Pot Task, Version 2, which asks students to identify the ins and outs for the first twenty stages rather than make the leap from Stage 5 to Stage 10 to Stage 100. There are years when I introduce the task with this format to the entire class. Such decisions will depend on the strengths and needs of your students as well as your particular mathematical objectives for the lesson.

Suggest pairs discuss the following talking points as they work through their initial T-chart.

- What will the pot do? Will it add, subtract, multiply, or divide?
- Will it do one operation? Or two?
- Where do you see the growth numerically when you move from stage to stage? Is the growth consistent and predictable?
- Have you created patterns within patterns?
- What happens when you put in an even number? Will this be the pattern for every even number? What happens when you put in an odd number? Will this pattern be the same for every odd number? What do you notice about your out values? Are they all even? All odd? Even and odd? Is there a pattern to their distribution?

The value of meaningful partner talk that can accompany this activity cannot be overemphasized. It is through the talk that questions, observations, and generalizations develop. Students begin to take ownership of these important mathematical ideas as well as develop confidence and competence in their ability to make sense of the mathematics.

As you move around the room, there will undoubtedly be some T-charts that catch your eye. Some may be mathematically interesting. Some might be mathematically incorrect. Choose a few interesting T-charts and ask the authors to reproduce just their T-chart (not the rule) on a blank transparency to share with the class. Conference with authors of T-charts characterized by incorrect mathematics to gain insights into their thinking. Asking, rather than telling, can be an important assessment and instructional tool. As the children field your questions, they will begin to self-assess and self-correct. I much prefer for children to work with their mistakes rather than to begin all over again. "How can we make this work?" is a question that honors the children's initial work but, at the same time, encourages them to rethink and rework. Once revisions have been made, encourage the pair to try out the rule with other in values to check for accuracy.

When each set of partners has completed at least two tasks, call the class together to share T-charts. Ask partners to keep track of the analyzed T-charts, their calculations, and the respective rules in their math notebooks. Also ask them to add three additional in values to each T-chart and calculate their respective out values according to the identified rule. Once again, partner talk should be encouraged and facilitated as you move around the room. Posing some of the following questions will support the conversations:

- What do you notice about the growth of this pattern?
- Is the growth constant between the out values from stage to stage?
- What do you notice about the in and out value of a specific stage? Is one value greater than the other? Is this relationship consistent with every stage?
- What is the relationship between the in value and the out value of each stage? Is this relationship consistent for every stage?
- Do you need one operation to get to the out value from the in value? Do you need two operations? How do you know?
- How do you know your rule works?
- If you were given the out value, how could you figure out the in value? What calculations would you use? Why does that make sense?
- Is your rule written as an equation? How do you know?

Figure 9–6 shows one recording page from Gracie's notebook.

The arithmetic embedded in this lesson is rich. As the children work to create their rules and in and out values, they practice and fine-tune basic calculation skills. Further calculation practice is carried out as

FIGURE 9–6 ▶

A recording page from Gracie's notebook.

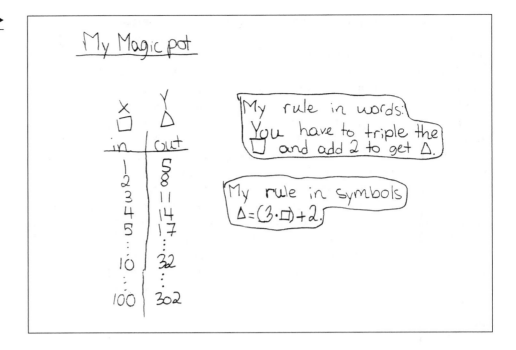

children work to identify each other's rules and add additional values. You may find it helpful to teach a minilesson on the use of parentheses as the children are creating rules from T-charts. The use of parentheses can help organize procedures and give greater clarity to the rule. Additional discussion about the teaching, learning, and use of parentheses can be found in the "Calculation Routines and Practices" section on page 331.

You may also wish to consider teaching a minilesson on using the variables x and y to represent respective in and out values. Our students will eventually move from the In and Out labels to the x and y labels as they enter the middle grades. Although the In and Out labels are developmentally appropriate and perfectly acceptable, being aware of how the T-chart relates to the axes of a coordinate graph may be helpful and even interesting to some children at this point in time.

Post daily in and out values as morning work throughout the month for students to complete in their math notebooks to provide further practice. This routine allows you the opportunity to introduce other function formats without formal instruction. Format options can include the following:

- giving out values and asking the children to calculate the in values
- using words or pictures rather than numbers
- presenting T-charts horizontally as well as vertically
- presenting in values in nonnumerical order

In	Out
27	9
12	4
30	10
?	7
?	12
90	?

In	Out
goose	geese
mouse	mice
wolf	wolves
?	sheep
aardvark	?
puppy	?

In	5	10	4	0	?	?
Out	11	21	9	?	15	101

Two of Everything Revisited is a lesson in *Lessons for Algebraic Thinking, Grades 3–5* (Wickett, Kharas, and Burns 2002) that extends the work completed with *Two of Everything*. In that lesson, students explore how plotting points on a coordinate graph produces a graph of a particular pattern. Students graph other patterns and investigate how graphs relate to the equations they represent. Too often children are introduced to function tables (T-charts), equations, and graphs in isolation. Our fourth graders are very capable of identifying and articulating the connections between all three representations when they are offered opportunities to make these connections visible.

TEACHER-TO-TEACHER TALK   The question inevitably arises: How hard can we push our fourth graders to think algebraically? Marilyn Burns reminds us that you cannot talk a child into learning or tell a child to understand (Burns 2007). But thinking algebraically is something most children already do! Mathematical investigations and conversations of our fourth graders already contain elements of algebraic thinking. They are intrigued by geometric and numerical patterns and are learning how to represent these patterns with words, symbols, tables, and graphs. They are able to think about how a change in one variable (in value) relates to a change in another (out value). They are learning how to make and test generalizations. They are exploring number properties and how they apply to whole number calculations. Exploring and articulating these ideas allow children to develop ways of thinking about arithmetic that are consistent with the expectations that the formal study of algebra will ask of them in later grades. It becomes our responsibility as teachers to facilitate explorations and conversations that help move children beyond the arithmetic that elementary school math curricula have traditionally presented. Students who are successful in mathematics are not simply better at computing. They are better able to make generalizations and recognize relationships between concepts and procedures. They can and do think algebraically.

The Banquet Table Problem: Representing Growing Patterns

Duration: 3–4 class periods

A great deal of time is spent in elementary mathematics classrooms describing and representing patterns. By examining patterns, we notice regularity, variety, and the interconnectedness of ideas. This lesson, which builds upon students' previous experiences with patterns, investigates a geometric pattern. Students use pictures, words, numbers, and a graph to represent growth patterns for perimeters of tables made from pattern blocks. Students measure perimeters as they place the blocks end-to-end. This lesson offers students opportunities to:

- explore, predict, and represent patterns that grow
- connect geometry, number, and algebra
- explore equivalent expressions and equations
- represent patterns with pictures (geometry), words, numbers (T-chart), symbols (equation), and graphs
- move flexibly from one representation of a pattern to another

Materials

- 1 tub of square, triangle, and trapezoid pattern blocks per group of students
- 1 set of overhead pattern blocks
- 1 sheet of 12-by-18-inch white construction paper or newsprint per child
- 1 sheet of 1-inch grid paper per student (see Blackline Masters)
- 1 colored pencil per student
- glue sticks
- 1 sheet of centimeter grid paper per child (see Blackline Masters)
- 1 piece of chart paper
- *Spaghetti and Meatballs for All!* by Marilyn Burns (1997)

A quick discussion and demonstration of repeating and nonrepeating patterns can set the stage for this investigation. I asked the children to continue the pattern with me when they could identify what it was. I snapped and clapped:

SCSCSC

We agreed to label this sequence a *repeating pattern* because the core of the pattern (*SC*) repeated over and over. I then moved to demonstrating a nonrepeating pattern. Once again I asked the children to join in when they could identify what it was.

SCSSCCSSSCCC

We labeled this sequence a *nonrepeating* or *growth pattern*. Growth patterns are more difficult to identify and articulate. Students not only have to determine what comes next but also must be able to generalize about the pattern from stage to stage within the sequence.

I distributed tubs of pattern blocks to each table. Free exploration time is always a good thing with pattern blocks. Every time I pull them out, my class always complains that we do not use them enough!

After a few minutes, I asked the children to place all of the blocks back in the tub in the middle of the table, with the exception of a collection of five squares per child. I always find it interesting to ask the children what they think we could investigate with these five squares. After the children offered several conjectures about what we could investigate, I informed them that we would be making banquet tables with our square blocks and representing how many people could sit at our tables as the tables grew.

My class always feels very grown-up when one of the students asks about the constraints of our investigation. (They love to use the word *constraint*.) For this activity, I presented the following constraints:

- One side of each polygon must completely touch a side of another polygon for each table.
- A "chair" can be placed at each open side of one unit, represented by the side length of the polygon.
- The formation of the tables is to be linear.

I placed one square on the overhead. "How many people can sit at this table?" I asked. All the children agreed that four people would be able to sit at this table. Even though the pattern block square offered a visual model of the table, I asked the children if we could represent the table and what the sides represented with greater clarity on the board. Matthew came up to the board and drew a square. We spent some time discussing representation—the symbols that we used in past work that could help us represent the available sides for chairs. Kira reminded us that we used hash marks to identify side lengths during our work with geometry. We all agreed that this made sense.

The visual representation on the board allowed many of the children to make the connection between sides of a table and perimeter, which is precisely what we were investigating! We agreed that this square had a perimeter of 4, or that this banquet table could seat four people.

Then I asked, "What about a table made from two squares? How many people could we seat now?" Before sending the students off to build the new table, I asked partners to discuss how many people could be seated at this new table. As you can imagine, many children responded with an answer of eight people because $2 \times 4 = 8$. As the class studied the diagram on the board or the single square in front of them, many children were able to articulate how adding a square actually took away the two internal sides of the new table.

I asked, a "What do you notice?" to encourage students to articulate what was happening mathematically when another square was added to the table. Once again, the drawing on the board as well as the blocks in front of them helped children visualize what was happening mathematically as well as geometrically.

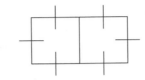

When asked about a new table made of three squares, many children will tell you what the perimeter will *not* be! Take advantage of these counterexamples with questions such as "How do you know that the perimeter will not be twelve? Why does that make sense?" Children need to hear and talk about the generalizations being made by their classmates.

Working with a neighbor, the children built banquet tables with three, four, and five squares, always making conjectures about the perimeter of each new table prior to building it. I often refer to each new table as a new *stage*. Because the stage number corresponds to the number of squares in a table, the children move between the two labels flexibly.

At this point in the investigation, I distributed large sheets of construction paper or newsprint and 1-inch grid paper to each child. Children continued to work with their partners, but each child constructed his own poster representing the growth of this pattern of tables. I asked the children to construct the first five tables at the top of their posters by outlining tables on 1-inch grid paper, coloring them in, and cutting them out. They glued these paper tables at the top of their posters and identified the available seating with slash marks. They also labeled each table stage: *Stage 1, Stage 2, Stage 3,* and so on. (See Figure 9–7.)

The geometric pictures that the children created told the story of the growth of this pattern. We had a quick discussion about the story of this growth. As the children offered descriptions of this particular growth story, I wrote their ideas on the board. Students might present the following ideas:

- The perimeter is *not* equal to the *total number of squares times four* that you use for your table.

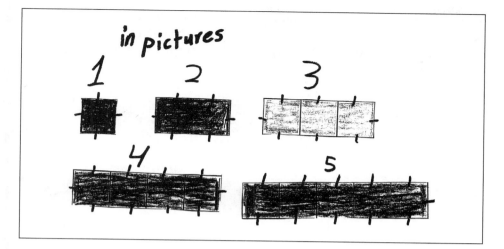

FIGURE 9–7 ◄

Kira's first five tables.

- Every time you add a square table, you add four sides, but then you have to take away some sides because they are inside the table and no one can sit there. So you are adding and then subtracting.
- You start with *four times the number of squares*; then you have to take away groups of two sides that are inside the new table.
- There will always be a *plus two* for the end perimeters of each table.
- You just *plus two* from the number of seats from the table before.

I posted snippets of their explanations on the board to help the children formulate a written representation of this pattern in words. I often model the writing with the children as we construct a group description. Together, we craft an explanation and I post it on the class poster. Although we eventually work toward a rule for the growth of this pattern, I prefer to keep the focus on a verbal description at this point in the investigation. The more the children talk about the growth and see the growth in their drawings, the more sense the rule will make when we are ready to move from words and pictures to symbols. (See Figure 9–8.)

Introducing the need for the numerical representation of this pattern now had a purpose. I drew a T-chart to help us keep track of and represent the numerical growth of the perimeters of the tables. At this point in the

FIGURE 9–8 ◄

Kira's written
representation of
the pattern.

in words

I found the way I see it
is the most efficient. My way is
you take the number of tables,
multiply it by 2 and then add
2 seats at the end. "..... There's a
+2 in there somewhere..."

year, do not be surprised if children have already constructed T-charts—be impressed! I asked the children to create T-charts on their posters to represent the growth numerically for this pattern. Because my students had experiences with creating T-charts in previous lessons, they knew what to do.

Squares	Perimeter
1	4
2	6
3	8
4	10
5	12
.	.
.	.
.	.
10	?
.	.
.	.
.	.
100	?

Once the first five stages were represented, we looked at the relationships found in the T-chart—both vertically and horizontally. I asked the children where they had seen T-charts before to help them connect prior work with function tables to this lesson. Children usually recognize the T-chart format, but they may not readily articulate that the chart also represents a functional relationship. A question such as "What can you tell me about this T-chart if I add these labels?" will help make the functional relationship accessible.

Squares In	Perimeter Out

Now that the in and out values were entered for Stages 1 through 5, I asked, "What do you notice?" to help the children identify and articulate patterns within the data. Students may offer the following observations:

- As the number of squares goes up by *one*, the perimeters go up by *two*.

- The perimeter is always *double the number of squares plus two* for the two end seats.

- All tables have an even number of seats/an even perimeter.

- A square has four sides, but there is *not* a *plus four* or a *times four* when you move from table to table!

- If you think of each additional table as having four sides, you actually have to take away sides because you cannot sit at those sides inside the table.

Ask, "What can you tell me about a banquet table made from ten squares?" to offer opportunities for the students to generalize about the pattern. Many children will say that the perimeter will be an even number because all the perimeters from the first five stages have been even numbers. Many will generalize that the perimeter will be 22 because that is double the number of squares plus two more. Many will add that the perimeter will *not* be 40! I often ask the children if they need to make a table of ten squares. The response is often varied. Some say yes. Some suggest making a table of six squares just to test out the generalization one more time. I ask the children to build, draw, and talk about representations to help them predict the perimeter for a table of ten squares with their neighbor. They then share their observations and conclusions.

Do not hesitate to make the connection between the geometry of the tables and the numbers of the T-chart explicit. Good questions such as the following will help make the connection deliberate, visible, and accessible.

- What do you notice?
- Where is the growth of the perimeters in your pictures? Where does that same growth show up in the T-chart? How and where is the *plus two* represented in the T-chart?
- Where is the growth in the T-chart from table to table? Where does that show up in the pictures of the tables? How and where does the *plus two* represent itself in the pictures?
- What relationship do you see between the number of squares and the perimeter? Is that relationship the same with every new table?
- Does the information in the T-chart represent the same information presented in the pictures of the tables? How do you know?

As we extended the T-chart to include a table made from one hundred squares, the children felt confident with the arithmetic and the beginning generalizations of a rule to predict the perimeter of any table. Asking children to predict the perimeters of tables made from other numbers of squares such as twenty-nine, thirty-five, and seventy-six can provide calculation practice as well as practice in solving equations by substitution.

Asking the children to simplify their oral observations into a rule that represents the growth of the pattern can be tricky business. Once again, keep in mind that this may be a stretch for some students. These children can draw the sequence, write about the sequence, and explain the growth in a T-chart, but may have difficulties stating a rule for the growth. Once a rule is suggested, such as *double the number of squares then add two*, ask the class to try out the rules with the values in the T-chart. Do the numbers make sense? Will a table with a perimeter of 18 be made from eight squares? What about a table made of one hundred squares? How many squares will make up a table with a perimeter of 24? Ask children about both the in values and the out values to encourage flexibility in their thinking. It will also stretch their understanding of the functional relationship represented in the T-chart between the in and out values. Equivalent representations of this rule may include:

$(2 \times \square) + 2 = \triangle$

$(2 \times in\ value) + 2 = out\ value$

$2\square + 2 = \triangle$

$2x + 2 = y$

Do not dismiss the children who continue to see the growth pattern as adding groups of four and then subtracting unused sides. Although the math may be a little messy and beyond most fourth graders, the $2x + 2$ rule can eventually be sifted out from this idea. The initial rule may be articulated as:

Start with the number of tables times four. The number of shared sides that has to be taken out will be one less than the total number of squares and then doubled because there are two shared sides.

If you put symbols to the words, the rule may look like the following:

$(\square \times 4) - 2(\square - 1) = \triangle$

This rule can be simplified to:

$(\square \times 4) - (2 \times \square) + 2 = \triangle$

This can then be simplified to:

$4\square - 2\square + 2 = \triangle$

Finally, it can be simplified to:

$2\square + 2 = \triangle$

This may appear to be a roundabout way to get to the rule, but the idea that this rule can be simplified from the ones above is very cool—and a very big idea of algebraic thinking. What we have here are different ways of seeing the growth with seemingly different representations that simplify to the same equation. Very cool.

Students can now complete the T-chart on their posters and post a rule below the T-chart. I try to keep the symbolic representation of the variables within the rule consistent with class accessibility. In some years, my class much prefers the use of □ and △. In other years, the class easily moves to the conventions of x and y. Once again, remind the children that all these representations tell the same story of the growth of perimeters of square banquet tables. They have now told the story in pictures, words, numbers, and symbols.

The final representation of this pattern to be explored is the graph. Graphs will be completed on centimeter grid paper. When completed, the graphs will be the final representation to be mounted on the posters. After distributing the graph paper, ask the children to turn their attention to the T-chart representing the growth of this pattern. Even though you have now labeled the number of squares as the in value and the respective perimeter as the out value, the ability to move from the T-chart to the graph may still be elusive. Ask the children if they can name the in values and out values with any other labels to move them a little closer to recognizing and identifying the connection. If a student suggests using a box and a triangle, respond by asking, "Would those labels make sense with this pattern?" to help the children access prior knowledge and experience with function tables.

Squares In □	Perimeter Out △
1	4
2	6
3	8
4	10
5	12
.	.
.	.
.	.
10	22
.	.
.	.
.	.
100	202

As my children talked with one another at their tables about adding the □ and △ labels, I added the labels to our class T-chart. When the class was called together, the children quickly agreed that adding these labels made sense; we were still dealing with ins and outs, and the □ and △ were just other names for these same ideas and relationships.

I informed the students that they would represent this growth on a graph that would contain the data from our T-chart. As I drew the axes for the class graph on chart paper, the children created their own axes and labeled them □ (x-axis) and △ (y-axis) on centimeter grid paper. In this situation, I ask the children to also represent each axis with its conventional label of x or y. Some children are ready to let go of the □ and △ labels and some are not. But at this point in the unit, I want the students to be at least familiar with the conventional notation. You also might consider moving from the □ and △ labels to S for number of squares and P for length (units) of perimeter. These contextual labels can scaffold the thinking necessary for children as they begin to move toward using the more abstract labels of x and y.

The class then began plotting ordered pairs from the T-chart. As the points were being plotted, I heard some students whispering about the shape of the graph. I explained to the children that this graph told the same story of the growth of this pattern as the pictures of the tables, the words, and the T-chart. I asked them to recount what they knew about the story of this pattern.

- Each time a square is added to the table, the perimeter goes up by two.
- The growth of the perimeters is constant.
- Table 1 starts with a perimeter of 4.

I asked the children to talk with a neighbor about where they could literally see this information in the graph. Once I called the class back together, we used the class graph to illustrate talking points. Sarah, who loved working with graphs, was quick to identify and articulate a staircase pattern: "You go over one, then up two, over one, then up two. It is just the same pattern as in the T-chart. Every time you go up to the next table, you plus two to get the perimeter." I mentioned that Sarah had described what mathematicians label as the *slope* of a line and we talked briefly about the term.

Use what you know about the culture of your class to help students make real-life connections to the term *slope*. Here in New England, those children who ski or sled have a context for the word. They use it freely and easily because it is part of their daily language. Your children may have experiences with hiking or skate boarding that allow them to make similar connections. Use them!

Once the graph was completed, we talked about whether or not to connect the points on the graph. Focusing on the context of the pattern helped me direct that conversation. When the points on a graph are connected, we can assume that every point along that graph represents a solution. I placed a point made of construction paper that could easily be attached and then removed from the graph on $(3\frac{1}{2}, 9)$. I asked the children to tell me about this table. Matthew said that the graph indicated that this table could exist, but we really couldn't have a table with $3\frac{1}{2}$ squares. In this case, our context presented *discrete* data. There were only whole number squares and whole number perimeters, so discrete points on a graph made sense according to the context of the problem. We agreed that within this context, our points should not be connected because it would not make any sense to do so. I often enlist the help of the science teacher to support this idea of when to connect or not connect the points on a graph. My children create graphs in science class to represent the growth of plants, and those points are connected because of the context of continual growth.

The children then glued their graphs onto their posters. Once again, I reminded them that all the representations on their posters told the same story. Fourth graders have all had experiences in creating these representations in isolation. But until we are deliberate in pulling them together and offering opportunities for children to move from one representation to the other, the connectedness of the representations remains unnoticed. (See Figure 9–9.)

The children will be delighted with an oral reading of Marilyn Burns's *Spaghetti and Meatballs for All!* (1997) at the conclusion of this lesson. The children will quickly recognize the banquet table context and the silliness of Mr. Comfort's thinking.

This is a time-consuming but algebraically powerful series of activities. Even so, you'll need to offer additional experiences in order for the children to make this knowledge and these practices their own.

Extension

You may wish to extend this lesson by asking the children to construct a pattern of growing banquet tables made from trapezoids and then triangles. I personally love the move from squares to trapezoids because the perimeter of the two pattern blocks is different even though they are both quadrilaterals. The move to triangles is equally interesting. What I always find so fascinating is the need the children have to test out their predictions and conjectures when working with triangles—and the mathematical insight that comes from it. There is something about three being an odd number or connected triangles being unusual shapes for tables that always causes children to second-guess their reasoning. This creates a natural need for mathematical proof. The children can use their posters about square tables as prototypes for additional posters made for other patterns. Once again, this extension works beautifully in a block period. You will need to decide whether students will work with partners or independently and how much time you will be able to allow for this extension. The extension can also be assigned as an out-of-school project for use as a formal assessment. As always, please be mindful to assign tasks that not only fit your curricular needs but can also fit into the lives of your children.

FIGURE 9–9   ▶

Kira's completed poster.

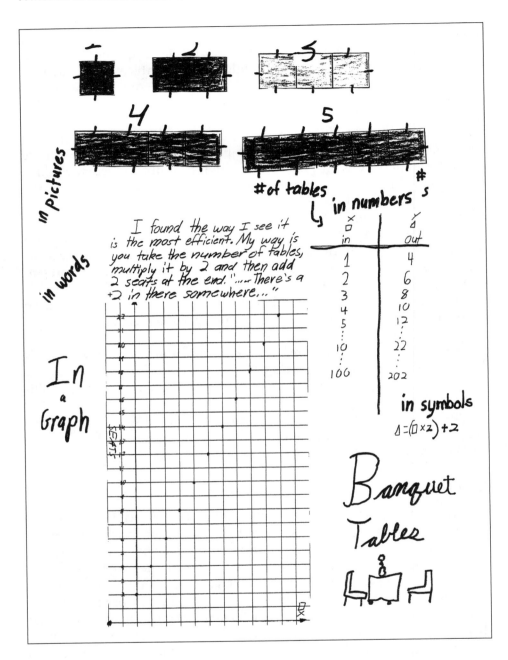

Minnie's Diner: Investigating Nonlinear Functions

Duration: 1–2 class periods

The Banquet Table Problem focuses on linear growth. Each of the tile patterns grows at the same predictable, consistent, and constant rate from stage to stage. Growth, however, does not always occur in a constant or regular manner. It can also be exponential. Like linear growth, exponential growth is predictable and consistent. But unlike linear growth, the rate of growth from stage to stage is not constant. This lesson offers a context within which to explore a pattern that presents a nonlinear function and graph. This lesson offers students opportunities to:

- identify and represent a nonlinear growth pattern
- organize information on a T-chart
- create a nonlinear graph

Materials
- *Minnie's Diner*, by Dayle Ann Dodds (2004)
- 1 piece of chart paper
- 1 graph paper notebook or piece of centimeter grid paper per student (see Blackline Masters)

Minnie's Diner (Dodds 2004) is a delightful story about the McFay boys and their inability to resist the aromas from Minnie's kitchen. One by one they succumb to the sweet aromas, with each brother being twice as hungry as the brother before. When Papa McFay realizes that his boys are gone and the chores are not done, he heads off to Minnie's, only to be enticed by her cooking as well.

I began the lesson with a read-aloud of *Minnie's Diner*. The children were immediately engaged by the illustrations and cadence of the book. They were also aware of the growth pattern of the menu items as each brother ordered from Minnie. Groans and giggles could be heard around the room as each new brother placed his order.

After the reading, I asked, "Where is the growth in this story?" Although I planned to investigate the growth of the menu items ordered, some students shared other examples of growth, such as the brothers' appetites, the muscles in Minnie's arm, and Papa McFay's anger.

As we discussed who ordered how much, I feigned confusion. The children agreed that charting each brother and how many menu items he ordered in a T-chart would help us keep track of who ordered what. As I drew the chart on the board, I asked the children for the column labels.

Brother	Menu Items Ordered
Will	1
Bill	2
Phil	4
Gill	8
Dill	16
Papa	32

I asked, "What do you notice?" to focus the children on the nuances and newness of this particular growth pattern and T-chart representation. Some of the student responses included the following:

- The growth is not constant; each brother doubles the menu items from the brother before.
- There are no numbers in the first column.
- The pattern ends with Papa.

These are all important observations. If they are not made by the students, you may wish to offer them as your own observations in order to encourage the children to think about them.

Asking the children to compare and contrast this growth pattern with the others they have used so far will open up a conversation about the doubling pattern. Jared was quick to identify the doubling pattern, but equally quick to recognize that he needed to know what the brother before had ordered so that he could double his menu items for the next brother. Jared identified the need and use of the iterative rule for this pattern.

Next I asked, "So what if an eighth brother came in? How could I figure out how many menu items he ordered?" Such a question may very well create some confusion. Many children will assume that the eighth brother will order sixteen menu items because $8 \times 2 = 16$. According to the T-chart, however, it is actually the fifth brother who orders sixteen menu items. Jared became quite animated in this discussion. He announced to the class that he had to know how many menu items the seventh brother ordered first. Then he could double that brother's items to figure out the number of menu items the eighth brother ordered. "I have to use the T-chart," explained Jared. "I have to follow the numbers from one brother to the next."

Jared was aware of the nuances of this pattern—and that it was not like the other patterns we had worked with so far. That was a wonderful observation. Representing this new type of pattern graphically helps make the nuances visible. Jared and his tablemates were already going for the graph paper!

It continues to be important to review where the ordered pairs can be found to graph this pattern. By this time in the unit, the children should be able to identify and articulate the power of the T-chart as a valuable and accessible mathematical tool. As I constructed a class graph on chart paper, the children drew graphs for themselves. As the children began to plot their points, several of them asked, "What the heck is this?" (See Figure 9–10.)

Several children were convinced a mistake had been made in the T-chart because this graph did not manifest itself in a straight line. We went back to rehash the story to make sure that a computational error had not been made as we checked the relationship between each brother and the

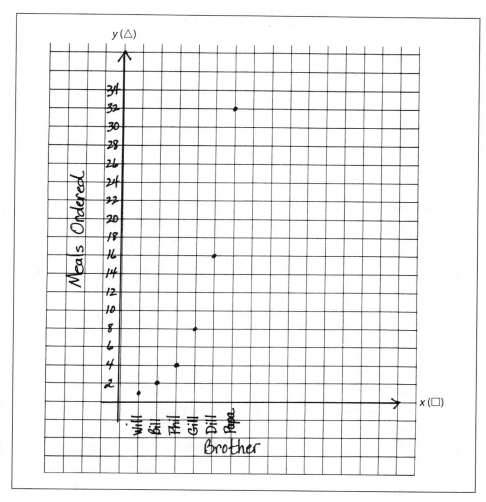

number of menu items ordered. We then agreed to extend the pattern to include more visitors to Minnie's diner. Nolan wanted to add Mama and Uncle Fred.

Brother	Menu Items Ordered
Will	1
Bill	2
Phil	4
Gill	8
Dill	16
Papa	32
Mama	64
Uncle Fred	128

We all agreed that the pattern made sense given the context of the story even though it was rather unrealistic.

We took some time to talk about what the students noticed and allow the children to ponder and articulate the characteristics of this pattern. Some of my students' observations included:

- The points of the graph do not make a straight line.
- The points curve upward.
- The number of menu items gets big in a hurry.

Take a few minutes to discuss the term *linear*. Discussing the root word, *line*, helps the children make sense of the word. Identifying and describing the graphs created in the *Banquet Tables* investigation as linear can help children identify and articulate nonlinear relationships such as those represented by the *Minnie's Diner* investigation. Keep in mind that the objective of this investigation is not for students to understand nonlinear functions but to become aware of them. Not all graphs represent linear functions and not all patterns represent constant growth. Guiding questions such as the following may help you direct the conversation:

- What can you tell me about the graphs in the *Banquet Tables* investigations?
- Where is the growth in the T-chart? Where is the growth in the graph?
- How is that growth different from the growth of the pattern in *Minnie's Diner*?
- How are the graphs the same? Why does that make sense?
- How are the graphs different? Why does that make sense?
- How are the T-charts of the two investigations the same? How are they different?
- How can you tell if a graph will be linear or nonlinear by looking at the T-chart?

Every so often an intrigued fourth-grade mathematician asks what the rule is for the *Minnie's Diner* investigation—or if there even is one! Some of your children may have been exposed to exponents and may be interested to see how the rule is represented in its symbolic form. Although the rule of this pattern is $2^{(x-1)}$, it is not necessary, nor do I suggest, that you go into detail about the rule with the children. Exponential rules and functions will be explored in greater detail and with developmental appropriateness in the later grades.

Balancing Number Puzzles: Exploring Equality

Duration: 2–3 class periods

According to the authors of *Thinking Mathematically*

[M]ost elementary students, and many other students as well, do not understand that the equal sign denotes the relation between two equal quantities. Rather, they interpret the equal sign as a command to carry out a calculation, much as a calculator does when we press the equal sign. This misconception limits students' ability to learn arithmetic ideas with understanding and their flexibility in representing using those ideas, and it creates more serious problems as they move to algebra. (Carpenter, Franke, and Levi 2003, 9)

In this series of lessons, students use their understanding of place value and computation skills to solve balancing number puzzles. The big idea of equality is explored as children calculate equivalent values and expressions in order to balance the two sides of a puzzle. These lessons offer students opportunities to:

- explore equivalency within a context requiring computational proficiency and creativity
- explore, identify, and articulate equivalence
- solve, create, and represent balancing number puzzles
- apply and practice estimation and calculation skills

Materials

- 1 *Balancing Number Puzzles* worksheet per student (see Blackline Masters)
- optional: several half sheets of plain paper per student

These lessons, adapted from *Teaching Arithmetic: Lessons for Extending Place Value* (Wickett and Burns 2005), meet the needs of fourth graders as they continue to develop their understanding of equality.

Balances are effective visual models that can be used to represent equality. A level balance is one with equivalent values or expressions on both sides. Initially, the equals sign is not used as balances are created and discussed. As the children begin to represent their equalities with equations, they will have greater understanding of the meaning of the equals sign and the relationship it represents between both sides of the balance.

I began the lesson with a discussion about the following balance, drawn on the board.

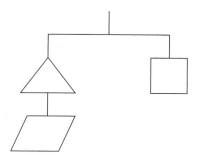

Even before I began to ask questions, Michael blurted out, "Do you want me to tell you what I notice?" The class giggled.

"As a matter of fact, I do!" I replied. Thanks to the science curriculum and our work with measurement in math class, my students were able to readily make the connection between the drawing and a balance scale. Simply identifying the structure as a balance, however, is not enough. Teasing out additional information about the nature of this particular balance is necessary, such as the following:

- The straight line at the top represents a balance.
- There are two unknowns on one side that balance one unknown on the other.
- The two unknowns on the left side have the same weight or value as the one unknown on the right side.

Then I added *100* to the right side of the balance.

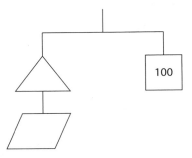

Because many of my students had been working with different shapes representing the unknowns in open number sentences since first grade, they were aware that this puzzle could contain three different quantities. Make sure your students understand that same shapes represent same quantities, but different shapes may or may not have the same value. In the balance above, the triangle and the parallelogram could have values of sixty and forty, but they could also have equal values of fifty. If no one suggests placing the same value in two different shapes, you may wish to present this idea to the children and ask them how they could make sense of this possibility.

Ask, "What can you tell me now about this balance?" to move the lesson forward. The idea that two unknowns must be equivalent to one hundred introduces the concept of equality. Before the concept of equality can be further discussed, it is important for children to have a context within which to discuss it. Ask the children to work in pairs to complete the balance by placing numbers on the left side that will satisfy the constraints of the problem. Tell students that they will be asked to defend and support their decisions. Because there are many solutions to this task, the children will begin to make generalizations about equality and equivalence based on a variety of addition models.

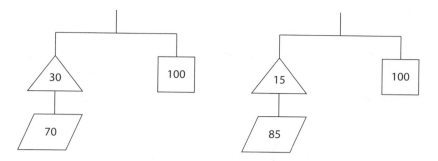

As my children were working, I drew five balances on the board. Once the children were ready to process, I asked various students to come to the board to place their numbers in the balances. The class was genuinely curious about the numbers other students used. The children quickly realized that there was no single correct solution.

Harry and Nick placed the following numbers on their balance.

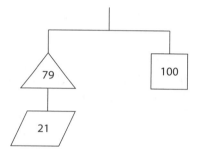

I asked the class to describe Harry and Nick's balance and wrote students' descriptions on the board to show the children how to represent this model in a more efficient and concise manner. The verbal and written descriptions are very necessary tools. A number sentence alone will not necessarily confirm a child's understanding of equivalence. "You have a seventy-nine and a twenty-one on one side. When you add them up, you get one hundred. One hundred is on the other side. So they balance." Listen for words such as *balance*, *left side*, *right side*, *the same as*, and *the same value*, which are all helpful as children make sense of equality.

"How do I know Harry and Nick are adding from this model?" I continued to highlight the need for clarity and efficiency. I asked the children to talk at their table groups about a way to represent this model with greater clarity so that I would know what Harry and Nick were doing without having to ask them. The class agreed that a number sentence would more clearly state what the balance represented.

Because the mathematical focus of this lesson is on equality, take some time to manipulate and discuss the components or terms of the number sentence.

$$79 + 21 = 100$$

- Is this number sentence an equation? How do you know?
- Is this number sentence true or false? How do you know?
- Where do we see this number sentence in the balance model?

$$21 + 79 = 100$$

- Is this number sentence an equation? How do you know?
- Is this number sentence true or false? How do you know?
- Where do we see this number sentence in the balance model?

$$100 = 100$$

- Is this number sentence an equation? How do you know?
- Is this number sentence true or false? How do you know?
- Where do we see this number sentence in the balance model?

A discussion of $100 = 100$ requires the children to simplify the sum to a single quantity. By simplifying $79 + 21$ to 100, we can now express this model as $100 = 100$, which demonstrates the equality of both sides of the balance or equation. The sentence $21 + 79 = 100$ can also represent the balance, but the different order of the addends illustrates the commutativity of addition. Ask the children how this language and work relate to previously studied concepts and procedures to make those connections explicit and accessible.

Attention can now turn to a new balance, such as the following.

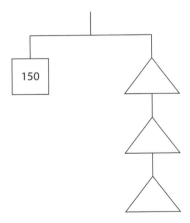

Ask the students to talk to their neighbors about this puzzle and the numbers that would make the two sides balance. The children will quickly acknowledge that three of the same number would need to be used for the three triangles. They should also quickly realize that in this puzzle, there is only one set of numbers that will work.

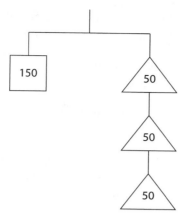

Once again, request a verbal description of this new balance from the children. Write it on the board and then translate it into an equation as before. The following number sentences can be generated and discussed:

$$150 = 50 + 50 + 50$$
$$150 = 3 \times 50$$
$$150 = 3(50)$$
$$150 = 50 \times 3$$
$$150 = 150$$

You might find that some of your students have difficulty with the operational symbol being to the right of the equals sign rather than to the left. It is important to expose your students to such models and engage them in conversations that can help those children make a shift in understanding. Offering puzzles that require operational work on both sides of the equals sign, such as the following, will also help them make greater sense of the equals sign and equivalent values.

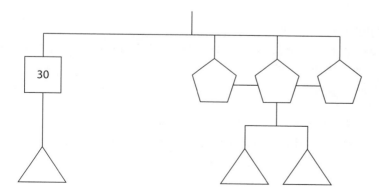

The *Balancing Numbers Puzzles* worksheet can be completed individually or with a partner. Devote some time to a whole-class discussion for processing the puzzles that your children found intriguing or challenging. The format for solving these puzzles remains the same:

1. Substitute and solve for equality.

2. Represent the puzzle with a number sentence.

3. Be able to identify the components of the number sentence and where each is represented in the model.

You can also ask students to create their own balancing number puzzles. They can draw each balance on the front of a half sheet of white paper and write the corresponding equation on the back. Student-generated puzzles can be shared with tablemates or placed at a math center for free choice time.

Follow-Up Journal Write

Create a balancing number puzzle that uses the following numbers: 4, 10, 4, 4, 10, 4, 4.
How do you know that your numbers work? Can you make more than one balance?

Are You a Square? Collecting, Representing, and Analyzing Data

Duration: 3–4 class periods

It is important for fourth graders to build upon experiences of data collection and representation that they have explored in earlier grades. Focus can now turn to the statistical terminology and interpretation of data sets that may or may not represent a relationship between one's arm span and height. These lessons offer students opportunities to:

- collect, represent, and analyze two sets of data and how they are related
- explore scatter plots
- make predictions and conjectures based upon inferences made from particular data set(s)

Materials

- 2 12-inch pieces of string per pair of students for each measurement
- 1 dark-colored marker per pair of students
- 1 measuring tape per pair of students
- 4 pieces of chart paper
- 3 different-colored markers (e.g., red, black, and green)
- small strips of dot stickers in three colors (to correspond with markers), 1 of each color per group of students

Measuring, representing, and analyzing one data set, then two, can build upon the statistical experiences children have had in the earlier grades. This exploration integrates an investigation often explored in science with the mathematics that can be used to represent and interpret the collected data.

I begin the lesson with a discussion of Leonardo da Vinci and his belief that many body parts were proportional, which made the drawing of the human body fascinating to him. Engage the class in a discussion about why this idea would be important to an artist. You may also need to talk about the meaning of *proportional*. Proportional reasoning involves a multiplicative rather than additive relationship. According to Van de Walle (2004), proportional reasoning is difficult to define. It is not something you can or cannot do. Thinking proportionally involves both quantitative and qualitative processes. Proportional thinkers understand relationships in which two quantities vary together and are able to articulate how one coincides with the variation in another. We are certainly not expecting our fourth graders to master the requirements of proportional thinking, but we can expose them to phenomena that present opportunities to explore and think about the relationship of two measurements.

Have the children choose partners with whom they will work for the entire investigation. With the aid of a 12-inch piece of string, one partner measures the circumference of the other partner's thumb by measuring the lowest part of the thumb. Instruct the measurer to mark the string with a dark marker at the point where the two sides of the string meet. Next, the measurer uses the second piece of string to measure the circumference of her partner's wrist. Using the mark on the first string, the pair compares the circumference of the model student's thumb and wrist and finds the proportion between the two measurements. Then the students can switch roles to compare two more body parts, such as the length of a foot and the length of a forearm. Suggest a few other ratios pairs can explore if they have time, such as neck circumference versus head circumference.

Before the children set off to work, discuss how they should record the proportions of their measurements. Following is one conventional notation for a proportion.

1:4 (read "one to four")

Students can use a table to record the proportions they find, such as the following:

Body Part : Body Part	Proportion

Although the measurement is informal, encourage children to be as accurate as possible. Consistency of measurement will be important so that the class can make meaningful comparisons among the sets of data. For example, as a class, agree on the procedure for measuring the length of a foot: Should students keep their shoes on or take them off? Should students step on the string and make a mark at the front and back of the foot? Once the class has collected its data, compare the ratios of body parts to find the most consistent ratio. The ratio 2:1 represents the proportional relationship between the thumb circumference and the wrist circumference. I am always amazed at how consistent that proportion is regardless of the subject's age! Here are the results for the other proportions:

Body Part : Body Part	Proportion
thumb circumference : wrist circumference*	2:1
foot* : forearm	1:1
neck circumference* : head circumference	2:1

*Unit of measure

Rates of growth may affect the consistency of the proportions. I also include my measurements on the class table as well as those of other adults in the school whom the children ask to measure. My principal is 6 foot 5, which makes for interesting measurements, but the proportions are very consistent with those of the rest of the class. You'll need to decide how many proportions to explore. I tend to stick to two—the thumb and wrist and the foot and forearm.

Next the class will explore the relationship between arm span and height. With measuring tapes, the students measure each other's height and arm span to answer the following question:

Is there a consistent and predictable relationship between people's arm span and height?

Give specific instructions for the representation of these measurements. Each child should record his measurement as an ordered pair with the arm span representing the x value and the height representing the y: (arm span, height).

Label three pieces of chart paper with different colors as follows:

Arm Span > Height (posted in **red** marker)	Arm Span = Height (posted in **black** marker)	Arm Span < Height (posted in **green** marker)

Have each child record her ordered pair on the appropriate chart with the appropriate color.

Once each member of the class has posted his ordered pair, ask, "What do you notice?" to begin a discussion about the collected data. I have been doing this activity for many years with my fourth graders, and the data seem to fluctuate from year to year. Keep in mind that these young mathematicians are growing, and the 1:1 ratio of arm span to height may or may not apply. Comparing some adult measures with those of your fourth graders may open up further conversations about the possibility of the ratio moving closer to 1:1 as the sample population matures.

Writing the measurements on the charts as ordered pairs is one way to represent the data. Now is a good time to repose the investigation question: "Is there a correlation between one's arm span and height? Can one help us predict the other?" Charting the data in this way helps us clump the data, but there may be a better representation to help us identify trends. Ask for ideas of other representations to push children to once again consider the importance of efficiency and the clarity of a chosen representation. Different representations help us view the collected data from different perspectives. Children may suggest using bar graphs because that is always a popular method. A coordinate graph, however, will allow you to look at two variables within the same representation.

Post on the board a grid drawn on chart paper. Work with the class to label the axes of the coordinate grid. I place the arm span on the x-axis because it makes sense visually. When you measure arm span, you measure horizontally. Height is placed on the y-axis because when you measure height, you measure vertically. Label the axes and number the intervals.

Numbering the intervals presents another opportunity for discussion. Should we start with 1 on both axes? The children quickly realize that the paper is not big enough to handle intervals of one. We also talk about the clumping of the data. Because many x and y values are so close in value, intervals of five or even two would make it difficult to plot and see all the data. So we move back to the idea of using intervals of one. Using the $\bigwedge$ symbol on both axes to identify missing numbers will solve this problem. The children love making and applying this new symbol! It is also important for the children to refer to the class data in order to determine what starting number should be used for both the axes. (See Figure 9–11 for an example graph.)

Give each group strips of red, black, and green dot stickers. Ask each student to take a dot that corresponds to the color of her ordered pair. Each child should write his ordered pair on his dot.

Inform the children that they are going to create a class *scatter plot* with their dots on the large coordinate graph. Scatter plots allow us to examine possible relationships between two variables using a coordinate graph structure. In this case, we are exploring the potential relationship between arm span and height. Starting with the class's $x = y$ (arm span = height) values, the children will construct a *diagonal* with which you can compare the other values. The more closely the red and green dots hug this diagonal, represented by the black dots, the greater confidence you can have in predicting that one's arm span is directly related to and can be predicted by one's height.

FIGURE 9–11   ▶

Setup for arm span vs. height.

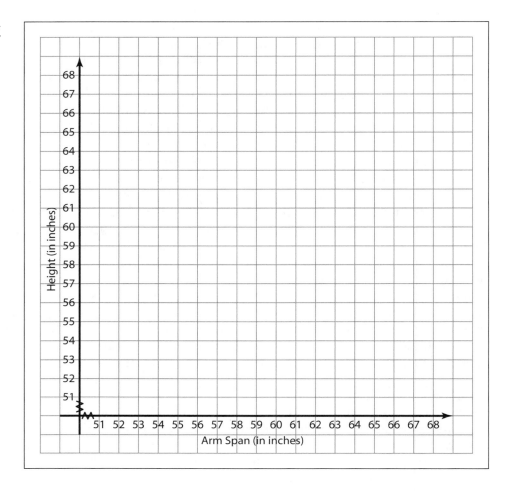

As those children with black dots place their values on the graph, the children will undoubtedly notice the diagonal line that is forming. Jane was quick to point out that this black line also cut the graph in half. When asked to make a prediction about the placement of the other ordered pairs, Jane suggested that the red dots would fall on one side of the line and that the green dots would fall on the other. Posing a question such as "Why would that make sense?" will push the children to make sense of the ordered pairs and how the x and y values are related.

I ask one child with a red dot to place her ordered pair on the graph. Before any other values are posted, we have a discussion about what we know about all the red and green values. Your students may offer the following observations:

- All the red dots will be above the black line and all the green will be below.
- All the red values represent children whose arm span is less than their height.
- All the green values represent children whose arm span is greater than their height.

- Most of the red and green dots will clump around the black line.
- The adults' black dots are outliers, but they are black. As we get older, our arm span catches up with our height or our height catches up with our arm span.

As these observations are made, write them on the graph. When the children identify the red values as representing the $x < y$ values, write $x < y$ in red marker within the respective region of the graph. Do the same with green marker for the $x > y$ values.

Ask one group at a time to plot their ordered pairs. There is something magical about the formation of this graph. The children watch for clumping and are quick to point out an incorrect placement of a point—respectfully, of course! The children see their conjectures about the graph coming to life before them. Once all the ordered pairs are plotted, I conclude the investigation with a discussion about what we notice about our class based on our scatter plot. Sharing graphs from previous years can offer additional opportunities to interpret and analyze characteristics of previous fourth grades. I had a very tall group about four years ago. My current class quickly noticed the shift in the ordered pairs on that class's graph. "Wow! They were tall!" the students surmised, based on the larger number of red dots and their placement well above the black diagonal.

Calculation Routines and Practices

Lessons that support and develop algebraic thinking skills can also support, enhance, and extend children's arithmetic learning. When we ask our students to think algebraically, we are asking them to draw upon their understanding of number relationships and operations as they predict and generalize.

Arithmetic equations can be identified as true or false because they contain no variables. Algebraic equations, on the other hand, contain variables and can be classified as *open* sentences. These sentences cannot be classified as true or false until a decision is made about the value of the variable.

Arithmetic Equation

$(4 + 8) \times 2 = 8 \times 3$

Algebraic Equation

$(4 + \Box) \times 2 = \Box \times 3$

Even at this point in the school year, I continue to use boxes and triangles as variable notation but begin to increase the use of letter variables. When a variable occurs more than once in an equation, it represents the same number each time.

Identifying arithmetic equations as true or false presents continued computational practice but also offers a context in which to continue discussions about equality. The act of identifying whether an equation is true or false is not enough. Students need to have many discussions about tasks requiring them to identify or create true and false number sentences in order to make meaning of the task as well as the equals sign. Posting and discussing number sentences also gives students exposure to different ways of representing mathematical relationships and writing mathematical sentences. Students can be presented with the following list of equations and asked to categorize each equation as true or false.

$$3 \times 6 = 18$$
$$25 = (20 - 10) + 5$$
$$2 + (4 \times 4) = (8 \times 2) + 1$$
$$4 + 1 = 10 - 4$$
$$7 = 21 \div (2 + 1)$$

You can ask students to label each sentence as T (true) or F (false) or to construct a two-column T-chart and post the equations under the appropriate heading.

True	False
$3 \times 6 = 18$	$2 + (4 \times 4) = (8 \times 2) + 1$
$7 = 21 \div (2 + 1)$	$4 + 1 = 10 - 4$
	$25 = (20 - 10) + 5$

Whatever the task, students should be encouraged to justify their label of true or false. Students can also generate their own lists of true and false number sentences. This is easier said than done! Deliberately writing a false equation takes some thought. My children claim that you have to think of a true sentence first and then turn it into a false sentence by adjusting the numbers, relationships, or operations. This strategy comes up year after year. I am always amazed about the thought, computational practice, and number sense that this simple task elicits.

Open number sentences contain a variable or variables, for example, $8 + \square = 14$. We cannot determine whether this sentence is true or false until we decide on a value for $\square$. If we place 6 in the $\square$, then the sentence is true. Any other number will make the sentence false. Any number that makes an open sentence true is called the *solution* of the sentence. Although open sentences can be solved and made true by calculation, number sense and relational generalizations can also be applied as children identify solutions. For example:

$$23 + 8 = 22 + \square$$

Some children may determine that the left side of the equation is equal to thirty-one. Therefore, the right side needs to be equal to the same value. Twenty-two plus nine is thirty-one, so nine would be the solution and make the sentence true. Other children may identify that twenty-two is one *less than* twenty-three. Therefore, the value of the □ will need to be one *more than* eight in order to balance the equation. These children are assessing and manipulating the number relationships found in the number sentence as they work to find a solution. As open sentences are solved and discussed, make sure to ask for other strategies and have students justify their solutions. The following is a list of open sentences you can present:

a. $21 - 8 = \square$

b. $13 \times \triangle = 13$

c. $\triangle = (23 + 7) + 5$

d. $5 + 8 = \square + 5$

e. $16 + (b - 7) = 16$

f. $12 + 9 = 10 + 8 + \triangle$

g. $12 = d + 12$

h. $8 \times 4 = (8 \times 3) + t$

i. $1{,}945 \times \square = 1{,}945$

j. $7 \times 5 = 5 \times a$

Creating your own list of open sentences to share with your class is a worthwhile mathematical task in itself. As you create open sentences, be aware of those properties to which your children have been exposed. Fourth graders should have an understanding of both the additive and multiplicative identities (see Items b, g, and i in previous list). Create open sentences that assess this understanding. Fourth graders should have an understanding of the commutative properties of both addition and multiplication (see Items d and j). Create open sentences that assess this understanding as well. Children need many opportunities to generalize about arithmetic. Solving deliberately constructed open sentences can help them do just that. Our fourth graders need to realize that number sense and the ability to assess and generalize about numerical relationships can often help them solve open sentences without the act of calculation.

Many fourth graders are familiar with calculations requiring the use of parentheses. A number sentence such as $15 - (3 \times 3) = \square$ tells us to do the work in the parentheses first. This number sentence can be simplified to $15 - 9 = \square$, with the final solution being 6. Presenting number sentences without parentheses and asking the children to identify whether each number sentence is true or false can move the children from a procedural to conceptual understanding of the use of parentheses. For example:

$$28 - 6 + 9 = 31$$

$$28 - 6 + 9 = 13$$

In the absence of parentheses, the convention is to first multiply and divide in order from left to right, and then add and subtract in order from left to right, and most fourth graders will choose to work from left to right. Parentheses could clarify how that process makes the first number sentence true.

$$(28 - 6) + 9 = 31$$
$$22 + 9 = 31$$

The second number sentence can also be true if we shift the placement of the parentheses.

$$28 - (6 + 9) = 13$$
$$28 - 15 = 13$$

Paying attention to notation and the order of that notation will affect calculation results. This is an important idea and practice for our young mathematicians. Children need opportunities to calculate and discuss how the grouping of numbers can affect solutions. Asking children to insert parentheses in pairs of number sentences to make them true will give them additional calculation opportunities. Sample routines could be modeled after the following examples.

Make a true sentence by inserting parentheses. Defend your thinking.

$8 + 14 \div 2 = 15$ $8 + 14 \div 2 = 11$

$4 \times 4 + 4 = 20$ $4 \times 4 + 4 = 32$

$1 = 24 \div 8 - 2$ $4 = 24 \div 8 - 2$

Make a true sentence by filling in the missing number. Defend your thinking.

$(30 - 15) \times 2 =$ _____ $30 - (15 \times 2) =$ _____

_____ $= (32 \div 8) \div 4$ _____ $= 32 \div (8 \div 4)$

$6 + (21 \div 3) =$ _____ $(6 + 21) \div 3 =$ _____

Equations in which parentheses are nested can give children additional computation practice.

$$(22 - (5 - 4)) + 7 = \underline{\hspace{1cm}}$$
$$\underline{\hspace{1cm}} = 2 \times (3 + (2 - 1))$$

Brackets can also be used as a second set of grouping symbols.

$$[22 - (5 - 4)] + 7 = \underline{\hspace{1.5cm}}$$

$$\underline{\hspace{1.5cm}} = 2 \times [3 + (2 - 1)]$$

It may be helpful to refer to your district or state standards to identify the preferred method of notation.

Variables are letters, symbols, or other placeholders that represent an unknown value. We can substitute values for unknown quantities as we work to solve open number sentences. This method of solving equations is commonly referred to as *substitution*. Routines requiring substitution offer valuable calculation practice.

Missing-number routines can offer substitution experiences.

Same shapes are same numbers.

$\square + \triangle + \square + \triangle = 20$

$\triangle + \triangle + \triangle + \triangle = 28$

What number is $\square$? ———

What number is $\triangle$? ———

How do you know?

Two-column T-charts can offer substitution practice as well. This format reinforces the big idea that a variable can *vary* in value.

b	$(b + 8) - 3$
6	11
0	5
22	27
1	?
4	?
15	?

These routines can easily be presented on worksheets. They can also serve well as daily class warm-ups. The Groundworks series (Greenes and Findell 1998, 2006) provides blackline masters of many activities requiring substitution.

The primary goal of embedding calculation routines and practices in lessons requiring algebraic thinking is not to teach children efficient ways to solve systems of equations, but rather to engage them in thinking flexibly about number operations and relationships (Carpenter, Franke, and Levi 2003).

Mathematics Writing

By this point in the year, you should hold students to high writing expectations. Completing journal entries with clarity, sound sentence structure, and supporting details such as diagrams and examples should be standard fare. Offering the opportunity for children to rethink, revise, and rewrite previous journal entries can help you assess how far they have come through a year of writing about their thinking. The process of rethinking, revising, and rewriting is sensitive and slow to develop. When our children demonstrate greater fluency in their writing, their willingness and ability to think more carefully and deeply about the mathematics are evident.

The following prompt is one that I have used in years past.

Final Journal Write

Choose any entry that you have completed this year and rewrite it. You might want to choose one that you feel you can better answer now. Or perhaps you would like to choose one in which the mechanics of your writing lacked attention.

Please pay attention to the original prompt. I will be comparing your first entry with your rewrite.

- *Reread your first response several times to identify ways in which it could be improved.*

- *Make sure diagrams are clean, clear, and well labeled.*

- *Pay attention to your use of mathematical vocabulary.*

- *Rewrite the prompt you are using under the "Prompt" section of your entry page.*

This rewrite will be worth the "price" of a test, so do your best! Demonstrate your strong mathematical writing skills!

Conversation prior to writing will set the tone for the revisions. Discuss what good mathematical writing looks like. As the mathematical thinking and reasoning of the children have developed over the year, so too should the expectations of their writing. This conversation can be very animated and insightful compared with conversations from earlier in the year. Children often overlook the importance of the mechanics of their writing because they are so focused on the mathematics, which is not a bad thing! Just remind your young mathematicians that the writing standards from language arts need to be applied to their mathematical writing as well. In other words, attention to capitalization, punctuation, and word choice continues to be important.

Each student's two writing samples can be posted side by side as an assessment of progress on the insides of a manila folder and added to each child's portfolio. Conferencing with children about these two pieces of writing gives them the opportunity to demonstrate and talk about how they have grown as mathematicians over the course of the year and how that growth is manifested in their writing.

Parent Communication

Once again, I create and distribute a parent information form to help parents support their children at home. (See Figure 9–12.)

You may also want to craft an end-of-year newsletter that can summarize the year as well as offer suggestions for summer activities to further develop and strengthen mathematical thinking skills and procedures. I often attach a bibliography such as the one on the next page to offer parents additional resources.

FIGURE 9–12 ◀

Parent information form for May.

Parent Information and Involvement Form

From: Lainie Schuster
To: Parents of Fourth Graders
Re: Mathematics Curriculum
Month: May

During the next unit, the major topic we will be studying is:

- algebraic thinking

My goal in studying this topic is for the students to be able to:

- identify, articulate, and represent numerical and geometric patterns
- represent growing patterns with words, pictures, graphs, and symbols
- identify and articulate functional relationships (rules) found in T-charts of growing patterns
- plot points on a coordinate graph
- solve for unknown quantities (variables) in equations and expressions
- identify number sentences as true or false

Parents can help at home by:

- asking children to explain how they *see* the growth of patterns: *How* is the pattern growing? (Expressing how they see growth in words first can then help them put numbers and symbols to their ideas.)
- asking children to identify the relationship between the in values and the out values of a T-chart in words before moving to symbols and equations; the function rule connecting the in values with the out values can often be uncovered and discovered in children's language!

You may wish to track down the following resources, which offer engaging problem-solving opportunities for the entire family.

Burns, Marilyn. 1975. *The I Hate Mathematics! Book*. Boston: Little, Brown.

———. 1982. *Math for Smarty Pants*. Boston: Little, Brown.

———. 1990. *The $1.00 Word Riddle Book*. Sausalito, CA: Math Solutions Publications.

Mokros, Jan. 1996. *Beyond Facts and Flashcards: Exploring Math with Your Kids*. Portsmouth, NH: Heinemann.

Stenmark, Jean Kerr, Virginia Thompson, and Ruth Cossey. 1986. *Family Math*. Berkeley: University of California.

Tang, Greg. 2001. *The Grapes of Math*. New York: Scholastic.

———. 2002. *Math for All Seasons*. New York: Scholastic.

———. 2003. *Math Appeal*. New York: Scholastic.

As the end of the school year quickly approaches, thoughts about the future loom large. As our fourth graders move on to become fifth graders, they'll experience new classrooms, new teachers, and new expectations. Many schools mandate an end-of-year report that can benefit everyone involved. Parents appreciate specific information about their children's strengths and challenges. Remember that effective reporting is far more a challenge in effective communication than simply a process of documenting student achievement (Guskey and Bailey 2001). Parents are most appreciative when information about their children is communicated clearly and easy to interpret. Whether reporting in the form of letter grades or narrative comments, you will need to decide whether to discuss other aspects of a student's learning in addition to providing evidence of mathematical achievement or performance. For example, you may wish to consider effort, work ethic, and participation when assigning a grade or writing a comment. Practical suggestions about what improvements can be made as their children move on to the fifth grade are also of great importance and help to parents. Many parents want to be involved their child's mathematical education and are highly dependent on the observations, assessments, and recommendations of the teacher.

Assessment

Because my students so enjoy *The Banquet Table Problem* (page 306), I often implement a final assessment project based on a growth pattern. I may have students investigate banquet tables built with triangle or trapezoid tables. I have also used a version of the *Piles of Tiles* investigation in *Lessons for Algebraic Thinking, Grades 3–5* (Wickett, Kharas, and Burns

Criteria	Point Value	Points Earned
I chose my banquet table and continued, labeled, and represented the growth of the seating for up to five tables. I posted this on my poster.	20	
I made a **T-chart** to represent the growth of the seating. I included 1–5 tables, as well as 10 and 100 tables. I posted this on my poster.	20	
I used **words** to describe the growth of the seating pattern. I posted this on my poster.	20	
I created a **rule** in mathematical symbols and numbers to represent the growth of the seating pattern. I posted this on my poster.	10	
I graphed the growth of the seating pattern with a labeled coordinate graph and did not connect my points. I posted this on my poster.	20	
My poster is neat, well organized, and really, really cool!	10	
Total Points	100	
Teacher Comments:		

FIGURE 9–13 ◀

Scoring rubric for banquet tables assessment.

2002) for a final assessment. These projects are completed in poster format and make for wonderful hall displays demonstrating the algebraic thinking of which fourth graders are capable. Figure 9–13 is a scoring rubric that I have used for the banquet table assessment.

As the year winds down, we often find ourselves in the throes of the mass hysteria of end-of-year routines. I must admit that as the end of the school year approaches, I often wonder if I have the energy to get through yet another May! As we have our sights on the summer months ahead, we must take the opportunity to look back on the months of mathematical study and growth that have taken place in our classrooms with our children. End-of-year reporting gives many of us the opportunity to do just that.

As we review portfolios and student progress, it becomes important to identify those mathematical habits of mind, routines, and practices that we have valued and implemented month in and month out. Whether your reporting format is a narrative, a letter grade, a standards-based checklist, or some combination of these, the message needs to be consistent and somewhat standardized from student to student. Identifying the process and progress of mathematical learning of each child with clarity and insight is a daunting task. I have found over the years that I focus on the same qualities of each child's learning as I formulate end-of-year reports in order to present clear descriptions of achievement, performance, and learning progress. I often organize my thoughts around a child's effort, clarity of thinking, clarity of writing, and arithmetic proficiency. Identifying a student's strengths as well as areas where improvement is needed is important. As long as the message can be accurately interpreted by those for whom it is intended, then our reporting system has served its purpose.

Resources

Math Matters (Chapin and Johnson 2006)—Chapter 9, "Algebra"
In-depth discussion of the study of algebra and the development of algebraic thinking in the elementary grades.

About Teaching Mathematics (Burns 2007)
The chapter on patterns, functions, and algebra offers whole-class lessons as well as independent (menu) activities.

Lessons for Algebraic Thinking, Grades 3–5 (Wickett, Kharas, and Burns 2002)
A must-have resource. Lessons, class vignettes, and author narration help teachers develop and support a wide variety of algebraic topics.

Groundworks: Algebraic Thinking (Greenes and Findell 2006)
A superb teacher-friendly book of blackline masters developing six big ideas of algebra through well-defined problem sets. The big ideas are representation, proportional reasoning, balance, variable, function, and inductive reasoning.

Thinking Mathematically (Carpenter, Franke, and Levi 2003)
Classroom dialogues and author narration describe how algebraic ideas emerge in children's thinking and what problems and questions can help elicit them. Includes an outstanding chapter on equality (Chapter 2).

Chapter 10

June

MULTIPLICATION AND DIVISION REVISITED

[Having children continue their thinking about multiplication and division] in a real-world context helps them link the idea of multiplication to the world around them. It also helps them avoid the pitfall of seeing mathematics as totally abstract and unrelated to their lives. Too often, math exists for children only on the pages of textbooks and worksheets. They need opportunities to see mathematics as integral to their daily experiences

About Teaching Mathematics
Burns 2007, 233

The Learning Environment

Continue to understand the thinking of your children and base your instruction on that understanding.

As you move into a unit whose purpose is to extend previous learning, the understanding and knowledge of your children become the guiding force as you help them build upon prior knowledge. A unit on extending multiplication and division may look different from year to year, depending on your class. It is important to offer tasks and facilitate conversations that encourage children to make connections and articulate relationships between concepts and procedures.

Engage students in tasks and discussions that help them develop better methods for solving problems.

Much classroom discussion revolves around exploring and analyzing methods for solving problems. As children describe and explain, they are empowered to improve their methods by making them more efficient and meaningful. Students may also opt to abandon previous methods for methods of others that make more sense to them. In a productive and healthy mathematical community, the give-and-take allows students to learn from each other. As we choose and guide activities, we need to provide opportunities that allow the children to apply, assess, and discuss methods for solving problems. By working together, members of a class can share information, pool expertise, and develop better methods of solution (Hiebert et al. 1997).

The Mathematics and Its Language

Children are introduced to rates and collect and compare rate data.

We use rates every day to make comparisons between quantities, for example, miles per gallon, wages per hour, and points per game. Rate problems involve a rate—a special type of ratio in which two quantities are compared (Chapin and Johnson 2006, 79). Many young students have little exposure to and experience with rates. Because of this, they are often unsure how to approach, interpret, represent, and solve problems involving rates. It is important for our fourth graders to informally explore rates in preparation for the significant time that will be spent developing these proportional reasoning concepts in the middle grades. We need to help students apply intuitive solutions based on understandings about multiplication and division as they move from additive to multiplicative thinking rather than rely on algorithms or formulas.

Children use rate tables to record rate information and to solve rate problems.

Rate tables can be used to aid in problem solving. Students may recognize rate tables as a special kind of in-and-out table. Rate tables are often horizontal, but can also be written vertically. Each format has its advantages and offers students opportunities to shift from one representation to the other, given the context or purpose of the information.

Children calculate and compare unit rates.

Per-unit rates can be calculated when rate information is given for a number of measurements and converted to an equivalent unit rate. Additional equivalent rates can then be calculated from the determined unit rate. A pricing and purchasing context is a familiar and engaging one for fourth graders.

Children review and apply multiplication and division strategies and procedures in problem-solving situations.

Presenting rich problems offers children opportunities to think about mathematical situations in ways that make sense and to make procedural decisions that have meaning in relation to a given context. This process supports the students' development of number sense, computation, and problem solving.

Children develop and apply strategies for multiplying and dividing more difficult problems without the use of a calculator or standard algorithm.

Children often perceive problems with large numbers as more difficult than those with smaller numbers. Because of this perceived reality, it is important for children to develop strategies with which to approach and solve more difficult problems. The more strategies children come to understand well, the more choices they will have when solving problems.

Investigations and Literature-Based Activities

Jump Roping Jacks and Jills: Introducing Rates

Duration: 2–3 class periods

Rates are introduced to students as they collect, record, and analyze jump roping data. This set of problem-solving activities, adapted from *Everyday*

Mathematics (Everyday Learning Corporation 2007a), offers students the opportunity to:

- collect, record, and analyze rate data
- apply and articulate the language of rates
- investigate the role of units of measure attached to the jump roping data
- review and apply previous understandings of statistical landmarks
- create and use rate tables to solve problems and answer questions

Materials
- 1 jump rope per group of three students
- 1 stopwatch per group of three students
- 1 sheet of chart paper
- *Rate Tables* record sheet (see Blackline Masters)

Rates are special types of ratios in which two different quantities are compared with different units of measure assigned for each value. For many fourth graders, as well as adults, everyday uses of rates pose difficulty. Much of the poor performance reported in the professional literature and popular press reflects difficulty with rate problems on inventory tests or an inability to apply proportional thinking in the workplace (Everyday Learning Corporation 2007a). As you work through this lesson and others, you may want to use some of the following rates as a source for problem ideas and conversations:

- store rates: price per dozen, price per ounce
- allowance: dollars per week, dollars per month
- rent payments: dollars per month
- heart rates: heartbeats per minute
- speed: miles per hour
- mileage: miles per gallon
- hotel rates: cost per night
- movies: cost per child, cost per adult
- rental car rates: cost per mile, cost per day, cost per week
- sports: minutes per half, minutes per period, minutes per quarter
- animals: number of legs per hippopotamus, number of legs per ostrich

The use of a physical activity such as jump roping can help give the children a real-world context within which to study rates. The third and fourth graders in my school participate in the American Heart Association's Jump Rope for Heart fund-raiser each spring. Having my fourth graders apply their newly acquired jump roping skills certainly makes the task of introducing rates an engaging one for my class. Other physical activities such as jumping jacks or ball bouncing can work just as well. Choose a task that is well suited for your class.

I introduce the lesson by showing the class a jump rope and a stopwatch. I inform the children that they are going to collect data about their jump roping skills. They will be working in threes; one child will have a jump rope, one will have a stopwatch, and one will count. The conversation quickly turns to what data we can collect with a jump rope and a stopwatch. As the children offer suggestions, I record on the board:

- *How many jumps can we do in a minute?*
- *How many jumps can we do in five minutes?*
- *Who can jump the longest—and for how long?*
- *How long will it take us to miss a jump?*

I present the following investigation to the class: *How many jumps can you jump in five minutes?* Because the children have had previous experiences with data collection and analysis, I encourage them to set up the guidelines of the investigation themselves with my help. Keep in mind that the knowledge and language that the children have acquired from previous work with data collection should be applied to this context. A student-generated set of investigation guidelines may look like the following:

You need:
- 1 jump rope
- 1 stopwatch
- a group of three students

Directions
1. Person A jumps for one minute.

2. Person B uses the stopwatch and says "Start" and "Stop."

3. Person C counts the number of jumps.

4. Person A jumps for one minute. You can miss jumps and still keep jumping until your minute is up. Only the "real" jumps will be counted.

5. Each person will jump three rounds. Out of those three rounds, the highest number of jumps will be posted on the class chart.

6. Once all three people have jumped three rounds, they will post each of their highest number of jumps on the class chart.

Before teaching the lesson, think about the essential components of the investigation, keeping in mind the mathematical objectives of the lesson.

Your students may not offer the idea of having three rounds. Is this something that you wish to add? You also may need to clarify what constitutes a "real" jump. I choose to have the children record their highest number of jumps from the three rounds. If your children have had previous experiences with mean calculations, you might want them to find their mean amount of jumps.

You might also wish to consider how long the children will jump. I discovered that two minutes is too long! One minute is long enough for some. Thirty seconds is an interesting option because the children will then have to determine how they can use that thirty-second jump to identify a jump rate for one minute. Many health care professionals will take a pulse for ten or fifteen seconds and then convert the rate to heartbeats/minute. You may find that sharing this information will help students apply a real-world context to this work with rates.

Perhaps the most important discussion of this lesson will be one focusing on the measurements and language used to record jumps on the class chart. The children may need to be reminded that once the data are collected, they will need to be recorded. To expedite time, you can draw a blank T-chart on the board. Because of their familiarity with T-charts, the children will quickly suggest that names can go on one side and number of jumps on the other.

Asking the children for a title for this T-chart will facilitate a beginning conversation about rates. After all, numbers in a T-chart are nothing more than numbers in a T-chart without appropriate headings and labels. Some children may suggest "Number of Jumps" for a title. Emphasize that although they are, in fact, counting the number of jumps, they are more importantly counting them within a framework of time, and that needs to be noted as well. What they are really measuring is how many jumps they can make per minute, which is what mathematicians refer to as a *rate*. A rate tells us how many there are of one thing (jumps) for a certain number of another thing (minutes). Rates often contain the word *per*, which means *for each*. In this case, you want to refer to jumps per one minute. A rate can also be written with a slash to represent the word *per*, as in *jumps/one minute*. Following this discussion, the class will probably agree that the title of the chart should be "Number of Jumps per One Minute."

The language of a *one*-minute rate can focus the conversation on *unit rates* and what they represent. Identifying a unit rate will give us a measurement of jumps/one minute, which is friendly and helpful when trying to find other unknowns within a rate table.

Ask the children to record their jumps of each round in T-charts in their math notebooks and circle their highest number of jumps, which they will then post on the class chart. (See Figure 10–1.)

Once all have agreed to the guidelines and questions to be answered, the children set off to jump and record in their notebooks. As the children are jumping, timing, and counting, create a class T-chart on chart paper for recording the highest jump counts.

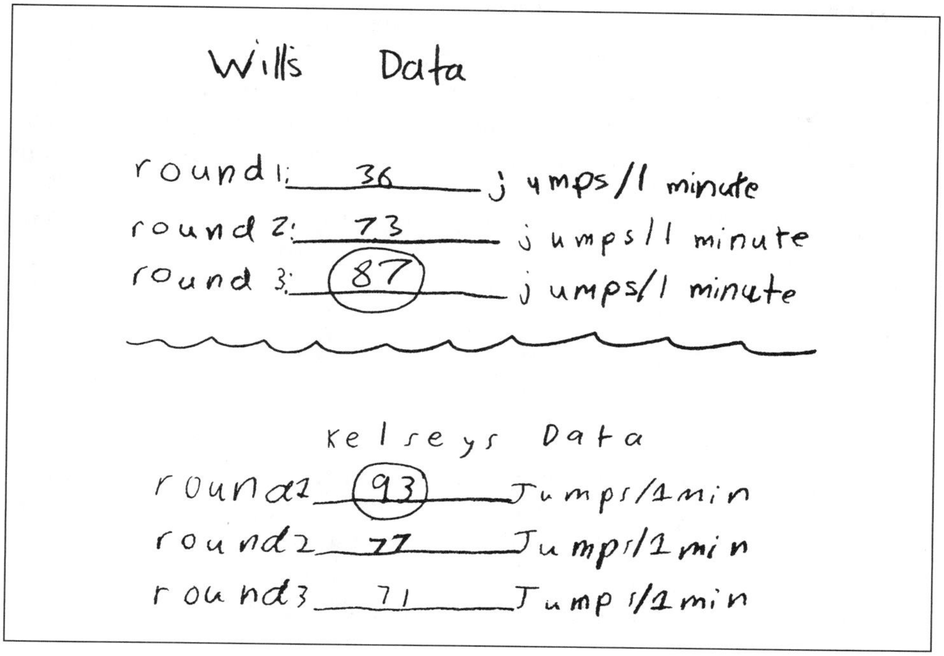

FIGURE 10–1 ◄

Will and Kelsey's jump roping data.

Will's Data

round 1: _____36_____ jumps/1 minute
round 2: _____73_____ jumps/1 minute
round 3: _____(87)____ jumps/1 minute

〜〜〜〜〜〜〜〜〜〜〜〜

Kelseys Data
round1 _____(93)____ Jumps/1min
round2 _____77_____ Jumps/1min
round3 _____71_____ Jumps/1min

Number of Jumps per One Minute

Student	Jumps

Once all the data have been collected and posted, ask, "What do you notice?" You may need to have a quick review of previously studied statistical landmarks such as median, mode, range, minimum, and maximum to remind students of applicable language with which to discuss the data. A questions such as "How could we best represent our class average of jumps per minute?" can move the children to applying their understandings of mean, median, and mode. Allowing the children to determine how best to identify the class average can elicit rich mathematical conversation and decision making. My classes tend to settle on the use of the median. They often apply the use of the organized list to identify the range and distribution of jumps. The median then makes the most sense to them for identifying a class average.

Once you have decided upon or calculated an average for the class, ask the students, "What does this information tell us?" I have heard everything from "We are great jump ropers" to "Maybe we should ask the Heart Association to change the challenge to Bounce Balls for Better Beats!"

Then ask the students how many jumps each member of the class could do in five minutes, given your average (e.g., 75 jumps/minute). Have students talk with a neighbor about how they could use the information that you already have to get the information you want. Because the collected data are recorded with a unit rate, multiplying the number of jumps by five will solve the problem.

Rate tables can offer a mathematical model within which to calculate equivalent rates.

Jumps					
Minutes	1	2	3	4	5

As with T-charts that represent growth patterns, functional relationships exist between horizontal values as well as vertical ones in a rate table. Because you have identified a unit rate, a rule to help to determine the number of jumps for any amount of time may be readily evident. Guiding questions such as the following can help children make sense of the numbers and relationships found in the rate table.

- What do we know?
- What do we need to know?
- What do you notice about the minutes?
- How can we extend this table? What values can be filled in for the minutes? Why do those numbers make sense? Do they fit the established pattern or relationship?
- If we know the minutes, how can we determine the jumps? What is the relationship between each successive number of jumps? How do you know?

TEACHER-TO-TEACHER TALK   Mindfully creating and choosing rate problems is a challenge. For example, as I was initially designing this lesson for my class, I posed the question, "How many jumps will be made, on average, in forty-eight minutes?" I chose forty-eight minutes because that is the length of one of our math periods. Initially, I concluded that forty-eight worked nicely; the children could relate to that number because they could identify its relevance to our daily schedule. I also realized, however, that some children might need to extend the rate table to 48 minutes, which would be tedious. And after all, this was a lesson to introduce rates, not to take up time extending a rate table. I settled on a rate table with only five values and a pattern based on the unit rate that the children could easily identify and continue. Thankfully, I was fortunate to catch this potential error in my planning before I presented the lesson. And I continue to remind myself that with the introduction of a new concept or procedure, less is often more!

I am not always that fortunate, however. We have all been in situations in which we have picked "bad" numbers for examples. There have been many times when I have had to ask the children to "rewind" a lesson so that I could choose better numbers to make what I was presenting clearer. I have learned over the years to prethink my lessons and identify groups of numbers that might work well. Perhaps I want to stay with even numbers, or single-digit numbers, or multiples of ten. It is actually an interesting thinking process for us as mathematicians to identify classifications of numbers that will work well within a given problem, procedure, or context.

Notice that the numbers are not complicated, nor difficult to manipulate, but the proportionality represented within the table can be. If a value such as five minutes is inserted into the table without discussion or representation of the rates of two, three, and four minutes, the number of jumps may quickly become elusive. The children usually agree that wanting to know how many jumps can be made in five minutes is a reasonable question to ask. Again, encouraging the students to use what they already know to figure out what they do not know can help make the pattern and proportionality between values visible.

A rate of jumps/minute allows us great flexibility within the rate table. Identifying the relationship between each additional minute will help the children articulate how to move in either direction on the rate table. The children are quick to recognize that knowing jumps/minute can allow us to determine the number of jumps for any increment of time.

When asked once again about the number of jumps/five minutes, Michael was quite confident in his response of 375 jumps. Before I could even ask, Michael continued his response with "And I know this makes sense because I know how many jumps we can make in one minute. So I just times the number of jumps by how many minutes I need to know about. I don't even need the rate table because I know the unit rate."

Offering additional rate scenarios will help children solidify their thinking about rates and the multiplicative relationship they represent. Remind the children that rate tables are tools to help them think about and extend a given rate. Rate tables will also help them move flexibly in both directions of the given rate, which can be helpful when trying to identify a unit rate. If more practice is needed, additional problems can be created based on the rates found and reported by the children in the follow-up journal write.

A building has a height of 72 feet. If each story is 12 feet high, how many stories does the building have? Sample rate table:

Height	12 ft							
Stories	1	2	3	4	5	6	7	8

In one week, Ava mowed 8 lawns and made $96. If she charged each customer the same amount, how much did she charge per lawn? Sample rate table:

Money Earned								96
Lawns	1	2	3	4	5	6	7	8

Matt receives $5 per week as an allowance. If he saves all his money, how much money will he save in four weeks? In a year? Sample rate table:

Total								
$	$5							
Week	1	2	3	4	5	. . .	52	

Follow-Up Journal Write

Look for examples of rates in newspapers, in magazines, and on labels. Cut out an example of a rate that you find interesting. Paste or tape it on top of your entry. For whom would this information be important to know? Why?

Solving and Creating Rate Problems

Duration: 1–2 class periods

Many fourth graders have had little experience with rates other than prices. As a result, they are often unsure how to approach, interpret, solve, or create these types of problems (Chapin and Johnson 2006, 79). This set of problem-solving activities, adapted from *Everyday Mathematics* (Everyday Learning Corporation 2007a), offers students opportunities to:

- develop and apply understandings about rates in problem-solving contexts
- create and use rate tables and charts to solve problems and answer questions

Materials

- 1 *Great Rates* worksheet per student (see Blackline Masters)
- 1 copy of "Mammal Heart Rates" chart per student (see Blackline Masters)
- optional: 1 sheet of chart paper

A rate chart is another type of rate table that can help children model and solve problems involving rate and time. To begin this lesson, post the following story problem on the board or chart paper.

A gray whale's heart rate is 8 beats/minute. At this rate, how many times does a gray whale's heart beat in five minutes?

Allow a few minutes of independent think time before beginning the whole-class conversation to offer children personal access to the mathematics and let them model the mathematics with paper and pencil. Do not be surprised if some children struggle with modeling or explaining the solution to this problem. Rate problems are difficult!

The children will recognize that this is a rate problem. Some students may proceed to construct a rate table. Some may move right to the multiplication or the division. And some may just be flummoxed!

After a few minutes, begin a class conversation by asking students what information they have and what information they need to know. Hayden reminded us that the rate actually gives us two pieces of information. We know how many beats a whale's heart beats in one minute. We need to know how many beats a whale's heart beats in five minutes.

Draw the following chart on the board.

8 beats per minute	5 minutes	

Ask the children how they could label these two cells. Students usually recognize the first cell as the rate. They also recognize the second cell as the time being asked about in the problem. They usually agree to label that cell *Time*.

Rate	*Time*	
8 beats per minute	5 minutes	

Review the initial problem to agree on a label for the final cell, such as Total Beats.

Because the children have had some prior experience with unit rates, they should be quick to articulate that multiplying eight and five will give you the total beats.

Rate	*Time*	*Total Beats*
8 beats per minute	5 minutes	40 beats

The unit labels of the cells are important. If the rate is beats per minute, then our time value and final solution value need to be consistent with the rate measure. In this context, the time needs to be reported in *minutes*, and the total beats needs to be reported as *beats*. The rate cell in such a model can help children identify the needed units of measure in order maintain consistency.

As you discuss the importance of the consistency of measures in rate problems, you may wish to present this same problem but with differing measures, such as the following:

Rate	Time	Total Beats
8 beats per minute	300 seconds	?

This example presents two different measures and this inconsistency needs to be resolved; the seconds need to be converted into minutes. By this time in the year, students should handle such conversions mentally and efficiently. Remember, however, to ask *why* and *how* the children know that three hundred seconds equals five minutes!

The *Great Rates* worksheet offers practice with different rates and measures within the same context. Students can work independently or with partners as they solve the problems and chart their solutions. Pulling the class together to process one or two of the problems is all that may be necessary at this point in the lesson. It will be more important for you to circulate and identify the level at which children are understanding, interpreting, and solving the problems. As with many new concepts, mathematical talk is extremely important as children bat around new ideas and language and work to make new concepts and procedures their own. Charting their thinking within a rate chart will also help children identify the meaning of the numbers, measures, and operations.

Rate problems involving speed and distance are a challenge for even our best mathematical thinkers. Not only are the concepts difficult to grasp, but these concepts are often referred to in a number of different ways—by using a rate (miles per gallon or miles per hour) or by using words and phrases such as *speed*, *distance*, *how fast*, and *how far* (Chapin and Johnson 2006, 79). You may wish to tackle some additional problems involving rate, time, and distance with your students. Using travel times within your geographic area can bring meaning to the mathematics. My students enjoy creating contexts and problems about travel times to New York, Philadelphia, and Washington, DC. When a family moved into our community from Chicago, we investigated that trip as well. Applying map skills will be necessary as you identify and agree upon distances from one city to another.

The children can now create their own rate problems and rate scenarios. The chart of mammal heart rates can be distributed to the children as a source of interesting rates to use in their problems. You may wish to differentiate the expectations of the task, given your particular time frame, in one of the following ways:

- Story problems are written on the front of a piece of paper. The solution and rate chart are written on the back. Children share problems with each other or in small groups.

- Story problems are written on lined paper. The story and an illustration are mounted on a piece of white construction or drawing paper. The solution is posted on the back.

- Story problems are written on the front of a piece of paper. The solution and rate chart are written on the back. The stories and their solutions are compiled into a class book with a cover, table of contents, and overview of rates and how to solve a rate problem written by the children. You can assign the writing of the overview to one or two children, or you can model the writing of the introduction in a whole-class format. Because the students have been exposed to mathematical writing all year, keep your expectations high! Expect concise language and evidence of understanding.

Encourage the children to extend their questions and thinking beyond the ever popular "How may beats will an elephant's heart beat in _____ minutes?" Children may wish to compare heart rates of various animals. They may wish to create strings of related story problems based on those rates. You may want to foster conversations about the relationship between the weight of a particular mammal and its heart rate. The children may also be interested in calculating an average heart rate for their class and comparing it with other mammal rates, remembering to keep consistent units of measure.

As we all know, time at the end of the school year is often scattered and interrupted. This activity can offer interdisciplinary experiences connecting work in science, language arts, and math and can easily be interrupted and restarted to fit your schedule. Teaming with another fourth-grade class can offer an additional social and cooperative dimension to thinking about, writing about, and calculating rates.

If You Hopped Like a Frog

Duration: 1–3 class periods

If You Hopped Like a Frog, by David Schwartz (1999), presents "What if . . . ?" propositions and activities that will engage your students with proportional thinking as they measure, calculate, and compare. This series of lessons, adapted from *The Marilyn Burns Classroom Math Library Teacher Handbook, Grades 4–6* (2005), offers students opportunities to:

- measure and compare measurements

- investigate measurement conversions: inches to feet, seconds to minutes

- reason proportionally about given measurements

- practice and apply multiplication skills and strategies within a problem-solving context

Materials

- *If You Hopped Like a Frog*, by David Schwartz
- 1 measuring tape or yard or meter stick per group of two to three students
- optional: 1 ruler per group of two to three students

Proportional reasoning is the ability to make *multiplicative* comparisons between quantities (Chapin and Johnson 2006). Proportionality is a complex topic. Many adults find it difficult to reason proportionately. It is necessary for students to informally explore ideas related to multiplicative relationships and how those relationships manifest themselves in problem-solving contexts. An engaging nonfiction context of animal feats can offer opportunities for children to shift from additive to multiplicative reasoning.

If you could hop like a frog, you could jump from home plate to first base in one leap. If you were as strong as an ant, you could lift an automobile. If you could swallow like a snake, you could gulp a hot dog thicker than a telephone pole. *If You Hopped Like a Frog* (Schwartz 1999) explores these intriguing facts as well as others about eleven different animals. Information at the back of the book explains how the author made his calculations and offers other interesting math problems to solve.

The lesson begins with a read-aloud of *If You Hopped Like a Frog*. Introduce the book by reading the "Dear Reader" preface, in which the author explains the "What if . . . ?" questions he pondered as a child when he realized that "answering these questions took just a little bit of math." Schwartz sets the stage for the comparisons that will be made between various animals and humans. This introduction to comparative thinking will scaffold the proportional reasoning required of the lesson. When you present the book to the class, however, refrain from sharing the information presented at the back of the book. The questions you pose for investigation will require the children to apply their measuring and proportional reasoning skills rather than consult the information at the end of the book. Their conclusions can then be compared with Schwartz's generalizations.

When introducing the book, do not focus on the mathematics, but rather on the fascinating facts and the language used to describe them. If a frog can jump *twenty times* its body length, for example, what does *twenty times* really mean? In this context of frogs and length, *twenty times* represents a multiplicative relationship that the children will need to apply when completing the initial investigation.

Once the book has been read, use the information presented at the back of the book to create investigations involving measurement and proportional reasoning. For the first investigation, pose the following questions on the board:

A frog can jump 20 times its body length.

- *How far could you jump if you jumped like a frog?*
- *From (about) where to (about) where could you jump?*

Asking the children what they need to know can help them establish the parameters of the investigation themselves. They will need to reach consensus about the measuring process. Either you or the class will also need to determine the unit of measure. I often choose U.S. customary units. Measuring in inches gives additional calculation opportunities as students convert from one unit of length to another. A conversation about the need to standardize the measurement process will help set the measuring directives. Some children may suggest that measurements be taken while lying on the floor while others suggest holding up tape measures. The method of choice in my class, however, always seems to be taping two yardsticks to the wall one above the other. The child being measured stands with her back against the yardsticks. Another student places a ruler on top of that child's head and reads the measure from the placement of the ruler. The students also need to agree on how precise the measure should be—to the nearest inch? Half inch? (The nearest inch works just fine!) Once the parameters are set, the children can begin measuring and calculating in groups of two or three. Each group must report its findings on paper and be prepared to share its methods of solving the problem. The artists in the group may enjoy drawing pictures to illustrate their findings.

Children are not allowed to use calculators for this investigation. By this time in the year, personal strategies of multiplying by multiples of ten should be established. Decomposing large factors into more manageable ones should be a common strategy. In this case, students can multiply by ten and then double the product. The frog investigation lends itself nicely to the use of a rate table. If the children do not make this connection, a leading question such as "Where have we seen these types of questions before?" will help students make the connection to rate tables.

Personal measurement references are important for children to establish. What does 20 feet look like? Fifty feet? One hundred feet? Taking the investigation outdoors can help them establish visual references for longer lengths. Marking these measures on an asphalt surface in sidewalk chalk can allow children further opportunities to compare, contrast, and visualize the distances they could jump if they hopped like a frog.

You can offer other investigations included at the end of Schwartz's book in various formats such as a menu or as whole-class investigations over several days. Choose various paragraphs from the back of the book. Pose other problems for pairs to investigate, such as the following:

An ant can lift fifty times its weight.

- *How much could you lift if you were as strong as an ant?*
- *What could you lift?*

A chameleon's tongue is half as long as its body.

- *How long would your tongue be if you had a tongue like a chameleon?*
- *What could you eat in one flick of your tongue?*

A snake can swallow something twice as big as its head.

- *What could you swallow if you could swallow like a snake?*
- *Why does your choice make sense? What measurement helped you make this decision?*

A shrew can eat three times its body weight.

- *How much would your food weigh?*
- *What could you eat if you could eat like a shrew?*

A spider can move thirty-three times the length of its body in one second.

- *How far can a spider move in two seconds? Three seconds? Ten seconds?*
- *How far could you run in one second if you could scurry like a spider? Two seconds? Three seconds? Ten seconds? One minute?*

Multiplication and Division Games to Revisit

Duration: 1–2 class periods or short explorations used as class warm-ups or closers

Replaying and rethinking previously played games offers students the opportunity to:

- extend previous understandings
- reevaluate previous strategies and develop new strategies grounded in deeper understanding

Materials
- directions and materials for the following games:
  - *Target 300* and *Target 600* (see Chapter 5)
  - *Silent Multiplication* (see Chapter 5)
  - *Rio* (see Chapter 5)
  - *Silent Division* (see Chapter 6)
  - *Division Dash* (see Chapter 6)

As mentioned throughout this book, games offer the children continued opportunities to practice number skills. Because the children are familiar with the rules of each game, revisiting them allows you the opportunity to differentiate each game's purpose according to the needs of the players. For example, children who continue to struggle with the sixes and sevens tables can be directed to play *Rio* with those tables. You can assign *Target 300* to those children still fragile with multiplication by multiples of tens. Assign *Target 600* to those children who are more comfortable with that process. Further extensions can be made for playing *Target 2,000, 3,000,* or *6,000* in which the children multiply by multiples of one hundred.

Additional explorations can be presented within the *Silent Multiplication* and *Silent Division* formats, such as the following.

Doubling both factors, resulting in a quadrupled product:

$$3 \times 5 = \qquad 4 \times 6 =$$
$$6 \times 10 = \qquad 8 \times 12 =$$
$$12 \times 20 = \qquad 16 \times 24 =$$

Halving factors or products, resulting in mixed numbers:

$$3 \times 5 =$$
$$1\tfrac{1}{2} \times 5 =$$
$$1\tfrac{1}{2} \times 2\tfrac{1}{2} =$$

Division with remainders:

$$11 \div 5 =$$
$$16 \div 5 =$$
$$21 \div 5 =$$
$$26 \div 5 =$$
$$31 \div 5 =$$

Multiplying and dividing the dividend by ten and doubling the divisor:

$$48 \div 8 =$$
$$480 \div 8 =$$
$$4,800 \div 8 =$$
$$4,800 \div 16 =$$
$$4,800 \div 32 =$$
$$480 \div 32 =$$
$$48 \div 32 =$$

Please be mindful of following up sessions of *Silent Multiplication* and *Silent Division* with conversation. Discussion will help relationships and patterns become visible and accessible.

Calculation Routines and Practices

I have yet to meet a fourth grader who did not benefit from continued practice of multiplication and division skills and procedures. Children are often more willing to carry out this practice in small amounts and if it is tailored to their needs and interests. Because so much of the in-class work that we are completing in June requires classroom discussion, multiplication and division packets once again have their place. If your children are like mine, you may find them more likely to work on practice in the form of logic puzzles or riddles. Over the years I have collected various books and blackline masters of such puzzles and riddles that I can compile in a packet for the children to complete independently over a certain period of days. One series I often use is Groundworks (Greenes and Findell 2006). Quality practice work may also be available from your prescribed curriculum. As you pick and choose work, continue to keep your instructional objectives in mind as well as the calculation needs of your children.

Minilessons can also be helpful at this time. Perhaps a few children cannot remember how to make a chunker for a double-digit multiplication problem (see Chapter 5, "Calculation Routines and Practices"), or some children are not remembering to place a zero in the ones place in their partial products, or some need additional instruction on multiplication by multiples of ten. Remember that a discussion of the *why* as well as the *how* should accompany minilessons. You'll find a wonderful set of activities in *Minilessons for Math Practice, Grades 3–5* (Bresser and Holtzman 2006) that can be used in various contexts and for various needs.

Mathematics Writing

As the year has progressed, so too have your children's mathematical writing skills and procedures. They have written about strategies and solutions. They have justified their reasoning and explained their thinking. They have responded to prompts in their journals and have created story problems for others to solve. Is this math or language arts? Personally, I like to see the lines blurred between the two at times. NCTM's *Principles and Standards for School Mathematics* (2000) reminds us that:

> communication is an essential part of mathematics and mathematics instruction. It is a way of sharing ideas and clarifying understanding. Through communication, ideas become objects of reflection, refinement, discussion, and amendment. The communication process also helps build meaning and permanence for ideas and makes them public. When students are challenged to think

and reason about mathematics and to communicate the results of their thinking to others orally or in writing, they learn to be clear and convincing. (60)

Revisiting what constitutes strong mathematical writing at year's end allows the children to acknowledge and document their journey through this mathematical writing process. Ask, "What do we know *now* about mathematical writing?" to begin a process of self-reflection and documentation. More times than not, all the children will have something to say in response to this prompt. Encouraging partner talk before a whole-class discussion will enable all the children to voice their opinions and beliefs. You can then create a class chart of expectations of good mathematical writing with the children. I have begun to type up and reproduce these expectations for the children to carry on with them to the fifth grade. I remind the children of the need to be respectful when sharing their ideas about good mathematical writing with their new fifth-grade teachers and classmates. "This is what *we* believe," I tell them. "This is what worked in *our* classroom. This is what *we* value. These may or may not be the beliefs, practices, and values of other classrooms. So please be respectful and mindful of the beliefs, practices, and values of other teachers and students."

What Good Fourth-Grade Mathematical Writing Looks Like
Mrs. Schuster's Class 2005–2006
Grade 4

- *It is neat and well organized.*
- *The work is written in pencil.*
- *Drawings can be in colored pencil (if you have the time).*
- *You can understand the problem by looking at the writing/work.*
- *Hardly any spelling mistakes—no misspelling of no-excuse words!*
- *Charts are labeled.*
- *Solutions are labeled. Sometimes the solution is written in a sentence.*
- *Numbers are legible. Zeros do not look like sixes!*
- *The writing is clear—words are not left out.*
- *Strong and appropriate math vocabulary is used.*
- *Strong introductory and concluding sentences are used.*

Parent Communication

You may wish to review the "Assessment" section on page 361 prior to reading this section. The self-reflection piece outlined in the "Assessment" section is the basis of this overview of suggested parental communication.

You may wish to distribute a parent information form for June. I often do not send out a June information form because of the fragmented schedule of June, which is full of end-of-year activities. I prefer to focus on self-reflection and closure as we move through June.

The selected portfolio piece for which each student writes a self-assessment and reflection can be copied and sent home to parents with a cover letter describing the child's progress and the requested parental involvement in the reflection process. Children love to talk about their work and share their work with their families. In this process, the child takes on the leadership role. It is, after all, his work and his growth. This is all very personal and important to the child, as it should be. My letter to parents is in Figure 10–2.

FIGURE 10–2 ▶

Parent cover letter for portfolio reflection.

Dear Parent(s),

Attached is a piece of completed work that your child has chosen from his or her yearlong collection of math work. The children were asked to choose a piece of work upon which they would reflect and subsequently assess. I offered guiding questions throughout the process to support the children as they assessed the mathematical process, their progress, and the quality of the completed work.

I am hopeful that you will take a few minutes out of your busy schedule to sit and talk with your child about her or his work and reflection. Please keep in mind that this is your child's assessment and that it is very personal. As adults, we may value aspects of work that you feel your child has overlooked. That conversation can be had at another time on another day! Some of the following questions may help facilitate the conversation with your child.

- Why did you choose this piece of work?
- Show me how you got started on the problem.
- What did you have to understand to complete this problem?
- What did you learn about the math while you worked through the problem?
- What did you learn about yourself as a mathematician?
- Is this a piece of your best work? Why or why not?
- What would you do differently if you were to solve a problem like this again?

If you have any questions about this exercise or your child's work, please feel free to contact me.

Thank you so much for your support this year. Happy summer-ing!

Mathematically yours,

Lainie Schuster

Lainie Schuster

It may also be helpful to model a parent conversation with a child in your class prior to sending home the work and reflection. The children can then pair up and share their work with each other as they practice this process. This is also a lovely time to invite your principal into your classroom if you have established such a relationship with him or her. It is a time of closure and celebration.

Assessment

Although self-assessment has been promoted and supported throughout the year in various formats and contexts, an end-of-year self-assessment allows children the opportunity to review their year's work, thinking, and progress. Wiggins and McTighe (2005) describe self-understanding as the most important facet of understanding for lifelong learning. Central to self-understanding is honest self-assessment based on the clarity of what we do understand and what we do not, what we have accomplished and what remains to be done.

Fourth graders are none too young to develop lifelong self-assessment practices and habits of mind. Our students have witnessed and experienced considerable cognitive and mathematical growth throughout the year. Asking the children to identify that growth and the process that supported it offers them the opportunity to assess their own progress rather than rely solely on external assessment indicators such as test scores, report cards, and adult feedback.

Asking children to self-assess requires mindful scaffolding and carefully crafted questions to guide the children through the process. I ask the children to review the work in their portfolios and math notebooks in pairs. There is often much animated discussion as the children review the year's earlier work and compare it with the more sophisticated thinking and writing completed at year's end. Allow the time for those conversations to happen. You may wish to post several guiding questions such as the following on the board prior to the children's perusal and discussion of their work. The questions will help the children focus on the task and think before they write.

- What was the purpose of this piece of work? Where and what was the mathematics involved?
- How was the math represented? In calculations? In writing? In a chart or diagram?
- Can your thinking be followed?
- Is this piece an example of quality work? Why or why not?
- If you did this piece again, what would you do differently?
- What would you like someone to notice about this piece of work?

Once the children have had ample time to review their completed work, I ask them to choose one piece of work about which they will write. I inform them that a copy of this piece of work and their written reflection will then be passed along to each of their respective fifth-grade teachers. Not only does this passed-along writing give each new teacher a mathematical snapshot of his new student, but it also gives that teacher a snapshot of our fourth-grade curriculum, expectations, practices, and routines. More often than not, meaningful conversations have evolved with colleagues in conjunction with this process of passing along work. The original work and reflection along with a cover letter can be sent home to the parents, as described in the "Parent Communication" section on page 359. I ask the children to sit down with their parents to review their work and reflection.

Developmentally, you may find that some fourth graders are more ready for the self-reflection that this type of work requires than others. Some children may confuse how they *feel* about a task with an *understanding* of the skills and knowledge required to complete that task successfully. Guiding questions and prompts can help children make this distinction. Creating a template with questions such as the one in Figure 10–3, which can then be attached to the piece of work, can help this self-reflective process along.

FIGURE 10–3 ▶

Adam's selected work and self-reflection.

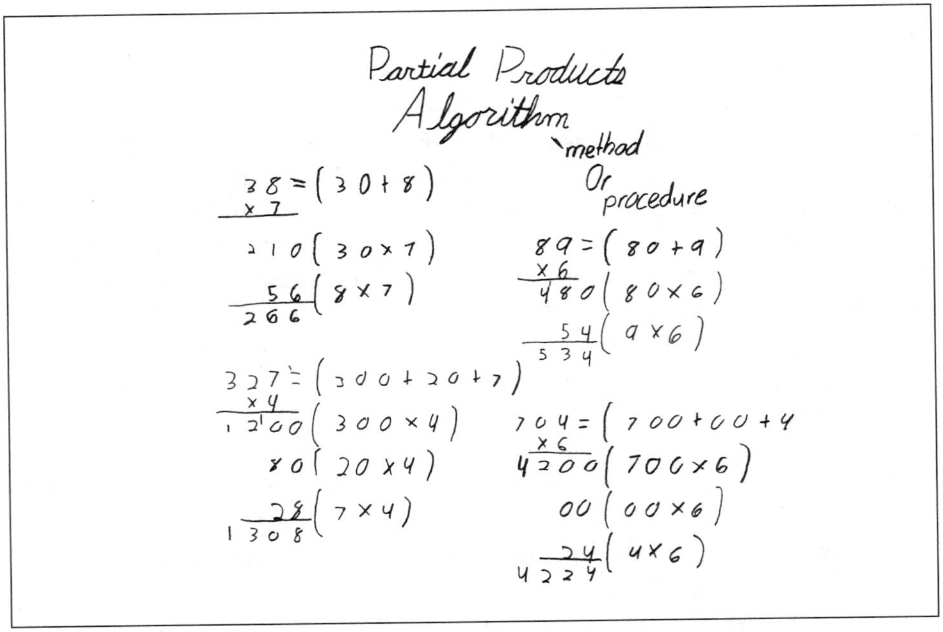

FIGURE 10–3 ◄

Adam's selected work and self-reflection, continued.

Math Learning Reflection

Subject Area: *Math/ Multiplication*

Assignment: *Partial Products Algorithm*

The purpose of this assignment was …

to learn another way to decompose big, hairy, scary multiplication facts. Also it was a more efficient way of multiplication than chunking.

This piece is an example of quality work because …

I really understood it and I used it very well in my work. For example, if I was stuck on a difficult problem I would use it and find the answer.

I selected this piece because I am proud of …

how I learned it so quick and efficient. When I was learning chunking it took awile, but I learned this no problem.

What I learned in the process of completing this piece …

■ about the subject/area/topic:

I learned that this way of doing multiplication is much more easier way than other ones I learned!

■ about myself as a learner:

I learned that I find partial product my numeral one way of figuring out multiplication facts.

If I did this assignment again, I would/would not …

I would do exactly what I did before. I would do this because I think I did very well on it.

Resources

Math Matters (Chapin and Johnson 2006)—Chapter 8, "Ratios"
An in-depth discussion of proportional reasoning. Geared more toward the upper grades, but extremely helpful in scaffolding the understanding and thinking necessary to manipulate the concepts of proportionality.

Chapter 4, "Multiplication and Division"
A discussion of rate problems and the importance of varying contexts and language.

About Teaching Mathematics (Burns 2007)
The chapter on expanding multiplication and division includes whole-class lessons as well as independent (menu) activities.

Seeing Fractions (Corwin, Russell, and Tierney 1991)
An exploration of rates reported as fractions can be found in Module 2.

Teaching Arithmetic: Lessons for Extending Multiplication (Wickett and Burns 2001)

Teaching Arithmetic: Lessons for Extending Division (Wickett and Burns 2003)
Activities, student vignettes, assessment recommendations, and superb narration make these must-have resources. Additional extensions are given for both *Silent Multiplication* and *Silent Division* in their respective books.

Groundworks: Algebraic Thinking (Greenes and Findell 2006)
Two excellent problem sets are offered that explore equivalent ratios and the use of ratio and rate tables.

The Groundworks Series (Grade 4) (Greenes and Findell 2006)

> *Reasoning About Measurement*
> *Reasoning with Numbers*
> *Reasoning with Geometry*
> *Reasoning with Data and Probability*
> *Algebraic Thinking*

Minilessons for Math Practice, Grades 3–5 (Bresser and Holtzman 2006)
Wonderful lessons that offer practice and reinforcement of math concepts, skills, and processes. Can be used as class warm-ups or during transition times during the schoolday.

Afterword
A Year in Review

The reports have gone out, the supply orders handed in, and the whiteboard given that one last cleaning. You snap the lid on the pattern blocks container and slide it into its designated spot. You throw out the markers with no caps and the gluesticks that have long since dried out. You sit at your desk and stare at the empty room and listen to the quiet hallways. You sigh. You are absolutely exhausted.

The school year is a long nine or ten months, but a successful school year feels even longer. It is hard work to keep up with wonderful mathematicians. It takes enthusiasm, thought, preparation, and more energy than any of us thinks that we could ever have! But as the years pass, I realize that it is the love of the children and the passion for the work that transcend the hours of planning, correcting, and reflection.

Even as we hear the warm days of summer calling, there is still work to do. This work, however, does not have the frenetic pace or urgency of our school year's, thank goodness! It is reflective in nature and can be done in a coffee shop, at the beach, or on the back porch. Take the time to think over the school year while it is still fresh in your mind. What worked? What didn't? What will you do differently next year? What unit needs tweaking? What new resources are you on the lookout for? Putting these ideas to paper will make them binding! Nothing formal is necessary—a simple spiral notebook or journal will do. But do document your thoughts. They are valuable.

NCTM's *Principles and Standards for School Mathematics* (2000) defines our charge as teachers of mathematics as enormous and essential. We have the daunting responsibility of preparing our children for a future of great and continual change. Mathematical experiences and practices that are rich in content and offer continual opportunities for children to make sense of what they are doing and thinking must be at the forefront of our charge. Even in this educational world of state-mandated testing and prescribed curricula, we do have the opportunity and responsibility to implement change in the teaching and learning of mathematics. That change may manifest itself in only one lesson or in only one unit in the upcoming year, but the seeds will have been sewn as we engage our fourth graders to think like mathematicians.

"Well," Miss Honey said, "it's only a guess, but here's what I think. While you were in my class you had nothing to do, nothing to make you struggle. Your fairly enormous brain was going crazy with frustration. It was bubbling and boiling away like mad inside your head. There was tremendous energy bottled up in there with nowhere to go, and somehow or other you were able to shoot out that energy through your eyes and make objects move. But now things are different. You are in the top form competing against children more than twice your age and all that mental energy is being used up in class. Your brain is for the first time having to struggle and strive and keep really busy, which is great. That's only a theory, mind you, and it may be a silly one, but I don't think it's far off the mark." (Dahl 1988, 229–30)

Matilda could very well have been a fourth grader with her "tremendous energy" and "fairly enormous brain." We very much want our fourth graders to use "all that mental energy . . . in class," just as Miss Honey wanted for Matilda.

Thank you for taking the time to accompany me on my journey through a year of teaching fourth-grade mathematics. I am hopeful that you have ended this journey with more questions than answers. Questions lead us to wonder, ponder, and ask, "What if . . . ?" And just like Matilda, "to struggle and strive and keep really busy."

Blackline Masters

Number Cards

Writing Prompts for *Martha Blah Blah*

How Many Cubes in Each Object? Record Sheet

Thinking in 3s

Thinking in 4s

Thinking About Thinking in 3s Record Sheet

Name That Number Directions

Close to 100 Directions

Close to 100 Score Sheet

Digit Draw Directions

Digit Draw Record Sheet

Parent Information and Involvement Form

Place-Value Mat

Digit Cards

A Million Taps . . . More or Less Record Sheet

What Would I Do with One Million? Worksheet

Close to 1,000 Directions

Close to 1,000 Score Sheet

Digit Place Directions

What Is a Polygon? Worksheet

Polygons: Must Be True and Cannot Be True Record Sheet

Polygon Shapes for Sorting Activities

Polygon Sorting Activity: This and That

Valuable Property and Target Mat

Polygon Sorting Activity: Out of Sorts

Polygon Sorting Activity: I Have a Secret

Polygon Sorting Activity: Guess My Rule

Classifying Triangles Record Sheet

Classifying Quadrilaterals Record Sheet

The Important Book About Polygons: Cover

The Important Book About Polygons: Page

The Important Book About Polygons: Author Page

Tangram Cutting Instructions

Constructing Polygons Worksheet

Pent-Tris Directions

Brainstorming Web

Measuring Up Directions

Down the Drain Directions

Number Cards

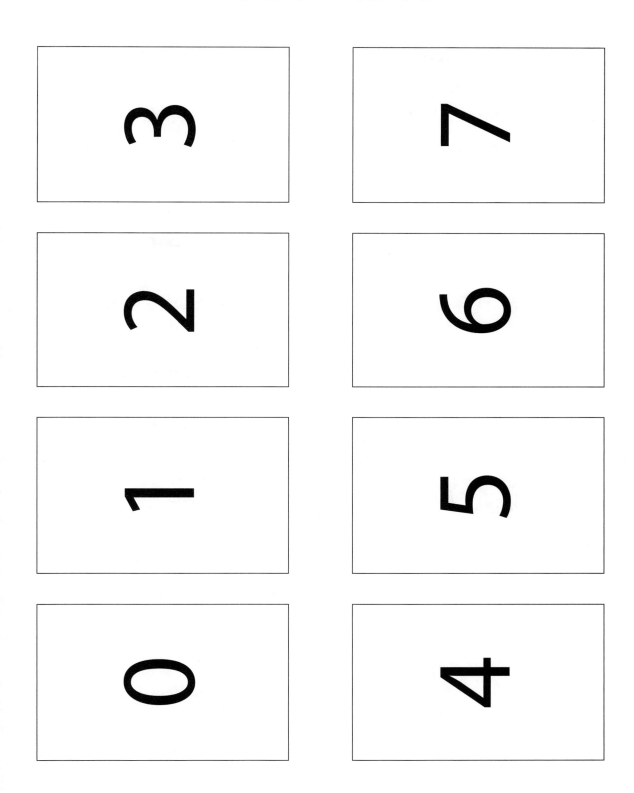

Number Cards (*Continued*)

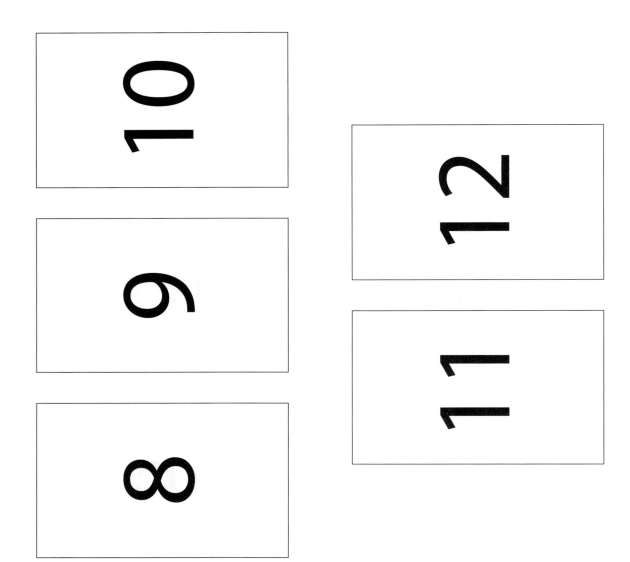

Writing Prompts for *Martha Blah Blah*

We would suggest that Granny Flo take out the following 7 letters:

_____

Why? _____

_____

_____

_____

_____

Without these 7 letters, it would be *difficult* for Martha to say the following words:

_____

_____

_____

Without these 7 letters, it would be *easy* for Martha to say:

_____

_____

_____

How Many Cubes in Each Object?
Record Sheet

Name of Builder	Name of Object	Estimate	Actual Count

How would you explain to someone not in this class how to estimate the number of cubes in an object?

Adapted from *Mathematical Thinking at Grade 4* by Cornelia Tierney (Dale Seymour Publications, 1998)

 From *A Month-to-Month Guide: Fourth-Grade Math* by Lainie Schuster. © 2009 Math Solutions Publications

Thinking in 3s

Cross out two of the numbers in the array below so that the sum of the numbers in each row and column is a multiple of 3.

1	3	5	6
4	9	2	1
2	3	9	4
8	7	5	8

From *A Month-to-Month Guide: Fourth-Grade Math* by Lainie Schuster. © 2009 Math Solutions Publications

Thinking in 4s

Fill in the array so that the sum of each row and column will be a multiple of 4.

Remember: You will need to cross out two of the numbers in the array when sums of rows and columns are identified as multiples of 4.

			1
	5		
		6	

Will any of the sums be odd? How do you know?

Thinking About Thinking in 3s
Record Sheet

1. Is a multiple of 3 always an odd number? Why or why not? Use examples to justify your thinking.

2. What numbers could you substitute for the crossed-out numbers to make sums of all the rows and columns divisible by 3? Are there other solutions?

3. Could you have a row (or column) of four *odd* numbers whose sum was a multiple of 3? Why or why not? Give examples to justify your thinking.

4. Could you have a row (or column) of four *even* numbers whose sum was a multiple of 3? Why or why not? Give examples to justify your thinking.

Name That Number

You need:
    1 deck of 0–12 number cards
    math notebook/paper
    2 or 3 players

Directions

1. Shuffle the cards. Deal five cards to each player. Place the remaining cards in the center of the table, number side down. Turn over the top card and place it beside the number deck. This is the *target number* for the round.

2. Players try to match the target number by adding, subtracting, multiplying, or dividing the numbers on as many cards as possible from their hand. A card may be used only once.

3. Players write their solutions on a piece of paper.

    ■ Each player shares his or her solution. Players check each other's accuracy.

    ■ Each player sets aside the cards that he or she has used.

    ■ Each player replaces the used cards with cards from the top of the deck in the middle of the table.

4. A new target number is drawn and play continues.

5. Play continues until there are not enough cards left to replace all the players' cards. The player who sets aside the most cards wins the game.

Adapted from *Everyday Mathematics: The University of Chicago School Mathematics Project, Grade 4, 3d ed.* (Everyday Learning Corporation, 2007)

From *A Month-to-Month Guide: Fourth-Grade Math* by Lainie Schuster. © 2009 Math Solutions Publications

Close to 100

You need:
   1 deck of 0–9 number cards
   1 *Close to 100* score sheet per player
   2 or 3 players

Directions

1. Shuffle the deck of cards. Place the deck in front of the players, facedown.

2. Player 1 flips over six cards from the deck. Player 1 makes two two-digit numbers from the cards whose sum will equal 100 or almost 100. The sum can be below or above 100. For example: $44 + 52 = 96$.

3. Player 1 writes his two numbers on his score sheet and calculates their sum. The score for that round is the difference between the sum and 100. For example, if the sum is 96, as in the previous example, the score is 4. If the sum is 100, the score is 0. If the sum is 107, the score is 7.

4. Player 1 places the four used cards in a discard pile.

5. Player 2 now chooses four cards to replace the cards Player 1 has discarded. Those four new cards are placed faceup along with the previous two cards that were not used. Player 2 now creates two two-digit numbers from the six cards in front of her.

6. Play continues until each child has played five rounds. Players total their scores. The player with the lowest score wins.

Adapted from *Mathematical Thinking at Grade 4* by Cornelia Tierney (Dale Seymour Publications, 1998)

From *A Month-to-Month Guide: Fourth-Grade Math* by Lainie Schuster. © 2009 Math Solutions Publications

Close to 100 Score Sheet

Game 1   **Score**

Round 1: _____ _____ + _____ _____ = _____   _____

Round 2: _____ _____ + _____ _____ = _____   _____

Round 3: _____ _____ + _____ _____ = _____   _____

Round 4: _____ _____ + _____ _____ = _____   _____

Round 5: _____ _____ + _____ _____ = _____   _____

                                              Total Score   _____

Game 2   **Score**

Round 1: _____ _____ + _____ _____ = _____   _____

Round 2: _____ _____ + _____ _____ = _____   _____

Round 3: _____ _____ + _____ _____ = _____   _____

Round 4: _____ _____ + _____ _____ = _____   _____

Round 5: _____ _____ + _____ _____ = _____   _____

                                              Total Score   _____

Adapted from *Mathematical Thinking at Grade 4* by Cornelia Tierney (Dale Seymour Publications, 1998)

From *A Month-to-Month Guide: Fourth-Grade Math* by Lainie Schuster. © 2009 Math Solutions Publications

Digit Draw

You need:
  card deck of 0–9 number cards, containing 2 of each number (for facilitator)
  1 *Digit Draw* recording sheet per player
  teams of 2–3 children

Directions

1. The teacher acts as facilitator of the game. The children are broken up in teams of two or three children. The children discuss their options when digits are drawn, but should work quietly and efficiently.

2. The facilitator asks for a target number between one hundred and two hundred.

3. Students post the target number on their record sheets.

4. The facilitator shuffles the number cards. The facilitator draws a card and reads it aloud (or places it on the overhead if using an overhead deck).

5. The teams discuss how to use the number and where to place it on their record sheets. The children place the digit in one of the squares representing placement in the tens place or ones place. The number may also be placed in a discard square if the children decide not to use it. Digits cannot be moved once placed in a position.

6. Play continues until eight digits are drawn and all squares on the record sheets are filled in.

7. Players add the resulting three two-digit numbers and record the sum.

8. The players then find the difference between their sum and the target number.

9. The team with the lowest difference wins the round.

Extension
Several rounds can be played. Once the rounds are completed, teams add the differences. The team with the lowest total wins.

Adapted from *Nimble with Numbers, Grades 4–5* by Leigh Childs and Laura Choate (Dale Seymour Publications, 1998)

From *A Month-to-Month Guide: Fourth-Grade Math* by Lainie Schuster. © 2009 Math Solutions Publications

Digit Draw Record Sheet

Total
☐☐ + ☐☐ + ☐☐ = _____

Discards ☐ ☐   Target #   Difference
_____   _____

Total
☐☐ + ☐☐ + ☐☐ = _____

Discards ☐ ☐   Target #   Difference
_____   _____

Total
☐☐ + ☐☐ + ☐☐ = _____

Discards ☐ ☐   Target #   Difference
_____   _____

Adapted from *Nimble with Numbers, Grades 4–5* by Leigh Childs and Laura Choate (Dale Seymour Publications, 1998)

From *A Month-to-Month Guide: Fourth-Grade Math* by Lainie Schuster. © 2009 Math Solutions Publications

Parent Information and Involvement Form

From: _____
To: **Parents of Fourth Graders**
Re: **Mathematics Curriculum**
Month: _____

During the next month, the major topics we will be studying are:

My goal in studying these topics is for the students to be able to:

Parents can help at home by:

Place-Value Mat

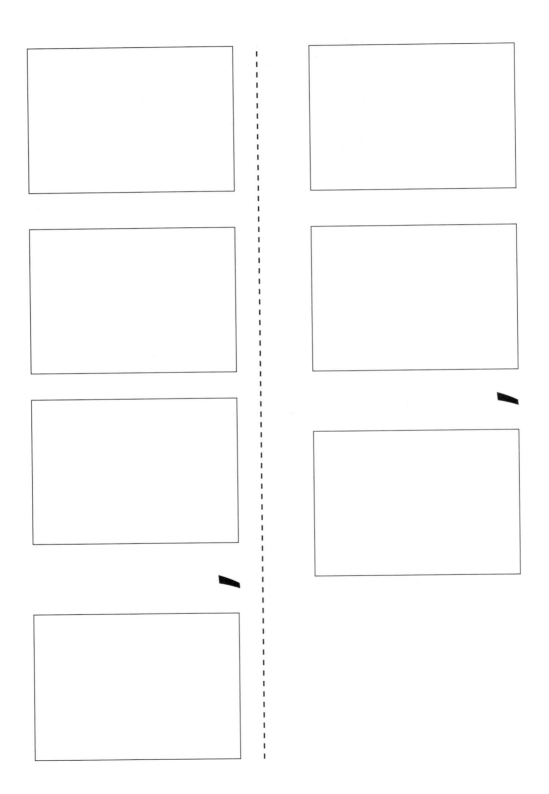

Digit Cards

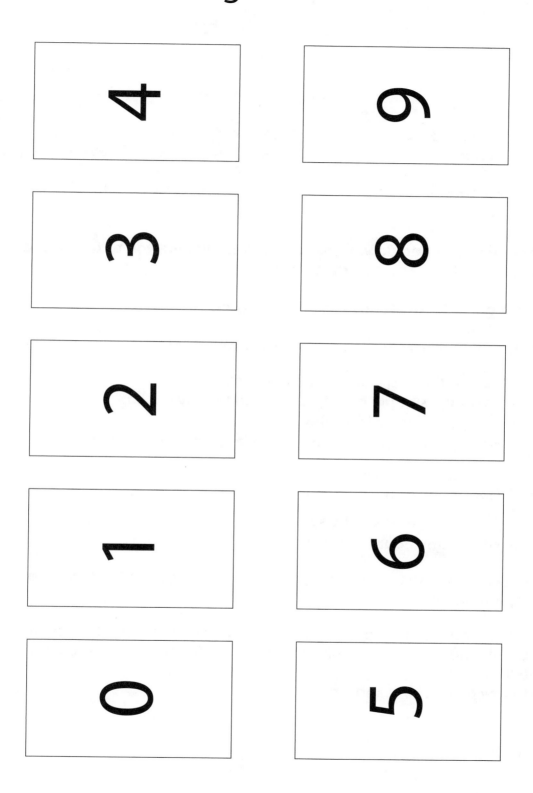

A Million Taps…More or Less
Record Sheet

Useful Information	
1 minute = 60 seconds	1 hour = 60 minutes
1 day = 24 hours	1 year = 365 days (366 days in a leap year)
100 × 10 = 1000	1000 × 1000 = 1,000,000

Make a guess: How long do you think that it would take you to tap your desk one million times without any interruptions? _____

Check your guess by the following investigation.
1. **Take a sample count.**
   Tap your desk for 10 seconds. Record the number of taps. _____

2. **Calculate the following from your sample count:**
   At the rate of my sample count, I expect to tap my desk:
   - _____ times in 1 minute
     (Hint: How many 10-minute intervals are there in 1 minute?)

   - _____ times in 1 hour.
     (Hint: How many minutes in 1 hour?)

   - _____ times in 1 day?
     (Hint: How many hours in 1 day?)

3. At this rate, it would take me ***about*** _____ full 24-hour days to tap my desk 1,000 times.

4. Using the amount of time it takes you to tap your desk 1,000 times, how could you predict how many full 24-hour days it would take you to tap your desk 1,000,000 times? _____
   (Hint: How many thousands in 1,000,000?)

Adapted from *Everyday Mathematics: The University of Chicago School Mathematics Project, Grade 5, 3d ed.*
(Everyday Learning Corporation, 2007)

From *A Month-to-Month Guide: Fourth-Grade Math* by Lainie Schuster. © 2009 Math Solutions Publications

What Would I Do with One Million?

I wish I had 1,000,000 . . .

_____

I would not want 1,000,000 . . .

_____

I can make 1,000,000 . . .

_____

I can eat 1,000,000,000 . . .

_____

I could never eat 1,000,000 . . .

_____

Having 1,000,000 _____ would be great!

Having 1,000,000 _____ would not be so great!

Close to 1,000

You need:
- 1 deck of 0–9 number cards
- 1 *Close to 1,000* score sheet per player
- 2–3 players

Directions

1. Shuffle the deck of cards. Place the deck in front of the players, facedown.

2. Player 1 flips over eight cards from the deck. Player 1 makes two three-digit numbers from his cards whose sum will equal 1,000 or near 1,000. The sum can be below or above 1,000. For example: $443 + 525 = 968$.

3. Player 1 writes his three numbers on his score sheet and calculates their sum. The score for that round is the difference between the sum and 1,000. For example, if the sum is 968, as in the previous example, the score is 32. If the sum is 1,000, the score is 0. If the sum is 1,007, the score is 7.

4. Player 1 places his six used cards in a discard pile.

5. Player 2 now chooses six cards to replace the cards Player 1 has discarded. Those six new cards are placed faceup along with the previous two cards that were not used. Player 2 now creates two three-digit numbers from the eight cards in front of her.

6. Play continues until each player has played five rounds. Players total their scores. The player with the lowest score wins.

Adapted from *Money, Miles, and Large Numbers, Grade 4* by Karen Economopoulos, Jan Mokros, Joan Akers, and Susan Russell (Scott Foresman, 2004)

 From *A Month-to-Month Guide: Fourth-Grade Math* by Lainie Schuster. © 2009 Math Solutions Publications

Close to 1,000 Score Sheet

Game 1   **Score**

Round 1: _____ _____ _____ + _____ _____ _____ = _____   _____

Round 2: _____ _____ _____ + _____ _____ _____ = _____   _____

Round 3: _____ _____ _____ + _____ _____ _____ = _____   _____

Round 4: _____ _____ _____ + _____ _____ _____ = _____   _____

Round 5: _____ _____ _____ + _____ _____ _____ = _____   _____

Total Score   _____

Game 2   **Score**

Round 1: _____ _____ _____ + _____ _____ _____ = _____   _____

Round 2: _____ _____ _____ + _____ _____ _____ = _____   _____

Round 3: _____ _____ _____ + _____ _____ _____ = _____   _____

Round 4: _____ _____ _____ + _____ _____ _____ = _____   _____

Round 5: _____ _____ _____ + _____ _____ _____ = _____   _____

Total Score   _____

Adapted from *Money, Miles, and Large Numbers, Grade 4* by Karen Economopoulos, Jan Mokros, Joan Akers, and Susan Russell (Scott Foresman, 2004)

From *A Month-to-Month Guide: Fourth-Grade Math* by Lainie Schuster. © 2009 Math Solutions Publications

Digit Place

You need:
  2 players

Directions
A chart such as the following is useful for keeping track of information:

Guess	Digit	Place
643	0	0
172	1	1
271	1	1
.	.	.
.	.	.
.	.	.

1. One partner (or the teacher) chooses a three-digit number with no two digits the same.

2. Ask for a guess as to what the number might be.

3. Write the guess in the Guess column. Specify how many digits are correct in the guess *and* how many of the correct digits are in the correct place. Do *not* tell which digits are correct or in the correct place, just how many.

4. Ask for another guess. Document the digit and place accuracy in the same way.

5. Continue the game until the target number is guessed.

6. Switch roles and play another round.

Adapted from *About Teaching Mathematics: A K–8 Resource, 3d ed.* by Marilyn Burns (Math Solutions Publications, 2007)

From *A Month-to-Month Guide: Fourth-Grade Math* by Lainie Schuster. © 2009 Math Solutions Publications

What Is a Polygon?

1.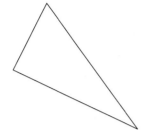

2.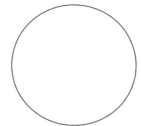

3.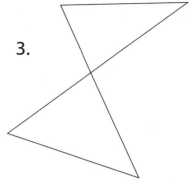

4.

5.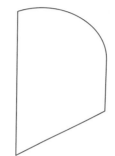

6.

7.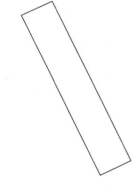

8.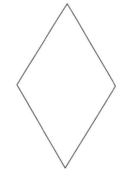

9.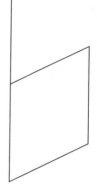

10.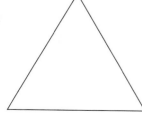

11.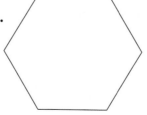

12.

Polygon Record Sheet

Must be true:	Cannot be true:

From *A Month-to-Month Guide: Fourth-Grade Math* by Lainie Schuster. © 2009 Math Solutions Publications

Polygon Shapes for Sorting Activities

This and That

You need:
   polygon cards

Directions
1. Place the polygon cards face down in the center of the table.

2. One at a time, each child randomly chooses two polygon cards and turns them over for everyone to see. Explain to your group members what is alike and what is different about those two shapes.

3. Move around the group having each member add to the list of similarities and differences between the two polygons.

4. Once all children have identified a similarity and difference between the two polygons, place the discussed polygons in the center of the table. The next child chooses two polygons and the process continues.

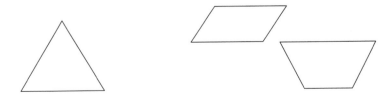

Adapted from *Elementary and Middle School Mathematics: Teaching Developmentally* by John A. Van de Walle (Pearson Education, 2004)

From *A Month-to-Month Guide: Fourth-Grade Math* by Lainie Schuster. © 2009 Math Solutions Publications

Valuable Property

You need:
   polygon cards
   target mat

Directions

1. Polygon cards are placed faceup in the center of the table.

2. A polygon card is taken from the center and placed on the target mat on the table for all to see.

3. The first child chooses a property of the chosen polygon and finds another polygon in the pile that fits that targeted property. One at a time, each child in the group does the same, explaining why her polygon fits the chosen property.

4. When all children have chosen a polygon, the second child identifies another property that could fit the target polygon.

5. Each child determines whether her chosen polygon can fit that property. If her polygon cannot, she can exchange her polygon for another.

Extension
Try a third sort!

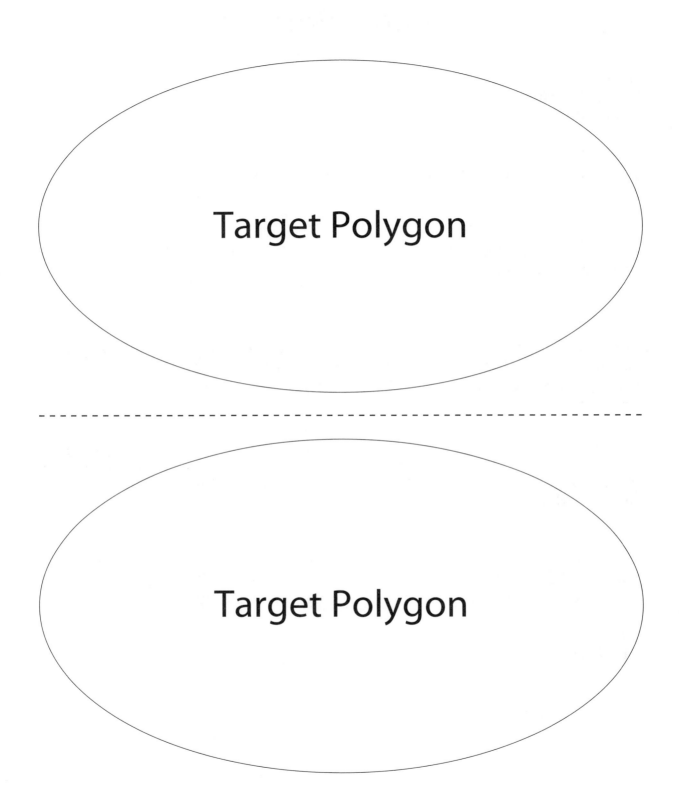

Target Polygon

Target Polygon

Out of Sorts

You need:
   polygon cards
   blank paper
   rulers

Directions

1. The polygon cards are placed faceup in the center of the table.

2. A child identifies a sorting rule.

3. Each child chooses a polygon that fits that rule and places it in the center of the table.

4. Each child writes the sorting rule on his paper and then constructs a polygon on his paper that fits that rule. Under the constructed polygon, each child is to write how his constructed polygon fits that rule.

5. Return the polygon cards to the center of the table. Another child chooses a sorting rule and the procedure continues.

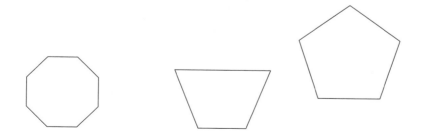

Adapted from *Elementary and Middle School Mathematics: Teaching Developmentally* by John A. Van de Walle (Pearson Education, 2004)

I Have a Secret

You need:
   polygon cards

Directions
1. The first child creates a collection of three polygons that fit a secret sorting rule for the group to see.

2. One at a time, the other members of the group try to add a polygon to the set. The child holding the secret agrees or disagrees with the added polygon. If the chosen polygon does not adhere to the secret property, the polygon must be removed from the set.

3. Once all the children have had a chance to add polygons to the set, the children try to guess the secret sorting rule. The child who guesses it correctly begins the process again with a new secret sort and a new collection of three polygons that fit the secret sorting rule.

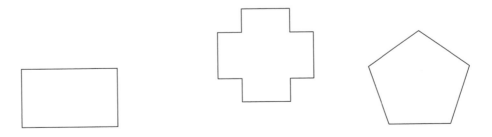

Adapted from *Elementary and Middle School Mathematics: Teaching Developmentally* by John A. Van de Walle (Pearson Education, 2004)

Guess My Rule

You need:
   polygon folders
   polygon cards

Directions

1. Polygon folders and polygon cards are placed in the center of the table.

2. The first child picks a polygon folder containing a polygon hidden from the other members of the group.

3. One at a time, each member of the group chooses a polygon that she thinks might match the shape in the folder. She can ask the leader one question about the polygon, but it can only be answered with a "yes" or "no." The members of the group *cannot* ask, "Is this the polygon?" If the polygon is not guessed, the polygon is returned to the pile and the next child has an opportunity to ask a question and guess the hidden polygon.

4. When a child guesses the matching shape, that child then becomes the leader, picks a new polygon folder, and the process continues.

Adapted from *Elementary and Middle School Mathematics: Teaching Developmentally* by John A. Van de Walle (Pearson Education, 2004)

Classifying Triangles Record Sheet

All Triangles	Some Triangles

From *A Month-to-Month Guide: Fourth-Grade Math* by Lainie Schuster. © 2009 Math Solutions Publications

Classifying Quadrilaterals Record Sheet

All Quadrilaterals	Some Quadrilaterals

The
Important Book
About
Polygons

words and pictures by

_____

The important thing about a _____

is _____

_____

_____

_____

_____

But the important thing about a _____

_____

is _____

_____

_____

About the Mathematician

_____

_____

_____

_____

_____

_____

_____

_____

_____

_____

Tangram Cutting Instructions

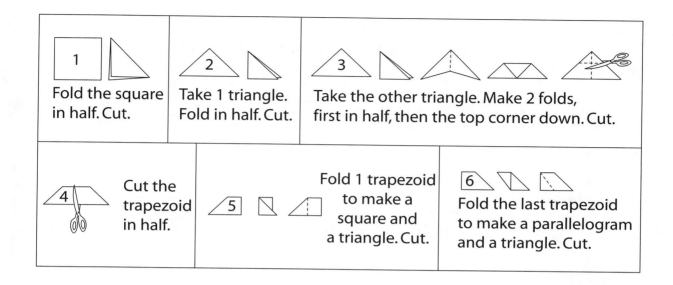

1 Fold the square in half. Cut.

2 Take 1 triangle. Fold in half. Cut.

3 Take the other triangle. Make 2 folds, first in half, then the top corner down. Cut.

4 Cut the trapezoid in half.

5 Fold 1 trapezoid to make a square and a triangle. Cut.

6 Fold the last trapezoid to make a parallelogram and a triangle. Cut.

From *A Month-to-Month Guide: Third-Grade Math* by Suzy Ronfeldt (Math Solutions Publications, 2003)

From *A Month-to-Month Guide: Fourth-Grade Math* by Lainie Schuster. © 2009 Math Solutions Publications

Constructing Polygons

	Square	Triangle	Rectangle	Trapezoid	Parallelogram
3 Small Triangles					
5 Small Pieces					
All 7 Pieces					
	Sketch ↑	**Sketch ↑**	**Sketch ↑**	**Sketch ↑**	**Sketch ↑**

From *A Month-to-Month Guide: Fourth-Grade Math* by Lainie Schuster. © 2009 Math Solutions Publications

Pent-Tris

You need:
    1 die
    outline of a 5 × 12, 6 × 10, 3 × 20, or 4 × 15 rectangle to use as a game board
    5 pentomino pieces
    1 colored pencil or marker per player
    2 players

Directions

1. Assign a number (1–5) to each pentomino. Create a key to show which piece corresponds with each number. You will roll a die to determine which piece you must play.

2. A roll of 6 earns the player a free choice.

3. Identify the bottom of the board. Two players will play on one board.

4. Each player chooses a color with which to color in his or her pentominoes.

5. Player 1 rolls the die. He chooses the placement of that piece and colors it in the board. Player 2 follows the same procedure. Each pentomino must touch either the bottom of the board or another pentomino.

6. Play continues until no other pentominoes can be placed on the board.

7. Each player adds up the total number of his or her colored-in squares on the board.

8. The winner is the player with the greatest number of squares colored in.

Adapted from *Flips, Turns, and Area: 2-D Geometry, Grade 3* by Susan Russell and Douglas H. Clements (Dale Seymour Publications, 1997)

From *A Month-to-Month Guide: Fourth-Grade Math* by Lainie Schuster. © 2009 Math Solutions Publications

Brainstorming Web

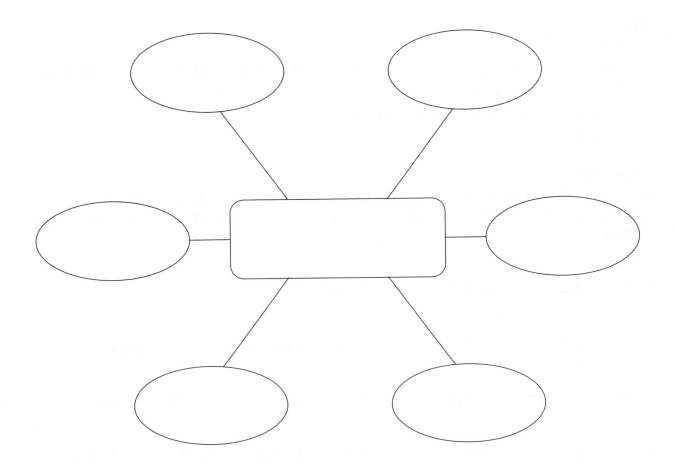

Measuring Up

How tall are most 4th graders? How long is the average 4th-grade arm span? Do 4th graders have big heads or small heads? What measurements are about the same? *In this project, you will learn about measuring lengths and determining the size of a typical 4th grader.*

In this project, you will answer the following questions:
- What does the word *typical* mean? How do you find an average?
- How do we measure length in the metric system?
- What tools do we use to measure length?
- What units do we use to measure length? What are their abbreviations?
- How tall is the typical 4th grader?
- What are two other typical 4th-grade measures?

You will need:
1 metric measuring tape
1 calculator
a pair of scissors

What you need to do:
- Learn about measuring length. Learn about centimeters and meters.
- Practice measuring different lengths using meters and centimeters.
- Decide on 3 measurements you will investigate.
- Decide how many students you must measure in order to find typical values.
- Collect and record your data.
- Make a poster that shows what you have learned. Remember to answer all of the questions on the poster.

Adapted from *MEGA Projects: Math Explorations and Group Activity Projects, Grade 4,* by Carole Greenes, Linda Schulman, Rika Spungin, Suzanne Chapin, Carol Findell, and Art Johnson (Dale Seymour Publications, 1996)

From *A Month-to-Month Guide: Fourth-Grade Math* by Lainie Schuster. © 2009 Math Solutions Publications

Down the Drain

How much water do you think that you use, on average, each time you brush your teeth? Do you leave the water running while brushing your teeth, or do you turn it off while the toothbrush is in your mouth? Are you wasting water? How much? *In this project, you will learn about measuring capacity and saving water.*

For this project, you will answer the following questions:
- What does the word *typical* mean? How do you find an average?
- How do we measure capacity in the metric system?
- What tools do we use to measure capacity?
- What units do we use to measure capacity? What are their abbreviations?
- How much water is needed to brush your teeth?
- How much water is wasted when brushing your teeth one time a day? Two times a day? Three times a day?
- How much water is wasted from brushing your teeth in a year?

You will need:
    4 toothbrushes
    1 calculator
    1 stopwatch
    metric measuring containers, 1,000 ml and 500 ml
    a sink

What you need to do:
- Learn about measuring liquids. Learn about liters and milliliters.
- Practice measuring different amounts of liquids.
- Decide how to measure the amount of water wasted.
- Collect and record your data.
- Make a poster that shows what you have learned. Remember to answer all of the questions on the poster.

Adapted from *MEGA Projects: Math Explorations and Group Activity Projects, Grade 4,* by Carole Greenes, Linda Schulman, Rika Spungin, Suzanne Chapin, Carol Findell, and Art Johnson (Dale Seymour Publications, 1996)

From *A Month-to-Month Guide: Fourth-Grade Math* by Lainie Schuster. © 2009 Math Solutions Publications

It Beats Me

How fast does your heart beat? What affects the number of heartbeats in a minute? *In this project, you will learn about heart rates and measuring time.*

For this project, you will answer the following questions:
- What does the word *typical* mean? How do you find an average?
- How do we measure time?
- What tools do we use to measure time?
- What units do we use to measure time? What are their abbreviations?
- What is a heart rate? How do you find someone's heart rate?
- What is your resting heart rate?
- How fast does your heart beat after jumping up and down 15 times?
- Does every 4th grader's heart beat the same after exercise?

You will need:
- 1 stopwatch
- 1 calculator
- 1 stethoscope

What you will need to do:
- Learn about heartbeats and heart rates. Learn about rates in math.
- Find your pulse in your wrist and neck. Practice measuring time and finding a pulse.
- Collect and record your data.
- Make a poster that shows what you have learned. Remember to answer all of the questions on the poster.

Adapted from *MEGA Projects: Math Explorations and Group Activity Projects, Grade 4,* by Carole Greenes, Linda Schulman, Rika Spungin, Suzanne Chapin, Carol Findell, and Art Johnson (Dale Seymour Publications, 1996)

From *A Month-to-Month Guide: Fourth-Grade Math* by Lainie Schuster. © 2009 Math Solutions Publications

Popcorn Madness

How much more space does popped popcorn take up than unpopped popcorn? If you popped an entire jar or bag of popcorn, how much space would the popped popcorn fill? *In this project, you will learn about volume and popcorn.*

For this project, you will answer the following questions:
- What does the word *typical* mean? How do you find an average?
- How do we measure volume in the metric system?
- What tools do we use to measure volume?
- What units do we use to measure volume? What are their abbreviations?
- What is the average volume of 100 cubic centimeters of popcorn kernels after popping?
- What is your estimate of the volume of the bag or jar of popcorn if you popped all of the kernels?

You will need:
> 1 jar or bag of popcorn
>
> metric containers for measuring volume; acrylic cubic decimeters (1 liter) work well
>
> an appliance for popping popcorn

What you will need to do:
- Learn about volume and measuring volume.
- Find out how cubic centimeters and milliliters are related.
- Get an adult to help you pop the popcorn.
- Collect and record your data.
- Make a poster that shows what you have learned. Remember to answer all of the questions on the poster.

Adapted from *MEGA Projects: Math Explorations and Group Activity Projects, Grade 4,* by Carole Greenes, Linda Schulman, Rika Spungin, Suzanne Chapin, Carol Findell, and Art Johnson (Dale Seymour Publications, 1996)

     From *A Month-to-Month Guide: Fourth-Grade Math* by Lainie Schuster. © 2009 Math Solutions Publications

Box It or Bag It

Every 4th grader keeps his or her pencils in something! The most common containers are pencil bags and pencil boxes. Decide which container you will investigate. What is the average weight of a 4th grader's pencil container? *In this investigation, you will learn about measuring weight.*

For this project, you will answer the following questions:

- What does the word *typical* mean? How do you find an average?
- How do you measure weight in the metric system?
- What tools do we use to measure weight?
- What units do we use to measure weight? What are their abbreviations?
- What is the range of the weight measures of full pencil containers?
- What is the typical weight measure of a 4th grader's full pencil container?

You will need:
  1 balance scale
  a set of metric weights

What you need to do:

- Learn about measuring weight. Learn about grams and kilograms.
- Practice measuring objects of different weights.
- Decide how many full pencil containers you will need to measure in order to find a typical weight.
- Collect and record your data.
- Make a poster that shows what you have learned. Remember to answer all of your questions on the poster.

From *A Month-to-Month Guide: Fourth-Grade Math* by Lainie Schuster. © 2009 Math Solutions Publications

Measures of Central Tendency

Averages

There are three *measures of central tendency,* or *averages.* Describe them:

Mode:

Median:

Mean:

How do we find:

a mode?

a median?

a mean?

If a sample of people blink 28, 29, 30, 31, 32, 33, 34, 35, and 36 blinks per minute, what is the mean number of blinks per minute?

If a sample of people blink 30, 29, 29, 31, and 29 blinks per minute, what is the mode of this data set?

What is the median score if six students scored 75, 86, 85, 80, 90, and 95 on their quizzes?

Target 300

You need:
   1 die
   2 players

Directions
The object of the game is to be the player whose total is closest to 300 after six rolls of the die. The total can be exactly 300, less than 300, or greater than 300. Each player must use all six turns.

1. Each player draws a two-column chart as a score sheet as shown, one column for each player.

Player 1	Player 2

2. Player 1 rolls the die and decides whether to multiply the number rolled by 10, 20, 30, 40, or 50, keeping in mind that each player will have six turns to reach the targeted amount of 300.

3. Both players write the multiplication sentence representing the first player's choice and product. For example, Player 1 rolls a 2 and chooses to multiply it by 20. Both players write the multiplication number model: $2 \times 20 = 40$.

Player 1	Player 2
$2 \times 20 = 40$	

4. Player 1 hands the die to Player 2. Player 2 follows the same steps as Player 1.

5. At the end of each turn, the player adds her new amount to the previous score to keep a running total.

6. At the end of six turns, players compare scores to see whose score is closest to 300. Each player records the following prompts under his or her chart:

   _____ won.

   _____ was _____ points away from 300.

   _____ was _____ points away from 300.

From *Teaching Arithmetic: Lessons for Extending Multiplication, Grades 4–5* by Maryann Wickett and Marilyn Burns (Math Solutions Publications, 2001)

From *A Month-to-Month Guide: Fourth-Grade Math* by Lainie Schuster. © 2009 Math Solutions Publications

Rio

You need:
- 1 game board
- 10 two-color counters or 5 counters in each of two different colors
- 2 dice
- 2 players

Directions

1. Player 1 rolls the dice and calculates the sum. The sum is then multiplied by the table number listed at the top of the game board. The player places one of his counters on the product.

2. Player 2 follows the same procedure as Player 1. If the product is covered by Player 1's chip, Player 2 can remove Player 1's chip and replace it with one of her own.

3. Chips can be bumped off the board and replaced at each turn when duplicate products are calculated.

4. The player who plays all his or her chips first is the winner.

From *A Month-to-Month Guide: Fourth-Grade Math* by Lainie Schuster. © 2009 Math Solutions Publications

Rio Game Board

**Rio Game Board
for the _____ Tables**

Multiplication Bingo

You need:
    1 deck of 1–10 number cards, 2 ten-sided dice, or 1 set of multiplication facts flash cards
    1 game board per player
    1 multiplication matrix
    2–3 players

Directions
Each player chooses sixteen products from the list below and writes each one in a square in the game board grid.

If using cards, shuffle the deck of number cards and place them facedown on the playing surface.

1. At each turn, a player takes two cards from the deck (or rolls the two dice) and calls out the product of the numbers. If there is a disagreement, the answer is checked with a multiplication fact table. If the answer is correct, the player can cross off the product if it appears on his grid. If the product called is not on the player's board, he loses his turn and the play turns to the next player.

2. The first player to cross off four products in a row horizontally, vertically, or diagonally, or to get eight crossed-off products anywhere on the grid, calls out "Bingo!" and wins.

3. If all the cards are used before someone wins, reshuffle the cards and continue playing until some one gets a bingo.

4. Create new game boards for each game.

Variation
Multiplication Bingo can be played in a whole-class format. Each child creates a bingo board from the listed products. The facilitator takes two cards from the deck and reads them to the class as a multiplication problem. Any child who has that product on her game board can cross it off. Play continues in the same way as above until a winner(s) calls "Bingo!"

Product List		
4	24	49
6	25	50
8	27	54
9	28	56
10	31	60
12	32	63
14	35	64
15	36	70
16	40	72
18	42	80
20	45	81
21	48	90
		100

Adapted from *Everyday Mathematics: The University of Chicago School Mathematics Project, Grade 4, 3d ed.* (Everyday Learning Corporation, 2007)

Multiplication Bingo Game Boards

Multiplication Bull's-Eye

You need:
   1 deck of 0–9 number cards
   a six-sided die
   a calculator
   2–3 players

Directions
Shuffle the number cards and place them facedown in a deck in the middle of the playing surface.

Players take turns. At each turn:

1. Roll the die. Look up the target range of the product in the table below.

2. Take four cards from the top of the deck. Use the cards to try to form two numbers whose product falls within the target range. *Do not use a calculator!*

3. You do not need to use all four cards. A number may not begin with a 0.

4. Multiply the two numbers on your calculator to check whether the product falls within the target range. If it does, you have hit the bull's-eye and score 1 point. If not, you score 0 points.

The game ends when each player has had five turns. The player who has scored the most points wins the game.

Number on Die	Range of Products
1	500 or less
2	501–1,000
3	1,001–3,000
4	3,001–5,000
5	5,001–7,000
6	More than 7,000

Adapted from *Everyday Mathematics: The University of Chicago School Mathematics Project, Grade 4, 3d ed.* (Everyday Learning Corporation, 2007)

Multiplication Tic-Tac-Toe

You need:
- 1 game board
- 2 large paper clips
- 13 colored counters or 1 colored pencil per player
- 2 players

Directions

1. The first player places two paper clips at the bottom of the game board, indicating two factors. The player multiplies the selected factors and places a counter on the resulting product in the grid (or colors in the square containing that number with a colored pencil).

2. The next player can move only one paper clip to a new factor. Player 2 then multiplies the two factors and places a counter on that product. It is permissible to have two paper clips on the same factor.

3. Play continues with players alternating turns, moving only one paper clip each time, multiplying the factors, and placing a counter on the game board.

4. A player loses his turn if a product is calculated that is not on the board.

5. The winner is the first player to have four counters in a row horizontally, diagonally, or vertically.

Adapted from *Nimble with Numbers, Grades 4–5* by Leigh Childs and Laura Choate (Dale Seymour Publications, 1998)

From *A Month-to-Month Guide: Fourth-Grade Math* by Lainie Schuster. © 2009 Math Solutions Publications

Multiplication Tic-Tac-Toe
Game Board, Version 1

1	2	3	4	5
6	7	8	9	10
12	14	15	16	18
20	21	24	25	27
28	30	32	35	36

1 2 3 4 5 6 7 8 9

From *A Month-to-Month Guide: Fourth-Grade Math* by Lainie Schuster. © 2009 Math Solutions Publications

Multiplication Tic-Tac-Toe
Game Board, Version 2

1	2	3	4	5	6
7	8	9	10	12	14
15	16	18	20	21	24
25	27	28	30	32	35
36	40	42	45	48	49
54	56	63	64	72	81

1 2 3 4 5 6 7 8 9

From *A Month-to-Month Guide: Fourth-Grade Math* by Lainie Schuster. © 2009 Math Solutions Publications

Questions for Snowmen

Represent each story problem with:
- a number model,
- an estimate,
- a calculation,
- a solution written in sentence form,
- a written explanation supporting your choice of calculation strategy, and
- an illustration.

----

1. How many marshmallows will be needed for each class member to make one snowman?

----

2. How many class sets of snowmen can be made from one bag of marshmallows?

----

3. How many snowmen can be made from the remaining marshmallows?

----

4. Each snowman needs a gumdrop hat. How many class sets can you make from a bag of gumdrops?

   From *A Month-to-Month Guide: Fourth-Grade Math* by Lainie Schuster. © 2009 Math Solutions Publications

Remainders of One

Circle all the numbers that when divided by ☐ **have a remainder of 1.**

1	2	3	4	5	6	7	8	9	10
11	12	13	14	15	16	17	18	19	20
21	22	23	24	25					

What do you notice?

Remainder Riddle 1

When you divide my number by 1, the remainder is 0.

When you divide my number by 2, the remainder is 0.

When you divide my number by 3, the remainder is 1.

When you divide my number by 4, the remainder is 2.

When you divide my number by 5, the remainder is 0.

When you divide my number by 6, the remainder is 4.

When you divide my number by 7, the remainder is 3.

 From *A Month-to-Month Guide: Fourth-Grade Math* by Lainie Schuster. © 2009 Math Solutions Publications

Remainder Riddle 2

When you divide my number by 1, the remainder is 0.

When you divide my number by 2, the remainder is 0.

When you divide my number by 3, the remainder is 1.

When you divide my number by 4, the remainder is 0.

When you divide my number by 5, the remainder is 1.

When you divide my number by 6, the remainder is 4.

When you divide my number by 7, the remainder is 2.

Remainder Riddle 3

When you divide my number by 1, the remainder is 0.

When you divide my number by 2, the remainder is 0.

When you divide my number by 3, the remainder is 2.

When you divide my number by 4, the remainder is 0.

When you divide my number by 5, the remainder is 3.

When you divide my number by 6, the remainder is 2.

When you divide my number by 7, the remainder is 1.

Remainder Riddles

You need:
- 1 piece of composition paper per riddle
- a mystery number from 1 to 25 for your first riddle
- a mystery number from 1 to 50 for remaining riddles
- clues for divisors from 1 to 7

The solution to your riddle will be written on the back of your paper. You will need to offer mathematical proof of the solution of your riddle on the back of your paper in the form of number models.

Riddle template

When you divide my number by 1, the remainder is _____.

When you divide my number by 2, the remainder is _____.

When you divide my number by 3, the remainder is _____.

When you divide my number by 4, the remainder is _____.

When you divide my number by 5, the remainder is _____.

When you divide my number by 6, the remainder is _____.

When you divide my number by 7, the remainder is _____.

An example of mathematical proof that 10 was the solution to our first riddle completed in class:

$$10 \div 1 = 10 \text{ R}0 \qquad \text{true}$$
$$10 \div 2 = 5 \text{ R}0 \qquad \text{true}$$
$$10 \div 3 = 3 \text{ R}1 \qquad \text{true}$$
$$10 \div 4 = 2 \text{ R}2 \qquad \text{true}$$
$$10 \div 5 = 2 \text{ R}0 \qquad \text{true}$$
$$10 \div 6 = 1 \text{ R}4 \qquad \text{true}$$
$$10 \div 7 = 1 \text{ R}3 \qquad \text{true}$$

Take Me Out to the Ballgame!

1. Twenty-five 4th graders are going to the Red Sox game. Four 4th graders can be seated in one car. How many cars will be needed to get the 4th graders to Fenway Park?

2. Howard, a baseballaholic, has $25.00 in his pocket. Red Sox pennants cost $4.00 each. How many pennants can Howard buy?

3. Remember Howard? He still has $25.00 in his pocket. And he still wants to buy pennants that cost $4.00 each. How much money will he have left to put toward a Fenway Frank (hot dog) if he buys 6 pennants?

4. Howard decided not to buy the pennants. Who needs 6 pennants, anyway? And he still has that $25.00. Howard realizes he can buy exactly 4 baseballs instead. How much does each baseball cost?

Adapted from Good Questions for Math Teaching: Why Ask Them and What to Ask, Grades 5–8 by Lainie Schuster and Nancy Canavan Anderson (Math Solutions Publications, 2005)

From *A Month-to-Month Guide: Fourth-Grade Math* by Lainie Schuster. © 2009 Math Solutions Publications

Leftovers with 25

You need:
   1 recording sheet
   2 players

Directions
1. Set up a recording sheet as shown:

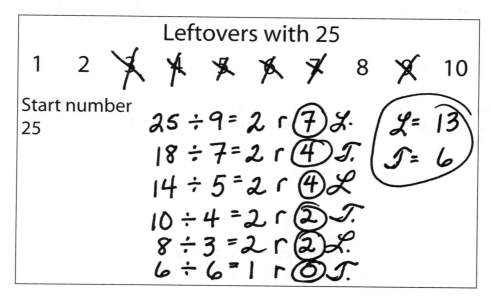

2. Player 1 chooses a divisor from 1 to 10 and divides the start number, 25, by the divisor chosen. Player 2 records the division, crosses out the divisor, and circles and labels the remainder with Player 1's initial.
3. Both players subtract the remainder from the start number to get the next start number. Subtracting the remainder is a way to check the subtraction.
4. Player 2 uses the new start number, chooses a divisor that has not yet been crossed out, and divides. Divisors can be used only once. Player 1 records the division, crosses out the divisor, and circles and labels the remainder. Both players subtract the remainder from the start number to get the next start number.
5. Players continue taking turns until either the start number reaches 0 or it is no longer possible for either player to score.
6. Players add up their remainders. The player with the larger sum wins.

Extensions
   ■ Increase the start number to 50 and use divisors from 1 to 20.
   ■ The player with the smaller sum of remainders wins.

From *A Month-to-Month Guide: Fourth-Grade Math* by Lainie Schuster. © 2009 Math Solutions Publications

Division Dash

You need:
    1 calculator with a square root key for each player
    1 score sheet
    2 players

Directions

1. Each player chooses a four-digit number and enters it on his calculator.

2. Each player presses the $\sqrt{}$ (square root) key. If the player's calculator display has fewer than three digits, the player needs to choose a new number and reenter it.

3. Each player:
   - uses the final digit of the display as the divisor
   - uses the two digits before the final digit as the dividend

4. Each player divides her dividend by her divisor and records the quotient. Remainders are ignored. Players must write down the number models for their calculations. Calculations can be done on paper or mentally.

5. For the following rounds, each player presses the $\sqrt{}$ key once again and repeats Steps 3 and 4 until the sum of a player's quotients is 100 or more. The winner is the first player to reach at least 100.

Adapted from *Everyday Mathematics: The University of Chicago School Mathematics Project, Grade 4, 3d ed.*
(Everyday Learning Corporation, 2007)

From *A Month-to-Month Guide: Fourth-Grade Math* by Lainie Schuster. © 2009 Math Solutions Publications

Division Dash Score Sheet

Game 1		Game 2		Game 3	
Player 1	*Player 2*	*Player 1*	*Player 2*	*Player 1*	*Player 2*

Adapted from *Everyday Mathematics: The University of Chicago School Mathematics Project, Grade 4, 3d ed.*
(Everyday Learning Corporation, 2007)

From *A Month-to-Month Guide: Fourth-Grade Math* by Lainie Schuster. © 2009 Math Solutions Publications

Menu Exit Slip

Name: _____

Partner: _____

Date: _____

Menu: _____

Games played:

Favorite game? _____

Why? _____

_____

_____

_____

_____

_____

From *A Month-to-Month Guide: Fourth-Grade Math* by Lainie Schuster. © 2009 Math Solutions Publications

Cover Up

You need:
  2 fraction kits
  a fraction die with faces marked $\frac{1}{2}, \frac{1}{4}, \frac{1}{8}, \frac{1}{8}, \frac{1}{16}, \frac{1}{16}$
  2 players

Directions

1. Take turns rolling the fraction die.

2. On your turn, the fraction that comes up on the die tells what size piece to place on your whole strip.

3. Check with your partner to be sure he agrees with what you did.

4. After finishing your turn, say, "Done," and pass the die to your partner.

5. The first player to cover her whole strip *exactly* wins.

6. If you need only a small piece to cover your whole strip ($\frac{1}{8}$ or $\frac{1}{16}$, for example) and you roll a larger fraction ($\frac{1}{2}$ or $\frac{1}{4}$, for example), you cannot play and will need to pass the die to your partner. You must roll a fraction smaller than or exactly what you need.

Adapted from *About Teaching Mathematics: A K–8 Resource, 3d ed.* by Marilyn Burns (Math Solutions Publications, 2007)

From *A Month-to-Month Guide: Fourth-Grade Math* by Lainie Schuster. © 2009 Math Solutions Publications

Uncover, Version 1

You need:
    2 fraction kits
    a fraction die with faces marked $\frac{1}{2}, \frac{1}{4}, \frac{1}{8}, \frac{1}{8}, \frac{1}{16}, \frac{1}{16}$
    2 players

Directions
1. Each player covers his whole strip with the two $\frac{1}{2}$ pieces.

2. Take turns rolling the fraction die.

3. On your turn, take one of three options:
   - remove a piece (only if you have a piece the size indicated by the fraction facing up on the die)
   - exchange any of the pieces on your whole strip for equivalent pieces
   - do nothing

4. Check with your partner to be sure she agrees with what you did.

5. After finishing your turn, say, "Done," and pass the die to your partner.

6. The first player who removes all the pieces from the whole strip wins.

Note 1: You may not remove a piece and exchange on the same turn; you can do only one or the other.

Note 2: You have to go out exactly. That means if you have only one piece left and roll a fraction that's larger, you may not remove the piece.

Adapted from *About Teaching Mathematics: A K–8 Resource, 3d ed.* by Marilyn Burns (Math Solutions Publications, 2007)

 From *A Month-to-Month Guide: Fourth-Grade Math* by Lainie Schuster. © 2009 Math Solutions Publications

Uncover, Version 2

The rules are the same as for the first version of *Uncover* except for the first option of Directive 3.

You need:
   2 fraction kits
   a fraction die with faces marked $\frac{1}{2}, \frac{1}{4}, \frac{1}{8}, \frac{1}{8}, \frac{1}{16}, \frac{1}{16}$
   2 players

Directions
1. Each player covers his whole strip with the two $\frac{1}{2}$ pieces.

2. Take turns rolling the fraction die.

3. On your turn, take one of three options:
   - **New Rule:** remove one or more pieces from your board as long as they add up to the fraction facing up on the die
   - exchange any of the pieces on your whole strip for equivalent pieces
   - do nothing

4. Check with your partner to be sure she agrees with what you did.

5. After finishing your turn, say, "Done," and pass the die to your partner.

6. The first player who removes all the pieces from the whole strip wins.

Note 1: You may not remove pieces and exchange on the same turn; you can do only one or the other.

Note 2: You have to go out exactly. That means if you have only one piece left and roll a fraction that's larger, you may not remove the piece.

Adapted from *About Teaching Mathematics: A K–8 Resource, 3d ed.* by Marilyn Burns (Math Solutions Publications, 2007)

From *A Month-to-Month Guide: Fourth-Grade Math* by Lainie Schuster. © 2009 Math Solutions Publications

Large Dot Paper Square

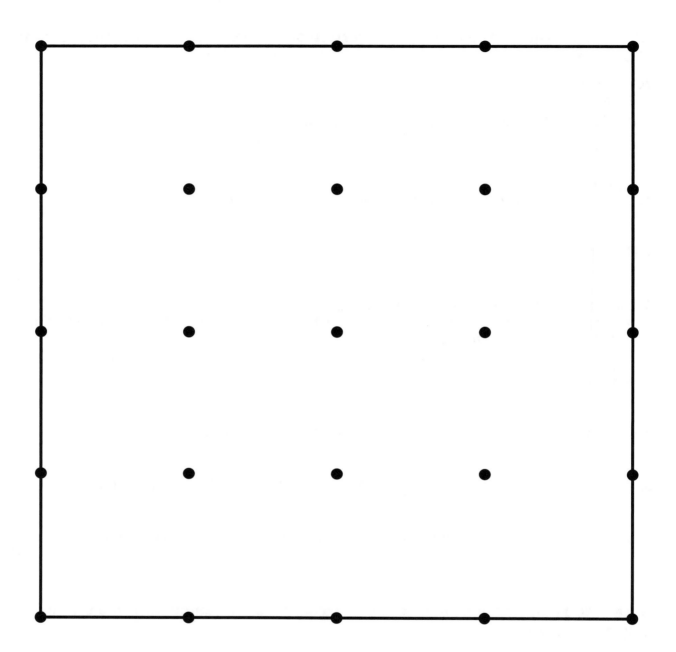

From *A Month-to-Month Guide: Fourth-Grade Math* by Lainie Schuster. © 2009 Math Solutions Publications

Small Dot Paper Squares

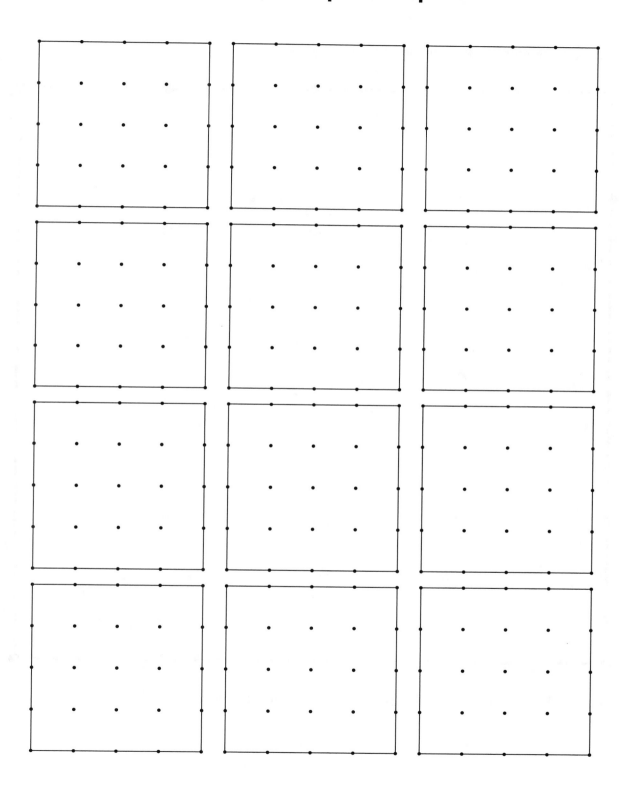

Fabulous Fourths

Draw one of your most interesting fourths.

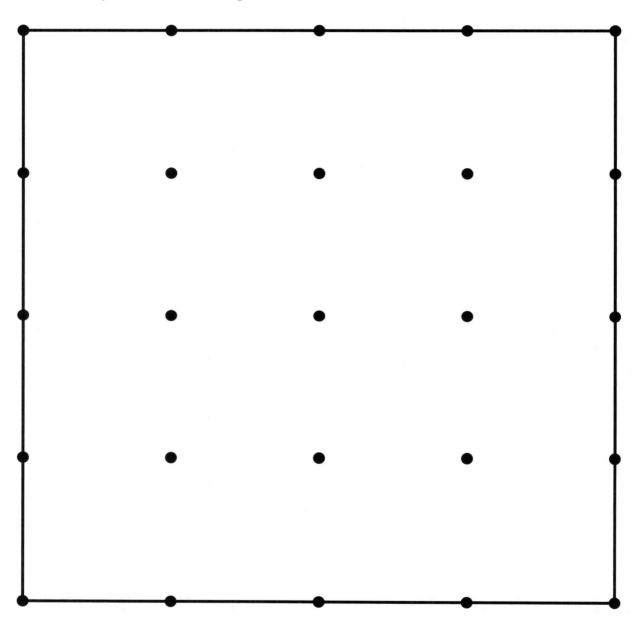

What makes this piece $\frac{1}{4}$? Explain in words and/or diagrams how you know.

 From *A Month-to-Month Guide: Fourth-Grade Math* by Lainie Schuster. © 2009 Math Solutions Publications

Awesome Eighths

Draw one of your most interesting eighths.

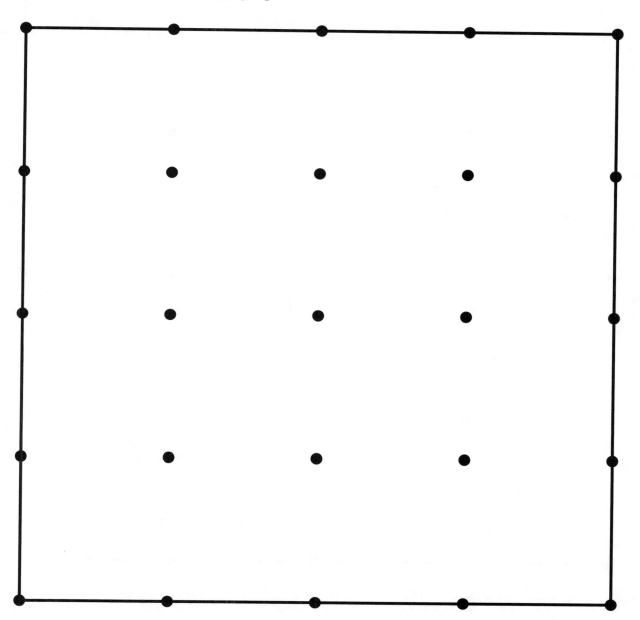

What makes this piece $\frac{1}{8}$? Explain in words and/or diagrams how you know.

Combining Fractions

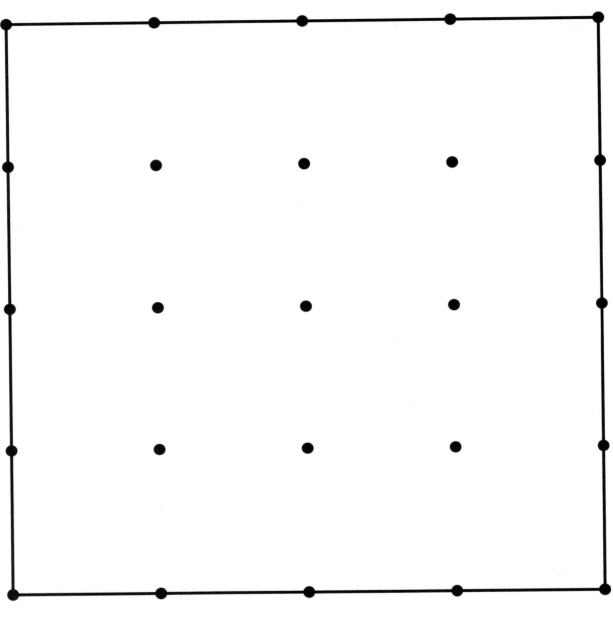

Number model: _____

From *A Month-to-Month Guide: Fourth-Grade Math* by Lainie Schuster. © 2009 Math Solutions Publications

Getting to One Whole

You need:
  1 *Getting to One Whole* record sheet per player
  1 fraction die with faces marked $\frac{1}{2}, \frac{1}{4}, \frac{1}{8}, \frac{1}{8}, \frac{1}{16}, \frac{1}{16}$
  1 colored pencil per player
  2 players

Directions

1. Take turns rolling the die.

2. On your turn, the fraction that comes up on the die tells what size fractional part to color in on your one whole. Partition your fractional part, label it, and color it in. Begin your addition number sentence, representing your roll. Continue your sentence with each fraction rolled.

3. Check with your partner to be sure that he agrees with what you did.

4. After finishing your turn, say, "Done," and pass the die to your partner.

5. The first person to fill in her whole *exactly* wins.

6. At the end of the game, *both* players will complete their number sentences with their final solution. The solutions may be:
   $a + b + c = 1$ (a winning game)
   $a + b + c < 1$ (a losing game)
   $a + b + c > 1$ (a losing game)

Extensions
  - Before the game begins, agree that equivalent pieces to those rolled on the die can be colored in.
  - Play *Getting to Two Wholes*.
  - Play with 8 × 4 dot paper rectangles and a new fraction die: $\frac{1}{2}, \frac{1}{4}, \frac{1}{3}, \frac{1}{6}, \frac{1}{8}, \frac{1}{12}$.

From *A Month-to-Month Guide: Fourth-Grade Math* by Lainie Schuster. © 2009 Math Solutions Publications

Getting to One Whole, Version 1
Record Sheet

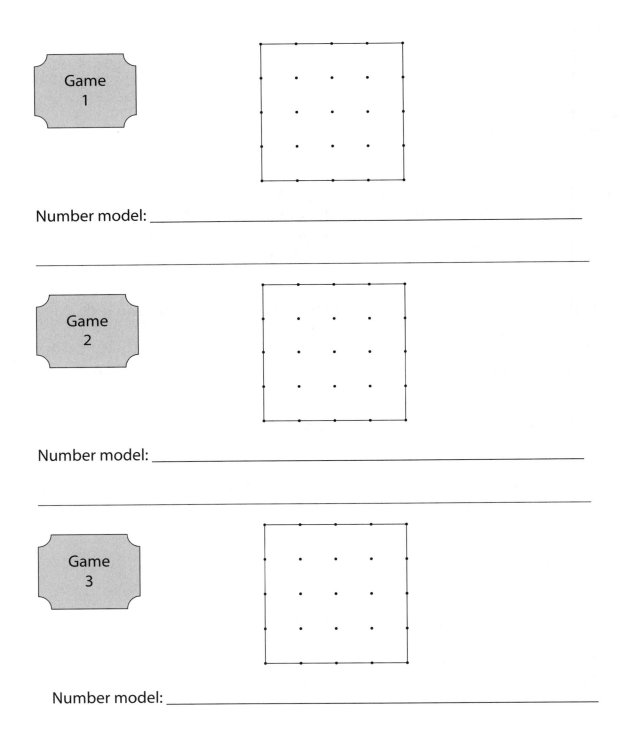

Game 1

Number model: _____

Game 2

Number model: _____

Game 3

Number model: _____

Getting to One Whole, Version 2
Record Sheet

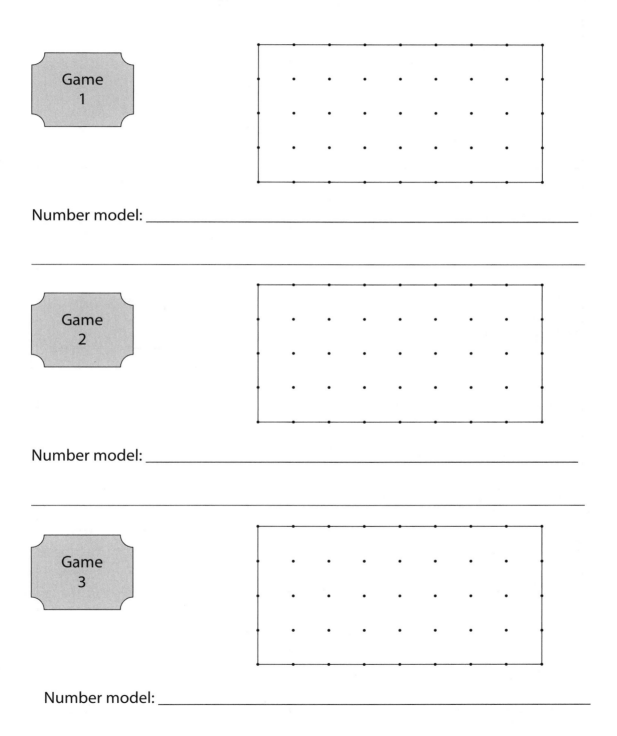

Game
1

Number model: _____

Game
2

Number model: _____

Game
3

Number model: _____

From *A Month-to-Month Guide: Fourth-Grade Math* by Lainie Schuster. © 2009 Math Solutions Publications

Dot Paper Rectangles

Fraction Spinners

A paper clip can be used as the spinning mechanism by placing it on the center point and holding it down with a pencil point.

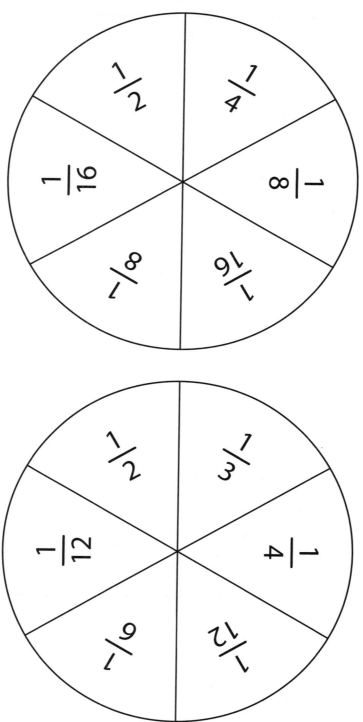

Place-Value Progression Grid: One Whole

From *A Month-to-Month Guide: Fourth-Grade Math* by Lainie Schuster. © 2009 Math Solutions Publications

Place-Value Progression Grid:
Tenths

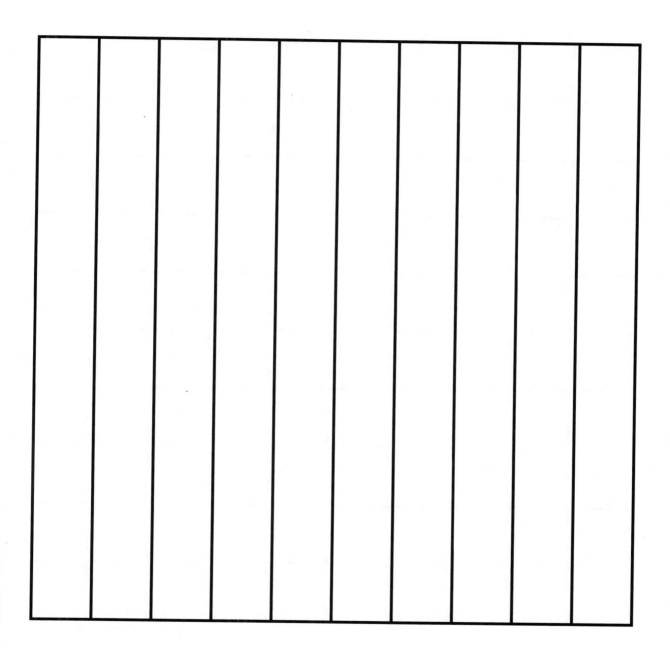

Place-Value Progression Grid: Hundredths

From *A Month-to-Month Guide: Fourth-Grade Math* by Lainie Schuster. © 2009 Math Solutions Publications

Place-Value Progression Grid:
Thousandths

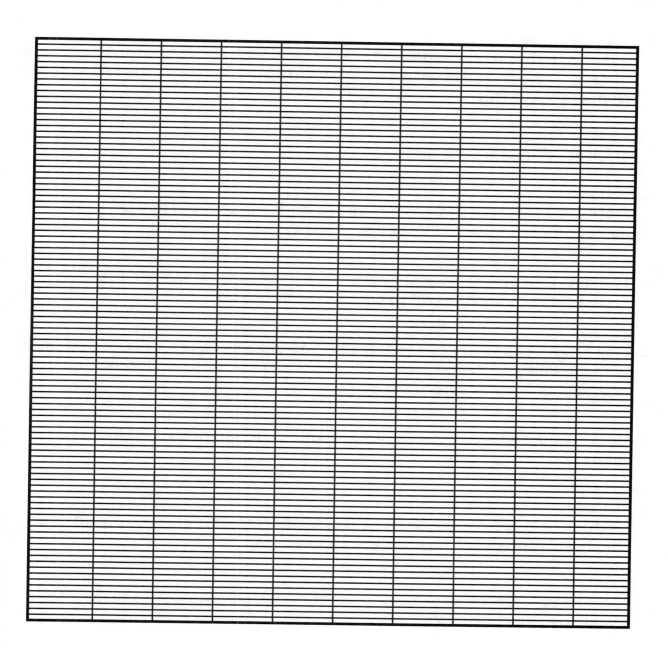

Decimal Bingo

Note: It is best to play this game in a whole-class format.

Each student needs:
9 tenths (red) and hundredths (green) Decimal Squares (can be mixed amounts of each); cards should be arranged faceup in a 3-by-3 array on the tabletop in front of the student

Teacher needs:
stack of Decimal Square cards

Directions

1. Teacher takes first decimal card from her stack and calls out that decimal number, for example, "Eight-tenths," "Twenty-five–hundredths."

2. Students turn over cards as they are called if they appear in their array. *Equivalent values of cards called may also be turned over.*

3. Play continues until a student gets a bingo horizontally, vertically, or diagonally. When a child yells "Bingo!" the teacher asks him to read each Decimal Square and/or equivalent square in the bingo.

4. Because this game can move quickly, continue play until two children earn bingos.

Variations

Flip and Switch: When a new game is ready to begin, the children flip up all of their cards and switch their order for a new array.

Switch Up: When a new game is to begin, each child switches a square with someone else at her table.

Tenths, Hundredths, and Thousandths: Add in thousandths (yellow) cards. Continue to play with 3-by-3 arrays of squares.

 From *A Month-to-Month Guide: Fourth-Grade Math* by Lainie Schuster. © 2009 Math Solutions Publications

Place-Value Chart

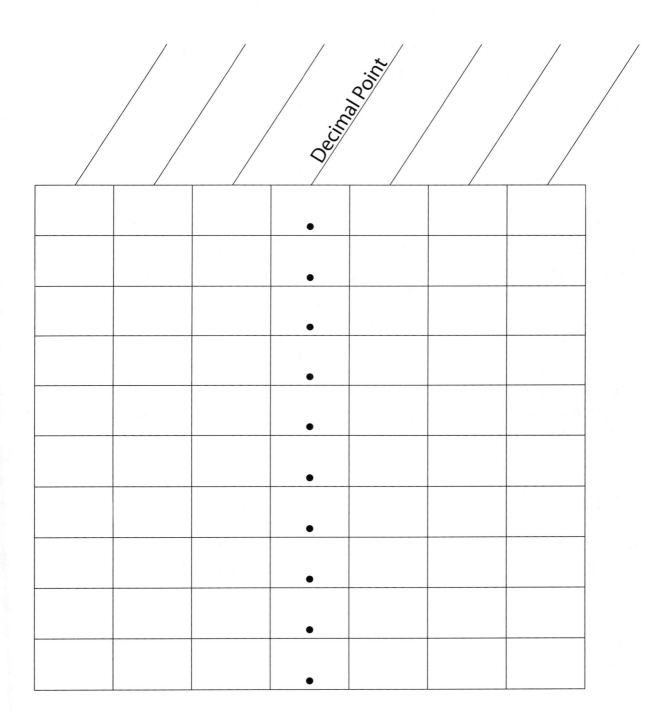

Decimal Point

Tenths Grids

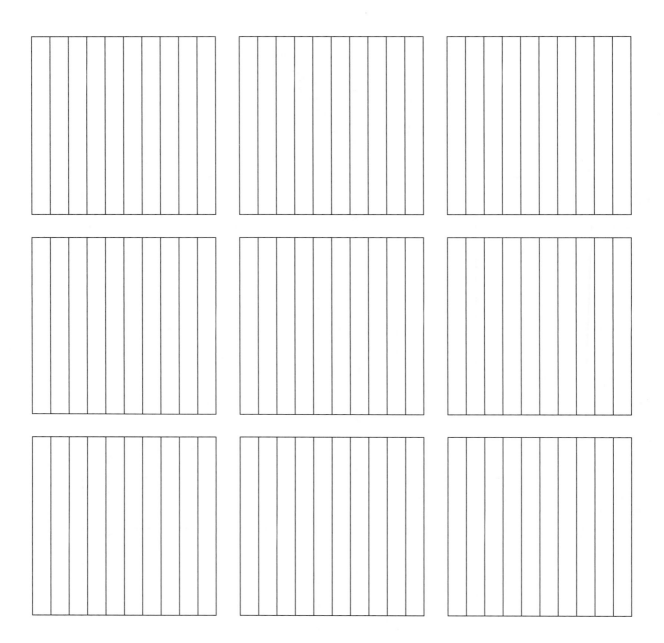

Hundredths Grids

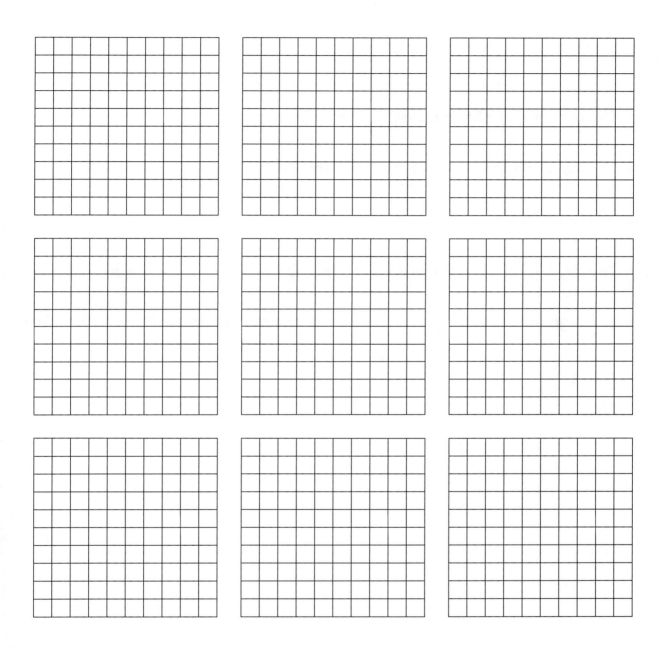

Place-Value Riddle Sample

- **The mystery number has no repeated digits.**

- **The mystery number falls between 6 and 7.**

- **All the digits are even.**

- **The digit in the ones place is three times the number in the hundredths place.**

- **The digit in the tenths place is two times the number in the hundredths place.**

From A Month-to-Month Guide: Fourth-Grade Math by Lainie Schuster. © 2009 Math Solutions Publications

Place-Value Riddle 1

- **The mystery number falls between 0 and 1.**

- **The digit in the hundredths place is a multiple of the the digit in the tenths place.**

- **There are no repeated digits.**

- **The number in the hundredths place is 6 more than the number in the tenths place.**

- **All the digits are even.**

Place-Value Riddle 2

- **The mystery number is greater than 8.**

- **Its ones digit is the sum of the tenths and hundredths digits.**

- **It is less than 9.**

- **All of its digits are even.**

- **Two of the digits are the same.**

- **One if its digits is 0.**

- **Its hundredths digit is the sum of its tenths and ones digits.**

- **Its hundredths digit is 8.**

Place-Value Riddle 3

- **The mystery number's tens digit is less than its ones digit.**

- **Its tens digit is less than its tenths digit.**

- **Its tenths digit is even.**

- **Its ones digit divided by its tens digit is 7.**

- **The product of two of its digits is 8.**

- **It has only one even digit.**

- **One of its digits is the sum of the other two digits.**

- **One of its digits is 7.**

From A Month-to-Month Guide: Fourth-Grade Math by Lainie Schuster. © 2009 Math Solutions Publications

Place-Value Riddle 4

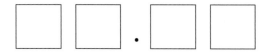

- The product of the mystery number's ones digit and tenths digit is 1.

- Its tens digit minus its tenths digit is 8.

- It has no even digits.

- The sum of its tens digit and its tenths digit is 10.

- There are only two different digits in the number.

- It is greater than 80.

- The sum of its tenths digit and its hundredths digit is 2.

- The mystery number's ones digit is 1.

From *A Month-to-Month Guide: Fourth-Grade Math* by Lainie Schuster. © 2009 Math Solutions Publications

Place-Value Riddle 5

- The mystery number's hundredths digit is an odd number.

- It has three different digits.

- Its tenths digit is a multiple of 4.

- Its thousandths digit is an even number.

- It is less than 0.8.

- The sum of all its digits is 17.

- Its hundredths digit is 5 more than its tenths digit.

- Its thousandths digit is 4.

- Its hundredths digit is 5 more than its thousandths digit.

The Place-Value Game

You need:
- 1 number generator, such as a 1–6 die, a 0–9 spinner, or a set of cards numbered 0–9
- 1 record sheet per player (see directions below)
- 2–4 players

Directions

1. Each player sets up a recording sheet as shown:

_____ _____ _____ . _____ _____   Discard _____

2. Players take turns rolling the die, spinning the spinner, or turning over cards from a deck.

3. Each time a number comes up, each player writes it in one space on his or her game board. Once written, the number cannot be changed or moved.

4. Continue until everyone has filled in all the places for his or her decimal.

5. The winner is the player with the largest number and must be able to read it.

Extension
Play for the smallest decimal number.

Adapted from *About Teaching Mathematics: A K–8 Resource, 3d ed.* by Marilyn Burns (Math Solutions Publications, 2007)

From *A Month-to-Month Guide: Fourth-Grade Math* by Lainie Schuster. © 2009 Math Solutions Publications

The Greatest Wins

You need:
   1 die

   record sheet (see directions below)

   2–4 players

Directions

1. Each player makes a recording sheet as shown:

   1) 0. _____ _____   Reject _____

   2) 0. _____ _____   Reject _____

   3) 0. _____ _____   Reject _____

   4) 0. _____ _____   Reject _____

   5) 0. _____ _____   Reject _____

   6) 0. _____ _____   Reject _____

   7) 0. _____ _____   Reject _____

   8) 0. _____ _____   Reject _____

   9) 0. _____ _____   Reject _____

   10) 0. _____ _____   Reject _____

2. Players take turn rolling the die, writing the number in a space in the first line, and passing the die to the next player. Continue until all players have filled in the first line. Once a number is recorded, its position cannot be changed.

3. Each player reads aloud her number. The group agrees on who has the largest number and wins the round.

4. Continue playing for nine more rounds. The overall winner is the player who wins the most rounds.

Extensions
- Add a third blank to each line to create a thousandths place.
- Play for the smallest decimal number.

Decimal Square Blackjack

You need:
> 15 chips for each player
> 1 cup for the collected chips per child, plus 1 for the dealer (teacher)
> a mixed deck of the tenths (red) and hundredths (green) Decimal Squares for the dealer from the original deck of 57 cards

Directions

1. Each player's goal is to use one or more decimal playing cards to get a sum as close to 1 as possible, without going over.

2. The dealer shuffles the deck. Each player places a chip into the dealer's cup to begin the round.

3. Each player receives one Decimal Square facedown. The players may look at their cards.

4. After the player has looked at his card, he may ask for another card by saying, "Hit me." He may be dealt a card of a different place value (a different color). To be dealt a card, each player must add another chip to the cup. The additional card is dealt faceup to the player.

5. If a player's sum is greater than 1, she must fold. To do so, she says, "I fold." Her cards are turned faceup and she is out of that round. If the sum is less than 1, the player may "hold" or ask for another card.

6. The round is completed when every player still in the round says, "I'm holding."

7. Cards are flipped over. The player whose sum is the closest to 1 but not over wins the round. The winner wins the chips in the dealer's cup.

8. After three games, the children count the number of chips in their cups. The child with the most chips wins the record.

9. All chips are returned to the dealer, and a new round starts with each child receiving fifteen chips.

Extension
Play for a sum of 2.

Adapted from *Decimal Squares: Step by Step Teacher's Guide* by Albert B. Bennett, Jr. (Scott Resources, 1992)

Centimeter Grid Paper

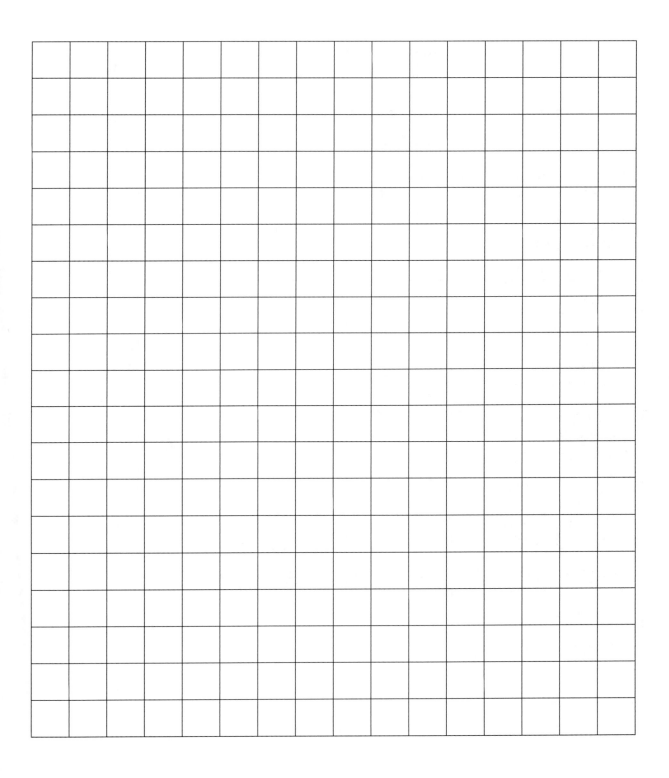

Graphing Tic-Tac-Toe One-Quadrant Grids

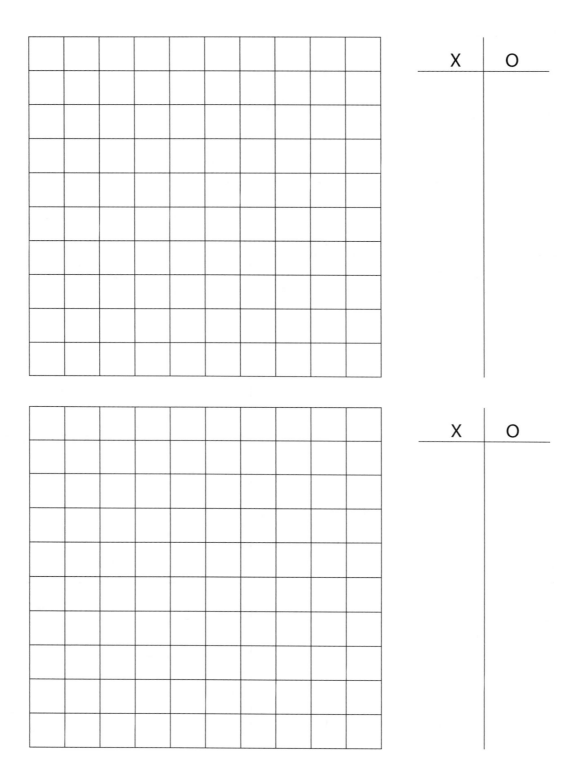

From *A Month-to-Month Guide: Fourth-Grade Math* by Lainie Schuster. © 2009 Math Solutions Publications

Graphing Tic-Tac-Toe Four-Quadrant Grids

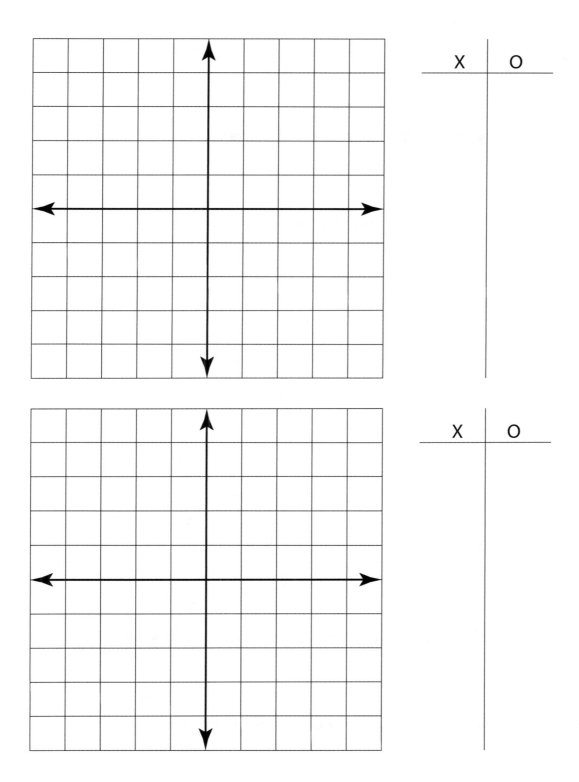

Magic Pot Task, Version 1

You need:
    a piece of paper
    2 players

Directions

1. **Discuss what your pot will do with your partner.**

2. **Construct a T-chart to represent the action of your pot.**

In □	Out △
1	
2	
3	
4	
5	
.	
.	
.	
10	
.	
.	
.	
100	

3. **On the back of your paper, write out the rule for your pot *in words*.**

4. **Below your description, rewrite your rule as an *equation*.**

From *A Month-to-Month Guide: Fourth-Grade Math* by Lainie Schuster. © 2009 Math Solutions Publications

Magic Pot Task, Version 2

You need:
- a piece of paper
- 2 players

Directions

1. Discuss what your pot will do with your partner.

2. Construct a T-chart to represent the action of your pot.

In $\square$	Out $\triangle$
1	
2	
3	
4	
5	
6	
7	
8	
9	
10	
11	
12	
13	
14	
15	
16	
17	
18	
19	
20	

3. On the back of your paper, write out the rule for your pot *in words*.

4. Below your description, rewrite your rule as an *equation*.

1-Inch Grid Paper

Balancing Number Puzzles

Complete the following number puzzles. Same shapes stand for same numbers. Represent each balance with an equation.

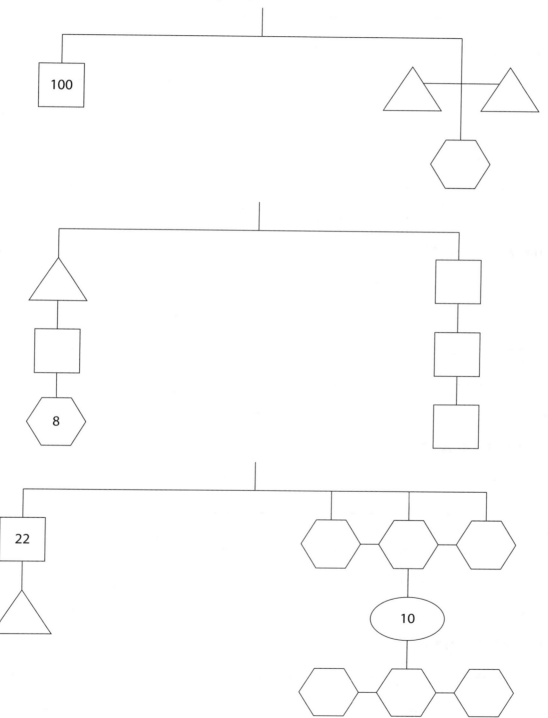

Rate Tables Record Sheet

Summary Statement:

_____

_____

Summary Statement:

_____

_____

Summary Statement:

_____

_____

Summary Statement:

_____

_____

Great Rates

Matthew loves hot dogs!

1. Hot dogs come in packages of 8. How many hot dogs will be in 6 packages?

Hot Dogs/Package	Number of Packages	Total Number of Hot Dogs

2. A package of hot dogs costs $2.99. How many packages of hot dogs did Matthew buy if he spent $17.94? (Can you use your number sense rather than a calculator to solve this?)

Price/Package	Number of Packages	Total Price

3. Hot dog buns come in packages of 12. How many buns would Matthew have if he bought 4 packages?

4. One package of hot dog buns costs $3.99. How much would Matthew spend if he bought 4 packages of hot dog buns? (Use your number sense rather than a calculator!)

5. Matthew is in charge of the fourth-grade picnic. Each fourth grader will get one hot dog and one bun. If 48 fourth graders are attending the picnic, how many packages of hot dogs and how many packages of buns will Matthew need? What will Matthew's total bill be for hot dogs and hot dog buns? Why do your answers make sense?

Mammal Heart Rates

Mammal	Heartbeats per Minute	Weight in Pounds
Pygmy Shrew	1,200	0.01
Mouse	650	0.25
Guinea Pig	280	0.75
House Cat	110	10
Tiger	40	500
African Elephant	25	12,000
Gray Whale	8	60,000
Human Rates	Heartbeats per Minute	Weight in Pounds
Newborn	110–160	7
7-Year-Old	90	50
Adult	60–80	160
Senior Citizen	50–65	140

Adapted from *Everyday Mathematics: The University of Chicago School Mathematics Project, Grade 4, 3d ed.*
(Everyday Learning Corporation, 2007)

From *A Month-to-Month Guide: Fourth-Grade Math* by Lainie Schuster. © 2009 Math Solutions Publications

References

Professional Resources

Bennett, Albert B. Jr. 1992. *Decimal Squares: Step by Step Teacher's Guide.* Fort Collins, CO: Scott Resources.

Bickmore-Brand, Jennie, ed. 1990. *Language in Mathematics.* Portsmouth, NH: Heinemann.

Bresser, Rusty. 2004. *Math and Literature, Grades 4–6.* 2d ed. Sausalito, CA: Math Solutions Publications.

Bresser, Rusty, and Caren Holtzman. 2006. *Minilessons for Math Practice: Grades 3–5.* Sausalito, CA: Math Solutions Publications.

Burns, Marilyn. 1975. *The I Hate Mathematics! Book.* Boston: Little, Brown.

———. 1982. *Math for Smarty Pants.* Boston: Little, Brown.

———. 1990. *The $1.00 Word Riddle Book.* Sausalito, CA: Math Solutions Publications.

———. 1995. *Writing in Math Class: A Resource for Grades 2–8.* Sausalito, CA: Math Solutions Publications.

———. 2001a. *Teaching Arithmetic: Lessons for Introducing Fractions, Grades 4–5.* Sausalito, CA: Math Solutions Publications.

———. 2001b. *Teaching Arithmetic: Lessons for Introducing Multiplication, Grade 3.* Sausalito, CA: Math Solutions Publications.

———. 2003a. "Marilyn Burns Demystifies Long Division." *Instructor Magazine* (April).

———. 2003b. The Marilyn Burns Fraction Kit, Grades 4–6. Sausalito, CA: Math Solutions Publications.

———. 2005. *The Marilyn Burns Classroom Math Library Teacher Handbook, Grades 4–6.* New York: Scholastic.

———. 2007. *About Teaching Mathematics: A K–8 Resource.* 3d ed. Sausalito, CA: Math Solutions Publications.

Burns, Marilyn, and Bonnie Tank. 1988. *A Collection of Math Lessons: From Grades 1 Through 3.* Sausalito, CA: Math Solutions Publications.

Carpenter, Thomas P., Megan Loef Franke, and Linda Levi. 2003. *Thinking Mathematically: Integrating Arithmetic and Algebra in Elementary School.* Portsmouth, NH: Heinemann.

Chapin, Suzanne H., and Art Johnson. 2006. *Math Matters: Understanding the Math You Teach, Grades K–8.* 2d ed. Sausalito, CA: Math Solutions Publications.

Chapin, Suzanne H., Catherine O'Connor, and Nancy Canavan Anderson. 2003. *Classroom Discussions: Using Math Talk to Help Students Learn, Grades 1–6.* Sausalito, CA: Math Solutions Publications.

Childs, Leigh, and Laura Choate. 1998. *Nimble with Numbers, Grades 4–5.* White Plains, NY: Dale Seymour Publications.

Clements, Doug, Cornelia Tierney, Megan Murray, Joan Akers, and Julie Samara. 2004. *Picturing Polygons: 2-D Geometry.* Investigations in Number, Data, and Space. Glenville, IL: Scott Foresman.

Collins, John J. 1992. *Developing Writing and Thinking Across the Curriculum: A Practical Program for Schools.* Boston: Collins Education Associates.

Corwin, Rebecca, Susan Russell, and Cornelia Tierney. 1991. *Seeing Fractions: A Unit for the Upper Elementary Grades.* Sacramento: California Department of Education.

De Francisco, Carrie, and Marilyn Burns. 2002. *Teaching Arithmetic: Lessons for Decimals and Percents, Grades 5–6.* Sausalito, CA: Math Solutions Publications.

Duckworth, Eleanor. 1987. *The Having of Wonderful Ideas and Other Essays on Teaching and Learning.* New York: Teachers College Press.

Economopoulos, Karen, Jan Mokros, Joan Akers, and Susan Russell. 2004. *Money, Miles, and Large Numbers, Grade 4.* Investigations in Number, Data, and Space. Glenview, IL: Scott Foresman.

Eliot, T. S. 1964. *The Waste Land.* In *T. S. Eliot: Selected Poems.* Orlando, FL: Harcourt Brace.

Ellett, Kim. 2005. "Making a Million Meaningful." *Mathematics Teaching in the Middle School* 10 (8): 416–23.

Everyday Learning Corporation. 1995. *Everyday Mathematics: Teacher's Reference Manual.* Chicago: Everyday Learning.

———. 2007a. *Everyday Mathematics: The University of Chicago School Mathematics Project, Grade 4.* 3d ed. Chicago: Everyday Learning.

———. 2007b. *Everyday Mathematics: The University of Chicago School Mathematics Project, Grade 5.* 3d ed. Chicago: Everyday Learning.

———. 2007c. *Operations Handbook: Grades 3–6.* 3d ed. Chicago: Everyday Learning.

Fosnot, Catherine Twomey, and Maarten Dolk. 2001a. *Young Mathematicians at Work: Constructing Multiplication and Division.* Portsmouth, NH: Heinemann.

———. 2001b. *Young Mathematicians at Work: Constructing Number Sense, Addition, and Subtraction.* Portsmouth, NH: Heinemann.

———. 2002. *Young Mathematicians at Work: Constructing Fractions, Decimals, and Percents.* Portsmouth, NH: Heinemann.

Gavin, M. Katherine, Carol Findell, Carole Greenes, and Linda Jensen Sheffield. 2000. *Awesome Math Problems for Creative Thinking: Grade 4.* Chicago: Creative Publications.

Greenes, Carole, Linda Schulman Dacey, and Rika Spungin. 2001a. *Hot Math Topics: Measurement and Geometry, Grade 4.* Parsippany, NJ: Dale Seymour Publications.

———. 2001b. *Hot Math Topics: Multiplication and Division, Grade 4.* Parsippany, NJ: Dale Seymour Publications.

Greenes, Carole, and Carol Findell. 1998. *Groundworks: Algebra Puzzles and Problems.* Chicago: Creative Publications.

———. 2006. *Groundworks: Algebraic Thinking, Grade 4.* Chicago: Creative Publications.

Greenes, Carole, Carol Findell, M. Katherine Gavin, and Linda Jensen. 2000a. *Awesome Math Problems for Creative Thinking: Grade 3.* Chicago: Creative Publications.

———. 2000b. *Awesome Math Problems for Creative Thinking: Grade 5.* Chicago: Creative Publications.

Greenes, Carole, Linda Schulman, Rika Spungin, Suzanne Chapin, Carol Findell, and Art Johnson. 1996a. *MEGA Projects: Math Explorations and Group Activity Projects, Grade 3.* Palo Alto, CA: Dale Seymour Publications.

———. 1996b. *MEGA Projects: Math Explorations and Group Activity Projects, Grade 4.* Palo Alto, CA: Dale Seymour Publications.

Guskey, Thomas R., and Jane M. Bailey. 2001. *Developing Grading and Reporting Systems for Student Learning.* Thousand Oaks, CA: Corwin.

Hiebert, James, Thomas P. Carpenter, Elizabeth Fennema, Karen C. Fuson, Diana Wearne, and Hanlie Murray. 1997. *Making Sense: Teaching and Learning Mathematics with Understanding.* Portsmouth, NH: Heinemann.

Jacobs, Heidi Hayes. 1997. *Mapping the Big Picture.* Alexandria, VA: Association for Supervision and Curriculum Development.

Kaplan, Andrew, Carol Debold, Susan Rogalski, and Pat Bourdreau, eds. 2004. *Math on Call: A Mathematics*

Handbook. Wilmington, MA: Great Source Education Group.

Kindlon, Dan, and Michael Thompson. 1999. *Raising Cain: Protecting the Emotional Life of Boys.* New York: Ballantine Books.

Litton, Nancy. 1998. *Getting Your Math Message Out to Parents: A K–6 Resource.* Sausalito, CA: Math Solutions Publications.

Massachusetts Department of Education. 2005. The Massachusetts Comprehensive Assessment System (MCAS) Released Spring Test Items. www.doe.mass.edu/mcas.

Math at Hand: A Mathematics Handbook. 2004. Wilmington, MA: Great Source Education Group.

Mokros, Jan. 1996. *Beyond Facts and Flashcards: Exploring Math with Your Kids.* Portsmouth, NH: Heinemann.

Mokros, Jan, Susan Jo Russell, and Karen Economopoulos. 1995. *Beyond Arithmetic: Changing Mathematics in the Elementary Classroom.* Parsippany, NJ: Dale Seymour Publications.

Molnar, Jane. 1999. *Logic Mysteries.* White Plains, NY: Dale Seymour Publications.

Moon, Jean. 1997. *Developing Judgment: Assessing Children's Work in Mathematics.* Portsmouth, NH: Heinemann.

Moon, Jean, and Linda Schulman. 1995. *Finding the Connections: Linking Assessment, Instruction, and Curriculum in Elementary Mathematics.* Portsmouth, NH: Heinemann.

National Council of Teachers of Mathematics (NCTM). 2000. *Principles and Standards for School Mathematics.* Reston, VA: National Council of Teachers of Mathematics.

———. 2006. *Curriculum Focal Points for Prekindergarten Through Grade 8 Mathematics: A Quest for Coherence.* Reston, VA: National Council of Teachers of Mathematics.

O'Connell, Sue. 2002. *Writing About Mathematics: An Essential Skill in Developing Math Proficiency, Grades 3–8.* Bellevue, WA: Bureau of Education and Research.

Post, Beverly, and Sandra Eads. 1996. *Logic, Anyone?* Torrance, CA: Fearon Teacher Aids.

Potok, Chaim. 1967. *The Chosen.* New York: Fawcett Crest Books.

Raphel, Annette. 2000. *Math Homework That Counts.* Sausalito, CA: Math Solutions Publications.

Rasmussen, Steven, and Spreck Rosekrans. 1985. *Key to Decimals: Decimal Concepts.* Berkley, CA: Key Curriculum Press.

Rectanus, Cheryl. 1993. *Math By All Means: Geometry, Grade 3.* Sausalito, CA: Math Solutions Publications.

———. 1997. *Math By All Means: Area and Perimeter, Grades 5–6.* Sausalito, CA: Math Solutions Publications.

Reeves, Noelene. 1990. "The Mathematics-Language Connection." In *Language in Mathematics,* ed. Jennie Bickmore-Brand (90–99). Portsmouth, NH: Heinemann.

Ronfeldt, Suzy. 2003. *A Month-to-Month Guide: Third-Grade Math.* Sausalito, CA: Math Solutions Publications.

Russell, Susan. 2002. "Developing Computational Fluency with Whole Numbers." *Teaching Children Mathematics* 7 (3): 154–58.

Russell, Susan, and Douglas H. Clements. 1997. *Flips, Turns, and Area: 2-D Geometry, Grade 3.* Investigations in Number, Data, and Space. Palo Alto, CA: Dale Seymour Publications.

Scavo, Thomas R., and Nora K. Conroy. 1996. "Conceptual Understanding and Computational Skill in School Mathematics." *Mathematics Teaching in the Middle School* (March–April): 684–87.

Schuster, Lainie, and Nancy Canavan Anderson. 2005. *Good Questions for Math Teaching: Why Ask Them and What to Ask: Grades 5–8.* Sausalito, CA: Math Solutions Publications.

Sherard, Wade H. 1998. *Logic Number Problems for Grades 4–8.* White Plains, NY: Dale Seymour Publications.

Stoessiger, Rex, and Joy Edmunds. 1993. "The Role of Challenges." In *Language in Mathematics,* ed. Jennie Bickmore-Brand (109–18). Portsmouth, NH: Heinemann.

Sullivan, Peter, and Pat Lilburn. 2002. *Good Questions for Math Teaching: Why Ask Them and What to Ask, K–6.* Sausalito, CA: Math Solutions Publications.

Tierney, Cornelia. 1998. *Mathematical Thinking at Grade 4.* Investigations in Number, Data, and Space Series. White Plains, NY: Dale Seymour Publications.

Tierney, Cornelia, Mark Ogonowski, Andee Rubin, and Susan Jo Russell. 2004. *Different Shapes, Equal Pieces.* Investigations in Number, Data, and Space Series. Glenville, IL: Scott Foresman.

Van de Walle, John A. 2004. *Elementary and Middle School Mathematics: Teaching Developmentally.* Boston: Pearson Education.

Wickett, Maryann, and Marilyn Burns. 2001. *Teaching Arithmetic: Lessons for Extending Multiplication, Grades 4–5.* Sausalito, CA: Math Solutions Publications.

———. 2003. *Teaching Arithmetic: Lessons for Extending Division,* *Grades 4–5.* Sausalito, CA: Math Solutions Publications.

———. 2005. *Teaching Arithmetic: Lessons for Extending Place Value, Grade 3.* Sausalito, CA: Math Solutions Publications.

Wickett, Maryann, Katharine Kharas, and Marilyn Burns. 2002. *Lessons for Algebraic Thinking, Grades 3–5.* Sausalito, CA: Math Solutions Publications.

Wiggins, Grant, and Jay McTighe. 2005. *Understanding by Design.* 2d ed. Alexandria, VA: Association for Supervision and Curriculum Development.

Children's Books

Brown, Margaret Wise. 1949. *The Important Book.* New York: HarperCollins.

Burns, Marilyn. 1997. *Spaghetti and Meatballs for All! A Mathematical Story.* New York: Scholastic.

Dahl, Roald. 1988. *Matilda.* New York: Penguin Books.

Dodds, Dayle Ann. 2004. *Minnie's Diner: A Multiplying Menu.* Cambridge, MA: Candlewick.

Ferris, Jean. 2002. *Once Upon a Marigold.* New York: Harcourt.

Fleischman, Sid. 1989. *The Ghost in the Noonday Sun.* New York: Harper Trophy.

———. 2006. *The Giant Rat of Sumatra: Or Pirates Galore.* New York: Harper Trophy.

Glass, Julie. 1998. *The Fly on the Ceiling.* New York: Random House.

Harshman, Marc. 1993. *Only One.* New York: Cobblehill Books.

Hong, Lily Toy. 1993. *Two of Everything.* Morton Grove, IL: Albert Whitman.

Meddaugh, Susan. 1998. *Martha Blah-Blah.* New York: Scholastic.

Pinczes, Elinor J. 1995. *A Remainder of One.* New York: Houghton Mifflin.

———. 1998. *One Hundred Hungry Ants.* New York: Houghton Mifflin.

Schwartz, David. 1985. *How Much Is a Million?* New York: Scholastic.

———. 1999. *If You Hopped Like a Frog.* New York: Scholastic.

Thompson, Lauren. 2001. *One Riddle, One Answer.* New York: Scholastic.

Tompert, Ann. 1990. *Grandfather Tang's Story.* New York: Crown.

Index

Continued from page iv.

Thinking in 3s activity: Adapted from *Awesome Math Problems for Creative Thinking, Grade 4*, by M. Katherine Gavin, Carol Findell, Carole Greenes, and Linda Jensen Sheffield (Creative Publications, 2000)

Color Tile Riddles activity: Adapted from *A Collection of Math Lessons: From Grades 1 Through 3*, by Marilyn Burns and Bonnie Tank (Math Solutions Publications, 1988)

Decimal Square Blackjack: Adapted from *Decimal Squares: Step by Step Teacher's Guide*, by Albert B. Bennett, Jr. (Scott Resources, 1992)

Dot Paper Fractions activity: Adapted from *Different Shapes, Equal Pieces*, by Cornelia Tierney, Mark Ogonowski, Andee Rubin, and Susan Jo Russell (Scott Foresman, 2004)

Polygon Sorting activities: Adapted from *Elementary and Middle School Mathematics: Teaching Developmentally*, by John A. Van de Walle (Pearson Education, 2004)

Multiplication Bingo, Multiplication Bull's-Eye, and Division Dash games, Division Dash score sheet, and the Jump Roping Jacks and Jills, Solving and Creating Rate Problems, and Mammal Heart Rates activities: Adapted from *Everyday Mathematics: The University of Chicago School Mathematics Project, Grade 4, Third Edition*, by Everyday Learning Corporation (Everyday Learning, 2007)

Name That Number game and A Million Taps . . . More or Less investigation: Adapted from *Everyday Mathematics: The University of Chicago School Mathematics Project, Grade 5, Third Edition*, by Everyday Learning Corporation (Everyday Learning, 2007)

Pent-Tris game: Adapted from *Flips, Turns, and Area: 2-D Geometry, Grade 3* by Susan Russell and Douglas H. Clements (Dale Seymour Publications, 1997)

Take Me Out to the Ballgame! story problems: Adapted from *Good Questions for Math Teaching: Why Ask Them and What to Ask, Grades 5–8*, by Lainie Schuster and Nancy Canavan Anderson (Math Solutions Publications, 2005)

Graphing Tic-Tac-Toe activity: Adapted from *Lessons for Algebraic Thinking, Grades 3–5*, by Maryann Wickett, Katherine Kharas, and Marilyn Burns (Math Solutions Publications, 2002)

If You Hopped Like a Frog activity: Adapted from *The Marilyn Burns Classroom Math Library Teacher Handbook, Grades 4–6*, by Marilyn Burns (Scholastic, 2005)

Remainder Riddles activity: Adapted from *Math and Literature, Grades 4–6, Second Edition*, by Rusty Bresser (Math Solutions Publications, 2004)

Area and Perimeter activities: Adapted from *Math By All Means: Area and Perimeter, Grades 5–6*, by Cheryl Rectanus (Math Solutions Publications, 1997)

Perimeters of Tangrams illustration: From *Math Matters: Understanding the Math You Teach, Grades K–8, Second Edition*, by Suzanne Chapin and Art Johnson (Math Solutions Publications, 2006)

Estimation Practice with Linking Cubes activity, How Many Cubes in Each Object? record sheet, Close to 100 game, and Close to 100 score sheet: Adapted from *Mathematical Thinking at Grade 4*, by Cornelia Tierney (Dale Seymour Publications, 1998)

Measuring Up, Down the Drain, It Beats Me, and Popcorn Madness investigations: Adapted from *MEGA Projects: Math Explorations and Group Activity Projects, Grade 4*, by Carole Greenes, Linda Schulman, Rika Spungin, Suzanne Chapin, Carol Findell, and Art Johnson (Dale Seymour Publications, 1996)

Close to 1,000 game and Close to 1,000 score sheet: Adapted from *Money, Miles, and Large Numbers, Grade 4*, by Karen Economopoulos, Jan Mokros, Joan Akers, and Susan Russell (Scott Foresman, 2004)

Digit Draw activity, Digit Draw record sheet, and Multiplication Tic-Tac-Toe game: Adapted from *Nimble with Numbers, Grades 4–5*, by Leigh Childs and Laura Choate (Dale Seymour Publications, 1998)

$1.00 Word Riddles activity: Adapted from *The $1.00 Word Riddle Book*, by Marilyn Burns (Math Solutions Publications, 1990)

The Greatest Wins game: Adapted from *Teaching Arithmetic: Lessons for Decimals and Percents, Grades 5–6*, by Carrie De Francisco and Marilyn Burns (Math Solutions Publications, 2002)

Silent Division lesson: Adapted from *Teaching Arithmetic: Lessons for Extending Division, Grades 4–5*, by Maryann Wickett and Marilyn Burns (Math Solutions Publications, 2003)

Checking for Multiplication Understanding, Target 300, Silent Multiplication, and Beans and Scoops activities: Adapted from *Teaching Arithmetic: Lessons for Extending Multiplication, Grades 4–5*, by Maryann Wickett and Marilyn Burns (Math Solutions Publications, 2001)

Balancing Number Puzzles: Adapted from *Teaching Arithmetic: Lessons for Extending Place Value, Grade 3*, by Maryann Wickett and Marilyn Burns (Math Solutions Publications, 2005)

Put in Order activity: Adapted from *Teaching Arithmetic: Lessons for Introducing Fractions, Grades 4–5*, by Marilyn Burns (Math Solutions Publications, 2001)

One Hundred Hungry Ants activity: Adapted from *Teaching Arithmetic: Lessons for Introducing Multiplication, Grade 3* by Marilyn Burns (Math Solutions Publications, 2001b)

Tangram Cutting instructions: From *A Month-to-Month Guide: Third-Grade Math* by Suzy Ronfeldt (Math Solutions Publications, 2003)

Chart of Double-Meaning Words: Adapted from *Writing About Mathematics: An Essential Skill in Developing Math Proficiency, Grades 3–8*, by Sue O'Connell (Washington Bureau of Education and Research, 2002)